THE GLOSSARY OF

Compiled & Edited By:
Manasi Pathak
Dr. Padmaja Saha

Rhythm

Independent
Publication

THE GLOSSARY OF DEVOPS

Compiled & Edited By:
Manasi Pathak
Dr. Padmaja Saha

ISBN:9798861984621

9798861984621

Published by:

Rhythm Independent Publication,

Jinkethimmanahalli, Varanasi, Bengaluru, Karnataka, India - 560036

For all types of correspondence, send your mails to the provided address above.

The information presented herein has been collated from a diverse range of sources, comprehensive perspective on the subject matter.

A/B Testing

A/B testing, also known as split testing, is a method used in the DevOps process to compare two different versions of a webpage or application in order to determine which one performs better in terms of user engagement, conversion rates, or other key metrics. This process involves dividing the users or traffic into two groups: the control group and the experimental group. The control group is presented with the original version of the webpage or application, while the experimental group is shown a modified version, often referred to as the "variant" or "treatment."

AIOps (Artificial Intelligence For IT Operations) Implementation

AIOps (Artificial Intelligence for IT Operations) is the implementation of AI technologies and techniques in the context of DevOps. It combines big data, machine learning, and analytics to enhance IT operations, automate tasks, and make data-driven decisions in real-time. AIOps leverages AI algorithms to monitor, analyze, and manage IT infrastructure, applications, and services, enabling organizations to detect and resolve issues proactively, optimize performance, and improve overall system reliability and availability.

AIOps (Artificial Intelligence For IT Operations) Platforms

AIOps (Artificial Intelligence for IT Operations) platforms are advanced software systems that leverage artificial intelligence (AI) and machine learning (ML) technologies to automate and optimize various aspects of IT operations within the context of DevOps. These platforms integrate with existing DevOps tools and systems to ingest and analyze vast amounts of operational data in real-time, including system logs, application performance metrics, network traffic, and user activity. By applying AI and ML algorithms to this data, AIOps platforms can detect patterns, anomalies, and correlations that human operators may overlook. One key feature of AIOps platforms is their ability to automatically identify and resolve IT incidents by predicting failures or service disruptions before they occur. They do this by continuously monitoring the infrastructure and flagging any abnormalities based on historical data and pre-defined thresholds. This proactive approach helps to prevent system outages and minimize downtime, allowing DevOps teams to focus on delivering new features and improving the overall user experience. AIOps platforms also provide intelligent automation capabilities, enabling organizations to streamline their IT processes and workflows. These platforms can autonomously perform routine tasks, such as log analysis, performance monitoring, and capacity planning. By offloading these manual tasks to AI-driven systems, DevOps teams can free up their time and resources to focus on more strategic initiatives. Furthermore, AIOps platforms enable organizations to gain in-depth insights into their IT infrastructure and application performance. By analyzing historical data and identifying trends, these platforms can help identify areas of improvement, such as bottlenecks or scalability issues. This data-driven approach empowers DevOps teams to make informed decisions and optimize their systems for better performance and reliability. In conclusion, AIOps platforms bring together AI, ML, and DevOps principles to automate and optimize IT operations. By leveraging advanced analytics and automation, these platforms help organizations streamline their processes, proactively prevent incidents, and gain valuable insights for continuous improvement.

AWS API Gateway

AWS API Gateway is a fully managed service provided by Amazon Web Services (AWS) that allows developers to create, deploy, manage, and scale APIs. It acts as a gateway that connects various backend systems or services with client applications. In the context of DevOps, AWS API Gateway plays a vital role in enabling continuous integration and deployment processes for APIs. DevOps is a set of practices that combines software development (Dev) and IT operations (Ops) to improve collaboration and increase the speed of software delivery. It focuses on

1

automating and streamlining the processes involved in building, testing, and deploying applications. AWS API Gateway fits into this DevOps mindset by providing a centralized platform to manage APIs and streamline their deployment. With AWS API Gateway, DevOps teams can easily define and configure APIs, set up authorization and access control, monitor API usage and performance, and handle different stages of the API lifecycle. It acts as a bridge between developers and operations teams, allowing them to collaborate efficiently and ensure a smooth integration and deployment process. API Gateway simplifies the release management process in a DevOps environment by providing features like API versioning, stage management, and deployment monitoring. Developers can create different versions of APIs and manage them separately to ensure backward compatibility and minimize disruption to existing clients. API stages can be used to represent different environments (e.g., development, testing, production), allowing teams to deploy and test APIs in controlled environments before making them available to the public. Furthermore, AWS API Gateway integrates seamlessly with other AWS services, such as AWS Lambda, Amazon S3, and AWS CloudWatch, allowing DevOps teams to build and deploy robust serverless architectures. It enables the use of Lambda functions as the backend for APIs, providing scalability, high availability, and cost efficiency. The integration with CloudWatch enables monitoring and alerting capabilities, allowing DevOps teams to proactively identify and resolve issues.

Accessibility Testing

Accessibility testing in the context of DevOps refers to the process of evaluating the usability and inclusivity of a software application for people with disabilities. It involves assessing whether the application is perceivable, operable, understandable, and robust enough to be used by individuals with various impairments or limitations. It is crucial for organizations to prioritize accessibility testing as part of their DevOps practices. By ensuring that their software is accessible to all users, they can foster inclusivity and comply with legal requirements, such as the Americans with Disabilities Act (ADA) and the Web Content Accessibility Guidelines (WCAG). During the accessibility testing process, different aspects of the application are examined to identify potential barriers that may hinder individuals with disabilities from fully utilizing the software. These aspects include visual elements, interactive components, multimedia content, navigation menus, forms, and other user interface elements. To conduct accessibility testing effectively, organizations often rely on a combination of automated tools and manual testing techniques. Automated tools can help identify common accessibility issues, such as missing alt text for images, inconsistent heading structures, or insufficient color contrast. Manual testing involves the use of assistive technologies, such as screen readers, magnifiers, or keyboard-only navigation, to simulate the experiences of users with disabilities. Accessibility testing should not be a one-time activity but an ongoing process integrated into the DevOps workflow. It is recommended to incorporate accessibility requirements into the software development lifecycle, from design and development to quality assurance and deployment stages. By considering accessibility early on and continuously monitoring and testing for accessibility throughout the development cycle, organizations can avoid costly retroactive fixes and ensure a more inclusive user experience. In conclusion, accessibility testing in DevOps involves evaluating the usability and inclusivity of software applications for individuals with disabilities. It helps organizations comply with legal requirements and promote inclusivity. By using a combination of automated tools and manual testing techniques, organizations can identify and address potential barriers for individuals with disabilities. Prioritizing accessibility testing throughout the development lifecycle is essential for fostering inclusivity and avoiding costly retroactive fixes.

Accountability

Accountability in the context of DevOps refers to the practice of taking responsibility for one's actions, decisions, and outcomes in the software development and operations processes. It involves holding individuals, teams, and organizations accountable for delivering high-quality software, meeting project deadlines, and aligning with the overall goals and objectives of the business. In a DevOps environment, accountability is a fundamental principle that emphasizes the need for transparency, collaboration, and open communication. It encourages individuals and teams to take ownership of their work, be proactive in problem-solving, and constantly strive for improvement. By being accountable, stakeholders are able to build trust, enhance collaboration, and create a culture of continuous learning and innovation.

Accurics

Accurics is a DevOps security platform that focuses on preventing security breaches in cloud native environments. It aims to ensure the security and compliance of infrastructure as code (IaC) and cloud resources throughout the development and deployment process. The platform offers an integrated approach to security by integrating into the DevOps workflow and providing continuous security throughout the software development lifecycle. Accurics analyzes IaC files, such as Terraform or CloudFormation templates, to detect misconfigurations, vulnerabilities, and policy violations that could lead to security breaches. It also monitors and alerts teams about any changes made to the cloud resources that may introduce security risks. Accurics provides organizations with actionable insights and recommendations on how to remediate security issues, enabling developers and DevOps teams to address vulnerabilities early in the development process. It offers a unified dashboard that shows the security posture of the entire cloud infrastructure, allowing teams to easily track and prioritize remediation efforts. The platform also facilitates collaboration between development, security, and operations teams by providing a common interface and language for discussing security concerns. It integrates with popular collaboration tools, such as Slack, Jira, and GitHub, to streamline communication and ensure timely remediation of security issues. Accurics supports the concept of "immutable security," which means maintaining a consistent and secure state of the cloud infrastructure by preventing unauthorized changes. It achieves this by applying self-healing principles, where it automatically rolls back any unauthorized changes and alerts the relevant teams about the incident. In summary, Accurics is a DevOps security platform that helps organizations ensure the security and compliance of their cloud native infrastructure. By scanning IaC files, monitoring cloud resources, and providing actionable insights, it enables teams to identify and address security issues early in the development process, promoting a secure and efficient DevOps workflow.

Adaptive Access Control

Adaptive Access Control is a security measure implemented in the context of DevOps that regulates access to resources based on dynamic and contextual factors. It is designed to enhance the security of an organization's applications and data by adapting access permissions in real-time to reflect the changing risk levels and user behavior. Traditional access control methods typically rely on static policies and predefined rules, granting or denying access based on predefined roles and permissions. However, in today's dynamic and rapidly changing DevOps environments, these static access control measures are no longer sufficient to address the evolving security threats. Adaptive Access Control takes a proactive approach to access management, continuously analyzing the contextual factors and risk indicators associated with each access request. These factors may include the user's identity, location, time of access, device being used, and previous access patterns, among others. By leveraging machine learning algorithms and advanced analytics, Adaptive Access Control can adaptively evaluate access requests and dynamically adjust the access permissions accordingly. For example, if a user attempts to access a critical resource from an unfamiliar location or device, the system may challenge the user with multi-factor authentication or restrict access until further authentication is provided. This adaptive and context-aware approach to access control allows organizations to strike a balance between security and usability. It helps prevent unauthorized access attempts by incorporating real-time risk assessments, while also reducing friction for legitimate users by adapting the authentication requirements based on their contextual factors. Adaptive Access Control supports the principles of least privilege and zero trust, ensuring that access permissions are continuously evaluated and adjusted as needed. It provides organizations with the ability to dynamically enforce security policies based on the current risk posture, reducing the likelihood of security breaches and unauthorized access to sensitive resources.

Agile

Agile is a software development methodology focused on iterative and incremental development, with a strong emphasis on collaboration and flexibility. In the context of DevOps, Agile principles and practices are essential for ensuring efficiency and effectiveness in the software development lifecycle. Agile practices help teams deliver high-quality software by breaking down large projects into smaller, manageable chunks called iterations or sprints. Each iteration typically lasts for a few weeks, during which cross-functional teams work collaboratively to deliver a working product increment. This iterative approach allows for continuous feedback and flexibility, enabling teams to adapt to changing requirements and customer needs.

Agility

Agility in the context of DevOps refers to the ability of an organization to quickly and efficiently respond to changing market conditions, customer needs, and business requirements. It is a key principle and practice that enables organizations to deliver software and services faster, increase customer satisfaction, and gain a competitive advantage. Agility in DevOps is facilitated by several key factors. Firstly, it emphasizes the importance of collaboration and communication between different teams involved in the software delivery process, including development, operations, and quality assurance. This promotes a shared understanding of goals and objectives, and encourages the identification and resolution of issues early in the development cycle. Secondly, agility is enabled by the implementation of continuous integration and continuous delivery (CI/CD) practices. CI/CD allows for the frequent and automated testing, integration, and deployment of software, reducing the time and effort required to deliver new features and updates to users. This iterative approach also enables organizations to receive feedback from users and stakeholders more quickly, allowing for faster iterations and improvements. Thirdly, agility is supported by the use of scalable and flexible infrastructure, such as cloud-based platforms and virtualization technologies. These allow for the rapid provisioning and scaling of resources, ensuring that the development and deployment of software can keep up with changing demands and requirements. Overall, agility in DevOps is crucial for organizations to remain competitive and meet the ever-evolving needs of their customers. By embracing collaboration, implementing CI/CD practices, and utilizing scalable infrastructure, organizations can achieve faster time-to-market, higher quality software, and increased customer satisfaction.

Airbrake

Airbrake is an application monitoring and error tracking tool that is commonly used in DevOps practices. It provides real-time visibility into errors and performance issues in software applications, allowing DevOps teams to quickly identify and resolve issues to ensure the stability and reliability of their systems. By integrating Airbrake into their development and operations workflows, DevOps teams can gain valuable insights into the health and performance of their applications. When an error occurs in an application, Airbrake automatically captures detailed information about the error, including its stack trace, request parameters, and environment information. This information is then aggregated and presented in a centralized dashboard, making it easy for DevOps teams to track and manage errors. One of the key features of Airbrake is its ability to alert DevOps teams in real-time when an error occurs. This allows teams to quickly respond and reduce the mean time to resolution (MTTR) for critical issues. By receiving immediate notifications, DevOps teams can prioritize and address errors based on their severity and impact on the application. In addition to error tracking, Airbrake also provides performance monitoring capabilities. It allows DevOps teams to measure key performance metrics of their applications, such as response time and throughput. By monitoring these metrics, teams can identify and optimize performance bottlenecks, ensuring that their applications are performing optimally. Airbrake can be easily integrated into popular DevOps tools and frameworks, such as Jenkins, GitHub, and Slack. This allows teams to streamline their workflows and collaborate more effectively. For example, when an error occurs in an application, Airbrake can automatically create an issue in a project management tool like JIRA, assign it to the appropriate team member, and notify the team via Slack. In summary, Airbrake is a powerful application monitoring and error tracking tool that helps DevOps teams gain visibility into the health and performance of their applications. By providing real-time error alerts, detailed error information, and performance metrics, Airbrake enables teams to quickly identify and resolve issues, ensuring the reliability and stability of their systems.

Alerting

Alerting in the context of DevOps refers to the practice of monitoring and notifying relevant individuals or teams about potential issues or anomalies in the system or application being developed or managed. It plays a crucial role in maintaining the reliability and stability of the system. The process of alerting involves setting up specific checks or indicators that

4

continuously monitor various aspects of the system, such as its performance, availability, security, or any other desired metrics. These checks can be configured to trigger alerts whenever certain predefined thresholds or conditions are met. For example, an alert can be triggered when the CPU usage exceeds a certain percentage, when the response time of an API call exceeds a specific threshold, or when a security vulnerability is detected. Alerts are typically sent through various communication channels, such as email, SMS, instant messaging, or other collaboration tools commonly used by the DevOps teams. The recipient of the alert is usually a member of the operations team or an on-call engineer responsible for handling incidents and ensuring the proper functioning of the system. Alerting provides several benefits in a DevOps environment. Firstly, it helps in proactive problem detection and resolution by notifying the responsible individuals or teams about potential issues before they escalate into major problems. By receiving timely alerts, the relevant stakeholders can quickly investigate the root cause of the issue and take appropriate actions to rectify it, minimizing the impact on users or customers. Furthermore, alerting enables effective incident response and management. When an alert is triggered, the responsible person can immediately start investigating the issue and coordinate with other team members to resolve it. This helps in reducing downtime and ensuring the system's availability and performance. In addition to issue detection and incident response, alerting also plays a crucial role in performance monitoring and capacity planning. By monitoring key performance metrics and receiving alerts when thresholds are breached, DevOps teams can identify potential bottlenecks or areas of improvement. This allows them to take proactive measures, such as scaling resources or optimizing code, to ensure optimal performance and reduce the risk of system failures. To summarize, alerting in DevOps is the practice of monitoring and notifying relevant individuals or teams about potential issues or anomalies in the system. It helps in proactive problem detection, incident response, performance monitoring, and capacity planning, contributing to the overall reliability and stability of the system.

Alignment

Alignment in the context of DevOps refers to the synchronization and coordination of different teams, processes, and goals within an organization. It involves ensuring that all stakeholders are working towards a common objective and are aware of each other's activities and progress.Alignment is a crucial aspect of DevOps as it enables seamless collaboration and integration between various functions such as development, operations, and quality assurance. It promotes effective communication, reduces inefficiencies, and enhances the overall efficiency and productivity of the organization.

AnthillPro

AnthillPro is a popular and powerful DevOps tool that enables organizations to automate their software build, test, and deployment processes. It is designed specifically for enterprise-level development teams, providing them with the necessary tools and features to streamline their software delivery pipeline. At its core, AnthillPro acts as a centralized platform for managing and orchestrating the entire software development lifecycle. It integrates seamlessly with various development, testing, and deployment tools to automate the different stages of the process, ensuring consistent and reliable software delivery. The key features of AnthillPro include: Build Automation: AnthillPro allows developers to automate the build process by defining and executing build scripts. It supports a wide range of build systems and technologies, making it versatile and adaptable to different development environments. Test Automation: AnthillPro facilitates the automation of testing activities by integrating with popular testing frameworks and tools. It enables the execution of tests in parallel, providing faster feedback on the quality of the software. Deployment Automation: With AnthillPro, organizations can automate the deployment of their software to multiple environments, such as development, staging, and production. It ensures consistent deployment processes, reduces manual errors, and enables faster release cycles. Visibility and Reporting: AnthillPro provides real-time visibility into the software delivery pipeline through its comprehensive reporting and dashboard capabilities. It captures key metrics and generates customizable reports, enabling teams to monitor and optimize their processes. Integration and Collaboration: AnthillPro integrates with various tools and systems in the DevOps ecosystem, including source code repositories, bug tracking systems, and team collaboration platforms. This allows for seamless collaboration and information sharing across different teams and workflows. In summary, AnthillPro is a robust DevOps tool that automates the build, test, and deployment processes within an organization. It promotes collaboration, improves efficiency, and helps deliver high-quality software faster and more reliably.

Apigee

Apigee is a leading DevOps platform that empowers organizations to design, build, secure, and manage their APIs. DevOps, short for Development and Operations, is a set of practices that aims to enhance software development and delivery processes by promoting collaboration and automation between development teams and IT operations teams. As a DevOps tool, Apigee offers several key features to support the API lifecycle. It enables developers to design and prototype APIs using a comprehensive set of tools and features. The platform also provides development teams with the ability to build, test, and deploy APIs using automated workflows and standardized programming languages. With Apigee, organizations can ensure the security of their APIs by implementing authentication, authorization, and access control mechanisms. Moreover, Apigee allows teams to manage APIs in a centralized manner, providing functionality for version control, documentation, and monitoring. This helps organizations track and analyze API usage and performance, enabling them to make informed decisions for improvements. The platform also facilitates the integration of APIs with other systems, enabling seamless data exchange and connectivity. Apigee supports the implementation of DevOps principles by streamlining the collaboration and communication between development and operations teams. The platform encourages the use of automation, enabling teams to automate repetitive tasks and increase efficiency. By utilizing tools and features provided by Apigee, organizations can reduce deployment errors, shorten release cycles, and improve overall software quality. In conclusion, Apigee is a powerful DevOps platform that supports organizations in designing, building, securing, and managing APIs. By leveraging the capabilities of Apigee, development and operations teams can collaborate effectively, automate processes, and enhance software delivery, ultimately accelerating digital transformation and innovation.

AppDynamics

AppDynamics is a comprehensive Application Performance Monitoring (APM) solution that enables organizations to effectively monitor and optimize their software application performance in a DevOps environment. It provides visibility into the entire application stack, from end-user experience to the underlying infrastructure, facilitating efficient collaboration between development, operations, and business teams. In the context of DevOps, AppDynamics plays a crucial role in ensuring the smooth operation and continuous delivery of software applications. It offers real-time monitoring and visibility into the performance of applications, allowing teams to detect and resolve issues proactively. By using AppDynamics, organizations can ensure that applications meet the desired performance thresholds, delivering an exceptional experience to end-users.

AppScan

AppScan is a security testing tool that is widely used in the context of DevOps. It is designed to help businesses scan and identify vulnerabilities in their applications and websites, ensuring that they are protected against potential threats and attacks. One of the key benefits of using AppScan in a DevOps environment is that it enables security testing to be seamlessly integrated into the software development lifecycle. With its automation capabilities, development teams can easily incorporate security scanning into their existing CI/CD pipelines, ensuring that vulnerabilities are detected and resolved early in the development process. AppScan offers a comprehensive set of features that cater to the specific needs of DevOps teams. It supports various types of security testing, including static, dynamic, and interactive application security testing (SAST, DAST, and IAST). These testing techniques help identify an array of vulnerabilities, such as SQL injections, cross-site scripting (XSS), and insecure configurations. Furthermore, AppScan provides developers with detailed and actionable reports that highlight the identified vulnerabilities and propose recommended remediation steps. By providing this information in a clear and concise manner, developers can easily understand the security risks associated with their applications and take appropriate actions to mitigate them. In addition to its scanning capabilities, AppScan offers integration with popular issue tracking and collaboration tools, such as JIRA and Slack. This enables seamless communication and collaboration between security teams and developers, facilitating the process of resolving vulnerabilities and ensuring a secure development process. Overall, AppScan is a valuable tool in the DevOps landscape, allowing organizations to proactively identify and address security vulnerabilities in their applications. By integrating security testing into the development process, businesses can ensure that their applications are well-protected, reducing the risk of security breaches and the associated financial and reputational damage.

Application Insights Tools Usage

Application Insights is a set of monitoring and diagnostic tools offered by Microsoft that helps developers gain insights into their applications and improve their overall health and performance. It is an essential component in the DevOps process, providing valuable information and metrics that can be used to optimize and enhance the development, deployment, and operations of applications. As a DevOps tool, Application Insights allows developers to collect and analyze data from their applications in real-time. It provides a comprehensive overview of the application's performance, availability, and usage, allowing developers to identify and troubleshoot any issues or bottlenecks quickly. This helps in ensuring that the application is running smoothly, meeting the required performance standards, and delivering an optimal user experience. Application Insights provides various features and capabilities that are valuable in the DevOps process. It offers deep monitoring capabilities, tracking key metrics such as response times, page views, and user sessions. This enables developers to understand how their application is performing and identify areas for improvement. They can easily monitor and analyze the impact of changes made to the application, ensuring that performance is not compromised and that the changes have the desired effect. Another important feature of Application Insights is its ability to provide detailed insights into application crashes and errors. Developers can view comprehensive error reports, including stack traces, to quickly diagnose and resolve issues. This helps in reducing application downtime and improving overall application reliability. Furthermore, Application Insights integrates seamlessly with other DevOps tools and workflows. It can be integrated with source control systems, build pipelines, and release management systems, providing a holistic view of the application lifecycle. This allows for efficient collaboration and communication between development, operations, and testing teams, ensuring smooth deployments and faster time to market. In conclusion, Application Insights is a powerful set of tools that plays a crucial role in the DevOps process. It provides developers with valuable insights and metrics, enabling them to monitor and optimize their applications effectively. By leveraging the capabilities of Application Insights, developers can enhance the performance, availability, and reliability of their applications, improving the overall user experience.

Application Insights Tools

Application Insights Tools are a set of monitoring and analytics tools provided by Microsoft as part of its Azure DevOps services. These tools are designed to help DevOps teams gain insights into the performance and usage of their applications, and to enable them to make more informed decisions to improve the quality and reliability of their software. Application Insights Tools offer a comprehensive suite of features that cover the entire application lifecycle, from development and testing to production and monitoring. These tools provide real-time monitoring and diagnostics capabilities, which allow DevOps teams to detect and diagnose issues quickly and efficiently. The tools also offer powerful analytics and reporting capabilities, which help teams gain insight into the overall health and performance of their applications, as well as identify potential areas for improvement.

Application Insights

Application Insights is a robust and comprehensive application performance monitoring (APM) and logging tool that is specifically designed for DevOps practices. It provides developers and operations teams with real-time insights into the performance, availability, and usage of their applications, helping them identify and resolve issues quickly and efficiently. With Application Insights, DevOps teams can effectively monitor and track the overall health and performance of their applications throughout the software development lifecycle. It enables teams to proactively identify and diagnose performance bottlenecks, exceptions, and errors, thereby allowing them to continuously improve and optimize their applications.

Application Performance Monitoring (APM) Strategies

Application Performance Monitoring (APM) strategies in the context of DevOps refer to the techniques and practices used to monitor and analyze the performance of applications throughout their lifecycle, with the goal of identifying issues and bottlenecks, optimizing performance, and ensuring overall system stability and availability. APM strategies encompass various tools, technologies, and methodologies that enable organizations to gain deep insights into the performance of their applications and associated infrastructure. These strategies focus on monitoring key performance indicators (KPIs) such as response times, throughput, error rates, resource utilization, and user experience metrics to proactively identify and resolve performance issues before they impact end users. One key aspect of APM strategies is the collection and monitoring of real-time performance data. This is achieved through the use of monitoring agents or instrumentation within the application code, which collect data on various performance metrics. This data is then transmitted to a centralized monitoring system or dashboard, where it can be analyzed and visualized in near real-time. The ability to capture and analyze this data enables DevOps teams to quickly identify performance bottlenecks, anomalies, and trends, allowing them to make informed decisions and take appropriate actions. Another important element of APM strategies is the correlation of performance data with business metrics. By aligning application performance with business goals, organizations can gain a deeper understanding of how performance impacts user satisfaction, customer retention, revenue generation, and overall business success. This enables teams to prioritize performance improvements based on their impact on the business, guiding their decision-making processes. Additionally, APM strategies often incorporate automated monitoring and alerting mechanisms. By setting thresholds and defining performance baselines, organizations can automate the detection of performance anomalies and trigger alerts to relevant stakeholders. This allows for timely response and remediation of performance issues, minimizing their impact on end users. In summary, APM strategies in the context of DevOps involve the comprehensive monitoring, analysis, and optimization of application performance throughout its lifecycle. By leveraging real-time performance data, correlating it with business metrics, and implementing automation, these strategies enable organizations to ensure high levels of application performance, stability, and user satisfaction.

Application Performance Monitoring (APM) Tools

Application Performance Monitoring (APM) Tools in the context of DevOps refer to software solutions that are designed to monitor and analyze the performance and availability of applications and services in a production environment. These tools are essential for ensuring that applications meet the desired performance goals and deliver an optimal user experience. APM tools provide visibility into the performance of applications by collecting and analyzing data from various sources such as server logs, infrastructure metrics, and user interactions. These tools capture information about response times, request rates, error rates, and other key metrics that can help identify performance bottlenecks and troubleshoot issues.

Application Performance Monitoring (APM)

Application Performance Monitoring (APM) is a vital practice in the field of DevOps that involves a set of tools and techniques used to monitor and optimize the performance and availability of software applications. APM helps organizations to ensure that their applications are running smoothly, efficiently, and without any disruptions or performance issues, thus enhancing the end users' experience. The main goal of APM is to provide real-time visibility into the performance of applications, as well as the underlying infrastructure and dependencies, allowing organizations to proactively identify and resolve any bottlenecks or issues that may impact the performance. By monitoring various metrics such as response time, throughput, resource utilization, errors, and user satisfaction, APM enables organizations to pinpoint the root cause of any performance-related problems and take appropriate actions to rectify them.

Aqua Security

Aqua Security is a software security platform designed to address the unique challenges of cloud-native and containerized environments in the context of DevOps. DevOps is a software development approach that combines software development (Dev) and information technology operations (Ops) to enable organizations to deliver applications and services at a high velocity. It emphasizes collaboration, automation, and continuous integration and delivery (CI/CD) to improve efficiency and speed up the software development lifecycle. In this context, Aqua Security helps organizations ensure the security of their cloud-native and containerized applications throughout the DevOps process. Cloud-native and containerized environments have become increasingly popular due to their scalability and agility. However, they also introduce unique security challenges. Aqua Security provides a comprehensive security platform that integrates into the DevOps pipeline, allowing organizations to build security into their applications and infrastructure from the beginning. The platform offers a range of security capabilities, including vulnerability management, container image scanning, runtime protection, and compliance controls. By integrating security into the DevOps process, Aqua Security enables organizations to identify and mitigate security risks early on, reducing the likelihood of security breaches and compliance violations. The platform automates security processes and provides real-time visibility into the security posture of cloud-native and containerized applications, allowing organizations to quickly identify and respond to potential threats. Aqua Security also provides tools and features that help organizations enforce security policies, ensure compliance with regulatory requirements, and streamline security operations. The platform integrates with popular DevOps tools and platforms, making it easy to incorporate security into existing workflows and processes. In summary, Aqua Security is a software security platform that helps organizations address the unique security challenges of cloud-native and containerized environments in the context of DevOps. By integrating security into the DevOps process, Aqua Security enables organizations to build secure applications and infrastructure from the beginning, reducing the risk of security breaches and compliance violations.

Argo CD

Argo CD is an open-source declarative continuous delivery (CD) tool that automates the deployment of applications and configurations to Kubernetes clusters. It is designed to simplify the complex and error-prone task of deploying and managing applications in a distributed environment. With its declarative approach, Argo CD allows DevOps teams to describe the desired state of their application deployments using Kubernetes manifests or other declarative formats. It then continuously monitors the actual state of the cluster and automatically reconciles any discrepancies, ensuring that the desired state is maintained at all times. Argo CD provides a powerful and intuitive user interface that allows teams to easily manage and visualize the deployment of their applications. It offers a comprehensive set of features, including multi-tenancy, RBAC (Role-Based Access Control), synchronization, and rollback capabilities. One of the key benefits of using Argo CD is its ability to promote a culture of GitOps, where the entire application deployment lifecycle is managed through Git repositories. This allows teams to leverage the familiar Git workflows and version control mechanisms for managing their application configurations, enabling better collaboration and traceability. Argo CD integrates seamlessly with other popular DevOps tools and practices, such as CI/CD pipelines, observability, and release management. It supports automation and integration through APIs and offers a CLI (Command-Line Interface) for powerful command execution and scripting capabilities. In summary, Argo CD is a powerful and flexible CD tool that enhances the DevOps workflow by automating the deployment and management of applications in Kubernetes clusters. Its declarative approach, GitOps principles, and integrations with other DevOps tools make it a valuable asset for teams looking to streamline their application deployment processes.

Argo Rollouts

Argo Rollouts is a progressive delivery tool that enhances the deployment process in a DevOps context. It facilitates the gradual rollout of new versions of an application, allowing teams to validate changes in a controlled and automated manner. By leveraging features such as automated canary analysis and blue-green deployments, Argo Rollouts ensures a smooth transition between versions and minimizes the impact of any potential issues. At its core, Argo Rollouts extends the functionality of Kubernetes, which is a popular container orchestration platform. It introduces additional resources and controllers that enable more sophisticated deployment strategies. Traditional deployments involve replacing the existing version of an application with a new one all at once. However, this can introduce a significant amount of risk, as any issues or bugs in the new version can potentially impact users and disrupt the stability of the system. With Argo Rollouts, teams can adopt a more incremental approach to deployment. Canary deployments allow for the gradual release of new versions to a subset of users or servers, reducing the blast radius in case of problems. This subset, or canary, receives only a

9

small portion of the traffic, while the majority of users continue to use the stable version. The tool provides automated analysis of metrics and user feedback to determine if the canary deployment is successful or if there are any regressions or issues that need to be addressed. Another useful feature of Argo Rollouts is blue-green deployments. In this strategy, a new version of the application is deployed alongside the existing one, which remains fully operational. Once the new version is fully tested and ready, traffic is switched to the new version, effectively transitioning from the blue environment (existing version) to the green environment (new version). This approach allows for quick rollbacks if any problems arise with the new version, as the existing version is still available and serving traffic. Overall, Argo Rollouts is a powerful tool that promotes safer and more efficient deployments in a DevOps environment. By offering enhanced deployment strategies and automated analysis, it enables teams to iterate on their applications with confidence, reducing the risks associated with traditional all-or-nothing deployments.

Artifact Repository

An artifact repository, in the context of DevOps, is a centralized location or system that stores and manages software artifacts such as compiled binaries, executable scripts, configuration files, documentation, and other components of a software project. It is a crucial component of the software development and delivery pipeline, serving as a version-controlled and accessible source of truth for all artifacts that are produced during the development process. The main purpose of an artifact repository is to enable efficient and reliable access to software artifacts by different stakeholders, including developers, testers, operations teams, and other collaborators involved in the software development lifecycle. It provides a single source of truth for all versions and revisions of the artifacts, ensuring traceability and reproducibility of software releases. This is particularly important in a DevOps environment where agility, collaboration, and automation are key principles. Artifact repositories typically support versioning, allowing different versions of the same artifact to coexist and be easily managed. This enables organizations to track and manage changes made to software artifacts over time, facilitating rollbacks, bug fixes, and the ability to recreate specific software releases as needed. Additionally, artifact repositories often provide metadata management capabilities, allowing users to associate additional information with the artifacts such as release notes, build information, dependencies, and licensing details. This metadata can help in cataloging, searching, and understanding the artifacts, ultimately enhancing the overall governance and visibility of the software delivery process. Furthermore, artifact repositories may also support access control mechanisms to ensure that only authorized individuals or automation processes can access or modify the artifacts. This helps in maintaining the integrity and security of the software artifacts. In summary, an artifact repository is a crucial component of the DevOps toolchain, providing a centralized and version-controlled store for software artifacts. It improves collaboration, traceability, and reproducibility, ultimately enabling organizations to deliver high-quality software more efficiently.

Asana

Asana is a web-based task and project management tool that is commonly used in the context of DevOps. It provides teams with a centralized platform for planning, organizing, and tracking their work, allowing for greater collaboration and efficiency in the software development and delivery process. Asana enables teams to create and assign tasks, set deadlines, and track progress in real-time. It offers a range of features that are specifically designed to support the principles and practices of DevOps, such as agile project management, cross-functional team collaboration, and automated workflows. One of the key advantages of Asana in the context of DevOps is its ability to facilitate seamless communication and collaboration between various teams and stakeholders involved in the software development lifecycle. By providing a single platform for everyone to access and update task information, Asana helps to eliminate silos and ensures that all relevant stakeholders are kept in the loop. With Asana, teams can create and manage their work in an agile manner, using features like kanban boards and customizable project templates. This allows for greater flexibility and adaptability, as teams can easily adjust their plans and priorities based on changing requirements or feedback. Furthermore, Asana offers integration capabilities with other popular DevOps tools, such as Jira, GitHub, and Slack. This allows teams to seamlessly connect their work across different platforms and leverage the benefits of these complementary tools. Overall, Asana serves as a valuable tool in the DevOps landscape, helping teams to streamline their workflows, enhance collaboration, and deliver high-quality software more efficiently. Its user-friendly interface, robust features, and integration capabilities make it a popular choice among DevOps teams looking to optimize their work processes and achieve their goals.

Audit Trail

Audit Trail is a vital aspect of the DevOps process that involves recording and monitoring all activities and changes made to a system or application. It provides a comprehensive record of events, actions, and transactions, enabling organizations to trace and understand the flow of operations, identify and analyze issues, and ensure compliance with security and regulatory policies. Every action or event in the DevOps environment, such as code deployments, configuration changes, infrastructure updates, and user access requests, is logged and stored in the audit trail. This trail serves as a repository of information that can be reviewed and analyzed to investigate incidents, troubleshoot problems, and maintain accountability.

Auditing

Auditing in the context of DevOps refers to the systematic examination of various processes, activities, and infrastructure within the DevOps environment to ensure compliance, identify areas for improvement, and promote transparency and accountability. DevOps auditing involves analyzing and evaluating the entire software development lifecycle, from code changes and deployments to monitoring and incident response. It aims to verify that each step is executed according to established standards, policies, and regulations. By conducting audits, organizations can mitigate risks, address gaps, and enhance the overall effectiveness of their DevOps practices.

Automated Deployment

Automated Deployment in the context of DevOps refers to the process of automatically deploying software or applications to production environments without manual intervention. It is a crucial aspect of continuous delivery and plays a vital role in streamlining and accelerating software development and deployment cycles. Traditionally, software deployments were time-consuming, error-prone, and required extensive manual effort. However, with the advent of DevOps practices and the introduction of automated deployment tools, organizations can now eliminate these challenges and achieve faster and more reliable deployments.

Automated Root Cause Analysis Techniques

Automated Root Cause Analysis Techniques in the context of DevOps refer to the use of automated tools and methods to identify and determine the underlying cause of issues or problems in software applications or system operations. This approach aims to streamline the analysis process and reduce the time and effort required to identify and resolve the root cause of issues. Root cause analysis is a crucial step in the DevOps lifecycle as it helps to address recurring incidents, improve system stability, and enhance the overall performance and reliability of software applications. By automating the root cause analysis process, organizations can accelerate troubleshooting activities, minimize human error, and ultimately optimize their software development and delivery processes.

Automated Root Cause Analysis

Automated Root Cause Analysis refers to the process of using automated tools and techniques to identify the underlying causes of issues or incidents in a DevOps environment. Root cause analysis is a critical component of DevOps, as it helps to identify and resolve the core problems that lead to failures or disruptions in software development and operations. In a DevOps setup, various systems, applications, and processes work together to deliver software and services. When problems occur, such as an application crash or a service outage, it is essential to determine the root cause to prevent future occurrences and minimize the impact on users and business operations. Traditional root cause analysis often involves manually investigating logs, system metrics, and other data sources to identify the factors contributing to an incident. However, in a DevOps environment, where speed and agility are crucial, manual analysis can be time-consuming and delay problem resolution. Automated Root Cause Analysis streamlines the process by leveraging intelligent algorithms, machine learning, and data analytics to analyze vast amounts of system and application data in real-time. These automated tools can detect patterns, anomalies, and correlations in data, helping to pinpoint the root cause of an incident accurately. By automating the root cause analysis process, DevOps teams can rapidly identify the underlying issues and take appropriate remedial actions. This automation reduces the Mean Time to Repair (MTTR) and allows for faster recovery from incidents, minimizing downtime and enhancing the overall reliability and performance of the software delivery pipeline. Additionally, automated root cause analysis facilitates continuous improvement in the DevOps environment. The insights gained from analyzing past incidents can be utilized to identify potential bottlenecks, weaknesses, or areas for optimization. This knowledge can then be used to implement proactive measures, improve system resilience, and prevent similar issues from occurring in the future. In conclusion, Automated Root Cause Analysis is an essential practice in DevOps as it enables faster incident resolution, reduces downtime, and fosters continuous improvement. By leveraging automated tools and techniques, DevOps teams can efficiently identify and address the root causes of issues, ultimately enhancing the reliability and performance of software development and operations.

Automated Testing Frameworks

An automated testing framework in the context of DevOps refers to a set of tools, libraries, and guidelines that enable the automation of testing activities throughout the software development process. It provides a structured approach for planning, designing, executing, and monitoring tests, allowing organizations to achieve continuous testing and integration with their DevOps practices. The primary goal of an automated testing framework in DevOps is to ensure the delivery of high-quality software at a faster pace and with more predictability. It helps teams reduce the time, effort, and manual intervention required for testing by automating repetitive and time-consuming tasks. This enables the development and operations teams to work in parallel, fostering collaboration and accelerating the overall delivery process.

Automation

Automation in the context of DevOps refers to the process of automating repetitive tasks, workflows, and processes in software development and IT operations. It involves the use of tools, scripts, and technologies to streamline and simplify manual tasks, reduce human error, and improve efficiency. DevOps focuses on the collaboration and integration between development teams (Dev) and operations teams (Ops). Automation plays a crucial role in the DevOps philosophy by enabling the rapid and continuous delivery of software. It ensures that software development and deployment processes are standardized, repeatable, and reliable.

Availability

Availability, in the context of DevOps, refers to the ability of a system or service to provide its intended functionality to its users without interruption or downtime. It is a fundamental characteristic that ensures continuous access and usability of applications, platforms, and infrastructure. An available system or service should be reliable, resilient, and accessible. Reliability implies that the system consistently performs its functions correctly and as expected. It should not experience failures or errors that result in unavailability. Resilience refers to the ability of the system to recover quickly and continue functioning after a disruption or failure. It involves implementing robust fault-tolerant mechanisms and redundancy to minimize downtime. Accessibility ensures that users can access the system easily and conveniently, regardless of their location or device used. Availability is crucial in the DevOps approach because it aligns with the goal of delivering continuous value and reducing time-to-market. When systems are available, users can rely on them to perform their tasks, resulting in improved productivity and user satisfaction. Achieving high availability requires a combination of proactive monitoring, automated testing, deployment practices, and infrastructure management. DevOps teams focus on ensuring availability through various practices and techniques. They implement continuous integration and continuous deployment (CI/CD) pipelines to automate the build, test, and deployment processes. This automation helps identify and prevent issues early in the development cycle, reducing the risk of deployment failures and minimizing downtime. They also leverage infrastructure-as-code (IAC) principles to manage infrastructure configuration and provisioning. This allows teams to quickly and reliably replicate environments, reducing the time required to recover from failures or scaling needs. In summary, availability in the context of

DevOps refers to the uninterrupted functioning and accessibility of systems or services. DevOps practices and principles aim to achieve and maintain high availability through proactive monitoring, automated testing, fault-tolerant design, and infrastructure management.

Bamboo

According to the context of DevOps, bamboo refers to a continuous integration and deployment tool that plays a significant role in automating the software development process. It is designed to facilitate collaboration and streamline the delivery of code changes, making it an essential component of a DevOps toolchain. Bamboo enables a continuous integration (CI) workflow by automating the build and testing processes. It helps software development teams to easily and consistently compile code changes into a deployable artifact. Bamboo achieves this by automatically triggering a build whenever changes are committed to the source code repository. It then compiles the source code, runs tests, and generates a build artifact, such as a binary or an executable. One of the key features of Bamboo is its integration with various version control systems, such as Git or Subversion. This integration allows Bamboo to monitor changes in the repository and trigger builds accordingly. Bamboo also supports parallel builds, which can accelerate the CI process by distributing the load across multiple build agents. Apart from CI, Bamboo also facilitates continuous deployment (CD). It provides tools for automating the release and deployment of software to various environments, such as development, testing, and production. Bamboo allows deployment plans to be defined and executed, ensuring consistent and reliable deployments. Bamboo's deployment capabilities include support for different deployment models, like manual or automated deployments, and the ability to roll back deployments if issues arise. It also integrates with configuration management tools, making it easier to manage infrastructure as code. In addition to its core CI/CD functions, Bamboo offers features like extensive reporting and analytics, enabling teams to gain insights into build and deployment processes. It provides dashboards and visualizations to monitor build statuses, test results, and deployment progress. Overall, Bamboo is a powerful tool for automating the software development lifecycle, from code compilation and testing to deployment and release management. Its integration with version control systems, support for parallel builds, and deployment automation capabilities make it a key component of an efficient DevOps workflow.

Behavior-Driven Development (BDD)

Behavior-Driven Development (BDD) is a software development approach that aligns the business goals, technical implementation, and user behavior to deliver high-quality software in a collaborative and iterative manner. It is an essential practice in the context of DevOps, where the focus is on continuous integration, delivery, and deployment. In BDD, the development process starts with defining the behavior of the software from the perspective of the user. This is achieved through collaborative discussions and the creation of executable specifications called "scenarios." These scenarios capture both the expected behavior and the edge cases that need to be considered. The scenarios are written in a natural language format that can be understood by stakeholders with varying technical backgrounds. This promotes effective communication and facilitates shared understanding between the development team, product owners, and other stakeholders. Moreover, the scenarios serve as living documentation, which can be referred to and updated throughout the software development lifecycle. Once the scenarios are defined, the development team can implement the corresponding functionality using an iterative and test-driven approach. The scenarios serve as the basis for writing automated tests, which are executed to ensure that the software behaves as expected. These tests are typically written using tools like Cucumber or SpecFlow, which provide frameworks for executing scenarios written in a natural language format. BDD promotes collaboration between different teams involved in the software development process, such as developers, testers, and operations. Through shared understanding and effective communication, potential issues and misunderstandings can be avoided or addressed early on. This reduces the likelihood of bugs and enhances the overall quality of the software. By integrating BDD into the DevOps workflow, software development teams can ensure that the software is developed and tested in alignment with the business goals. BDD empowers teams to continuously deliver valuable features, mitigate risks, and make informed decisions based on user behavior. Ultimately, BDD enables organizations to deliver high-quality software at a faster pace while maintaining a focus on business value.

Behavioral Analytics

Behavioral Analytics, in the context of DevOps, refers to the practice of collecting, analyzing, and interpreting data on user behavior to gain insights and make informed decisions to optimize software development and deployment processes. DevOps is a software development methodology that aims to improve collaboration and communication between software development and operations teams, with the goal of delivering high-quality software at a faster pace. Behavioral analytics plays a crucial role in this methodology by providing valuable insights into user behavior, which can be used to identify potential bottlenecks, optimize processes, and enhance the overall user experience.

Black Duck

Black Duck is a comprehensive software and security solution designed specifically for DevOps teams. It offers a range of tools and functionalities aimed at helping organizations manage and secure their open source code and third-party components. Black Duck's primary purpose is to aid DevOps teams in identifying and managing potential security vulnerabilities, licensing issues, and code quality concerns in their software development process. It achieves this by automatically scanning codebases, including open source components and their dependencies, to generate a detailed inventory of all the components used in an application.

Blameless Post-Mortems

Blameless post-mortems, in the context of DevOps, refer to thorough and objective retrospective analyses of incidents or failures that have occurred within a software or system development process. These post-mortems aim to identify and understand the root causes of the incidents, as well as to propose and implement effective solutions to prevent similar issues from recurring in the future. Blameless post-mortems follow the principles of blameless culture, which focuses on fostering a blame-free environment where individuals are encouraged to share their experiences, insights, and concerns openly without fear of negative repercussions. The purpose is to shift the focus from attributing blame or seeking punishment to promoting learning, collaboration, and improvement.

Bleeding Edge Technology Adoption

Bleeding Edge Technology Adoption refers to the practice of integrating and implementing cutting-edge technologies in the field of DevOps. It involves embracing and utilizing the latest and most innovative tools, methodologies, and frameworks to optimize the software development and delivery process. DevOps, which is a combination of software Development and IT Operations, aims to streamline and automate the software development lifecycle, from planning and coding to testing, deployment, and monitoring. Embracing bleeding-edge technologies in a DevOps environment allows organizations to gain a competitive advantage by leveraging the most advanced solutions available in the market.

Bleeding Edge Technology

Bleeding Edge Technology refers to the most advanced and innovative tools, software, methodologies, and practices that are currently being developed and have not yet been widely adopted or proven in the industry. In the context of DevOps, bleeding edge technology represents the latest and most cutting-edge technologies and approaches used to enable seamless collaboration, continuous integration, delivery, and deployment of software applications. DevOps is a set of practices that combines software development (Dev) and IT operations (Ops) to improve the speed, quality, and agility of software delivery. It focuses on breaking down silos between development and operations teams, automating processes, and fostering a culture of collaboration and continuous improvement. By adopting bleeding edge technology in DevOps, organizations can stay at the forefront of innovation and gain a competitive edge. These technologies often involve leveraging advancements in cloud computing, containerization, microservices, automation, artificial intelligence, machine learning, and analytics. For example, containerization technologies like Docker and Kubernetes have revolutionized the way applications are deployed and managed. They provide lightweight, isolated environments that enable faster development, deployment, and scalability. Using bleeding edge technology like containers, organizations can achieve greater flexibility, portability, and efficiency in their software delivery pipelines. Bleeding edge technology also includes the use of Infrastructure as Code (IaC) tools such as Terraform and Ansible. These tools enable the automation and management of infrastructure resources through code, eliminating manual configurations and reducing time-consuming and error-prone processes. By adopting IaC, organizations can achieve greater consistency, scalability, and reliability in their infrastructure provisioning and management. However, it is important to note that bleeding edge technology comes with its own set of challenges. As these technologies are relatively new and untested, there may be limited documentation, community support, and best practices available. Organizations should carefully evaluate the risks and benefits of adopting bleeding edge technology and consider factors such as stability, compatibility, security, and skillset requirements before implementation. In conclusion, bleeding edge technology in the context of DevOps represents the latest and most advanced tools and practices used to enhance software delivery processes. While it offers the potential for improved efficiency and innovation, organizations must carefully assess the risks and consider the specific requirements of their environment before embracing bleeding edge technology.

Blue-Green Deployment

Blue-Green Deployment is a software release technique used in the context of DevOps to minimize downtime and risk during the deployment process. It involves maintaining two separate and identical environments, referred to as the blue environment and the green environment, running concurrently. The blue environment represents the production environment, handling the live traffic and user requests. It is the stable and tested version of the application that is currently in use. The green environment, on the other hand, represents the new version of the application that is being deployed. It is an identical replica of the blue environment, running the updated code that needs to be rolled out. With the blue-green deployment approach, the release process is as follows: 1. Initially, the blue environment is serving the application to the users, and the green environment is inactive. 2. The new version of the application is deployed to the green environment, allowing it to be thoroughly tested and verified before being made live. 3. Once the green environment passes all the tests and is deemed stable, a router or load balancer is updated to direct the incoming traffic to the green environment instead of the blue environment. 4. Users are now accessing the new version of the application in the green environment, while the blue environment remains intact and ready to handle potential rollbacks if any issues arise. 5. In case of any problems or unexpected behavior, the router or load balancer can be switched back to redirect the traffic to the stable blue environment, effectively rolling back the deployment with minimal downtime. This deployment technique enhances the reliability and availability of the application during updates, as any issues can be quickly addressed by reverting back to the stable blue environment. It also reduces the risks associated with a faulty deployment and allows for thorough testing of the new version in an identical environment. Overall, the blue-green deployment approach provides a controlled and seamless transition between application versions, ensuring minimal disruption to the end users and maximizing the overall software delivery process.

Bridgecrew

Bridgecrew is a crucial component of a DevOps strategy, specializing in cloud security and compliance. It is an automated platform that integrates security into the software development lifecycle, ensuring that security and compliance are consistently incorporated from the initial stages. Bridgecrew provides real-time security insights, automating security controls, and enables developers to address vulnerabilities as part of their everyday workflow. By integrating seamlessly with popular DevOps tools such as GitHub, GitLab, and Bitbucket, Bridgecrew empowers developers to proactively identify and remediate security issues early on.

Buddy

DevOps is a software development approach that focuses on establishing close collaboration between software developers, operations teams, and other stakeholders involved in the product lifecycle. The term "DevOps" is a combination of "development" and "operations," representing the convergence of these two traditionally separate areas. In the DevOps model, development and operations teams work together throughout the software development process, from planning and design to coding, testing, deployment, and monitoring. This collaboration is enabled by implementing a set of practices, tools, and cultural norms aimed at breaking down silos and fostering efficient communication and cooperation between teams.

BuildMaster

BuildMaster is a comprehensive DevOps tool that streamlines and automates the software development and release process. It serves as a powerful platform for managing and controlling the entire application lifecycle, from initial code commit to final deployment. With BuildMaster, organizations can achieve efficient and reliable software delivery by automating key processes such as building, testing, and deploying applications. It enables teams to collaborate easily and consistently across various stages of the development lifecycle, ensuring that software is delivered on time and with high quality. BuildMaster provides a centralized platform for managing and versioning source code, allowing developers to efficiently collaborate and track changes. It supports integration with popular version control systems, such as Git and Subversion, enabling teams to easily synchronize their codebase. BuildMaster offers flexible and customizable build and release pipelines, empowering teams to define and automate their unique workflows. It automatically pulls code from version control, compiles it, runs tests, and packages applications for deployment. Teams can easily configure and manage deployment environments, such as development, testing, and production, ensuring consistent and repeatable deployments. BuildMaster incorporates best practices of continuous integration and continuous delivery (CI/CD). It integrates seamlessly with popular build systems, such as Jenkins and Azure DevOps, allowing teams to leverage their existing infrastructure investments. It provides extensive configuration options, allowing teams to integrate with a wide range of tools and systems required for their unique development process. Key features of BuildMaster include release management, environment promotion, artifact management, release pipeline visualization, and deployment automation. It provides comprehensive reporting and auditing capabilities, allowing teams to track and analyze the progress and quality of their software releases. In summary, BuildMaster is a robust DevOps tool that simplifies and automates the software delivery process. It enables teams to collaborate effectively, accelerate release cycles, and ensure reliable and consistent deployments. By leveraging BuildMaster's capabilities, organizations can streamline their development process, reduce errors, and deliver software faster and with higher quality.

Buildkite

Buildkite is a powerful continuous integration and delivery platform designed specifically for DevOps teams. It provides a streamlined and efficient way to automate the process of building, testing, and deploying software applications. With Buildkite, developers can easily set up pipelines that define the various stages of the software development lifecycle. These pipelines act as a chain of command, determining the order in which tasks are executed. Each task within the pipeline represents a specific action, such as compiling code, running tests, or deploying to production. One of the key features of Buildkite is its flexibility and extensibility. It supports a wide range of programming languages, tools, and third-party integrations, allowing teams to tailor their workflows to suit their specific needs. Buildkite seamlessly integrates with popular development platforms like GitHub, Bitbucket, and GitLab, making it easy to trigger builds based on code changes. Buildkite also provides a rich set of features to support collaboration and visibility within the development team. It enables real-time notifications, so team members can stay informed about the progress of builds and deployments. Buildkite's user interface provides a clean and intuitive dashboard that displays detailed information about each build, including logs, artifacts, and test results. Furthermore, Buildkite fosters a culture of transparency and accountability by storing all pipeline configurations and build histories in version control. This means that every change made to the pipeline is tracked and auditable, which helps teams identify and resolve issues quickly. In summary, Buildkite is a comprehensive and flexible continuous integration and delivery platform that empowers DevOps teams to build, test, and deploy software efficiently. Its powerful features, extensive integrations, and intuitive UI make it an excellent choice for organizations looking to streamline and automate their software development processes.

Canary Deployment

A Canary Deployment is a deployment strategy in the context of DevOps that aims to minimize the risk associated with rolling out new software versions or updates to a production environment. It involves gradually redirecting a small subset of user traffic to the new version of an application, while the majority of traffic still goes to the stable, existing version. The term "Canary" is inspired by the practice of using canaries in coal mines to detect toxic gases. In a similar vein, a Canary Deployment functions as an early warning system, allowing the development team to observe and assess the behavior and performance of the new version in a real-world environment before fully committing to its release.

Capacity Management

Capacity Management, in the context of DevOps, refers to the process of ensuring that an organization has the necessary resources and capabilities to effectively meet the demands of its IT infrastructure and achieve its goals. Capacity Management involves planning, monitoring, and optimizing the allocation and utilization of various resources, including hardware, software, network bandwidth, storage, and human resources. The goal is to ensure that the organization has the right amount of capacity, neither too little nor too much, to deliver IT services efficiently and cost-effectively.

Capacity Planning

Capacity planning is a strategic process within the context of DevOps that involves assessing and forecasting the computing resources and infrastructure required to meet the demands of an application or system. It helps organizations ensure that they have the appropriate amount of resources available at any given time to support their operations and deliver reliable and efficient services to their customers. The goal of capacity planning is to strike a balance between providing enough resources to meet current demands without underutilizing or overprovisioning the infrastructure. By accurately estimating the required capacity, organizations can optimize resource allocation, minimize downtime, and achieve cost-efficiency by avoiding unnecessary hardware or cloud expenses.

Change Advisory Board (CAB)

A Change Advisory Board (CAB) is a crucial component of the DevOps process that is responsible for reviewing, evaluating, and approving or rejecting proposed changes to the IT environment. The CAB plays a significant role in ensuring that all modifications made to the system align with the organization's objectives and do not negatively impact its stability or performance. The primary objective of the CAB is to minimize risk and disruption to the IT infrastructure by carefully assessing and controlling changes. This board comprises representatives from various departments or teams within the organization, including those responsible for application development, infrastructure operations, security, and business units. By bringing together individuals with diverse expertise and perspectives, the CAB facilitates a comprehensive evaluation of proposed changes. The CAB operates as a decision-making body that evaluates the impact of proposed changes on both technical and business aspects. This evaluation includes assessing the financial implications, potential risks, resource requirements, and impact to the existing systems and applications. The board evaluates whether the proposed change is necessary, feasible, and aligned with the organization's overall strategy. The CAB follows a well-defined process to ensure transparent and efficient decision-making. This process typically includes the submission of change requests, evaluation of the requests by the board members, and collaborative discussions to reach a consensus. The CAB may request additional information or documentation to support the evaluation process and may involve technical experts or stakeholders for their insights. Ultimately, the CAB is responsible for either approving or rejecting proposed changes. If a change is approved, the CAB may also define the specific conditions or prerequisites that must be met before implementation. During the change implementation phase, the CAB is kept informed about the progress and may provide further guidance or support if necessary. In summary, the Change Advisory Board (CAB) is an essential governing body within the DevOps process. It ensures that changes are thoroughly reviewed, evaluated, and aligned with the organization's objectives. By minimizing risks associated with changes, the CAB contributes to the successful delivery of reliable and stable IT services.

Change Failure Rate (CFR)

The Change Failure Rate (CFR) is a metric used in the context of DevOps to measure the rate at which changes made to a software system fail. It quantifies the percentage of changes that do not meet the intended objectives and cause negative outcomes. This metric is crucial in evaluating the effectiveness of the DevOps practices and identifying areas for improvement. The CFR is calculated by dividing the number of failed changes by the total number of changes made within a specific time period. The result is expressed as a percentage, providing a clear understanding of the success or failure rate of changes. A lower CFR indicates a higher success rate and, consequently, a more efficient and reliable software delivery process.

Change Management

Change Management in the context of DevOps refers to the systematic approach and process that is implemented to manage and control any changes made to the software development and deployment lifecycle. It aims to ensure that changes are effectively planned, implemented, tracked, and controlled, minimizing any potential negative impacts on the business and its customers. Change Management in DevOps involves a structured set of activities and procedures that are followed to assess, authorize, and implement changes in software systems without causing disruptions or compromising the stability and reliability of the overall development and operations process. It focuses on managing risk, minimizing downtime, and optimizing the release and deployment of software changes. The primary goal of Change Management in DevOps is to facilitate a smooth and seamless transition from one state to another, whether it is the introduction of new features, bug fixes, infrastructure updates, or configuration changes. It ensures that changes are carefully planned and tested, and that the impact on all stakeholders, including developers, operations teams, end-users, and business units, is taken into consideration. Change Management practices in DevOps typically involve the following key steps: 1. Request and Evaluation: Changes are initiated through a formal request process, where their impact and feasibility are assessed. This involves evaluating the potential risks, benefits, and dependencies associated with the proposed changes. 2. Change Authorization: Once a change request is evaluated, it needs to be authorized by the appropriate stakeholders. This step ensures that the change aligns with the business objectives and is in accordance with the overall DevOps strategy. 3. Change Planning: Detailed planning is crucial to ensure that changes are implemented in a controlled manner. This includes defining the scope, identifying the resources required, creating a schedule, and establishing communication channels. 4. Change Implementation: The actual execution of the change is carefully managed, ensuring that best practices are followed and any potential risks are mitigated. This can involve activities such as code deployment, configuration updates, infrastructure changes, or any other necessary actions. 5. Change Monitoring and Review: Once the change is implemented, it is closely monitored to ensure that it meets the desired objectives and does not cause any unexpected issues. Regular reviews and feedback are essential to continuously improve the change management process. In conclusion, Change Management in the context of DevOps is a disciplined approach to handle changes in software development and deployment processes. It ensures that changes are carefully planned, authorized, and implemented, reducing the risks and maximizing the efficiency of the overall DevOps lifecycle.

Chaos Engineering Experiments Planning

Chaos Engineering is a discipline that aims to proactively identify and address weaknesses in a system's resilience. It involves conducting controlled experiments to simulate real-world failure scenarios and observe how the system behaves under stress or unpredictable conditions. These experiments are typically performed in the context of a DevOps environment where continuous integration and deployment practices are followed. The goal of Chaos Engineering is to uncover vulnerabilities and risks before they occur in production, allowing organizations to build more reliable and resilient systems. By deliberately injecting failures, such as shutting down servers, increasing network latency, or introducing faulty code, Chaos Engineering enables teams to gain insights into how their systems react to these events. This information can then be used to make informed improvements, such as implementing better monitoring, redundancy, or failover mechanisms.

Chaos Engineering Experiments

Chaos Engineering is a DevOps practice that involves conducting controlled experiments on a system or application to assess its resilience and ability to withstand unexpected disruptions or failures. These experiments aim to simulate real-world scenarios and identify potential weaknesses or vulnerabilities in the system, with the ultimate goal of improving its overall reliability and stability. The process of Chaos Engineering typically involves intentionally injecting failures or perturbations into a system and closely monitoring its behavior and performance during these disruptions. By deliberately causing failures in a controlled environment, teams can gain valuable insights into how their systems respond under stress and uncover potential issues or bottlenecks that may not be apparent under normal conditions.

Chaos Engineering

Chaos Engineering is a practice rooted in the DevOps philosophy that aims to proactively identify weaknesses and potential vulnerabilities in complex distributed systems. It involves intentionally and safely injecting controlled forms of chaos into the system to uncover any weaknesses and potential failure points. The primary goal of Chaos Engineering is to build resilient systems that can withstand unexpected failures or disruptions without impacting the overall system performance. By deliberately introducing controlled chaos, organizations can identify and address potential points of failure, thereby increasing the system's overall reliability and stability.

ChatOps Tools Adoption

ChatOps tools adoption refers to the process of integrating and implementing tools that enable teams to collaborate and execute tasks within the context of a DevOps environment. These tools are specifically designed to leverage chat platforms or messaging applications, allowing users to interact with various systems and tools through a conversational interface. By adopting ChatOps tools, organizations can streamline and automate their DevOps workflows, enabling teams to communicate, coordinate, and perform tasks more efficiently. These tools facilitate real-time communication, collaboration, and visibility, creating a centralized and transparent environment where teams can work together seamlessly.

ChatOps Tools

ChatOps tools are software applications designed to facilitate collaboration and communication between development and operations teams in the context of DevOps. These tools integrate with chat platforms such as Slack, Microsoft Teams, or Mattermost to provide a central hub for team members to interact, share information, and execute tasks in real-time. With ChatOps tools, developers and operations personnel can leverage the power of chat platforms to streamline their workflows and enhance collaboration. Through the integration of various DevOps tools, such as CI/CD pipelines, version control systems, monitoring systems, and issue trackers, these tools enable teams to perform a wide range of tasks directly from their chat interface. One of the key features of ChatOps tools is their ability to enable real-time notifications and alerts. Team members can receive automated notifications about events and changes in the development and operations processes, ensuring everyone stays up-to-date and can take immediate action if needed. By centralizing this information in a chat platform, team members can access and react to these notifications without having to switch between different tools or interfaces. Another important aspect of ChatOps tools is the ability to execute commands and perform actions through chat commands or interactive bots. These tools allow team members to trigger actions, deploy software, initiate tests, and perform various other tasks by simply typing commands in the chat platform. This not only saves time but also reduces the chances of human error by removing the need for manual interventions in complex processes. Furthermore, ChatOps tools often include features for sharing information and knowledge among team members. They provide a platform for sharing links, documents, code snippets, and other resources, fostering a culture of knowledge sharing and collaboration within the team. By keeping the conversation history and shared resources accessible, these tools also help new team members get up to speed quickly and provide a reference for future discussions and decisions. In summary, ChatOps tools are essential for fostering collaboration, streamlining workflows, and enhancing communication between development and operations teams in a DevOps environment. By integrating with chat platforms, automating notifications, enabling command execution, and facilitating knowledge sharing, these tools empower teams to work more efficiently and effectively towards their common goals.

ChatOps

ChatOps is a practice within the DevOps culture that aims to enhance collaboration, automation, and monitoring by integrating communication tools directly into the operational workflow. It involves using chat platforms as a central hub for managing and controlling various aspects of the development and operation processes. With ChatOps, teams can perform a wide range of actions and tasks, such as code deployments, infrastructure provisioning, incident management, and monitoring, all from within the chat interface. This approach promotes real-time communication, transparency, and traceability, enabling teams to work more efficiently and effectively.

Checkmarx

Checkmarx is a static application security testing (SAST) tool that is used in the context of DevOps. It helps organizations identify and address vulnerabilities in their software code early in the development process. As part of the DevOps workflow, Checkmarx integrates seamlessly into the software development cycle, providing developers with the ability to automatically scan their code for potential security flaws. It analyzes the source code to identify potential vulnerabilities, such as injection attacks, cross-site scripting (XSS), and improper authentication. The tool offers a wide range of features to assist developers in securing their code. It provides detailed reports and alerts on vulnerabilities, allowing developers to quickly identify and remediate any issues. Checkmarx also integrates with popular development environments, such as IDEs, build tools, and version control systems, allowing developers to easily incorporate security testing into their existing workflows. Checkmarx's SAST approach offers several advantages in the DevOps context. By catching security vulnerabilities early in the development process, developers can address them before they become more critical and costly to fix. This helps organizations reduce the risk of potential security breaches and improve the overall security posture of their software applications. In addition to its scanning capabilities, Checkmarx supports collaboration and communication between development, security, and operations teams. It provides a centralized platform for developers and security professionals to work together on resolving vulnerabilities and implementing secure coding practices. This collaboration helps foster a culture of security and ensures that security concerns are addressed throughout the software development lifecycle. Overall, Checkmarx is a valuable tool in the DevOps landscape, enabling organizations to integrate security testing seamlessly into their development processes. By helping developers identify and resolve security vulnerabilities early on, it contributes to the creation of secure, high-quality software applications.

Chef Automate

Chef Automate is a DevOps tool that allows organizations to manage and automate their infrastructure and applications in a seamless and efficient manner. It provides a consolidated platform for teams to collaborate, manage, and monitor their entire DevOps workflow, from development to deployment to production. With Chef Automate, organizations can define their infrastructure as code, using Chef's declarative language, known as Chef Infra. This allows for consistent and reproducible configurations, reducing the risk of errors and enabling quick and easy updates and rollbacks.

CircleCI

The CircleCI is a continuous integration and continuous delivery (CI/CD) platform that helps software development teams automate their build, test, and deploy processes. It is a cloud-based solution that allows developers to integrate their code changes frequently and reliably into a shared repository, enabling early detection of bugs and issues. As part of the DevOps culture, CircleCI plays a crucial role in automating the pipeline and ensuring the efficient delivery of software. It provides a seamless integration with popular version control systems like GitHub and Bitbucket, allowing teams to trigger builds automatically whenever changes are pushed to the repository. By adopting CircleCI, development teams can set up comprehensive pipelines to facilitate the building, testing, and deployment of their applications. The platform supports various programming languages, frameworks, and tools, making it versatile for a wide range of projects. CircleCI offers a highly scalable and flexible infrastructure, where developers can define their build and test processes using a configuration file. This file, typically stored at the root directory of the project, describes the required steps, dependencies, and environment variables for the CI/CD pipeline. It enables teams to reproduce the build and test environment accurately, thereby reducing errors caused by inconsistencies. CircleCI triggers automated builds whenever new commits or pull requests are made to the repository. It carries out a series of tasks such as code compilation, running unit tests, and creating deployable artifacts. The platform provides extensive logging and reporting capabilities, allowing teams to inspect the build process and identify any failures or bottlenecks. With its deployment capabilities, CircleCI helps teams deliver their applications to various environments such as staging, production, and cloud platforms. It integrates seamlessly with popular deployment options like AWS, Google Cloud, and Heroku, streamlining the process of releasing software to end-users. In conclusion, CircleCI is a powerful CI/CD platform that empowers development teams to automate their build, test, and deployment processes. By simplifying and accelerating the software delivery life cycle, CircleCI enables organizations to deliver high-quality software faster and with fewer errors.

Circuit Breaker Pattern

The Circuit Breaker Pattern is a DevOps design pattern that aims to improve the resilience and stability of a system by managing the impact of remote service failures. It is inspired by electrical circuit breakers, which automatically interrupt the flow of electricity when there is an overload or a short circuit to prevent damage to the electrical system. In a DevOps context, the Circuit Breaker Pattern is used to handle the integration of microservices or distributed systems. It provides an abstraction layer between the caller and the remote service, protecting the caller from cascading failures caused by the unavailability or poor performance of the service.

ClickUp

ClickUp is a comprehensive project management tool designed for DevOps teams. It serves as a central hub for collaboration, task management, and workflow automation, enabling teams to streamline their development processes and deliver high-quality software products. With ClickUp, DevOps teams can easily manage their projects and tasks by creating custom workflows, assigning responsibilities, setting due dates, and tracking progress. The tool offers a wide range of features, including task lists, Kanban boards, Gantt charts, and calendars, providing teams with the flexibility to choose the most suitable view for their projects. One of the key features of ClickUp is its seamless integrations with popular DevOps tools and services. DevOps teams can connect ClickUp with their preferred version control systems, such as Git or SVN, to streamline code management and ensure smooth collaboration between developers. Furthermore, ClickUp integrates with CI/CD platforms, allowing teams to automate their build, test, and deployment processes, resulting in faster and more efficient delivery of software updates. ClickUp also includes communication and collaboration tools that facilitate effective teamwork among team members. It provides real-time chat functionality, enabling instant messaging and file sharing, fostering quick discussions and decision-making. Additionally, ClickUp allows teams to create and assign comments to specific tasks, ensuring clear communication and a centralized space for discussions. Furthermore, ClickUp offers powerful reporting and analytics capabilities for DevOps teams. It provides customizable dashboards and charts, allowing teams to monitor project status, track key performance indicators, and identify areas for improvement. By leveraging these insights, teams can make data-driven decisions and continuously optimize their development processes. In summary, ClickUp is a feature-rich project management tool that caters specifically to the needs of DevOps teams. By providing a centralized workspace, seamless integrations, effective collaboration tools, and insightful analytics, ClickUp empowers teams to enhance their productivity, improve communication, and successfully deliver software products in an agile and efficient manner.

Cloud-Native Security

Cloud-Native Security refers to the set of practices and measures implemented in the DevOps context to protect cloud-native applications and infrastructure from potential cybersecurity threats and vulnerabilities. As organizations increasingly adopt cloud-native architectures and leverage cloud technologies to develop, deploy, and manage their applications, the need for robust security mechanisms becomes imperative. Cloud-Native Security focuses on mitigating both known and unknown risks inherent to cloud-native environments by integrating security measures seamlessly into the entire DevOps pipeline.

Code Promotion

Code promotion in the context of DevOps refers to the process of moving software code from one environment to another in a controlled manner. It involves promoting code changes through various stages such as development, testing, staging, and production, ensuring a smooth and reliable deployment. In a typical DevOps workflow, code promotion follows a systematic approach to ensure quality and stability. It involves several steps, including code review, build and packaging, automated testing, and deployment. Each step aims to validate the code changes and minimize the risk of introducing errors or defects into the production environment.

Code Review

Formal Definition of DevOps: DevOps is a software development and operations methodology that aims to bridge the gap between development and IT operations teams by fostering a culture of collaboration, automation, and continuous delivery. It seeks to improve software development and delivery processes, ensuring faster and more reliable releases, better quality software, and increased customer satisfaction. DevOps emphasizes close collaboration and communication between developers, system administrators, and other stakeholders involved in the software development lifecycle. It encourages breaking down silos and integrating development and operations teams into a single entity, often referred to as a DevOps team or a DevOps culture.

Codefresh

Codefresh is a DevOps platform that enables developers to streamline and automate the software delivery process. It provides a comprehensive set of tools and features to help organizations adopt and implement DevOps best practices. At its core, Codefresh simplifies the development and deployment workflows by offering seamless integration with popular source code repositories, such as GitHub and Bitbucket, as well as with leading containerization platforms like Docker and Kubernetes. This tight integration allows developers to easily build, test, and deploy their applications within a standardized and automated pipeline. One of the key benefits of Codefresh is its ability to accelerate the software delivery process. By automating the build, test, and deployment steps, developers can greatly reduce the time and effort required to release new features or bug fixes. This speed and efficiency enable teams to iterate on their code more frequently, resulting in faster time to market and enhanced overall product quality. Furthermore, Codefresh supports continuous integration and continuous delivery (CI/CD) methodologies, which are fundamental principles of DevOps. It allows teams to define and enforce consistent development and release processes, ensuring that every change goes through a comprehensive set of automated tests before being deployed to production. This automation not only increases the software's reliability but also helps to catch any bugs or issues early in the development cycle. Additionally, Codefresh enables collaboration and coordination among team members. It provides a centralized platform where developers, DevOps engineers, and other stakeholders can collaborate, share code, and track progress. This fosters better communication, improves transparency, and allows for more effective teamwork, leading to higher productivity and better outcomes. In conclusion, Codefresh is a powerful DevOps platform that helps organizations integrate and automate their software delivery pipelines. By providing a seamless and efficient way to build, test, and deploy applications, it enables teams to deliver high-quality software at a faster pace, while also fostering collaboration and coordination among team members.

Collaboration Tools

A collaboration tool in the context of DevOps refers to software or platforms that facilitate communication, coordination, and collaboration among individuals or teams involved in the development, testing, deployment, and maintenance of software. These tools help streamline various aspects of the DevOps process by enabling real-time communication, efficient task management, and seamless integration with other DevOps tools. The primary goal of collaboration tools in DevOps is to bring together individuals with diverse expertise and responsibilities and provide them with a centralized platform for effective collaboration. These tools enable developers, testers, operations teams, and other stakeholders to work together, share information, and coordinate their efforts towards achieving common objectives.

Collaboration

The concept of collaboration in the context of DevOps refers to the practice of bringing together individuals with different expertise, roles, and backgrounds to work together towards achieving common goals and objectives in the software development and operations process. Collaboration is a fundamental aspect of DevOps culture and is essential for promoting effective communication, fostering a sense of ownership and shared responsibility, and ultimately achieving faster and more efficient software delivery. In a DevOps environment, collaboration involves breaking down silos and encouraging cross-functional teams to work collaboratively throughout the entire software development lifecycle. This includes activities such as planning, development, testing, deployment, and monitoring. By promoting collaboration, DevOps aims to eliminate the traditional barriers and handoffs between different teams or departments, such as developers, operations, quality assurance, and security, in order to foster a culture of shared understanding, accountability, and continuous improvement.

Collaborative Version Control Systems

Collaborative Version Control Systems are tools used in the context of DevOps to manage and organize the development of software projects through collaborative and controlled versioning of code and other digital assets. These systems enable multiple developers to work on the same project simultaneously, providing mechanisms for merging and integrating changes made by different team members. By acting as a central repository for code, Collaborative Version Control Systems allow developers to track and manage changes, revert to previous versions, and maintain a clear history of modifications.

Collaborative Version Control

Collaborative Version Control, in the context of DevOps, refers to the practice of managing and tracking changes to software source code and other development assets in a collaborative and efficient manner. The process of software development often involves multiple team members working simultaneously on different features or bug fixes. Collaborative Version Control enables these team members to work together seamlessly by providing a centralized repository where all changes are stored and tracked. This ensures that everyone on the team has access to the latest version of the code and can contribute to its development. One of the key components of Collaborative Version Control is the ability to manage different versions of the code. This is achieved through the use of branching and merging techniques. Branching allows team members to create separate branches of the codebase to work on specific features or bug fixes without affecting the main codebase. Once the changes in a branch are tested and approved, they can be merged back into the main codebase, ensuring that the final version contains all the necessary changes. Collaborative Version Control also provides mechanisms for resolving conflicts that may arise when multiple team members make changes to the same piece of code simultaneously. Through the use of tools and processes, these conflicts can be detected and resolved in a systematic manner, ensuring that the integrity of the codebase is maintained. Furthermore, Collaborative Version Control enables team members to track the history of changes made to the code. This can be crucial for troubleshooting issues, understanding the evolution of the codebase, and ensuring compliance with regulatory requirements. By keeping a comprehensive record of all changes, Collaborative Version Control helps maintain transparency and accountability throughout the development process. Overall, Collaborative Version Control plays a critical role in facilitating collaboration, coordination, and efficiency in an agile DevOps environment. It ensures that developers can work on code simultaneously, manage different versions effectively, resolve conflicts, and track changes systematically. By adopting Collaborative Version Control practices, organizations can enhance their development processes and deliver high-quality software products faster.

Communication

DevOps is a software development and delivery approach that focuses on bridging the gap between software development and operations teams to enable faster and more efficient software delivery. It is characterized by collaboration, automation, continuous integration and delivery, and monitoring. The main objective of DevOps is to break down the traditional barriers and silos between developers and operations teams and create a more collaborative and integrated environment. By fostering collaboration and communication, DevOps aims to improve efficiency and productivity throughout the software development lifecycle. Automation is a key aspect of DevOps, as it helps streamline and accelerate the software development and delivery processes. Automation tools and frameworks are used to automate various tasks, such as building, testing, and deploying software, reducing the likelihood of errors and speeding up time to market. Continuous integration and delivery are core principles of DevOps and involve the integration and delivery of small, frequent changes to the software. Continuous integration focuses on integrating code changes into a shared repository and running automated tests to detect issues early on. Continuous delivery takes it a step further by ensuring that the software is always in a releasable state, allowing for quick and frequent deployments. In addition to automation and continuous practices, monitoring plays a crucial role in DevOps. Continuous monitoring helps identify and address performance issues, bottlenecks, and failures in real-time. It provides valuable insights into the health and performance of the software, enabling teams to proactively respond to any issues and ensure a high level of reliability and availability. In summary, DevOps is a collaborative and automation-driven approach to software development and delivery that aims to break down silos, streamline processes, and foster continuous improvement. By enabling closer collaboration between developers and operations teams and leveraging automation and monitoring, DevOps enables organizations to deliver software faster, with higher quality, and increased reliability.

Compliance Automation

Compliance automation in the context of DevOps refers to the process of streamlining and automating compliance tasks and procedures within the software development lifecycle. It involves integrating compliance requirements into the existing DevOps processes, workflows, and toolchains, with the aim of ensuring that software products and systems meet the necessary regulatory, security, and industry standards. By automating compliance, organizations can minimize the manual effort and human errors traditionally associated with compliance management. Compliance automation allows for continuous monitoring, enforcement, and reporting of compliance controls throughout the software delivery pipeline, enabling faster and more efficient software development cycles while mitigating compliance risks.

Compliance As Code

Compliance as Code is a methodology that integrates compliance requirements into the software development process in the context of DevOps. It focuses on automating compliance checks and validations as part of the code delivery pipeline, ensuring that applications meet regulatory and security standards. In DevOps, where software development and delivery are highly automated, compliance can often be a bottleneck due to manual, time-consuming processes. Compliance as Code addresses this challenge by treating compliance requirements as code artifacts, just like any other software components. By defining compliance rules and policies as code, organizations can enforce consistent and scalable compliance checks throughout the software development lifecycle. Compliance checks can be integrated into the continuous integration and continuous delivery (CI/CD) pipeline, allowing for automated verification and enforcement at each stage of the development process. Compliance as Code leverages infrastructure as code (IaC) principles to enforce compliance requirements. By expressing compliance rules in a human-readable and machine-executable format, organizations can automatically assess and validate their infrastructure and applications against industry standards and regulatory frameworks. With Compliance as Code, compliance checks become repeatable, auditable, and scalable. By incorporating compliance checks into the CI/CD pipeline, organizations can ensure that applications are continuously and automatically validated against compliance requirements. This helps reduce manual effort, improve consistency, and increase the speed of compliance validation. Furthermore, Compliance as Code promotes collaboration between development, operations, and compliance teams. It encourages the use of standardized compliance libraries and frameworks that can be shared and reused across different projects and teams. This simplifies the adoption and maintenance of compliance requirements, while fostering a culture of collaboration and shared responsibility. In summary, Compliance as Code is a methodology that integrates compliance requirements as code artifacts into the software development process. It automates compliance checks and validations, making them repeatable, auditable, and scalable. By incorporating compliance checks into the CI/CD pipeline, organizations can ensure that their applications meet regulatory and security standards without sacrificing speed or efficiency.

Compliance

Compliance in the context of DevOps refers to adhering to the rules, regulations, and policies set forth by governing bodies, industry standards, and internal organizational requirements. It involves ensuring that the development and operation processes align with these guidelines and meet the necessary security, privacy, and quality standards. DevOps teams strive to achieve compliance by integrating the necessary controls, practices, and tools into their workflows. This entails establishing standardized procedures, implementing robust security measures, conducting regular audits, and maintaining thorough documentation. By building compliance into their processes, DevOps teams can mitigate risks, improve transparency, and demonstrate accountability to stakeholders.

Concourse CI

Concourse CI is a cloud-native, open-source continuous integration (CI) and continuous delivery (CD) platform, designed to automate software development processes within the DevOps framework. It provides a scalable and flexible solution for building, testing, and deploying software applications efficiently and reliably. Concourse CI acts as a central hub for managing and executing CI/CD pipelines, which are sequences of automated steps that enable the development, testing, and release of software in a streamlined and automated manner. These pipelines define the stages and tasks required to build, test, and deliver applications, ensuring that the software is continuously integrated, tested, and deployed throughout the development process. One of the key features of Concourse CI is its declarative configuration approach. Developers define the desired state of their pipelines using a simple, human-readable syntax, known as "YAML" (YAML Ain't Markup Language). This allows for easy collaboration and version control of pipeline configurations, as they can be stored and managed alongside the software codebase. Concourse CI provides a web-based user interface, allowing developers and operations teams to monitor the status and progress of pipelines, as well as view logs and troubleshoot issues. The web interface also facilitates the management of resources, such as source code repositories, build artifacts, and deployment targets. Furthermore, Concourse CI emphasizes the principles of reproducibility and isolation. Each task within a pipeline is executed within its own isolated container, ensuring that dependencies are well-defined and consistent. This approach enables reliable and reproducible builds and tests, regardless of the underlying infrastructure or environment. In summary, Concourse CI is a powerful CI/CD platform that helps automate software development processes within a DevOps environment. Its cloud-native architecture, declarative configuration approach, web-based user interface, and focus on reproducibility and isolation make it a versatile and efficient tool for building, testing, and delivering software applications.

ConfigCat

ConfigCat is a configuration management tool that operates within the context of DevOps. It simplifies the process of managing feature flags and configuration settings in software development projects. Within the DevOps cycle, ConfigCat facilitates seamless configuration management, including the continuous delivery and deployment of features, as well as A/B testing and experimentation. It provides a centralized platform for managing configuration settings and feature toggles, ensuring that changes can be made and deployed without requiring code changes or new releases of the software.

Configuration Drift Detection Tools Selection

Configuration drift refers to the gradual deviation from the desired state of a system's configuration over time. In the context of DevOps, configuration drift can occur as a result of manual interventions, uncontrolled changes, or inconsistencies between different environments. Detecting and addressing configuration drift is crucial for maintaining the stability, reliability, and security of the system. To identify and rectify configuration drift, organizations can leverage various tools specifically designed for this purpose. These configuration drift detection tools monitor and compare the actual state of the system's configuration with the intended or desired state, notifying the DevOps team of any discrepancies or deviations. By automating this process, these tools help ensure that the system stays aligned with the desired configuration and reduce the risk of drift-related issues.

Configuration Drift Detection Tools

Configuration drift refers to the gradual divergence between the actual configuration of an environment and its desired or expected configuration. In the context of DevOps, where continuous integration and continuous delivery practices are adopted, configuration drift can become a major challenge to maintaining application infrastructure and ensuring consistent performance across different environments. Configuration drift detection tools are specifically designed to identify and alert teams about any deviations or discrepancies in the configuration of systems or infrastructure. These tools continuously monitor the state of various components, such as servers, networks, databases, and other resources, to detect any changes that may have occurred over time. They compare the current configuration with a predefined baseline or desired configuration to pinpoint drift and ensure that the environment remains within compliance and operational standards.

Configuration Drift Detection

Configuration drift detection is a concept in DevOps that refers to the process of identifying and tracking changes in the configuration of a system or infrastructure. It involves comparing the current state of the system or infrastructure with its desired or intended state, and detecting any discrepancies or deviations that may have occurred over time. The desired state of a system or infrastructure is typically defined using configuration management tools or scripts, which specify how different components should be configured and how they should interact with each other. These configurations may include settings, parameters, dependencies, and other properties that need to be maintained in order for the system to function properly. Configuration drift can occur due to various reasons, such as manual changes made by administrators or developers, software updates or patches that modify system configurations, hardware or network changes that affect the environment, or even malicious activities that alter system settings. These changes may be intentional or unintentional, but they can result in the system deviating from its desired state and potentially causing performance issues, security vulnerabilities, or other problems. Configuration drift detection involves regularly assessing and comparing the current state of the system or infrastructure with the desired state, and flagging any discrepancies or deviations that are detected. This can be done through automated processes that capture and analyze configuration data, such as configuration management databases (CMDBs), monitoring tools, or version control systems. By continuously monitoring and detecting configuration drift, organizations can identify and address any issues or risks before they escalate and impact the overall stability and reliability of their systems. In conclusion, configuration drift detection is a critical aspect of DevOps that helps ensure the consistency and integrity of system configurations. By regularly comparing the actual state of the system with its desired state, organizations can proactively identify and resolve any configuration drift, minimizing the risks and challenges associated with evolving infrastructures.

Configuration Drift

Configuration drift refers to the phenomenon where the configuration of a system or environment gradually becomes inconsistent or deviates from its intended state over time. In the context of DevOps, configuration drift can occur in various aspects of the software development and deployment lifecycle, such as infrastructure, networks, applications, or even code. When a system is initially set up, its configuration is carefully defined and documented. However, as changes are made to the system over time, whether intentional or not, these changes can accumulate and result in configuration inconsistencies. These inconsistencies can lead to a wide range of issues, including reduced system stability, degraded performance, security vulnerabilities, and ultimately, hindered efficiency in the development and deployment processes. Configuration drift can occur due to several reasons. One common cause is manual configuration changes made by different individuals or teams involved in the development and deployment process. As the system evolves, each change may be made with good intentions, but the collective impact can result in configuration discrepancies. Moreover, system updates, patches, or upgrades can also contribute to configuration drift if they are not properly tested or validated against the existing configuration. To mitigate configuration drift, an effective DevOps

26

practice includes proper configuration management. This involves establishing robust and automated mechanisms for maintaining and enforcing configuration consistency. By leveraging infrastructure as code (IaC) and configuration management tools, organizations can define and enforce desired configurations, automate deployments, and detect and remediate drift in a systematic and efficient manner. Configuration management tools, such as Ansible, Chef, or Puppet, provide capabilities to define and provision system configurations, enforce compliance, and continuously monitor and manage the configuration state. These tools enable organizations to automate the process of configuration deployment, ensure consistency across environments, and detect and remediate drift through periodic configuration checks and automated remediation workflows.

Configuration Management Tools

Configuration Management Tools in the context of DevOps refer to software solutions or platforms that assist in automating and managing the configuration of complex and dynamic IT infrastructure and application environments. These tools enable organizations to achieve greater efficiency, scalability, and reliability in their deployment and management processes. Configuration management plays a critical role in DevOps by ensuring that the entire system, including hardware, software, and network components, is properly configured and optimized for performance. It involves documenting and managing the configuration settings and parameters across different stages of the software development lifecycle, from development to testing, staging, and production environments.

Configuration Management

Configuration Management in the context of DevOps refers to the practice of systematically managing the configurations of software systems and infrastructure throughout their lifecycle. It involves the coordination and control of all elements that make up a system, including hardware, software, network components, and documentation. The main goal of Configuration Management is to ensure consistency and stability in the software development and deployment process. It helps teams to effectively manage and automate changes in their environments, reducing the risk of errors and improving the overall efficiency of software delivery.

Conflict Resolution

Conflict resolution in the context of DevOps refers to the process of identifying, addressing, and resolving conflicts that arise within a DevOps team or between different teams involved in the development and operations of software products. DevOps is a collaborative approach that brings together software development and IT operations teams, aiming to streamline and accelerate the delivery of high-quality software products. However, the collaboration and integration of different teams and their unique perspectives and goals can lead to conflicts. In the DevOps context, conflicts can arise due to various reasons, including differences in priorities, goals, communication styles, and technical choices. These conflicts can result in delays, quality issues, and a strained working environment. Effective conflict resolution strategies are essential to maintain a productive and harmonious DevOps culture. The first step in conflict resolution is to identify the underlying causes of the conflict. This requires open and transparent communication between the parties involved. Each party should have the opportunity to express their concerns and viewpoints without fear of judgment or retribution. Once the causes of the conflict are understood, the next step is to address the conflict by finding a mutually agreeable solution. This often involves compromise, collaboration, and negotiation. Both parties should be willing to listen to each other's perspectives and consider alternative approaches to resolve the conflict. It is important to note that conflict resolution in DevOps is not about eliminating all conflicts. Healthy conflicts can actually lead to innovation and improvement. The goal is to resolve conflicts in a constructive manner, where all parties feel heard and their concerns are taken into account. Additionally, conflict resolution in DevOps should focus on facilitating knowledge sharing and learning from the conflict. Through reflection and continuous improvement, teams can identify patterns of conflict and develop strategies to prevent or mitigate similar conflicts in the future.

Consul

A Consul is a service discovery and configuration management tool that is commonly used in the context of DevOps. It helps automate and organize various aspects of a distributed system, providing features such as service discovery, health checking, key-value storage, and distributed coordination. With Consul, DevOps teams can easily discover and connect services running within a distributed architecture. It provides a central registry where services can be registered, allowing other services to dynamically discover and communicate with them. This enables the automation of service-to-service communication, making it easier to build and scale complex applications. In addition to service discovery, Consul also offers health checking functionality. It periodically checks the health of registered services, ensuring that they are running properly and available to handle requests. If a service becomes unhealthy, Consul can automatically remove it from the registry or trigger an alert, allowing for proactive monitoring and maintenance. Consul's key-value store allows for the storage and retrieval of dynamic configurations, making it easy to manage configuration parameters for applications deployed within a distributed environment. This allows DevOps teams to decouple configuration from code, making it easier to update and manage configurations without redeploying the entire application. Furthermore, Consul provides distributed coordination primitives, such as leader election and distributed locks, which can be used to build resilient and highly available systems. These primitives enable distributed applications to elect a leader, coordinate tasks, and handle concurrency, ensuring that the system remains reliable even in the event of failures. Overall, Consul plays a crucial role in the DevOps ecosystem by simplifying the management and automation of distributed systems. It enables efficient service discovery, ensures the health and availability of services, allows for dynamic configuration management, and provides distributed coordination capabilities, empowering DevOps teams to build and maintain robust and scalable applications.

Container Orchestration

Container orchestration in the context of DevOps refers to the process of managing and coordinating the deployment, scaling, and operation of containerized applications. It involves automating the creation, scheduling, and scaling of containers across a cluster of machines or a distributed infrastructure. The goal of container orchestration is to streamline the management of containerized applications, allowing DevOps teams to efficiently deploy and manage large-scale container environments. It simplifies the process of deploying applications by abstracting away the complexity of managing individual containers and their dependencies, enabling teams to focus on application development rather than infrastructure management.

Container Registry

A container registry, in the context of DevOps, is a centralized repository that stores and manages container images. It serves as a reliable source for distributing container images across different stages of the software development lifecycle. In a modern DevOps environment, containers are widely used to package and deploy applications. A container image contains everything needed to run an application, including the code, runtime, system tools, and libraries. The container registry acts as a storehouse for these images, providing a secure and scalable solution for storing, sharing, and retrieving container images.

Container Security Scanning Best Practices

Container Security Scanning Best Practices in the context of DevOps refer to the recommended methods and approaches to assess and enhance the security of containerized applications within a DevOps environment. In the fast-paced and dynamic world of software development, containers have gained significant popularity due to their lightweight nature and efficient deployment capabilities. However, with the increasing adoption of containers, it becomes crucial to ensure the security of the underlying container images and the overall containerized application. One of the key practices in container security scanning is the regular and automated scanning of container images for known vulnerabilities. This involves using specialized tools and services that analyze the container images and their dependencies to identify any known security issues or weaknesses. By scanning containers at various stages of the DevOps pipeline, from development to deployment, organizations can identify and address vulnerabilities early on, reducing the risk of security breaches or exploits in production environments. Another important aspect of container security scanning is enforcing image integrity and authenticity. This is achieved through the use of digital signatures and container image registries with built-in security features. Digital signatures help verify the authenticity and integrity of container images, ensuring that only trusted and authorized images are deployed. Container image registries, on the other hand, provide centralized repositories for storing and distributing container images, enabling version control, access control, and vulnerability scanning. Implementing access controls and least privilege principles is also essential in container security scanning. By enforcing strict access controls, organizations can limit the actions and permissions granted to containers, reducing the potential impact of a compromised container. Additionally, following the principle of least privilege ensures that containers only have the necessary permissions and resources to perform their intended tasks, minimizing the attack surface and improving the overall security posture. Continuous monitoring and logging play a significant role in container security scanning. By monitoring containers and the surrounding infrastructure in real-time, organizations can detect and respond to security incidents promptly. Monitoring container activity, resource usage, and network communications helps identify any suspicious or unauthorized behavior. Logging container events and activities allows for forensic analysis and provides valuable insights into potential security breaches. In conclusion, container security scanning best practices in a DevOps environment aim to ensure the security and integrity of containerized applications throughout their lifecycle. By incorporating regular vulnerability scanning, enforcing image integrity, implementing access controls, and adopting continuous monitoring, organizations can mitigate the risks associated with container security and enhance the overall security posture of their DevOps pipelines.

Container Security Scanning

Container Security Scanning is an essential component of the DevOps process, aimed at identifying vulnerabilities and threats in container-based applications. It involves the systematic analysis of container images or runtime environments to detect any security weaknesses, misconfigurations, or potential risks that may compromise the security and stability of the overall infrastructure. This scanning process is typically carried out using specialized container security tools or services, which leverage various techniques such as static analysis, dynamic analysis, and machine learning algorithms. These tools extensively examine the container images or runtime environments, meticulously checking for known vulnerabilities, outdated dependencies, insecure configurations, and potential malware or malicious code. The primary objective of container security scanning is to proactively identify and mitigate security risks during the development and deployment stages of containerized applications. By integrating security scanning into the DevOps pipeline, organizations can ensure that their containers are thoroughly examined for potential security flaws before they are deployed to production environments. This helps to prevent security incidents and streamline the remediation process, reducing downtime and minimizing the impact on business operations. Container security scanning provides DevOps teams with actionable insights and recommendations to strengthen the security posture of their containerized applications. Depending on the severity of the identified vulnerabilities or risks, teams can prioritize and address them accordingly, adopting suitable security measures such as patching, configuration changes, or applying security best practices. Additionally, container security scanning enables organizations to meet regulatory compliance requirements and enforce security standards across their container-based infrastructure. In conclusion, container security scanning plays a critical role in the DevOps landscape by helping organizations identify and address security vulnerabilities and threats in containerized applications. By integrating this scanning process into the development and deployment pipeline, DevOps teams can enhance the security and reliability of their container-based infrastructure, ensuring the overall integrity of their applications.

Container Security

Container security in the context of DevOps refers to the practice of securing and protecting the various aspects of containers used in the software development and deployment process. Containers are lightweight and isolated environments that package an application and its dependencies, allowing for easy portability and scalability. However, they also introduce new security challenges that need to be addressed to ensure the overall security of the DevOps pipeline. Container security encompasses several aspects, including: Firstly, vulnerability management is crucial in container security. Containers rely on various software packages and libraries, which may have vulnerabilities that can be exploited by attackers. Regularly scanning containers for known vulnerabilities and keeping them up to date with security patches is essential to mitigate these risks. Secondly, access control and segregation of duties play a significant role in container security. Implementing strong access controls ensures that only authorized personnel can access and modify containers. Additionally, segregating duties ensures that different teams have limited access to specific containers, reducing the risk of unauthorized changes or potential security breaches. Thirdly, monitoring and logging are essential in container security. Monitoring the behavior of containers and collecting relevant logs can help identify any abnormal activities or potential security incidents. This information is valuable for detecting and responding to security threats in a timely manner. Fourthly, network security is a critical aspect of container security. Containers communicate with other containers, hosts, and external services, and securing these network connections is crucial. Implementing network segmentation, encryption, and strong authentication protocols help protect the communication channels and prevent unauthorized access. Fifthly, runtime security involves continuously monitoring the containers during execution. Real-time monitoring can detect malicious activities or unauthorized changes, enabling prompt actions to mitigate any security risks. Finally, secure container deployment practices are essential for container security. Following secure configurations and best practices when building and deploying containers can significantly reduce the attack surface and enhance their overall security.

Containerization

Containerization is a software development approach that is widely used in the context of DevOps. It involves packaging an application along with its dependencies in a container, allowing it to run consistently and reliably across different environments. A container is a lightweight, isolated, and portable environment that contains everything needed to run an application, including the code, runtime, system tools, libraries, and configurations. It provides a standardized and consistent way to package and deploy software, eliminating the need for manual interventions and ensuring consistency between development, testing, and production environments.

Continuous Accessibility Testing

Continuous Accessibility Testing is a process incorporated within the DevOps methodology to ensure that digital products and services are accessible to all users, including those with disabilities. It involves regularly and systematically evaluating the accessibility features and characteristics of a product or service throughout its development lifecycle, from design to deployment. By integrating accessibility testing into the iterative and automated DevOps workflow, organizations can identify and address accessibility issues early on, reducing the risk of non-compliance and improving the user experience for individuals with disabilities. Continuous Accessibility Testing typically involves the following key components: 1. Automated Testing: Automated accessibility testing tools are utilized to scan web pages or digital interfaces for potential accessibility violations. These tools analyze the HTML, CSS, and JavaScript code and provide reports on accessibility issues, such as missing alternative text for images, improper heading structure, or non-descriptive link texts. 2. Manual Testing: Human testers with expertise in accessibility guidelines and best practices manually review the application or website to identify accessibility barriers that automated tools may have missed. This involves testing with assistive technologies, like screen readers, keyboard-only navigation, or voice recognition software, to simulate the experiences of users with disabilities. 3. Integration with CI/CD: Continuous Integration/Continuous Deployment (CI/CD) pipelines are leveraged to automatically trigger accessibility tests as part of the build and deployment process. This ensures that accessibility checks are performed regularly and consistently throughout the development lifecycle, allowing for rapid identification and resolution of issues. 4. Tracking and Reporting: Accessibility issues detected during testing are logged as defects or issues in the bug tracking system, enabling developers and designers to track their resolution. Organizations often use accessibility testing tools that provide detailed reports and metrics, allowing stakeholders to monitor progress and measure the accessibility compliance of their products or services. In conclusion, Continuous Accessibility Testing is an essential practice within the DevOps framework, aiming to ensure that digital products and services meet established accessibility standards. By seamlessly integrating accessibility testing into the development process, organizations can create inclusive and user-friendly experiences for all individuals, regardless of their abilities or disabilities.

Continuous Agility

Continuous Agility in the context of DevOps refers to the ability of an organization to respond quickly and effectively to changing market demands and customer needs. It is a key principle of DevOps that emphasizes the importance of continually adapting and improving the software development and deployment processes. This approach involves a combination of agile practices, continuous integration, continuous delivery, and rapid feedback loops. It requires a mindset shift towards embracing change and continuous improvement, and a collaborative culture that encourages experimentation and learning.

Continuous Alerting

Continuous Alerting, in the context of DevOps, refers to the practice of proactively monitoring and receiving real-time alerts about any abnormalities or issues that may arise during the software development and deployment process. It is a crucial aspect of a successful DevOps culture, ensuring that teams can rapidly respond to incidents, maintain system availability, and deliver high-quality software to end-users. In a DevOps environment, where automated CI/CD pipelines and frequent deployments are the norm, continuous alerting helps teams detect and respond to problems promptly, minimizing any potential downtime or impact on the end-user experience. It involves the use of various monitoring tools, such as application performance monitoring (APM) solutions, log analyzers, and infrastructure monitoring systems. Continuous alerting allows developers, operations teams, and other stakeholders to receive immediate notifications whenever a predefined threshold or criteria is exceeded, anomalies are detected, or critical events occur. These alerts can be in the form of email notifications, SMS messages, or integrated into collaboration tools like Slack or Microsoft Teams. To implement continuous alerting effectively, teams need to establish clear monitoring objectives and define alerting rules based on key performance indicators (KPIs) and business requirements. This involves setting up monitoring metrics, thresholds, and escalation paths to ensure that the right individuals or teams are alerted at the appropriate time. By leveraging continuous alerting, DevOps teams can identify potential issues early on, such as performance bottlenecks, resource constraints, security breaches, or infrastructure failures. This enables them to take proactive measures, such as rolling back deployments, scaling resources, or resolving issues before they impact the end-user experience. Moreover, continuous alerting also facilitates post-incident analysis and improvement. By collecting and analyzing alert data, teams can gain insights into recurring problems, trends, and patterns, allowing for continuous optimization and refinement of the software development and delivery process.

Continuous Alignment

Continuous Alignment in the context of DevOps refers to the ongoing process of ensuring that the goals and objectives of development and operations teams are in sync and aligned towards the common goal of delivering high-quality software products. It involves regular and open communication between the development and operations teams, allowing them to share information, make informed decisions, and collaborate effectively. Continuous Alignment helps bridge the gap between these two teams, fostering a culture of collaboration and shared responsibility.

Continuous Auditing

Continuous Auditing in the context of DevOps refers to the ongoing and automated process of evaluating, monitoring, and assessing the effectiveness and security of an organization's software development and delivery practices. It involves the use of technology-driven tools and frameworks to continuously gather and analyze data related to the development, testing, deployment, and operation of software systems. These tools and frameworks enable auditors to identify potential risks, vulnerabilities, and non-compliance issues throughout the software development lifecycle.

Continuous Automation

Continuous Automation in the context of DevOps refers to the practice of automating various aspects of the software development and delivery process to enable faster and more efficient release cycles. It involves the use of tools, scripts, and processes to automate repetitive tasks, minimize manual intervention, and ensure consistent and reliable software delivery. Continuous Automation is a fundamental principle of DevOps, aiming to streamline the software development lifecycle by automating repetitive tasks such as code compilation, automated testing, and deployment. By automating these tasks, organizations can reduce human errors, increase productivity, and facilitate faster time-to-market for their applications.

Continuous Capacity Planning

Continuous Capacity Planning is an essential aspect of DevOps, aimed at ensuring that an organization's systems and infrastructure have the required capabilities to meet current and future business demands seamlessly. It involves constantly monitoring and evaluating the resources, such as compute power, memory, storage, and network bandwidth, to ensure they align with the changing needs of the application and user base. The core concept behind Continuous Capacity Planning is to avoid any potential capacity bottlenecks that might hinder system performance or cause downtime. By continuously evaluating the existing infrastructure and comparing it with the anticipated growth and usage patterns, organizations can proactively identify and address any potential capacity shortfalls before they become critical issues.

Continuous Change Management

Continuous Change Management in the context of DevOps refers to the ongoing process of managing and implementing changes to software systems or infrastructure using a continuous and iterative approach. It is an essential component of the DevOps lifecycle, ensuring that changes are smoothly integrated into the system with minimal disruption to the overall workflow. In Continuous Change Management, the focus is on fostering a culture of collaboration, communication, and automation to streamline the change process and address any potential risks or issues that may arise. It involves a combination of technical practices, tools, and organizational strategies to support a continuous flow of changes while maintaining stability and reliability. The key principles of Continuous Change Management are: 1. Continuous Integration: Changes are regularly and automatically integrated into the main code base, allowing for early detection of conflicts or issues. 2. Continuous Testing: Comprehensive testing is conducted throughout the change process to ensure that new features or updates do not introduce critical bugs or regressions. 3. Continuous Deployment: New changes are automatically deployed to production environments, eliminating the need for manual intervention and reducing the time between development and deployment. 4. Continuous Monitoring: Real-time monitoring and logging are implemented to track the impact of changes and promptly identify and resolve any performance issues or anomalies. Continuous Change Management also involves establishing a robust change management process that includes proper documentation, version control, change tracking, and regular communication among all stakeholders. Effective collaboration and communication between developers, operations teams, and other relevant stakeholders are crucial to ensure that changes are properly planned, reviewed, and implemented. Overall, Continuous Change Management enables organizations to embrace a DevOps culture and effectively manage the complexities of frequent software deployments and system changes. By automating processes, fostering collaboration, and integrating feedback loops, organizations can achieve faster time-to-market, improved software quality, and increased customer satisfaction.

Continuous Code Review

Continuous Code Review is a critical component of the DevOps approach, designed to ensure the quality, consistency, and maintainability of code throughout the software development lifecycle. It involves the ongoing examination and analysis of code by developers, peers, and tools to identify potential issues, improve code quality, and promote best practices. Continuous Code Review serves as a pro-active and collaborative process that aims to catch potential bugs, security vulnerabilities, and performance bottlenecks early in the development cycle. It helps in enhancing code readability, modularity, and adherence to coding standards, leading to better maintainability and easier collaboration among team members.

Continuous Collaboration Tools

Continuous Collaboration Tools in the context of DevOps refer to the software tools and platforms that facilitate real-time communication and collaboration among team members involved in the software development and deployment processes. These tools are designed to enable seamless and efficient sharing of information, coordination of tasks, and integration of workflows, ultimately promoting a culture of collaboration and teamwork within the DevOps environment. Continuous Collaboration Tools play a crucial role in DevOps by breaking down silos and bringing together developers, operations personnel, and other stakeholders involved in the software development lifecycle. These tools provide a centralized platform for team members to communicate, collaborate, and share information throughout the entire software development pipeline, from planning and design to testing, deployment, and monitoring.

Continuous Communication

Continuous Communication, in the context of DevOps, refers to an ongoing and seamless flow of information and feedback between different teams and stakeholders involved in the software development and operations lifecycle. In traditional software development models, there are often distinct silos between development, testing, operations, and other teams, resulting in fragmented communication and collaboration. This can lead to delays, misunderstandings, and inefficiencies, ultimately affecting the quality and delivery of software. DevOps aims to break down these silos by fostering a culture of continuous communication. This means that all teams involved in the software delivery process, including developers, testers, operations personnel, business stakeholders, and customers, should be in constant contact, exchanging information, updates, and feedback. One aspect of continuous communication in DevOps is the use of collaboration tools and technologies. These tools facilitate real-time communication, enabling teams to easily share information, documents, and updates. Examples of such tools include messaging platforms like Slack, project management tools like Jira, and version control systems like Git. Another crucial element of continuous communication is the practice of regular meetings and stand-ups. For example, daily stand-up meetings allow team members to quickly share their progress, discuss any challenges or blockers, and align their goals. This promotes transparency, accountability, and collaboration among team members. Continuous communication also involves proactive feedback loops. This means that teams should actively seek and provide feedback throughout the software development cycle. For instance, developers may seek feedback from testers to ensure the quality of their code, while operations teams may provide feedback on the performance and stability of the deployed software. Overall, continuous communication in DevOps fosters collaboration, enhances transparency, and promotes a culture of agility and shared responsibility. By breaking down silos and promoting ongoing information exchange, teams can work together more effectively, resulting in faster delivery of high-quality software that aligns with the needs and expectations of stakeholders.

Continuous Compliance Strategies

Continuous Compliance Strategies refer to the implementation of processes and practices within DevOps that ensure ongoing adherence to regulatory requirements, security guidelines, and other compliance standards throughout the development and deployment lifecycle.These strategies are essential for organizations that operate in highly regulated industries such as finance, healthcare, or government, where compliance with various regulations and industry standards is a critical requirement.

Continuous Compliance Tools

Continuous Compliance Tools in the context of DevOps refer to software solutions or frameworks that enable organizations to automate compliance checks and integrate them seamlessly into their continuous deployment and delivery processes. These tools are designed to ensure that software deployments comply with the relevant regulatory, security, and policy requirements throughout the development and deployment lifecycle. By using Continuous Compliance Tools, organizations can ensure that their software systems adhere to required standards and regulations, reducing the risk of non-compliance and potential security breaches. These tools typically involve a combination of policy definition, automated testing, and reporting mechanisms to offer real-time visibility into compliance status.

Continuous Compliance

Continuous Compliance, in the context of DevOps, refers to the practice of continuously ensuring that all software development and deployment processes comply with relevant regulations, security standards, and industry best practices. Compliance is an essential aspect of any software development and deployment process, particularly in industries that are heavily regulated or deal with sensitive data. Traditional compliance processes involve manual audits and periodic assessments, which can be time-consuming, costly, and often lead to delays in software delivery. In contrast, continuous compliance integrates compliance checks and validations into the DevOps pipeline, enabling organizations to maintain compliance throughout the software development lifecycle.

Continuous Conflict Resolution

Continuous Conflict Resolution in the context of DevOps refers to the ongoing process of identifying, addressing, and mitigating conflicts that arise within a DevOps environment. It is a proactive approach to managing conflicts and promoting collaboration among team members. In DevOps, conflicts can arise due to various factors, such as differences in opinions, conflicting goals, miscommunication, or resource constraints. These conflicts can hinder the progress of projects, lower team morale, and negatively impact the overall success of DevOps initiatives. The continuous conflict resolution process involves several key steps. Firstly, conflicts need to be identified and acknowledged. This can be done through regular communication and by creating an environment where team members feel comfortable expressing their concerns. It is important to promote open and honest dialogue to encourage the early detection of conflicts. Once conflicts are identified, the next step is to address them in a timely manner. This requires active listening and understanding of each team member's perspective. By validating and acknowledging individual concerns, it becomes easier to find common ground and work towards a resolution that satisfies all parties involved. To effectively resolve conflicts, collaboration and compromise are essential. By involving all relevant stakeholders, such as developers, operations personnel, and management, a diverse range of perspectives can be considered. This collaborative approach fosters a sense of ownership and shared responsibility, leading to more sustainable and satisfactory resolutions. Continuous conflict resolution in DevOps also involves the implementation of constructive feedback mechanisms. Through regular performance evaluations and retrospectives, team members can provide feedback on areas that need improvement and contribute to a culture of continuous learning and growth. This allows conflicts to be dealt with proactively, before they escalate and negatively impact the workflow. In summary, continuous conflict resolution in the context of DevOps is an ongoing process of identifying, addressing, and mitigating conflicts that arise within a DevOps environment. By promoting open communication, collaboration, compromise, and the implementation of feedback mechanisms, DevOps teams can create a harmonious and productive work environment that leads to successful project outcomes.

Continuous Cross-Functional Skills

Continuous cross-functional skills in the context of DevOps refer to the ability of individuals or teams to possess and continuously develop a diverse set of skills across various functional areas within the software development and operations processes. DevOps is a collaborative approach that aims to bridge the gap between development and operations teams, breaking down traditional silos and fostering a culture of collaboration and continuous improvement. In order to effectively implement DevOps principles and practices, it is essential for individuals and teams to have cross-functional skills.

Continuous Customer Focus

Continuous customer focus in the context of DevOps refers to the ongoing commitment to understanding and meeting the needs and expectations of customers throughout the software delivery lifecycle. DevOps is an approach to software development and delivery that emphasizes collaboration, communication, and integration between software development and IT operations teams. It aims to create a culture of shared responsibility and continuous improvement to deliver high-quality software at a faster pace. In this context, continuous customer focus is an essential principle that ensures the software being developed and delivered aligns with the needs and desires of the end users.

Continuous Decision-Making

34

Continuous decision-making in the context of DevOps refers to the ongoing process of making informed choices and taking actions to improve software development and delivery practices. It involves actively analyzing data and feedback, identifying areas for improvement, and making decisions based on real-time information. In DevOps, continuous decision-making is closely linked to the concept of continuous improvement. It emphasizes the need for teams to continuously evaluate their processes and systems, and make adjustments to optimize efficiency, quality, and delivery speed. This approach is essential in fast-paced software development environments where agility and responsiveness are critical.

Continuous Delivery (CD)

Continuous Delivery (CD) is a software development approach and a key practice in the DevOps methodology. It focuses on the automation and streamlining of the software release process, enabling frequent and reliable deployments of new code changes to production environments. In Continuous Delivery, code changes are made in small increments, typically through version control systems like Git. Developers commit their changes to the main branch, triggering automated build and integration tests to ensure the code's integrity. This helps identify any issues or conflicts early in the development cycle. Once the code changes pass the automated tests, they are deployed to a production-like environment for further testing and quality assurance. This environment closely resembles the production environment and allows for thorough testing and validation of the code changes. Automated deployment pipelines are used to deploy the code to the environment, ensuring consistency and repeatability. Continuous Delivery also involves configuration management, as the underlying infrastructure and application configurations need to be managed and versioned alongside the code. This helps ensure that the application can be reliably and consistently deployed to any environment, taking into account its specific configuration requirements. The main goal of Continuous Delivery is to minimize risk and enable faster, more frequent releases of software. By automating the release process and investing in extensive testing and validation, teams can reduce the chances of errors or bugs in production. Furthermore, Continuous Delivery supports a culture of continuous improvement, allowing teams to continuously learn from their releases and make iterative improvements based on user feedback and metrics.

Continuous Delivery Pipeline

Continuous Delivery Pipeline is a key concept in the field of DevOps, where it refers to a set of automated processes and practices that enable teams to continuously and reliably deploy software changes to production. It represents an end-to-end workflow from source code to production, encompassing activities such as building, testing, and deploying software. The Continuous Delivery Pipeline is designed to streamline software delivery and ensure that changes can be released rapidly and with confidence. It helps to minimize risks, such as introducing bugs or disrupting the stability of the production environment, by providing a structured and repeatable process for delivering software changes.

Continuous Deployment

Continuous Deployment is a DevOps practice that involves automatically deploying software changes to production environments as soon as they pass a series of automated tests. This approach eliminates the need for manual intervention, reduces the time between development and deployment, and enables organizations to quickly iterate and deliver new features to users. In Continuous Deployment, the entire deployment process is automated and streamlined. Once code changes are committed to the version control system, they go through a series of automated tests to ensure that they meet the predefined quality and functional criteria. These tests typically include unit tests, integration tests, regression tests, and performance tests. If the code changes pass all the tests, they are automatically deployed to the production environment. This continuous deployment process offers several benefits to organizations. Firstly, it reduces the time and effort required for deployment, as there is no need for manual intervention or coordination. This leads to faster and more frequent releases, enabling organizations to respond quickly to market demands and user feedback. Additionally, it minimizes the risk of human errors during the deployment process, as the entire process is automated and consistent. Continuous Deployment also promotes a culture of continuous improvement and experimentation. Since changes can be deployed rapidly and easily, teams can iterate and release new features more frequently. This enables organizations to gather feedback and data from users quickly, allowing them to make informed decisions and prioritize future development efforts. However, Continuous Deployment requires careful planning and robust infrastructure. Organizations must have a reliable and automated testing framework in place to ensure the integrity and quality of the software. Additionally, continuous monitoring and rollback mechanisms should be implemented to address any issues that may arise in the production environment. In conclusion, Continuous Deployment is a DevOps practice that automates the deployment of code changes to production environments as soon as they pass a series of automated tests. This practice enables organizations to release software updates quickly, reduce manual intervention, and foster a culture of continuous improvement.

Continuous Disaster Recovery Testing

Continuous Disaster Recovery Testing is a process within the DevOps framework that involves regularly and systematically evaluating the effectiveness and reliability of a disaster recovery plan. It is a proactive approach to ensure that the necessary measures are in place to recover IT systems and operations in the event of a major disruption or outage. In a DevOps context, continuous disaster recovery testing is an essential component of the overall strategy for managing and mitigating risks. It involves conducting regular tests, simulations, and drills to assess the preparedness and responsiveness of an organization's disaster recovery plan. The goal is to validate the plan's effectiveness, identify any potential weaknesses or gaps, and make necessary improvements to enhance the overall resilience of IT systems. Continuous disaster recovery testing typically involves the following steps: 1. Scenario Design: Define and design specific disaster scenarios that could potentially impact the organization's IT systems. This could include natural disasters, cyber-attacks, hardware failures, or other catastrophic events. 2. Test Execution: Conduct controlled tests and simulations to assess the effectiveness of the disaster recovery plan in responding to each defined scenario. This may involve suspending production operations, switching to backup systems, and restoring data and services. 3. Evaluation and Analysis: Analyze the results of each test to evaluate the performance and effectiveness of the disaster recovery plan. Identify any vulnerabilities, bottlenecks, or weaknesses that may need to be addressed. 4. Plan Improvement: Based on the findings from the evaluations, make necessary improvements to the disaster recovery plan to enhance its effectiveness and overall capability to recover IT operations in the face of a disaster. Continuous disaster recovery testing ensures that the organization is better prepared to minimize downtime and service disruptions in the event of a disaster. It helps maintain business continuity and reduces the potential impact on customers, partners, and stakeholders. By regularly assessing and updating the disaster recovery plan, organizations can build resilience and confidence in their ability to recover rapidly from any major disruptions or outages.

Continuous Documentation

Continuous Documentation is a fundamental practice in DevOps that involves the ongoing creation, maintenance, and improvement of documentation throughout the software development lifecycle. It is a collaborative effort that aims to provide accurate and up-to-date information about the software system, its components, and configurations. Continuous Documentation ensures that the knowledge and understanding of the software system are captured and shared among team members, enabling them to make informed decisions, troubleshoot issues, and effectively collaborate in a DevOps environment. It emphasizes the creation of clear, concise, and accessible documentation that can be easily understood by both technical and non-technical stakeholders.

Continuous Empowerment

Continuous empowerment, in the context of DevOps, refers to an ongoing process of enabling and supporting individuals and teams to take ownership and responsibility for their work, decisions, and outcomes. It emphasizes creating an environment that fosters trust, collaboration, and continuous learning, allowing individuals to actively contribute and make meaningful contributions to the organization's goals and objectives. Continuous empowerment is a fundamental principle that underpins the DevOps philosophy, which aims to break down silos and empower cross-functional teams to work together seamlessly. It encompasses the principles of autonomy, mastery, and purpose, focusing on providing individuals with the freedom, skills, and motivation they need to excel in their roles. Autonomy is a key aspect of continuous empowerment, as it provides individuals with the authority and decision-making capabilities to drive their work. It allows them to make decisions in real-time, respond to emerging challenges, and take ownership of their tasks, fostering a sense of accountability and responsibility. Mastery is another crucial element of continuous empowerment, as it focuses on providing individuals with the necessary skills, knowledge, and resources to excel in their roles. It emphasizes continuous learning, professional development, and the acquisition of new competencies, enabling individuals to grow and thrive in their positions. Purpose is the final pillar of continuous empowerment, emphasizing the importance of aligning individuals' work with the organization's goals and objectives. It seeks to create a sense of purpose and meaning in individuals' work, inspiring them to contribute their best efforts and actively participate in achieving the organization's vision. By embracing continuous empowerment, organizations can foster a culture of ownership, innovation, and collaboration, empowering individuals and teams to take initiative, make autonomous decisions, and continuously improve their work practices. It breaks down traditional hierarchical structures, promoting a flat, collaborative organizational model that encourages transparency, communication, and empowerment at every level. In essence, continuous empowerment in DevOps encourages organizations to create an environment that enables individuals to become active contributors, decision-makers, and problem solvers. It emphasizes trust, collaboration, and autonomy, allowing individuals to take ownership of their work, continuously learn and improve, and actively contribute to the organization's success.

Continuous Experimentation

Continuous Experimentation is a fundamental aspect of the DevOps methodology that involves continually iterating, testing, and refining software applications in order to drive innovation, enhance user experience, and deliver value to customers. At its core, Continuous Experimentation encompasses the agile principles of constant feedback, collaboration, and learning. It is a proactive approach that enables organizations to rapidly and incrementally introduce new features, evaluate their effectiveness, and gather valuable insights from real user interactions. This iterative process allows teams to make informed decisions based on empirical evidence rather than relying solely on assumptions or intuition. The key objective of Continuous Experimentation in the context of DevOps is to foster a culture of continuous improvement and enable organizations to embrace a fail-fast mindset. By regularly experimenting and gathering data, teams can identify previously unknown opportunities, uncover potential issues, and quickly adapt their software to meet changing market demands. The Continuous Experimentation process typically involves the following steps: - Hypothesis Generation: Teams formulate testable hypotheses and define the desired outcome of an experiment. - Experiment Design: Teams plan and execute controlled experiments to collect data and validate their hypotheses. - Data Collection and Analysis: Teams collect relevant data through instrumentation and tracking mechanisms, analyze the results, and draw conclusions. - Insights and Learning: Teams use the insights gained from the analysis to inform future decisions and refine their software. - Rapid Deployment: Teams use deployment pipelines and automation tools to swiftly release changes and updates based on their learnings. By continuously experimenting, teams gain a deep understanding of their users' preferences, behaviors, and needs. This knowledge allows them to align their development efforts with customer expectations, leading to higher-quality products, increased customer satisfaction, and ultimately, business success.

Continuous Feedback Loops

A continuous feedback loop in the context of DevOps refers to an iterative process of gathering and incorporating feedback at every stage of the software development and deployment lifecycle. It involves establishing mechanisms to capture feedback from various stakeholders, including customers, users, developers, testers, and operations teams, and using that feedback to drive continuous improvement and enhancement of the software product or service. The continuous feedback loop in DevOps is characterized by the following key elements: Firstly, it emphasizes the importance of early and frequent feedback. Rather than waiting until the end of the development cycle or deployment phase, feedback is sought as early as possible to identify and address any issues or bottlenecks promptly. Secondly, it promotes a culture of collaboration and communication among different teams and stakeholders. Feedback is not limited to a single point of contact but involves continuous interaction and information sharing between developers, testers, operators, and end-users. Thirdly, the continuous feedback loop relies on the integration of feedback into the development and deployment processes. This means that feedback is not only collected but actively used to make improvements and adjustments to the software product or service. This integration may involve modifying code, updating configurations, designing new features, or refining user experience based on the received feedback. Fourthly, the continuous feedback loop is supported by automated feedback mechanisms and tools. Automated testing, monitoring, and analytics play a critical role in not only capturing feedback but also providing real-time insights and actionable data to support decision-making and corrective actions. Overall, the continuous feedback loop in DevOps is an ongoing and dynamic process that enables organizations to detect and address issues or shortcomings in their software products or services quickly. By leveraging continuous feedback, DevOps teams can continuously learn, adapt, and improve, ultimately delivering higher quality software that aligns closely with user needs and expectations.

Continuous Feedback

Continuous feedback in the context of DevOps refers to the ongoing and regular communication and evaluation of the software development and deployment processes. It involves the timely exchange of information, observations, and insights between different teams and stakeholders involved in the DevOps lifecycle, such as developers, testers, operations, and customers. Continuous feedback plays a crucial role in the iterative and collaborative nature of DevOps, aiming to drive continuous improvement and enhance the quality, performance, and reliability of software products. It allows for the identification and resolution of issues, bugs, and bottlenecks at early stages, ultimately leading to faster, more efficient, and more streamlined development and delivery processes.

Continuous Improvement Plan

A Continuous Improvement Plan, in the context of DevOps, refers to an ongoing process that aims to enhance and optimize the development and operations practices within an organization. It involves identifying areas of improvement, defining actionable steps, and implementing changes to drive efficiency, quality, and collaboration across teams. The Continuous Improvement Plan is a fundamental principle in the DevOps philosophy, which focuses on breaking down silos, fostering effective communication, and streamlining processes throughout the software development lifecycle. It is a systematic approach that encourages continuous learning, experimentation, and adaptation to achieve better results and meet the evolving needs of users and stakeholders.

Continuous Improvement In DevOps Culture

Continuous Improvement in DevOps culture refers to the ongoing process of identifying and implementing improvements in the way software is developed, tested, and delivered within a DevOps environment. It is a key principle that focuses on constant enhancement and refinement of practices, processes, and tools to achieve higher levels of efficiency, quality, and customer satisfaction. In a DevOps culture, continuous improvement is based on the philosophy of "Kaizen", which is a Japanese term meaning "change for the better". It emphasizes the importance of small, incremental changes that are continuously applied over time to achieve significant improvements. Rather than relying on major overhauls or big-bang changes, it encourages teams to make regular, iterative enhancements to their processes and technologies. Continuous improvement in DevOps culture encompasses several key elements: 1. Collaboration: To achieve continuous improvement, collaboration and feedback loops between cross-functional teams are vital. This involves close collaboration between developers, operations personnel, and other stakeholders throughout the software development lifecycle. 2. Automation: Automation plays a crucial role in DevOps culture, enabling faster and more efficient delivery of software. Continuous improvement focuses on automating manual tasks, streamlining workflows, and optimizing processes to eliminate waste and reduce errors. 3. Measurement and Feedback: Continuous improvement in DevOps culture relies on data-driven decision making. Metrics are used to measure the performance of various processes and identify areas for improvement. Feedback loops, such as retrospectives and post-incident reviews, provide valuable insights to drive enhancements. 4. Continuous Integration and Deployment: Continuous improvement encourages the adoption of practices such as continuous integration and continuous deployment, which enable frequent and incremental delivery of software. These practices ensure that changes are tested, integrated, and deployed in a timely and automated manner, reducing lead time and enabling faster feedback loops. By embracing continuous improvement in DevOps culture, organizations can foster a culture of learning and experimentation. It empowers teams to adapt and evolve their practices, processes, and tools to meet the changing demands of software development, ultimately resulting in improved efficiency, quality, and customer satisfaction.

Continuous Improvement In DevOps

Continuous Improvement in DevOps refers to the iterative process of identifying and implementing measures to enhance the efficiency, quality, and productivity of software development and deployment practices. It involves a relentless pursuit of ongoing improvements to optimize processes, eliminate waste, and deliver value to customers more effectively. In the context of DevOps, continuous improvement is guided by several key principles: 1. Automation: Continuous improvement emphasizes automating repetitive and time-consuming tasks to increase efficiency and reduce human error. By automating processes such as build, test, and deployment, organizations can enhance productivity and reliability. 2. Feedback: Continuous improvement relies on gathering feedback from stakeholders, including developers, operations teams, and end-users. Feedback provides valuable insights into areas that need improvement and helps to identify opportunities for enhancing the software development and delivery lifecycle. 3. Collaboration: Continuous improvement fosters a collaborative culture where development and operations teams work together to identify areas for improvement and implement changes. Collaboration helps break down silos and ensures that improvements are made across the entire software delivery pipeline. 4. Metrics: Continuous improvement relies on the measurement and analysis of key metrics to evaluate the effectiveness of changes and track progress over time. Metrics such as lead time, deployment frequency, and defect rates enable organizations to identify bottlenecks, spot areas of improvement, and make data-driven decisions. 5. Continuous Learning: Continuous improvement recognizes the importance of learning from both successes and failures. By promoting a culture of learning and experimentation, organizations can continuously adapt and improve their processes to deliver better results. By embracing continuous improvement in DevOps, organizations can achieve several benefits, including faster time-to-market, higher quality software, more efficient collaboration between teams, and enhanced customer satisfaction. The iterative nature of continuous improvement ensures that organizations are constantly evolving and adapting to changing business needs and technological advancements.

Continuous Improvement

Continuous Improvement in the context of DevOps refers to the ongoing process of enhancing software delivery and operational practices through iterative and incremental improvements. It is a fundamental principle that promotes a culture of learning, collaboration, and evolution within an organization. Continuous Improvement aims to achieve higher efficiency, quality, and customer satisfaction by continuously assessing and refining all aspects of the software development and deployment lifecycle. This involves identifying areas for improvement, implementing changes, measuring the impact, and incorporating feedback to drive further enhancements.

Continuous Incident Response

Continuous Incident Response in the context of DevOps refers to the ongoing and iterative process of identifying, mitigating, and resolving incidents that occur within the software development and operations lifecycle. Unlike traditional incident response approaches, which are typically reactive and only activated when an incident occurs, continuous incident response is proactive and integrated into the overall DevOps process. It involves continuously monitoring, detecting, and responding to potential incidents in real-time, with the goal of minimizing their impact and preventing their recurrence.

Continuous Innovation

Continuous Innovation in the context of DevOps refers to the ongoing process of consistently introducing new ideas, practices, and technologies to improve software development and delivery. It encapsulates the philosophy of continuously iterating, experimenting, and refining software development processes to drive innovation and stay ahead in the fast-paced technology landscape. DevOps, which stands for Development and Operations, is a software development methodology that emphasizes collaboration and communication between development teams and operations teams. It aims to streamline the software development lifecycle by integrating development and operations processes, enabling faster and more frequent releases, improved quality, and increased customer satisfaction. In the context of DevOps, continuous innovation involves several key aspects: 1. Change Management: DevOps encourages a culture of embracing change and taking calculated risks. Continuous innovation involves efficiently managing and implementing changes across the entire software development pipeline. It requires effective planning, monitoring, and communication to ensure that changes are implemented smoothly without disrupting the development and deployment process. 2. Automation: Continuous innovation in DevOps relies heavily on automation. By automating repetitive tasks and processes, such as building, testing, and deploying software, development teams can focus on more creative and innovative solutions. Automation enables faster feedback loops, shorter development cycles, and higher productivity. 3. Monitoring and Feedback: Continuous innovation in DevOps requires constant monitoring and feedback. By tracking and analyzing key performance indicators and metrics, teams can identify areas for improvement and make data-driven decisions. Continuous monitoring helps teams to measure the effectiveness of their innovations and make adjustments accordingly. 4. Collaboration and Communication: Continuous innovation is deeply rooted in collaboration and communication between development and operations teams. By fostering a culture of open communication, sharing ideas, and learning from each other's experiences, teams can drive innovation and collectively find new solutions to challenges. In conclusion, continuous innovation in the context of DevOps is an ongoing process of introducing new ideas, practices, and technologies to improve software development and delivery. It involves change management, automation, monitoring, and feedback, as well as collaboration and communication between development and operations teams.

Continuous Inspection

Continuous Inspection refers to the practice of automatically analyzing and evaluating code quality and compliance to established guidelines throughout the software development lifecycle in the context of DevOps. In DevOps, Continuous Inspection is an essential component of the continuous delivery pipeline that focuses on uncovering potential issues and defects early on in the development process. It aims to proactively identify code quality, security vulnerabilities, adherence to coding standards, and overall system health to ensure the timely delivery of high-quality software.

Continuous Integration (CI)

Continuous Integration (CI) is a key practice in the context of DevOps, aimed at improving the efficiency and quality of software development, by merging code changes from developers into a shared repository frequently, and automatically building, testing, and validating these changes as soon as they are integrated. CI plays a crucial role in enabling teams to collaborate and work more effectively, by providing a consistent and automated process for integrating code changes into a central codebase. Without CI, developers often face challenges in managing code conflicts, ensuring consistency, and verifying the stability and quality of their changes, leading to delays, inefficiencies, and potential integration issues. In a CI environment, developers regularly commit their code changes to a version control system, such as Git, which serves as a central repository. The CI system continuously monitors this repository for new code changes and triggers an automated build process as soon as a change is detected. During the build process, the CI system compiles the code, runs unit tests, and performs other necessary tasks, depending on the project requirements. Once the build is complete, the CI system generates reports and notifies the development team about the build status. These reports provide valuable insights into the health and quality of the codebase, allowing developers to identify issues early and address them promptly. In case of build failures, the CI system helps in pinpointing the exact cause, facilitating faster debugging and resolution of the issues. CI also encourages the adoption of other best practices, such as automated testing, code review, and continuous delivery. By automating the process of building and validating code changes, CI reduces the manual effort and human errors involved in these activities, ultimately leading to faster development cycles and improved software stability. In conclusion, Continuous Integration (CI) is an essential practice in DevOps that promotes collaboration, efficiency, and code quality by automating the process of integrating, building, and validating code changes. It enables teams to detect and address issues early, ensuring a more stable and reliable software development process in a fast-paced and collaborative environment.

Continuous Integration And Continuous Deployment (CI/CD)

Continuous Integration (CI) is a practice in DevOps where developers frequently integrate their code changes into a shared repository. The main objective of CI is to identify and address any issues or conflicts that occur during the integration process as early as possible, ensuring that the code remains stable and ready for deployment. CI involves automating the build, test, and validation processes to achieve continual feedback on the quality of the codebase. By implementing CI, teams can detect and resolve issues quickly, leading to faster development cycles and improved software quality. Continuous Deployment (CD) is an extension of CI that focuses on automating the release and deployment of application changes. It involves automatically taking the successfully tested and validated code from the CI process and deploying it to production or staging environments. CD aims to reduce the manual effort needed for release management, minimize the risk of human errors, and enable faster and more frequent deployments. By implementing CD, organizations can achieve shorter time-to-market, increased agility, and improved customer satisfaction.

Continuous Knowledge Base

A continuous knowledge base refers to a centralized repository of information that is continuously updated and accessible to all stakeholders involved in the DevOps process. It serves as a single source of truth for knowledge related to the development, deployment, and operations of software systems, facilitating collaboration and enabling continuous improvement. The continuous knowledge base acts as a knowledge sharing platform, showcasing best practices, lessons learned, and documentation of various processes and procedures. It contains a wide range of information, including architectural diagrams, system requirements, deployment scripts, troubleshooting guides, and performance tuning guidelines. It also includes code snippets, reusable components, and configuration templates that can be readily used or adapted for different projects. By having a continuous knowledge base, organizations are able to foster a culture of learning and knowledge sharing, enabling teams to leverage existing knowledge and avoid reinventing the wheel. It promotes cross-functional collaboration and breaks down silos, ensuring that all stakeholders have access to the latest information and are aligned with the overall goals and objectives of the DevOps workflow. Furthermore, the continuous knowledge base supports the concept of continuous improvement by enabling teams to capture and share lessons learned from previous projects or incidents. It serves as a valuable resource for problem-solving and troubleshooting, providing guidance on how to resolve common issues or challenges that may arise during the development, deployment, or operation of software systems. In summary, a continuous knowledge base is a vital component of the DevOps process, providing teams with a centralized and up-to-date source of knowledge and information. It promotes collaboration, facilitates continuous learning, and supports the overall objectives of the DevOps workflow.

Continuous Knowledge Sharing

Continuous Knowledge Sharing is a key principle of DevOps that promotes the regular and ongoing dissemination of knowledge among team members, fostering collaboration, innovation, and continuous improvement. In the context of DevOps, continuous knowledge sharing involves creating a culture and environment that encourages and enables the sharing of information, skills, and experiences across teams and individuals. It goes beyond traditional knowledge transfer methods, such as formal training sessions or documentation, and emphasizes the importance of informal and spontaneous knowledge exchange. This principle recognizes that every team member possesses unique perspectives, insights, and expertise, and it encourages individuals to actively contribute their knowledge and learn from others. By facilitating the flow of information throughout all stages of the software development lifecycle, continuous knowledge sharing helps break down silos, enhance collaboration, and drive cross-functional learning.

Continuous knowledge sharing encompasses various practices and techniques, including pair programming, peer code review, regular team meetings, knowledge sharing sessions, and documentation in easily accessible formats. It promotes the use of transparent communication channels, such as chat platforms, online collaboration tools, and shared repositories, to ensure that information is readily available and easily discoverable. This principle also emphasizes the importance of learning from both successes and failures. Team members are encouraged to share their triumphs, challenges, and lessons learned, fostering a culture of continuous improvement and enabling the entire team to benefit from these experiences. By embracing continuous knowledge sharing, organizations can tap into the collective intelligence of their teams, foster a learning culture, and drive innovation. It not only enhances individual skills and capabilities but also strengthens the overall resilience, adaptability, and effectiveness of the DevOps practice.

Continuous Learning From Failure

Continuous learning from failure, in the context of DevOps, refers to the practice of actively seeking, analyzing, and applying lessons learned from failures in order to improve and optimize the software development and delivery processes. DevOps is an approach that combines software development and IT operations to enhance collaboration, increase efficiency, and accelerate the delivery of high-quality software products. Continuous learning from failure is a crucial component of the DevOps philosophy, as it enables teams to identify and address issues early on, fosters a culture of innovation, and promotes continuous improvement.

Continuous Learning

Continuous Learning is a fundamental principle of DevOps, which refers to the ongoing process of acquiring knowledge, improving skills, and evolving practices that enable organizations to adapt, innovate, and continuously improve their software development and delivery processes. It encompasses a mindset and culture of continuous improvement and learning throughout the entire DevOps lifecycle. In the context of DevOps, Continuous Learning entails the following key aspects: Firstly, it involves fostering a learning culture within the organization, where individuals and teams are encouraged to actively seek and share knowledge, skills, and experiences. This requires creating a safe environment that values experimentation, collaboration, and open communication, enabling everyone to learn from failures and successes. Secondly, Continuous Learning in DevOps emphasizes the importance of continuously acquiring and refining technical skills and domain knowledge. This includes staying up-to-date with the latest tools, technologies, frameworks, and methodologies relevant to software development, operations, and delivery. It also involves gaining a deeper understanding of the business domain and customer needs to deliver value more effectively. Thirdly, Continuous Learning involves regularly assessing and reflecting upon current practices and processes to identify areas for improvement and innovation. This includes embracing a mindset of curiosity and a willingness to challenge the status quo, seeking new ways to deliver software faster, with higher quality, and greater efficiency. It also involves leveraging data, metrics, and feedback loops to measure and validate the impact of changes and innovations. By embracing Continuous Learning in DevOps, organizations can foster a culture of innovation, adaptability, and resilience. It enables teams to continuously enhance their capabilities, drive continuous improvement, and respond to changing market demands effectively. Continuous Learning empowers individuals and teams to collaborate, learn from each other, and share knowledge and best practices, leading to better outcomes, higher productivity, and increased customer satisfaction.

Continuous Load Testing

Continuous Load Testing is a key aspect of implementing a DevOps methodology, where load and stress tests are performed continuously throughout the software development lifecycle. It involves simulating real-world user traffic and testing the application's performance under different load conditions to identify and address performance issues early on. Continuous Load Testing helps teams in the DevOps environment ensure that their applications can handle the expected user load and perform well under high stress scenarios. By conducting load tests continuously, teams can quickly detect any degradation in performance and take necessary actions to optimize the application's performance.

Continuous Measurement

Continuous Measurement, in the context of DevOps, refers to the ongoing process of collecting and analyzing data to gain insights and make informed decisions regarding the performance, efficiency, and quality of software development and delivery processes. This approach involves the systematic and automated monitoring of various metrics and key performance indicators (KPIs) at every stage of the software development life cycle (SDLC), including planning, coding, testing, deployment, and operations.

Continuous Monitoring

The term Continuous Monitoring refers to the process of regularly and consistently collecting, analyzing, and reviewing data from various systems and applications in order to assess and maintain the performance, security, and compliance of these systems throughout the DevOps lifecycle. In the context of DevOps, Continuous Monitoring allows organizations to continuously monitor and track the health, performance, and security of their software systems and infrastructure. It enables teams to proactively identify and address potential issues, vulnerabilities, and deviations from established baselines before they become critical or impact the end-user experience.

Continuous Optimization

Continuous optimization in the context of DevOps refers to the ongoing process of making improvements and fine-tuning various aspects of software development and deployment to achieve optimal performance and efficiency. DevOps is a methodology that combines development (Dev) and operations (Ops) teams to streamline software development and deployment processes. Continuous optimization is an integral part of the DevOps approach, as it aims to ensure that the software being developed and deployed is constantly refined and optimized to meet the evolving needs of end users and the business.

Continuous Performance Testing

A short formal definition of Continuous Performance Testing in the context of DevOps is: Continuous Performance Testing is a practice in DevOps that involves monitoring the performance and scalability of an application or system throughout its development and deployment lifecycle. It aims to identify and address performance issues early on, ensuring that the application or system performs optimally and meets the required performance standards.

Continuous Post-Incident Review

Continuous Post-Incident Review is a practice within the DevOps approach that focuses on analyzing and learning from incidents that occur in the operational environment. It involves conducting regular and systematic reviews of incidents with the aim of identifying and understanding the root causes, determining the necessary remedial actions, and implementing improvements to prevent similar incidents from happening again in the future. The purpose of Continuous Post-Incident Review is to foster a culture of learning and improvement within the organization. It emphasizes the importance of treating incidents as opportunities for growth and development, rather than solely as disruptions or failures. By conducting post-incident reviews continuously, teams can gain insights into the underlying issues, challenges, and dependencies that contribute to incidents, enabling them to enhance their understanding of their systems and processes.

Continuous Problem Solving

Continuous problem-solving in the context of DevOps refers to the ongoing and iterative process of identifying, analyzing, and resolving issues that arise during the development, deployment, and operations of software systems. It is a fundamental principle of DevOps that aims to enable teams to deliver high-quality software products with minimal disruptions and downtime. Continuous problem-solving involves several key steps. First, it requires a proactive and vigilant approach to monitoring and observing the infrastructure and applications in real-time. This may involve the use of various monitoring and logging tools to track performance metrics, detect anomalies, and identify potential problems before they impact end-users. Once an issue is identified, teams must analyze and diagnose the root cause of the problem. This often requires collaboration and communication between different teams, such as developers, operations, and quality assurance. The goal is to gain a comprehensive understanding of the issue and determine the most effective solution. The next step is to implement a solution to address the problem. This may involve making code changes, configuring infrastructure, or adjusting system settings. It is crucial to ensure that the solution is thoroughly tested and validated before deploying it to production to avoid introducing new problems or issues. Continuous problem-solving also emphasizes the importance of learning from past experiences and preventing similar issues in the future. This includes documenting and sharing knowledge about problems and their solutions, conducting post-mortem analyses to understand the underlying causes, and implementing preventive measures to mitigate the risk of recurrence. To support continuous problem-solving in DevOps, organizations often adopt various practices and tools. This may include implementing automated monitoring and alerting systems, using incident management and tracking tools to streamline issue resolution processes, and fostering a culture of collaboration, learning, and experimentation. In summary, continuous problem-solving in the context of DevOps is the ongoing, iterative process of identifying, analyzing, and resolving issues in software systems. It involves proactive monitoring, collaborative analysis and diagnosis, effective solution implementation, and continuous learning from past experiences. By embracing this approach, organizations can improve the reliability, availability, and quality of their software products while enabling faster delivery and better customer satisfaction.

Continuous Product Ownership

Continuous Product Ownership, in the context of DevOps, refers to the ongoing responsibility and accountability for the product being developed and delivered. It is a concept that emphasizes the continuous involvement of the product owner throughout the entire lifecycle of a software product. Traditionally, product ownership has been seen as a one-time activity where the product owner defines the requirements and hands them over to the development team. However, in a DevOps environment, continuous product ownership recognizes that product development is a continuous and iterative process, and the product owner's role extends beyond just defining initial requirements.

Continuous Resilience

Continuous resilience refers to the ability of a DevOps team or system to adapt and recover quickly from failures or disruptions in order to maintain consistent performance and delivery of software products or services. It encompasses a set of practices, processes, and technologies aimed at building and sustaining robust systems that can withstand and recover from various challenges, including hardware or software failures, security breaches, infrastructure outages, or other unexpected events. In a DevOps context, continuous resilience is closely related to the concept of resilience engineering, which focuses on designing and implementing systems that can operate effectively and recover quickly from disruptions or failures. It involves proactive measures to anticipate and prevent failures, as well as reactive measures to respond promptly and effectively when failures occur.

Continuous Review

Continuous Review is a practice in the context of DevOps that emphasizes the ongoing monitoring and assessment of software development processes and outcomes. It involves the regular and systematic evaluation of the various stages of the software development lifecycle to identify areas of improvement and ensure that the defined targets and objectives are being achieved. As part of Continuous Review, DevOps teams implement continuous feedback loops and measure key performance indicators (KPIs) to gain insights into the effectiveness of their processes. This allows them to identify bottlenecks, inefficiencies, and areas for optimization, enabling them to make informed decisions and take corrective actions as needed.

Continuous Risk Management

Continuous Risk Management (CRM) in the context of DevOps is a proactive approach to identifying, assessing, and addressing risks throughout the software development lifecycle. It involves integrating risk management practices seamlessly into the DevOps processes to ensure that risks are continuously monitored and managed effectively. The main goal of CRM is to enable organizations to identify potential risks early on and implement mitigation strategies in a timely manner, thereby reducing the impact and probability of negative outcomes. This helps to maintain a stable and secure software delivery pipeline, with minimal disruption to operations and customer satisfaction. CRM involves several key steps: 1. Risk Identification: This step involves systematically identifying and documenting potential risks that may impact the software development and delivery process. This can include risks associated with technology, security, compliance, project management, and stakeholder expectations. 2. Risk Assessment: Once risks are identified, they need to be assessed in terms of their potential impact and likelihood of occurrence. This includes evaluating the severity of the risk, determining its priority, and understanding the context in which it might arise. 3. Risk Mitigation: After assessing the risks, mitigation strategies need to be formulated and implemented. This involves taking proactive steps to reduce the likelihood of risk occurrence or minimizing its impact. Mitigation strategies can include implementing security controls, conducting regular vulnerability assessments, performing code reviews, and incorporating feedback loops for continuous improvement. 4. Risk Monitoring and Reporting: Continuous monitoring of risks is essential to ensure their effectiveness and address any emerging risks. This includes regular reporting on the status of risks, their impact, and the effectiveness of mitigation measures. Monitoring can be done through automated tools, data analysis, and regular communication among DevOps teams. By integrating CRM into DevOps processes, organizations can ensure that risks are identified and managed efficiently throughout the software development lifecycle. This helps to build a culture of risk awareness and proactive risk management, ultimately leading to improved software quality, customer satisfaction, and overall business performance.

Continuous Root Cause Analysis

Continuous Root Cause Analysis (CRCA) in the context of DevOps refers to an ongoing process of identifying and addressing the underlying causes of problems or incidents that occur within a DevOps environment. It involves a systematic approach to analyzing incidents, identifying their root causes, and implementing corrective actions to prevent similar issues from happening in the future. The goal of CRCA is to create a culture of learning and improvement within a DevOps team, where problems are seen as opportunities for growth rather than as failures. It encourages cross-functional collaboration and knowledge sharing, as multiple perspectives are considered during the analysis process. CRCA involves several key steps. Firstly, when an incident occurs, it is important to collect data and gather information about the problem. This can include logs, metrics, and other relevant data that can help in the analysis. Next, the incident is thoroughly investigated to determine the immediate cause of the issue. Once the immediate cause is identified, the focus shifts to finding the root cause. This involves asking "why" multiple times to uncover the underlying factors that contributed to the incident. The goal is to go beyond surface-level explanations and uncover the fundamental issues that need to be addressed. After the root cause is identified, appropriate corrective actions can be developed and implemented. These actions can range from process improvements to changes in infrastructure or tooling. The effectiveness of these actions is then monitored to ensure that they have the desired impact. CRCA is an iterative process, where incidents are continuously analyzed and improvements are made over time. It helps in creating a more resilient and reliable DevOps environment, where issues are proactively addressed, and the overall system becomes more stable.

Continuous Security Practices

Continuous Security Practices, in the context of DevOps, refer to an ongoing and integrated approach to security that is seamlessly incorporated into the entire software development lifecycle. It is a set of processes and techniques that aim to ensure the security and compliance of the software being developed, deployed, and operated, with a focus on enabling frequent and rapid release cycles without compromising security. Continuous Security Practices involve the implementation of security measures and controls early in the development process, as well as integrating security tasks and responsibilities throughout the entire DevOps pipeline. This enables security to be a shared responsibility among all members of the development and operations teams, instead of being considered as an afterthought or standalone process. The key principles of Continuous Security Practices include: - Security by design: Embedding security considerations into the design and architecture of the software, ensuring that security controls and measures are integrated from the start. - Automated security testing: Leveraging automated tools and technologies to perform regular security checks and vulnerability assessments throughout the development and deployment stages. This helps to identify and fix security gaps and vulnerabilities early on, preventing the introduction of potential security risks into the software. - Security as code: Treating security configurations and policies as code, utilizing version control systems and automated deployment tools to manage and enforce security controls consistently across different environments. This allows for improved traceability, repeatability, and auditability of security measures. - Continuous monitoring and incident response: Implementing proactive monitoring and detection mechanisms to identify security incidents and breaches in real-time. Coupled with a well-defined incident response plan, this helps to minimize the impact of security incidents and enables rapid mitigation and recovery. - Continuous compliance and governance: Incorporating compliance requirements and control frameworks into the development and deployment processes, ensuring that the software meets relevant regulatory and security standards. This includes regular audits, assessments, and documentation of security controls and measures. - Collaboration and knowledge sharing: Fostering a culture of collaboration and knowledge sharing among all stakeholders involved in the DevOps process, including developers, operations, security teams, and other relevant parties. This helps to improve awareness, understanding, and adherence to security practices throughout the organization.

Continuous Security Testing Practices

Continuous Security Testing Practices refer to the integration of security testing processes and techniques into the development and deployment pipelines of a DevOps environment. DevOps is a software development methodology that emphasizes collaboration, integration, and automation between development (Dev) and IT operations (Ops) teams. Continuous Security Testing Practices, within the context of DevOps, aim to ensure that security testing is conducted throughout the software development lifecycle, from the initial phase of code development to the final phase of production deployment. Continuous Security Testing Practices involve the use of various security testing tools and techniques such as static code analysis, vulnerability scanning, penetration testing, and security code review. These practices allow organizations to identify and address security vulnerabilities and weaknesses in their software applications in a timely manner, reducing the risk of potential security breaches and data leaks. By integrating security testing into their DevOps pipelines, organizations can minimize security risks and ensure the continuous delivery of secure and reliable software products.

Continuous Security Testing

Continuous Security Testing, in the context of DevOps, refers to the practice of continuously assessing and validating the security posture of software applications, systems, and infrastructure throughout the entire software development lifecycle (SDLC). It is a proactive approach that aims to identify vulnerabilities, weaknesses, and potential threats early on and allow for prompt remediation. This ongoing process of security testing is integrated seamlessly into the DevOps pipeline, focusing on automation, collaboration, and feedback loops to deliver secure software at the speed of DevOps. By incorporating security into every stage of the SDLC, from planning and design to coding, testing, and deployment, Continuous Security Testing helps to ensure that security is not an afterthought but an integral part of the development process.

Continuous Security

Continuous Security in the context of DevOps refers to an ongoing and automated approach to ensuring the protection and integrity of software applications throughout the entire software development lifecycle (SDLC). It involves seamlessly integrating security practices and measures into the DevOps pipeline, without creating bottlenecks or hindering the rapid delivery of software. This continuous approach to security aims to prevent, detect, and remediate potential vulnerabilities and threats throughout the software development process, enabling organizations to deliver secure software at the speed and scale required in today's fast-paced digital world. By incorporating security practices early on, continuous security mitigates risks and helps organizations proactively address security concerns, reducing the likelihood of security breaches and the associated business impacts.

Continuous Stress Testing

Continuous Stress Testing is a practice in DevOps that involves continually subjecting a system or application to varying levels of stress in order to assess its performance, reliability, and resilience under real-world conditions. By simulating high user loads, excessive traffic, or resource-intensive scenarios, the objective is to identify and address bottlenecks, weaknesses, and potential failure points before they impact end-users and business operations. Continuous Stress Testing is an essential component of the DevOps approach as it enables teams to proactively detect and fix performance-related issues early in the development cycle. It goes beyond traditional load testing by not only examining how a system performs under expected loads but also testing its limits and robustness under extreme conditions. This practice helps in validating system scalability, response times, error handling, and overall stability.

Continuous Testing

Continuous Testing is a fundamental practice in the context of DevOps that enables the seamless and automated verification of software quality throughout the software development lifecycle. It involves the frequent and iterative testing of application components, aiming to identify and address issues as soon as possible, ensuring that software meets the desired quality levels and is fit for production deployment. Continuous Testing is deeply integrated into the DevOps workflow, as it supports the principles of continuous integration and continuous delivery. It provides developers and operations teams with prompt feedback on the quality of the code, allowing them to detect and rectify defects early in the development cycle.

Continuous Threat Monitoring

Continuous Threat Monitoring is a crucial component of the DevOps practice that focuses on ensuring the security and protection of applications, systems, and infrastructure throughout the software development lifecycle. DevOps is an approach that combines development and operations teams to deliver high-quality software at a faster pace, and Continuous Threat Monitoring is a fundamental step in this process to identify, analyze, and mitigate any potential security threats or vulnerabilities that may arise. The practice involves the continuous monitoring of security controls, such as firewalls, intrusion detection systems, and vulnerability scanners, to detect any suspicious activities, unauthorized access attempts, or security breaches. These monitoring activities can be automated, leveraging tools and technologies like security information and event management (SIEM) systems, log management systems, and penetration testing tools. Continuous Threat Monitoring helps organizations maintain a proactive security posture by enabling real-time detection and response to security incidents. It allows teams to quickly identify vulnerabilities, misconfigurations, or weaknesses in their applications or infrastructure and take immediate corrective actions. To effectively implement Continuous Threat Monitoring, organizations must establish a comprehensive security strategy, including the definition of security standards, policies, and procedures. They must also ensure proper integration of security practices within the DevOps pipeline, such as incorporating security testing into the continuous integration and continuous delivery (CI/CD) process. By continuously monitoring for threats, DevOps teams can minimize the risk of security breaches, data leaks, and service disruptions, ultimately leading to increased customer trust and satisfaction. Additionally, Continuous Threat Monitoring allows for compliance with industry regulations and standards, as it enables organizations to identify and address any security vulnerabilities or weaknesses that may prevent them from meeting the required security criteria.

Continuous Validation

Continuous Validation in the context of DevOps refers to the ongoing process of testing and verifying code changes and updates throughout the software development lifecycle. It is a fundamental principle of the DevOps approach, which aims to deliver better quality software at a faster pace. Continuous Validation involves continuously running automated tests against the software application to identify any bugs, issues, or inconsistencies. This process begins as soon as a code change is made and continues throughout the entire development and deployment process. By doing so, any potential issues can be detected early on, allowing for quicker resolution and reducing the likelihood of these issues reaching production environments. The objective of Continuous Validation is to ensure that the software is functioning as intended and meeting the expected requirements and quality standards. It involves a combination of different testing techniques, such as unit testing, integration testing, system testing, and performance testing. These tests are typically automated and incorporated into the continuous integration and continuous delivery (CI/CD) pipelines. Continuous Validation is closely tied to Continuous Integration (CI) and Continuous Delivery (CD), as it relies on the frequent and automated integration of code changes into a shared repository and the rapid deployment of these changes into production environments. With each code change, the automated tests are executed to check if the changes have introduced any regressions or defects. By adopting Continuous Validation practices, development teams can detect and fix issues early on, reducing the amount of rework required and improving the overall software quality. It also enables teams to release new features and updates to end users more frequently while maintaining a stable and reliable software system. Continuous Validation is not a one-time activity but rather an ongoing process that continues even after the software is deployed to production. By continually monitoring the application's performance and user feedback, developers can make necessary improvements and updates to ensure the software remains reliable, secure, and user-friendly. In conclusion, Continuous Validation is an essential component of the DevOps methodology, ensuring that the software is thoroughly tested and validated throughout its lifecycle. By continuously running automated tests, development teams can identify and address issues early on, resulting in higher-quality software delivered at a faster pace.

Continuous Verification

Continuous Verification, in the context of DevOps, refers to the ongoing process of automatically validating software changes and infrastructure updates to ensure their compliance with predefined quality standards and desired functionality. It is an essential component of the continuous integration and continuous delivery (CI/CD) pipeline, where it acts as a quality gate to prevent faulty code and configurations from reaching production environments. The primary goal of continuous verification is to minimize the risk of introducing defects and regressions into the software development process by continuously monitoring and validating the changes made to the codebase and the associated infrastructure, such as cloud resources or network configurations. This is achieved through a combination of automated tests, monitoring tools, and observability practices. Continuous verification involves running different types of tests at various stages of the CI/CD pipeline. These tests include unit tests, integration tests, regression tests, performance tests, security tests, and acceptance tests. The tests are designed to cover different aspects of the software and infrastructure, ensuring that they function as intended and meet the specified requirements. By continuously verifying software changes, development teams can quickly detect and resolve issues, preventing them from reaching production environments and causing disruptions or customer dissatisfaction. It enables fast feedback loops, allowing developers to make iterative improvements based on test results and user feedback. Additionally, continuous verification helps identify any inconsistencies or discrepancies between the environment in which the software is tested and the production environment, reducing the likelihood of deployment-related issues. Continuous verification also contributes to the overall reliability and stability of the software system. By continuously validating changes, teams can maintain a high level of confidence in the quality and performance of their applications and infrastructure. It enables proactive identification of potential issues before they become critical problems, ensuring smoother operations and better user experiences.

Continuous Version Control

Continuous Version Control, in the context of DevOps, refers to an approach where changes made to software code and other artifacts in a development project are systematically managed and tracked throughout the entire development process. This includes the seamless integration of version control tools and practices into the DevOps pipeline to ensure that code changes are recorded, monitored, and easily accessible for collaboration, troubleshooting, and continuous improvement. The core principles behind Continuous Version Control align with the broader goals of DevOps, which aim to automate and streamline the software delivery lifecycle. By integrating version control practices into the DevOps pipeline, development teams can ensure that changes made to the code are tracked and documented in a controlled and structured manner. This enables enhanced collaboration, improved visibility, and increased traceability of code changes, leading to better code quality, reduced development time, and increased software reliability.

48

Contrast Security

Contrast Security is an application security company that focuses on providing solutions for DevOps teams. In the context of DevOps, Contrast Security offers a unique platform that integrates security seamlessly into the software development process. The primary goal of DevOps is to enable collaboration and streamline the development, deployment, and operation of software systems. However, in this fast-paced environment, security often takes a back seat, leading to vulnerabilities and potential breaches. Contrast Security addresses this challenge by offering a comprehensive application security solution that is specifically designed for DevOps workflows. Contrast Security's platform offers continuous protection by embedding its security capabilities directly into the application. It does not rely on external security scans or delayed testing cycles, ensuring that applications are protected in real-time throughout the entire development process. The platform analyzes the code as it executes, identifying and blocking any malicious activity. This approach allows DevOps teams to detect and remediate vulnerabilities early on, reducing the risk of security incidents. The platform provides visibility into the security posture of applications, empowering developers and security teams with actionable insights. It offers detailed reports and dashboards that highlight vulnerabilities and their potential impact, enabling teams to prioritize and address issues efficiently. Contrast Security also provides alerts and notifications, ensuring that teams are immediately aware of any security issues that arise. One of the key advantages of Contrast Security is its ability to integrate seamlessly into existing DevOps workflows. It supports a wide range of development languages and frameworks, making it compatible with diverse technology stacks. The platform also integrates with popular development and collaboration tools, such as CI/CD pipelines and issue trackers, enabling teams to incorporate security into their existing processes without significant disruption. In summary, Contrast Security is an application security platform that caters specifically to the needs of DevOps teams. Its continuous protection, real-time analysis, actionable insights, and seamless integration capabilities make it an effective solution for addressing security concerns in the fast-paced DevOps environment.

Control-M

Control-M is a powerful workload automation tool used in the context of DevOps. It enables the automation and orchestration of tasks and processes across different systems and platforms. Control-M provides a centralized platform for managing and monitoring workflows, ensuring the efficient execution of jobs and providing visibility into the status and performance of critical business processes.

Crisis Management

Paragraph 1: Crisis management in the context of DevOps refers to a set of practices and strategies implemented by organizations to effectively respond to and mitigate incidents or crises that may occur during the software development and deployment process. It involves a proactive approach to identifying and resolving potential issues, as well as reactive measures to contain and address problems that arise. Paragraph 2: Crisis management in DevOps is focused on minimizing the impact of incidents on the development, testing, deployment, and maintenance of software applications. It includes activities such as incident detection, response, resolution, and recovery. The goal is to minimize downtime, maintain service availability, and restore normal operations as quickly as possible. Crisis management in DevOps involves several key components. Firstly, it requires the establishment of clear incident response processes and procedures. This includes defining roles and responsibilities, creating escalation paths, and ensuring that the necessary resources and tools are available to effectively respond to and resolve incidents. Another important aspect of crisis management in DevOps is proactive monitoring and alerting. This involves continuously monitoring the system for potential issues or anomalies and setting up alerts to notify the appropriate individuals or teams when abnormalities are detected. This allows for early detection and intervention, minimizing the impact of incidents on the overall system. Furthermore, crisis management in DevOps includes effective communication and collaboration among team members. This involves maintaining open lines of communication, sharing information and updates, and coordinating efforts to resolve incidents. Collaboration tools and platforms are often utilized to facilitate this process, ensuring that all team members can work together efficiently and effectively. In addition, crisis management in DevOps involves conducting post-incident reviews and analysis. This allows organizations to identify the root cause of incidents, learn from the experience, and implement necessary improvements or preventive measures to prevent similar incidents from occurring in the future. Overall, crisis management in DevOps plays a crucial role in ensuring the stability, reliability, and resilience of software systems. By implementing effective crisis management practices and strategies, organizations can minimize the impact of incidents, maintain high service availability, and deliver quality software products to customers.

Cross-Functional Skills

Cross-functional skills in the context of DevOps refer to the abilities and knowledge required to collaborate and work effectively across different functional areas or teams involved in the development and operation of software systems. In a DevOps environment, teams with different expertise, such as developers, operations engineers, quality assurance specialists, and business analysts, need to work together seamlessly to deliver high-quality software products efficiently. Cross-functional skills enable individuals to bridge the gaps between these diverse teams, facilitating effective collaboration, communication, and problem-solving.

CruiseControl

CruiseControl is a software tool that is implemented in the DevOps context to facilitate continuous integration and automation of software build and release processes. It is an open-source framework that helps development teams automate the integration and testing of code changes, ensuring that the software remains in a releasable state at all times. CruiseControl acts as a central hub for managing and executing the continuous integration processes within a development environment.

Cucumber

Cucumber is a testing tool widely used in the field of DevOps. It is an open-source software that allows collaboration between developers, testers, and business stakeholders to create and execute automated acceptance tests in a behavior-driven development (BDD) approach. With Cucumber, tests are written in a language called Gherkin, which uses plain, natural language statements that are easy to understand and visualize. These statements are structured into scenarios and features, which represent different aspects and functionalities of the software being tested. Gherkin syntax provides a common language that can be understood by technical and non-technical team members, facilitating communication and collaboration.

Customer Focus

Customer Focus is the foundational principle of DevOps that emphasizes on understanding and continuously improving the experience of customers throughout the development and operational processes of a software product or service. DevOps is a software development methodology that combines software development (Dev) and IT operations (Ops) to promote collaboration, automation, and continuous delivery of high-quality software. Central to the philosophy of DevOps is the concept of Customer Focus, which places the customer at the core of the development and delivery process. By adopting a customer-focused approach, DevOps teams prioritize meeting the needs and expectations of the end-users, whether they are internal stakeholders or external customers. This involves actively seeking feedback from customers, empathizing with their pain points, and aligning development efforts to enhance the product or service based on their requirements. Customer Focus in the context of DevOps entails designing and delivering software solutions that not only meet functional requirements but also provide a seamless user experience. This involves gathering user feedback early in the development cycle, involving customers in the decision-making process, and iterating on the product based on their input. Additionally, Customer Focus in DevOps also involves considering the operational aspects of the software, such as ease of deployment, monitoring, and maintenance. By designing and delivering products with a focus on customer satisfaction and ease of use, DevOps teams can minimize downtime, reduce support calls, and improve overall operational efficiency. Furthermore, Customer Focus also drives continuous improvement by leveraging metrics and analytics to measure customer satisfaction, identify areas of improvement, and make data-driven decisions. By constantly monitoring and analyzing customer feedback and usage patterns, DevOps teams can proactively address issues and enhance the product to better align with customer expectations. In conclusion, Customer Focus is a critical principle in DevOps that emphasizes the importance of understanding and continuously improving the experience of customers throughout the software development and delivery process. By placing the customer at the core, DevOps teams ensure that the software meets their needs, provides an exceptional user experience, and evolves to drive customer satisfaction and operational efficiency.

CyberArk Conjur

CyberArk Conjur is a privileged access management (PAM) tool that is specifically designed to address the unique challenges faced in a DevOps environment. It provides a comprehensive solution for securely managing credentials, secrets, and other sensitive information that is used by applications and infrastructure in a DevOps workflow. At its core, Conjur works by implementing a centralized secrets management system. It allows organizations to securely store, retrieve, and rotate secrets such as API keys, passwords, tokens, and certificates. These secrets are encrypted and protected at rest and in transit, ensuring that they are secure from unauthorized access. One of the key features of Conjur is its ability to manage secrets dynamically. It integrates with popular DevOps tools and provides APIs and plugins that can be easily integrated into existing workflows. This enables automated, on-demand access to secrets, eliminating the need for hardcoded credentials in code repositories or configuration files. Secrets can be retrieved programmatically during runtime, both in development and production environments. Conjur also provides fine-grained access controls and audit capabilities. It offers role-based access control (RBAC), allowing organizations to define and enforce policies around who can access and manage secrets. User actions and access attempts are logged and can be audited to maintain compliance with regulatory requirements. In addition, Conjur supports secrets rotation, ensuring that credentials are regularly changed to prevent unauthorized access. It provides automation capabilities to rotate secrets without affecting running applications or workflows. By utilizing CyberArk Conjur in a DevOps environment, organizations can enhance security and compliance without impeding the speed and agility of the development and deployment processes. It allows for secure, automated management of secrets, reduces the risk of credential leakage, and provides an auditable trail of access and usage.

Dark Launching

Dark launching, in the context of DevOps, refers to a deployment strategy that allows for testing new features or changes in a production environment without exposing them to end users. It involves releasing the new feature or change to a subset of the production environment, typically hidden behind feature flags or toggles, to ensure that it works as intended before making it available to the entire user base. The main purpose of dark launching is to minimize the impact of potential issues or bugs on end users. By isolating the new feature or change to a limited set of users, developers can gather real-time data and feedback to identify and fix any issues that may arise. This approach mitigates the risk of introducing a flawed or disruptive feature to the entire user base, resulting in a better user experience and increased system stability.

Dark

The term "dark" in the context of DevOps refers to the practice of performing operations or experiments in an isolated and controlled environment without impacting the production system. This approach allows teams to test new features, infrastructure changes, or performance enhancements in a safe environment before deploying them to the live production system. In a typical DevOps setup, the production environment is critical and serves as the backbone of a business. Any unexpected behavior or failure in the production system can result in downtime, revenue loss, and damaged reputation. Therefore, making changes without thoroughly testing them can be a risky endeavor. The dark practice mitigates these risks by providing a separate environment where developers and operations teams can experiment and validate changes.

Data Loss Prevention (DLP)

Data Loss Prevention (DLP) refers to a set of practices and technologies implemented in the context of DevOps to prevent sensitive data from being lost, stolen, or leaked. It is a crucial aspect of information security that aims to protect both the organization and its customers from the potential consequences of data breaches. The primary goal of DLP in DevOps is to ensure the confidentiality, integrity, and availability of sensitive data throughout its lifecycle. This involves identifying and classifying sensitive data, implementing appropriate controls and policies to protect it, and monitoring and detecting any potential data leakage or unauthorized access.

Datadog

Datadog is a monitoring and analytics platform that helps organizations gain valuable insights into their infrastructure and applications. It is designed to support the needs of DevOps teams by providing a unified view of performance metrics, logs, and traces. DevOps is a set of practices that combines development (Dev) and operations (Ops) to improve collaboration and streamline software delivery. The goal of DevOps is to bridge the gap between developers and IT operations teams, making it easier to build, test, and release software at a faster pace. Datadog is an important tool for DevOps teams because it enables them to monitor and troubleshoot their applications and infrastructure in real-time. With Datadog, DevOps teams can collect and analyze data from a wide variety of sources, including servers, containers, databases, and cloud services. Datadog provides a centralized dashboard that displays metrics, logs, and traces in a visually appealing and easy-to-understand format. This allows DevOps teams to quickly identify issues, track performance trends, and make informed decisions to improve the reliability and efficiency of their applications. In addition to monitoring, Datadog also offers a range of other features that support the DevOps workflow. For example, it includes comprehensive alerting capabilities, which can be used to notify teams of any performance issues or anomalies. It also supports collaboration by allowing team members to annotate and share dashboards, making it easier to work together and troubleshoot problems. Overall, Datadog plays a crucial role in the DevOps process by providing the necessary visibility and insights into an organization's infrastructure and applications. It helps DevOps teams proactively identify and resolve issues, optimize performance, and deliver high-quality software at a faster pace.

Decision-Making

Decision-making in the context of DevOps refers to the process of making choices and taking actions within a DevOps environment. It involves the analysis and evaluation of various options, considering their potential impact on software development, deployment, and operations. In DevOps, decision-making plays a crucial role in ensuring that teams can effectively collaborate and deliver value to end-users. It involves making decisions about the selection and implementation of technologies, tools, and methodologies that will support the overall DevOps goals and objectives.

Deep Learning For Anomaly Detection Methods

Deep Learning for Anomaly Detection methods refer to a set of techniques that utilize deep neural networks to detect and identify unusual patterns or anomalies in DevOps systems and processes. DevOps, a combination of development and operations, involves the integration and collaboration of development and operations teams to enhance software delivery speed, quality, and reliability. Anomaly detection plays a crucial role in ensuring the smooth functioning of DevOps practices by identifying unexpected behaviors that can potentially impact the system's performance or security. The deep learning approach to anomaly detection involves training deep neural networks on large amounts of historical data to capture the normal behavior of a DevOps system. These networks are capable of learning complex patterns and relationships in the data, enabling them to identify deviations from the norm accurately. The process typically involves the following steps: 1. Data Collection: Relevant data from different sources in the DevOps environment, such as log files, performance metrics, and system events, is collected and preprocessed for further analysis. 2. Network Architecture Design: A deep neural network architecture is designed based on the characteristics of the DevOps data and the specific anomaly detection task. This architecture consists of multiple layers of interconnected neurons that enable the network to learn hierarchical representations of the data. 3. Training: The designed network is trained on labeled data that includes both normal and anomalous instances. During training, the network learns to minimize a predefined loss function by adjusting its internal parameters to improve its ability to distinguish between normal and anomalous patterns. 4. Testing and Evaluation: The trained network is evaluated on unseen data to assess its performance in detecting anomalies. Various evaluation metrics, such as precision, recall, and F1-score, are used to measure the network's accuracy and effectiveness in identifying anomalies. Deep Learning for Anomaly Detection methods provide a powerful and efficient solution for identifying deviations or irregularities in DevOps systems. By leveraging the ability of deep neural networks to learn complex patterns, these methods can greatly enhance the overall reliability and security of DevOps practices.

Deep Learning For Anomaly Detection

Deep Learning for Anomaly Detection is a technique used in the field of DevOps to identify abnormal patterns or behaviors in data collected from various sources such as system logs, performance metrics, and user activities. It involves training a deep learning model to learn the normal patterns in the data and then using that model to detect any deviations from those patterns. DevOps is a set of practices that combines software development and IT operations to deliver high-quality software products quickly and efficiently. In such a dynamic environment, it is crucial to quickly identify and address any anomalies or issues that may arise, as they can have a significant impact on the overall performance, availability, and reliability of the software systems. Deep Learning, a subset of machine learning, is well-suited for anomaly detection in DevOps as it can handle large volumes of complex and unstructured data. It involves training deep neural networks with multiple layers to automatically extract meaningful features from the data and make predictions. By leveraging the power of deep learning, DevOps teams can develop sophisticated models that can detect anomalies with high accuracy and efficiency. The process of applying deep learning for anomaly detection in DevOps typically involves the following steps: 1. Data Collection: Gather data from various sources such as system logs, performance metrics, user activities, and other relevant sources. 2. Data Preprocessing: Clean, transform, and normalize the collected data to make it suitable for training the deep learning model. 3. Model Training: Use the preprocessed data to train a deep learning model, such as a deep neural network. The model learns the normal patterns in the data during training. 4. Anomaly Detection: Apply the trained model to new, unseen data to detect any deviations or anomalies from the learned patterns. The model assigns a score or probability to each data point, indicating its likelihood of being anomalous. 5. Alerting and Remediation: Take appropriate actions based on the detected anomalies, such as raising alerts, investigating the root causes, and implementing necessary fixes or optimizations. By leveraging the power of deep learning for anomaly detection, DevOps teams can proactively identify and address anomalies in their systems, ensuring smooth operations, optimal performance, and high-quality software products.

Dependency Management

Dependency management, in the context of DevOps, refers to the process of identifying, tracking, and resolving dependencies that exist between components of a software application or system. These dependencies may include libraries, frameworks, modules, plugins, or other artifacts that are required for the application to function correctly. In a DevOps environment, where software development and operations teams work together to deliver reliable and efficient software, dependency management plays a crucial role in ensuring smooth and seamless deployment and delivery processes. It allows teams to manage the complex web of dependencies and ensure that all necessary components are available and compatible with each other.

Dependency Scanning

Dependency scanning is a crucial component of the DevOps workflow that aims to identify and manage dependencies within software applications. It involves the automated analysis of software dependencies to identify any potential vulnerabilities or issues that may exist. In the context of DevOps, dependency scanning is a security practice that helps teams identify and mitigate risks associated with the use of external libraries, frameworks, or other software components in their applications. It helps ensure that the software being developed or deployed does not contain known vulnerabilities or threats.

DeployHub

DeployHub is a software delivery platform that aids in the efficient deployment of applications in a DevOps environment. It is designed to simplify the release management process, allowing teams to automate and orchestrate application deployments across various environments. With DeployHub, development teams can easily manage their application release pipeline, enabling a continuous delivery approach. It provides a centralized repository for storing and versioning application components, allowing users to track changes and dependencies throughout the software development lifecycle.

Deployment Automation Tools

Deployment Automation Tools, in the context of DevOps, are software solutions that facilitate the process of deploying software applications and infrastructure changes in an automated and repeatable manner. These tools are designed to streamline the deployment process by reducing manual effort, enabling faster and more reliable deployments, and promoting collaboration between development and operations teams. Deployment automation tools typically offer a range of features and functionalities that support the various stages of the deployment process, including packaging, versioning, configuration management, orchestration, and monitoring. They provide a centralized platform for managing the deployment pipelines and ensure that the software applications are consistently deployed across different environments, such as development, testing, staging, and production.

Deployment Automation

Deployment automation in the context of DevOps refers to the process of automating the deployment of software applications, configurations, and infrastructure changes to various environments, such as development, testing, staging, and production. The goal of deployment automation is to streamline and accelerate the deployment process while ensuring consistency and reducing human error. By automating the deployment process, organizations can achieve quicker time-to-market, increased deployment frequency, and more reliable releases. Manual deployment processes are often time-consuming, error-prone, and require significant manual intervention. Deployment automation replaces these manual steps with automated scripts, tools, and workflows that enable organizations to consistently and reliably deploy software changes to different environments. Deployment automation involves several key components and practices. These include: Version control: The use of version control systems, such as Git, helps to manage source code and configurations, enabling teams to track changes, collaborate effectively, and ensure that the correct versions are deployed. Infrastructure as code: Infrastructure as code (IaC) is an approach to managing and provisioning infrastructure through code. By defining infrastructure elements, such as servers, networks, and storage, as code, deployment automation can deploy and configure infrastructure resources consistently and reliably. Continuous integration and continuous deployment: Deployment automation is closely tied to the concepts of continuous integration (CI) and continuous deployment (CD). CI involves integrating code changes into a shared repository frequently, while CD is the practice of automatically deploying changes to production environments. These practices ensure that changes are integrated and deployed regularly, reducing the risk of issues and enabling faster feedback loops. Deployment pipelines: Deployment pipelines are a series of steps and stages that software changes pass through before being deployed to production. These pipelines typically include stages for building, testing, and deploying applications. Automation tools can facilitate the creation and management of deployment pipelines, ensuring that changes are thoroughly tested and validated before being released. Monitoring and feedback loops: Deployed applications and infrastructure should be monitored to detect issues and gather feedback. Automation can enable the automatic collection of metrics, logs, and other data, which can be used to improve the deployment process and identify areas for optimization. In conclusion, deployment automation plays a vital role in DevOps by enabling organizations to streamline and accelerate the deployment of software changes. By automating processes, organizations can achieve faster time-to-market, increased deployment frequency, and improved reliability, ultimately leading to more efficient software delivery and customer satisfaction.

Deployment Frequency

Deployment Frequency refers to the frequency at which a software application or system is released or deployed into production. In the context of DevOps, it represents the pace and frequency at which development teams can deliver changes to the production environment.

Deployments can range from small code changes to major feature updates or bug fixes. DevOps emphasizes delivering software updates in smaller, more frequent increments to enable faster time-to-market, higher customer satisfaction, and quicker feedback loops. Deployment Frequency is an essential metric in measuring the effectiveness of a DevOps practice and the agility of an organization. By increasing the deployment frequency, teams can rapidly respond to market demands, reduce the time between identifying a user need and delivering a solution, and mitigate risks associated with larger, less frequent deployments.

Deployment Patterns

Deployment patterns refer to the strategies or approaches used in the deployment phase of software development within the context of DevOps. They outline the best practices and guidelines for deploying software applications or updates to production environments, ensuring a seamless and efficient process. These deployment patterns are essential in DevOps as they help streamline the deployment process, automate tasks, minimize downtime, and improve collaboration between development and operations teams. By following established deployment patterns, organizations can achieve faster release cycles, higher quality software, and better customer satisfaction.

Deployment Pipeline

A deployment pipeline is a fundamental concept in the field of DevOps. It refers to an automated process that enables the continuous delivery of software applications from development to production environments. This pipeline encompasses various stages, such as coding, building, testing, and deploying the application. The main objective of a deployment pipeline is to ensure quick and reliable software releases by facilitating frequent and automated feedback loops. The deployment pipeline typically starts with the code being committed to a version control system. Once committed, the pipeline automatically triggers a series of actions, beginning with the code being built into an executable version. This build phase ensures that all necessary dependencies are satisfied and that the code is compiled correctly. After the build phase, the application undergoes a series of tests. These tests can include unit tests, integration tests, and even performance tests. By automating these tests and running them after every code change, the deployment pipeline helps catch bugs and issues early in the software development process. This enables quick resolution and ensures a high level of software quality. Following the testing phase, the application is deployed to a staging environment, where it can be further validated before being released to the production environment. This staging environment closely resembles the production environment, allowing for comprehensive testing and acceptance before the final release. Once the application passes all the necessary tests in the staging environment, it can be released to the production environment. The deployment pipeline automates this process, making it easier and less error-prone. This automation also provides the opportunity for continuous deployment, where changes are deployed to the production environment as soon as they pass the necessary tests in the pipeline. In conclusion, a deployment pipeline in the context of DevOps refers to an automated and efficient process that facilitates the continuous delivery of software applications. It involves various stages, including coding, building, testing, staging, and deployment. By automating these stages, the deployment pipeline ensures quick and reliable software releases, improving efficiency and enhancing software quality.

DevOps

DevOps is a set of practices that combines software development (Dev) and IT operations (Ops) in order to improve collaboration and communication between the two teams. This approach seeks to automate and streamline the processes involved in delivering software applications, from development to deployment and maintenance. The main goal of DevOps is to bridge the gap between development and operations, creating a more efficient and reliable software delivery lifecycle. By breaking down the silos between these two traditionally separate teams, DevOps seeks to foster a culture of collaboration, feedback, and continuous improvement.

DevOps Assessment Tools Evaluation

DevOps Assessment Tools Evaluation is the process of analyzing and evaluating different tools and technologies that can aid in the implementation and execution of DevOps practices. DevOps is an approach to software development and delivery that emphasizes collaboration, automation, and continuous integration and delivery. DevOps Assessment Tools Evaluation involves assessing various tools based on their features, capabilities, and compatibility with existing infrastructure and workflows. These tools can include but are not limited to configuration management tools, containerization tools, continuous integration and delivery tools, monitoring and logging tools, and security and compliance tools.

DevOps Assessment Tools

DevOps Assessment Tools are software tools used in the DevOps process to evaluate and measure various aspects of an organization's DevOps practices and performance. These tools provide valuable insights and feedback to help identify areas of improvement, optimize processes, and enhance the overall efficiency and effectiveness of DevOps workflows. To successfully implement DevOps principles and practices, continuous assessment and monitoring are essential. DevOps Assessment Tools play a crucial role in this continuous improvement cycle by providing objective and data-driven assessments. These tools enable organizations to assess their alignment with DevOps principles, measure the effectiveness of their DevOps practices, and identify bottlenecks and areas for improvement. DevOps Assessment Tools typically offer a range of assessment capabilities and metrics. They assess various factors such as development practices, deployment processes, automation levels, collaboration, and cultural aspects. These tools also evaluate the effectiveness of tools and technologies used in the DevOps pipeline, including version control systems, continuous integration/continuous deployment (CI/CD) tools, and monitoring and logging systems. The assessments performed by these tools help organizations gain insights into their DevOps maturity level, identify gaps in their practices, and facilitate data-driven decision-making. They provide a basis for setting goals and establishing metrics to track progress and measure success in DevOps adoption. The benefits of using DevOps Assessment Tools are numerous. These tools enable organizations to identify areas of improvement and make data-driven decisions for process optimization. They help teams deliver quality software faster, improve collaboration and communication between development and operations teams, and enhance overall efficiency and productivity. Additionally, these tools promote a culture of continuous improvement and enable organizations to benchmark their DevOps practices against industry best practices. In conclusion, DevOps Assessment Tools are essential components of the DevOps toolkit. They enable organizations to assess their DevOps practices and performance, identify areas of improvement, and make data-driven decisions to optimize their development and operations workflows. By using these tools, organizations can enhance their DevOps maturity, continuously improve their practices, and achieve greater success in their DevOps initiatives.

DevOps Bootcamps

DevOps Bootcamps are intensive training programs designed to equip individuals with the skills and knowledge needed to thrive in a DevOps environment. The term "DevOps" refers to a set of principles and practices that promote collaboration, integration, and automation between software development and IT operations teams, with the goal of achieving faster and more efficient software delivery. These bootcamps typically cover a wide range of topics and technologies related to DevOps, including version control systems, continuous integration and delivery, infrastructure as code, cloud computing, containerization, monitoring and logging, and security. They are often delivered in a focused and hands-on format, featuring a combination of lectures, workshops, and real-world projects.

DevOps Case Studies Analysis

DevOps Case Studies Analysis refers to the process of examining and assessing various real-world examples of implementing DevOps practices and principles in organizations to understand their effectiveness and impact. DevOps, which combines development and operations, aims to improve collaboration, communication, and efficiency between software developers and IT operations teams. Through case studies analysis, organizations can gain insights into successful DevOps implementations, identify best practices, and learn from the challenges faced by others. This analysis involves studying different aspects of DevOps adoption, including the tools used, cultural changes, team structure, automation, and continuous integration/continuous delivery (CI/CD) approach.

DevOps Case Studies

DevOps case studies refer to documented examples of the implementation and success of the DevOps methodology in real-world scenarios. DevOps is a software development approach that combines development (Dev) and operations (Ops) teams to streamline the software delivery process, foster collaboration, and increase efficiency and speed. A DevOps case study typically presents a detailed analysis of an organization's journey towards adopting DevOps practices, highlighting the challenges faced, strategies implemented, and outcomes achieved. It provides insights into how different companies have leveraged DevOps principles and tools to transform their software development and deployment processes.

DevOps Center Of Excellence (CoE)

The DevOps Center of Excellence (CoE) refers to a specialized team or group within an organization that establishes and promotes best practices for the implementation and adoption of DevOps principles. Its primary function is to ensure the successful implementation and continuous improvement of DevOps methodologies across the organization. The CoE serves as a centralized hub of knowledge and expertise in the field of DevOps, bringing together professionals from various disciplines including software development, systems administration, quality assurance, and operations. It provides guidance, support, and resources to teams and individuals who are involved in DevOps initiatives within the organization. The key objective of a DevOps CoE is to drive collaboration and alignment between development teams and operations teams, breaking down silos and fostering a culture of shared responsibility. It helps organizations achieve faster and more frequent software releases, reduced time-to-market, increased reliability, and improved customer satisfaction. The CoE achieves its objectives through a range of activities, including conducting training sessions and workshops to educate teams about DevOps practices, facilitating the adoption of automation tools and technologies, and promoting the use of continuous integration and continuous delivery (CI/CD) pipelines. It also establishes metrics and performance indicators to measure the success of DevOps initiatives and facilitates the sharing of knowledge and best practices across teams. A DevOps CoE operates as a catalyst for cultural transformation, promoting a shift from traditional siloed approaches to a more collaborative and integrated software delivery model. It helps organizations overcome challenges related to communication, collaboration, and the coordination of activities between development and operations teams. In summary, the DevOps Center of Excellence is a dedicated team or group within an organization that drives the adoption of DevOps practices and principles. It serves as a centralized hub of knowledge and expertise, providing guidance and support to teams involved in DevOps initiatives. Its key objective is to foster collaboration and alignment between development and operations teams, enabling organizations to achieve faster and more reliable software delivery.

DevOps Certifications Pursuit

DevOps Certifications Pursuit refers to the process of acquiring certifications that validate an individual's knowledge and skills in the field of DevOps. DevOps is a collaborative approach that combines the principles of software development (Dev) and IT operations (Ops) to improve the efficiency and effectiveness of delivering software products and services. In today's technology-driven world, where organizations are constantly striving for digital transformation and agility, DevOps has emerged as a crucial practice. It enables organizations to deliver software at a faster pace, while ensuring reliability, stability, and quality. Consequently, the demand for professionals with expertise in DevOps has significantly increased, leading to the popularity of DevOps certifications. DevOps certifications provide individuals with a formal recognition of their knowledge and skills in various aspects of DevOps. These certifications are offered by reputable organizations and typically involve passing an examination or completing a training program. The curriculum of these certifications typically covers a wide range of topics, including DevOps principles, Agile methodologies, continuous integration and continuous delivery (CI/CD), infrastructure automation, cloud technologies, and collaboration tools. By pursuing DevOps certifications, professionals can enhance their career prospects and increase their market value. These certifications validate their understanding of DevOps practices and demonstrate their ability to effectively implement DevOps methodologies in real-world scenarios. Furthermore, DevOps certifications provide individuals with a competitive advantage, as they differentiate them from their peers and serve as proof of their expertise in this rapidly evolving field. Moreover, DevOps certifications also benefit organizations by ensuring that their teams are equipped with the necessary skills to successfully adopt DevOps practices. Certified professionals can contribute to improving the organization's software development and delivery processes, leading to increased efficiency, reduced risk, and better collaboration between development and operations teams. In conclusion, DevOps Certifications Pursuit is the process of acquiring certifications that validate an individual's knowledge and skills in DevOps. These certifications provide formal recognition, enhance career prospects, and contribute to the successful adoption of DevOps practices within organizations.

DevOps Certifications

DevOps certifications refer to the recognition and validation of an individual's knowledge and skills in the field of DevOps. DevOps, an abbreviation for Development and Operations, has emerged as a widely adopted approach in the software development industry. It aims to bridge the gap between software development and IT operations, promoting collaboration, communication, and automation to deliver high-quality software products rapidly and efficiently. DevOps certifications are designed to assess the proficiency of professionals in various aspects of DevOps, including tools, practices, methodologies, and principles. These certifications typically cover a range of topics, such as continuous integration and deployment, infrastructure as code, containerization, orchestration, monitoring, and collaboration. They often require candidates to demonstrate their ability to apply DevOps principles in real-world scenarios, solve problems, and make informed decisions.

DevOps Challenges And Pitfalls Avoidance

DevOps challenges refer to the obstacles, hurdles, or difficulties that organizations may face when implementing or adopting DevOps practices and principles. DevOps is a collaborative approach that emphasizes communication, collaboration, and integration between software development and IT operations teams. It aims to improve the efficiency, speed, and quality of software development and delivery processes. One of the main challenges of DevOps is cultural resistance or organizational resistance. This refers to the resistance or reluctance of employees or teams to change their traditional ways of working and to embrace the DevOps mindset. It may involve resistance to sharing knowledge, adopting automation tools, or breaking down silos between development and operations teams. Overcoming cultural resistance requires strong leadership, open communication, and a focus on building a collaborative culture.

DevOps Challenges And Pitfalls

DevOps Challenges DevOps is a practice that combines software development (Dev) and information technology operations (Ops) to ensure seamless collaboration and communication between development teams and operations teams. It aims to automate the processes involved in software delivery and infrastructure management to improve efficiency, reliability, and scalability. However, implementing and adopting DevOps practices can present several challenges and pitfalls that organizations must overcome to achieve successful outcomes. One major challenge is cultural resistance and organizational silos. DevOps requires a shift in mindset and collaboration between traditionally separate teams, such as developers, operations, quality assurance (QA), and security. Overcoming resistance to change and breaking down silos is crucial for fostering a culture of collaboration, trust, and accountability. Another challenge is the complexity of the technical environment and legacy systems. Many organizations have complex infrastructure setups and legacy applications that are not designed for automation and continuous integration/continuous delivery (CI/CD). Adapting and integrating these systems into a DevOps pipeline can be challenging and require significant effort in terms of refactoring, rearchitecting, or even rebuilding from scratch. Inadequate tooling and automation capabilities can also pose challenges. DevOps heavily relies on automation to streamline and standardize processes, reduce manual errors, and enable faster deployments. However, selecting the right tools and setting up effective automation frameworks can be overwhelming and time-consuming. Additionally, maintaining security and compliance in a DevOps environment can be challenging. With continuous integration and frequent deployments, it is crucial to ensure that security measures are not compromised. Implementing proper security controls, conducting regular vulnerability assessments, and adhering to compliance standards can be complex in a fast-paced DevOps environment. Furthermore, scaling DevOps practices across large organizations or in projects with diverse teams can present challenges. Coordinating and aligning teams, processes, and tools across different departments, locations, and time zones can be difficult and require strong communication, coordination, and collaboration mechanisms. To overcome these challenges and avoid common pitfalls, organizations must focus on creating a culture of collaboration, invest in training and upskilling, automate processes effectively, select appropriate tools, prioritize security and compliance, and establish effective communication and coordination mechanisms across teams and departments.

DevOps Coach

A DevOps Coach is a professional who helps organizations implement and improve their DevOps practices and culture. DevOps is a set of practices that combine software development (Dev) and IT operations (Ops) to foster collaboration, efficiency, and continuous delivery of high-quality software. The primary role of a DevOps Coach is to guide and mentor teams through the transition to DevOps, helping them understand the principles and benefits of DevOps and align their workflows and processes accordingly. They work closely with development, operations, and other teams to identify areas for improvement and provide the necessary guidance and support to implement DevOps practices effectively. A DevOps Coach typically starts by assessing the current state of an organization's software development and IT operations and identifying the gaps and bottlenecks that hinder collaboration, automation, and continuous delivery. They then work with the relevant teams to define and implement strategies and techniques that address these challenges and support the adoption of DevOps. Some of the key responsibilities of a DevOps Coach include: - Educating teams on DevOps principles, best practices, and tools - Facilitating cross-functional collaboration and communication - Encouraging and guiding the automation of repetitive processes and tasks - Promoting a culture of continuous integration, testing, and deployment - Establishing performance metrics and monitoring systems to measure improvements - Providing ongoing guidance, coaching, and support to teams - Facilitating the adoption of DevOps tools and technologies A successful DevOps Coach possesses a deep understanding of DevOps principles, practices, and tools, as well as the ability to effectively communicate and collaborate with different stakeholders. They should have strong problem-solving and analytical skills to identify and overcome obstacles to DevOps adoption. In conclusion, a DevOps Coach plays a vital role in helping organizations transform their software development and IT operations through the implementation of DevOps practices and culture. They guide and mentor teams, promote collaboration and automation, and drive continuous delivery of high-quality software.

DevOps Communities Of Practice Formation

A DevOps Community of Practice (CoP), in the context of DevOps, is a group of individuals who come together to share knowledge, exchange ideas, and collaborate on improving DevOps practices within an organization. The formation of a DevOps CoP is driven by the need to foster a culture of collaboration, continuous learning, and improvement. It aims to bring together cross-functional teams, including developers, operations personnel, quality assurance engineers, and other stakeholders, to encourage collaboration and break down silos.

DevOps Communities Of Practice

A DevOps Community of Practice is a group of individuals who share a common interest and passion for practicing DevOps principles and methodologies. This community is formed with the purpose of fostering knowledge sharing, collaboration, and continuous improvement within the organization. The primary goal of a DevOps Community of Practice is to facilitate the adoption of DevOps practices across teams within the organization. This is achieved by providing a platform for individuals to engage in discussions, share best practices, and learn from each other's experiences. The community acts as a centralized hub for experts, enthusiasts, and beginners to come together and collectively work towards the successful implementation of DevOps practices. Members of a DevOps Community of Practice typically possess a diverse range of skills and experiences. They may include developers, system administrators, quality assurance engineers, and other IT professionals who are involved in the software development and

59

delivery lifecycle. By bringing together individuals from different roles and perspectives, the community aims to foster cross-functional collaboration and knowledge sharing. The activities of a DevOps Community of Practice may include regular meetings, workshops, webinars, and knowledge-sharing sessions. These events provide opportunities for members to discuss challenges, share success stories, and exchange ideas on how to improve and optimize the software development and deployment processes. Additionally, the community may maintain a repository of resources, such as articles, case studies, and guidelines, that can help members stay updated with the latest DevOps trends and practices. In summary, a DevOps Community of Practice is an inclusive and collaborative group that aims to drive the adoption of DevOps principles and practices within an organization. It serves as a platform for individuals to come together, share knowledge, and work towards the common goal of achieving faster, more reliable software delivery.

DevOps Competitions

DevOps Competitions, in the context of DevOps, refer to organized events or challenges where teams or individuals showcase their skills and abilities in applying DevOps principles and practices. These competitions aim to encourage collaboration, innovation, and continuous improvement in software development and IT operations. The primary goal of DevOps Competitions is to foster a culture of teamwork and learning in the DevOps community, while also promoting the adoption of DevOps methodologies and tools. Participants usually compete by taking part in various tasks or scenarios that simulate real-world development and deployment scenarios.

DevOps Conferences And Events Attendance

DevOps Conferences and Events Attendance refers to the participation of individuals, teams, or organizations in conferences and events that focus on the principles, practices, and tools related to DevOps. DevOps, short for Development and Operations, is an approach that emphasizes collaboration, communication, and integration between software development and IT operations teams. It aims to streamline the software delivery process and foster a culture of continuous improvement. DevOps conferences and events provide a platform for professionals, experts, and enthusiasts to share knowledge, exchange ideas, and learn from each other's experiences in implementing DevOps practices. These events often feature a range of activities such as keynote speeches, panel discussions, workshops, and networking sessions. They cover various aspects of DevOps including automation, infrastructure as code, continuous integration and deployment, monitoring, security, and cultural transformation.

DevOps Conferences And Events

The term "DevOps conferences and events" refers to industry gatherings and meetings that focus on the principles, practices, and tools related to DevOps. DevOps, a combination of "development" and "operations," is a software development methodology that emphasizes collaboration, communication, and automation between software developers and IT operations teams. DevOps conferences and events provide a platform for professionals from various organizations, backgrounds, and roles to come together and exchange knowledge, insights, and experiences related to DevOps. These events often feature keynote presentations, panel discussions, workshops, and networking opportunities.

DevOps Cultural Assessment

The DevOps Cultural Assessment refers to the process of evaluating and analyzing the cultural aspects within an organization with respect to the implementation of DevOps practices. It involves understanding and assessing the current cultural norms, values, and behaviors within the organization, and identifying any cultural barriers or challenges that may hinder the adoption and success of DevOps. This assessment aims to promote a cultural shift towards collaboration, transparency, and continuous improvement in order to foster a DevOps mindset and enable successful DevOps implementation. It helps identify areas where cultural changes are required, and provides insights into how to align the organization's culture with the principles and practices of DevOps.

DevOps Hackathons

A DevOps Hackathon is a collaborative event in the context of DevOps where individuals or teams come together to work on developing, testing, and implementing solutions that align with the principles and practices of DevOps. It offers a platform for cross-functional teams to exchange ideas, experiment with new technologies, and solve specific challenges related to software development, operations, and infrastructure management. In a DevOps Hackathon, participants typically have a limited amount of time, ranging from a few hours to a couple of days, to work intensively on a given problem or objective. The event promotes a hands-on approach, encouraging participants to apply their skills and knowledge to build innovative solutions. During a DevOps Hackathon, participants may work on tasks such as automating the deployment pipeline, improving monitoring and alerting systems, optimizing infrastructure provisioning, or integrating various tools and technologies to enhance collaboration and efficiency. The focus is on fostering a culture of collaboration, continuous learning, and experimentation, thereby fostering the adoption of DevOps principles and practices within an organization. Teams formed during a DevOps Hackathon often consist of individuals from different backgrounds, including developers, system administrators, operations engineers, quality assurance professionals, and other relevant roles. This diversity allows for the integration of different perspectives and experiences, leading to more creative and well-rounded solutions. The goal of a DevOps Hackathon is not only to deliver tangible outcomes but also to promote knowledge sharing, skill development, and team bonding. It provides an opportunity for participants to learn from each other, overcome technical challenges, and work collaboratively towards a common goal. The event may conclude with presentations or demos of the solutions developed, allowing teams to showcase their work and share the knowledge gained with the wider audience.

DevOps Leadership

DevOps leadership is the practice of guiding and managing a DevOps team in order to effectively implement and deliver DevOps principles and practices within an organization. It involves fostering a culture of collaboration, continuous improvement, and automation, while promoting cross-functional teams and a shared responsibility for the entire software development lifecycle. DevOps leadership entails establishing a clear vision and strategy for DevOps adoption, aligning it with organizational goals and objectives. It involves defining and communicating the DevOps vision to the team, advocating for its adoption, and gaining buy-in from stakeholders across the organization. The leader should also set clear expectations and goals for the team, as well as provide the necessary resources and support to enable them to succeed. DevOps leaders are responsible for creating an environment that encourages collaboration and open communication among team members. They promote cross-functional teamwork, bringing together members from different disciplines, such as development, operations, and quality assurance, to work together towards a common goal. This includes breaking down silos, fostering a blameless culture, and promoting knowledge sharing and learning. Continuous improvement is a key aspect of DevOps, and leaders play a crucial role in driving this mindset within the team. They encourage experimentation and innovation, while providing the necessary support and feedback to facilitate learning from failures. They also champion automation, driving the adoption of tools and processes that enable the team to automate manual and repetitive tasks, thereby increasing efficiency and reducing errors. DevOps leadership involves promoting a sense of ownership and accountability among team members. Leaders empower the team to make decisions and take ownership of their work, while providing guidance and support when needed. They promote a culture of learning from mistakes, encouraging reflection and improvement, rather than blame. In summary, DevOps leadership is about guiding and managing a DevOps team to effectively implement and deliver DevOps principles and practices. It involves creating a collaborative, cross-functional environment, promoting continuous improvement and automation, and fostering a sense of ownership and accountability among team members.

DevOps Learning Resources Exploration

DevOps is a software development methodology that combines software development (Dev) and information technology operations (Ops) to create a collaborative and efficient approach for delivering high-quality software products. It aims to bridge the gap between developers and IT operations teams, enabling them to work together seamlessly throughout the entire software development lifecycle. At its core, DevOps focuses on automating and streamlining the software delivery process, from code development and testing to deployment and operation. It promotes a culture of collaboration, communication, and continuous improvement, ensuring that software is delivered faster, more reliably, and with fewer errors.

DevOps Learning Resources

DevOps is a practice that aims to unify software development (Dev) and IT operations (Ops). It is a collaborative and iterative approach that emphasizes communication, collaboration, and automation throughout the software development lifecycle. The goal of DevOps is to enable organizations to deliver high-quality software products at a fast pace, while maintaining stability, reliability, and security. It brings together the development and operations teams to work closely together, breaking down the traditional silos and fostering a culture of collaboration and shared responsibility.

DevOps Maturity Models Assessment

A DevOps maturity model is a framework or model that is used to assess and evaluate an organization's level of maturity in adopting and implementing DevOps practices and principles. It provides a structured approach to measure an organization's readiness for DevOps, identify areas of improvement, and guide the organization towards achieving higher levels of maturity in their DevOps journey. The assessment is based on a set of defined criteria or indicators that cover various domains of DevOps, including culture, collaboration, automation, measurement, sharing, and continuous improvement. These criteria are typically grouped into different levels or stages of maturity, ranging from initial or ad hoc practices to advanced or optimized practices. The assessment process involves gathering data and evidence about the organization's current capabilities, practices, and processes related to DevOps. This can be done through interviews, surveys, observations, and analysis of existing artifacts such as documentation, metrics, and tooling. The collected data is then compared against the criteria defined in the maturity model to determine the organization's maturity level in each domain. Based on the assessment results, organizations can identify their strengths and weaknesses in adopting DevOps and prioritize their improvement efforts. The maturity model provides a roadmap or set of recommendations for organizations to progress from one maturity level to the next, with the ultimate goal of achieving higher levels of integration, automation, and efficiency in their software development and delivery processes. It is important to note that the objective of a DevOps maturity model is not to label or categorize organizations as "good" or "bad" but rather to provide a means of assessing their current state and identifying areas for improvement. It should be seen as a tool for self-assessment and continuous improvement rather than a benchmark for comparing organizations.

DevOps Maturity Models

A DevOps Maturity Model is a framework used to assess and measure the level of maturity and effectiveness of an organization's DevOps practices. It provides a structured and systematic approach to evaluate the organization's capabilities in terms of collaboration, automation, continuous delivery, and culture. The model consists of multiple levels or stages that represent different levels of maturity in the organization's DevOps journey. Each stage represents a set of practices and characteristics that define the level of maturity and effectiveness in implementing DevOps principles.

DevOps Mentoring

DevOps Mentoring is a practice within the realm of DevOps that involves providing guidance, support, and expertise to individuals or teams in order to help them improve their skills, efficiency, and knowledge in implementing DevOps principles and practices. Mentoring is a collaborative and interactive process that aims to bridge the gap between theory and practical application, enabling mentees to gain hands-on experience and a deeper understanding of DevOps concepts. The primary objective of DevOps Mentoring is to foster continuous learning and development, facilitating the growth and maturation of individuals or teams in their DevOps journey. Mentors play a crucial role in this process, utilizing their extensive knowledge and industry experience to provide mentees with valuable insights, advice, and best practices in areas such as automation, continuous integration and delivery, infrastructure as code, and agile methodologies.

DevOps Metrics And KPIs Monitoring

DevOps Metrics and KPIs Monitoring refers to the process of measuring and tracking key performance indicators (KPIs) and metrics in a DevOps environment to gain insights into the efficiency, quality, and productivity of the software development and operations practices. In a DevOps context, metrics and KPIs play a crucial role in enabling teams to make data-driven decisions, understand the impact of their actions, and continuously improve their processes. By monitoring relevant metrics and KPIs, organizations can identify bottlenecks, areas for improvement, and trends that affect the overall success of their DevOps initiatives.

DevOps Metrics And KPIs

DevOps Metrics and KPIs refer to the quantitative measures and indicators used to track, analyze, and assess the performance and effectiveness of DevOps practices within an organization. These metrics and KPIs provide valuable insights into various aspects of the DevOps lifecycle, allowing teams to identify areas for improvement, optimize processes, and drive continuous improvement. Metrics are objective and measurable data points that provide a snapshot of the current state of a specific aspect of the DevOps process. They help teams gain visibility into operational performance and identify bottlenecks or areas of inefficiency. Examples of DevOps metrics include deployment frequency, lead time for changes, mean time to recovery (MTTR), and customer satisfaction. Key Performance Indicators (KPIs), on the other hand, are a set of metrics that are aligned with organizational goals and objectives. KPIs provide a high-level overview of the performance and success of the DevOps practices in meeting business objectives. They help teams evaluate the overall effectiveness of their DevOps initiatives and make strategic decisions to drive improvement. Examples of DevOps KPIs include uptime, release frequency, change failure rate, and time to market. DevOps metrics and KPIs enable organizations to gauge the impact of their DevOps practices on operational efficiency, software quality, and customer satisfaction. By collecting and analyzing these metrics, teams can identify trends, measure progress over time, and make data-driven decisions to improve their DevOps processes. They also promote transparency, collaboration, and accountability within cross-functional teams, as stakeholders can easily monitor performance and communicate areas of concern or success. In conclusion, DevOps metrics and KPIs provide organizations with valuable insights into the performance and effectiveness of their DevOps practices. By tracking and analyzing these metrics, teams can identify areas for improvement, optimize processes, and drive continuous improvement. The use of metrics and KPIs also promotes transparency, collaboration, and accountability within cross-functional teams, enabling organizations to achieve their business objectives more effectively.

DevOps Metrics

DevOps metrics refer to the quantitative data collected and analyzed to measure the performance, efficiency, and effectiveness of a DevOps practice. These metrics provide insights into the continuous integration and delivery processes, enabling teams to identify areas for improvement, track progress, and make data-driven decisions. DevOps metrics can be classified into several categories, including lead time, deployment frequency, change failure rate, mean time to recovery, and availability. Lead time measures the time taken from initiating a change to its deployment, reflecting the speed at which new features and fixes are delivered. Deployment frequency, on the other hand, focuses on the number of deployments made in a given timeframe, signaling the frequency and efficiency of code releases. The change failure rate indicates the percentage of unsuccessful changes deployed, highlighting the stability and quality of the system. Mean time to recovery (MTTR) is a critical metric in DevOps, representing the average time required to restore the system to a normal state after an incident occurs. A lower MTTR signifies faster incident response and resolution. Availability measures the uptime and accessibility of a system, reflecting its reliability and ability to meet user demand. Other important DevOps metrics include test coverage, test automation percentage, error rates, feedback loop duration, customer satisfaction, and resource utilization. Test coverage measures the proportion of the codebase that is covered by automated tests, assessing the comprehensiveness of the test suite. Test automation percentage evaluates the extent to which tests are automated, reducing manual effort and ensuring rapid feedback. Error rates reflect the

63

frequency and severity of errors, providing insights into code quality and stability. Feedback loop duration measures the time taken to collect and act upon feedback from stakeholders, enhancing collaboration and continuous improvement. Customer satisfaction metrics gauge user satisfaction and the value delivered by the product or service. Resource utilization metrics, such as CPU and memory usage, disk space, and network traffic, help optimize infrastructure efficiency and cost-effectiveness.

DevOps Staff Augmentation

DevOps staff augmentation refers to the practice of hiring external DevOps professionals on a temporary basis to work alongside an existing team and fill skill gaps or project demands. This approach allows organizations to quickly scale their DevOps capabilities without the need for long-term commitments or extensive hiring processes. The main objective of DevOps staff augmentation is to enhance the efficiency and effectiveness of a DevOps team by leveraging the expertise of external professionals. These individuals are usually highly skilled and experienced in various DevOps tools, practices, and methodologies, making them valuable assets for organizations looking to accelerate their DevOps transformation. When implementing DevOps staff augmentation, organizations typically outline their specific requirements and project goals, and then seek out professionals who possess the necessary skill set and experience to address those needs. The process involves identifying the areas where additional expertise is required and finding the right candidates to temporarily fill those positions. DevOps staff augmentation offers several benefits to organizations. Firstly, it provides immediate access to highly skilled professionals who can start contributing to projects right away. This speeds up the development and deployment processes, helping organizations deliver products and services to market faster. Additionally, staff augmentation allows organizations to fill skill gaps without the need for extensive training or hiring processes, saving time and resources. Furthermore, DevOps staff augmentation promotes knowledge sharing and cross-pollination of ideas between external professionals and existing team members. This collaboration can lead to the adoption of new tools, processes, and methodologies, ultimately improving the overall effectiveness of the DevOps team. In conclusion, DevOps staff augmentation is a practice that involves hiring external DevOps professionals on a temporary basis to fill skill gaps or project demands. It allows organizations to quickly enhance their DevOps capabilities and achieve faster development and deployment cycles. By leveraging the expertise of external professionals, organizations can benefit from immediate access to highly skilled individuals, fill skill gaps without extensive training, and foster knowledge sharing within the team.

DevOps Success Stories Celebration

DevOps is a set of practices and principles that combines software development (Dev) and operational tasks (Ops) to improve collaboration, communication, and integration between teams. It focuses on automating processes, reducing deployment time, and ensuring smooth delivery of software products. One of the key components of DevOps is the use of continuous integration and continuous delivery (CI/CD) pipeline. This pipeline allows for automated and frequent integrations and deployments, ensuring that new features and bug fixes are quickly and reliably released to production. By automating these processes, DevOps teams can increase productivity, reduce errors, and improve overall software quality. DevOps success stories are examples of organizations that have successfully implemented DevOps practices and achieved significant improvements in their software delivery and operations. These success stories highlight the benefits of adopting DevOps, such as faster time to market, increased efficiency, and improved customer satisfaction. For example, a well-known DevOps success story is the transformation of Amazon from a traditional retail company to a technology-driven organization. By implementing DevOps practices, Amazon was able to significantly improve its software development and delivery processes. The company now releases new features and updates multiple times a day, ensuring that its online services remain up-to-date and competitive. Another notable DevOps success story is the case of Netflix. By embracing a DevOps culture, Netflix was able to achieve continuous deployment and increase its release frequency. This allowed the company to quickly respond to customer needs and preferences, resulting in a highly personalized and seamless user experience. Netflix also implemented chaos engineering, a DevOps practice that deliberately introduces failures to test the resilience of its systems. This approach has helped Netflix improve its fault tolerance and ensure high availability.

DevOps Success Stories

DevOps is a set of practices and cultural beliefs that aims to enhance collaboration and communication between software development and operations teams. It emphasizes the use of automation, continuous integration, and continuous delivery to achieve the goal of delivering software quickly, reliably, and at scale. Successful implementation of DevOps can lead to numerous benefits for organizations. Here are a few examples of DevOps success stories: 1. Netflix: Netflix is a leading video streaming service that relies heavily on DevOps practices. By adopting a DevOps culture, Netflix has been able to rapidly release new features and updates to its platform, ensuring a seamless user experience. Their use of automated testing and deployment has enabled them to achieve a high velocity of software delivery while maintaining high quality standards. 2. Amazon: Amazon, one of the largest e-commerce companies in the world, has embraced DevOps principles to improve its software development and delivery processes. Through automation and continuous integration, Amazon has been able to reduce the time it takes to deploy new features and updates to its website and infrastructure. This has allowed them to quickly respond to market demands and stay ahead of their competitors. 3. Google: Google, a technology giant, is known for its reliable and scalable products. DevOps practices play a critical role in enabling Google to deliver highly available and efficient services to millions of users worldwide. By automating their infrastructure management and using continuous integration and delivery, Google can quickly deploy updates and minimize downtime. 4. Etsy: Etsy, an e-commerce marketplace for handmade and vintage items, has achieved great success through the implementation of DevOps principles. By building a culture of collaboration and sharing, Etsy has been able to improve its software quality, reduce time to market, and increase the frequency of deployments. Their use of infrastructure automation has allowed them to scale their platform rapidly to meet growing user demands. In conclusion, DevOps is a set of practices that can bring substantial benefits to organizations. These success stories demonstrate how organizations across various industries have leveraged DevOps principles to improve their software delivery processes, increase productivity, and deliver value to their customers.

DevOps Talent Acquisition

DevOps Talent Acquisition refers to the process of finding, attracting, and hiring individuals with the necessary skills and experience to work in a DevOps environment. It involves identifying and evaluating candidates based on their technical proficiency, as well as their ability to collaborate and adapt to a fast-paced, team-oriented culture. In a DevOps context, talent acquisition focuses on recruiting individuals who possess a unique combination of technical skills, such as software development, systems administration, and automation, as well as soft skills, including communication, problem-solving, and collaboration. These individuals are typically responsible for bridging the gap between development and operations teams, enabling the seamless integration and delivery of software solutions.

DevOps Training And Certification

DevOps Training and Certification is a process of acquiring knowledge and skills related to the DevOps methodology and obtaining a formal recognition of competency through a certification program. DevOps is a software development approach that combines development (Dev) and operations (Ops) teams to improve collaboration, efficiency, and the delivery of high-quality software products. DevOps Training aims to educate individuals on the principles, practices, and tools used in the DevOps lifecycle. It focuses on enhancing collaborative efforts between developers, system administrators, quality assurance professionals, and other stakeholders involved in the software development process. The training covers various aspects such as coding, testing, deployment, monitoring, and infrastructure management. Moreover, it emphasizes the automation of repetitive tasks, continuous integration, and continuous delivery practices to achieve faster and more reliable software releases. DevOps Certification validates the proficiency and expertise of individuals in implementing DevOps practices. It serves as a proof of their ability to support software development teams in employing efficient and reliable DevOps workflows. The certification process involves passing a standardized assessment that evaluates the candidate's understanding of DevOps principles, tools, and best practices. By obtaining a certification, professionals can demonstrate their commitment to continuous learning and professional growth in the field of DevOps. DevOps Training and Certification programs are offered by various organizations, including industry associations, training institutions, and technology vendors. These programs typically include instructor-led training sessions, hands-on exercises, and assessments to evaluate the learners' knowledge and skills. The training may also cover case studies, real-world scenarios, and industry-specific use cases to provide practical insights into implementing DevOps in different contexts. Overall, DevOps Training and Certification play a vital role in equipping individuals with the necessary knowledge and skills to effectively embrace and implement the DevOps methodology. It enables professionals to advance their careers, contribute to organizational success, and drive continuous improvement in software development processes.

DevOps Transformation Roadmap

A DevOps transformation roadmap is a strategic plan that outlines the steps and activities required to successfully adopt the principles and practices of DevOps within an organization. DevOps is an approach to software development and delivery that emphasizes collaboration, automation, continuous integration, and continuous deployment. The transformation roadmap typically begins with an assessment of the organization's current software development and delivery processes, including identifying areas of inefficiency, bottlenecks, and pain points. This assessment helps to create a baseline understanding of the organization's current state and sets the stage for defining the desired future state. Once the current state has been established, the next step in the roadmap is to identify the specific goals and objectives of the DevOps transformation. These goals may include improving software quality, increasing deployment frequency, reducing lead time, enhancing collaboration between development and operations teams, and increasing overall organizational agility. After the goals have been defined, the roadmap focuses on the activities and initiatives required to achieve those goals. This includes identifying the necessary tools and technologies, building or enhancing the required infrastructure, implementing best practices for collaboration and communication, and establishing metrics and monitoring systems to track progress. Key components of a DevOps transformation roadmap may include the introduction of automation tools for building, testing, and deployment; the implementation of continuous integration and continuous deployment processes; the adoption of agile development practices; the creation of cross-functional teams; the establishment of feedback loops and metrics; and the development of a culture of continuous learning and improvement. The roadmap should also account for potential challenges and risks that may arise during the transformation process. This includes identifying and addressing cultural resistance to change, managing the complexity of integrating new tools and technologies, and ensuring that the necessary skills and knowledge are developed throughout the organization.

DevOps Transformation

A DevOps Transformation refers to the process of implementing and adopting a set of practices, tools, and cultural changes to enhance collaboration, communication, and integration between software development (Dev) and IT operations (Ops) teams. The goal of a DevOps Transformation is to streamline and automate the software delivery process, enabling organizations to rapidly and continuously deliver higher-quality software. During a DevOps Transformation, organizations typically undergo a series of changes to break down silos, foster cross-functional collaboration, and enable seamless integration between developers, testers, system administrators, and other stakeholders involved in the software development and deployment lifecycle. This involves adopting agile development methods, implementing continuous integration and continuous delivery (CI/CD) pipelines, and leveraging infrastructure-as-code (IaC) tools for automating infrastructure provisioning and management. A key aspect of a DevOps Transformation is the cultural shift towards shared responsibility and accountability among teams, as well as a focus on continuous learning and improvement. This includes promoting a blameless culture, encouraging knowledge sharing and collaboration, and fostering a mindset of iteration and experimentation. By fostering a DevOps culture, organizations can enable faster feedback loops, identify and resolve issues more quickly, and continuously adapt and improve their software delivery processes. In addition to cultural changes, a DevOps Transformation also involves adopting various tools and technologies to support the automation and integration of development and operations activities. This includes version control systems, build servers, automated testing frameworks, containerization platforms, monitoring and logging tools, and cloud platforms. These tools help automate manual tasks, enable faster and more reliable deployments, and provide visibility and insights into the software delivery pipeline. Overall, a DevOps Transformation represents a holistic approach to software development and delivery, emphasizing collaboration, automation, and continuous improvement. By breaking down traditional barriers between development and operations teams, organizations can achieve faster time-to-market, increase software quality, and enhance overall business agility.

DevOps Workshops

DevOps workshops are interactive training sessions designed to equip participants with the knowledge, skills, and tools required to implement and optimize the DevOps methodology within their organizations. The workshops typically cover a wide range of topics, including the fundamental principles and best practices of DevOps, as well as specific techniques and tools used in the various stages of the DevOps lifecycle. During these workshops, participants are introduced to the cultural shift that DevOps brings, emphasizing collaboration, communication, and integration between development and operations teams. They gain a deep understanding of the key concepts of DevOps, such as continuous integration, continuous delivery, and automated testing, and learn how to apply these principles effectively in their own environments. Participants also have hands-on opportunities to work with popular DevOps tools and technologies, such as Git, Jenkins, Docker, and Kubernetes. They learn how to leverage these tools to automate various tasks, streamline software development, and enhance the overall efficiency and quality of their delivery pipelines. DevOps workshops provide a platform for participants to exchange ideas, share experiences, and learn from industry experts and peers. They often include discussions and case studies that highlight real-world challenges and solutions, allowing participants to gain practical insights and apply them to their own contexts. By attending these workshops, individuals and organizations can gain a competitive edge by adopting and implementing a DevOps approach. They can improve collaboration between teams, accelerate time-to-market for software releases, enhance the quality and stability of their applications, and ultimately drive business growth and innovation.

DevOps For Mainframes Integration

DevOps for Mainframes Integration is a software development approach that aims to streamline the collaboration and integration between mainframe systems and the rest of the DevOps ecosystem. It encompasses a set of practices, tools, and cultural changes that enable mainframe development teams to adopt DevOps principles and methodologies, and effectively integrate their workflows with the broader DevOps pipeline. Traditionally, mainframe systems have operated in silos, with separate development, testing, and deployment processes. This lack of integration and collaboration often leads to longer release cycles, increased risk of errors, and a slower pace of innovation. DevOps for Mainframes Integration addresses these challenges by breaking down the barriers between mainframe and non-mainframe development teams, and fostering a culture of continuous integration, delivery, and feedback. One of the key aspects of DevOps for Mainframes Integration is the automation of mainframe-related tasks throughout the software development lifecycle. This includes the provisioning and configuration of mainframe environments, the deployment of mainframe artifacts, and the testing and validation of mainframe applications. By automating these processes, organizations can reduce manual errors, accelerate the delivery of mainframe changes, and improve the overall reliability and stability of their mainframe systems. In addition to automation, DevOps for Mainframes Integration also emphasizes the importance of collaboration and communication between mainframe and non-mainframe development teams. This involves breaking down organizational silos, establishing shared goals and metrics, and fostering a culture of knowledge sharing and cross-team collaboration. By integrating mainframe development processes into the larger DevOps workflow, organizations can benefit from shorter feedback loops, faster time-to-market, and improved visibility and traceability across the entire software delivery process.

DevOps For Mainframes

DevOps for Mainframes is the practice of applying DevOps principles and practices to mainframe systems and software development processes. It aims to improve collaboration, efficiency, and agility in mainframe development and operations teams, while ensuring the reliability, security, and performance of mainframe applications. Traditionally, mainframe development and operations have been managed separately, with siloed teams and manual processes. DevOps for Mainframes seeks to break down these barriers and promote a more integrated and automated approach to mainframe software development and delivery. One key aspect of DevOps for Mainframes is the adoption of continuous integration and continuous delivery (CI/CD) practices. This involves integrating mainframe code changes early and often, automating build, test, and deployment processes, and enabling frequent and reliable releases of mainframe applications. Another important aspect of DevOps for Mainframes is the use of infrastructure as code (IaC) and configuration management tools. These enable teams to define and manage mainframe infrastructure and configurations in a version-controlled and automated manner, reducing manual errors and ensuring consistency across environments. DevOps for Mainframes also emphasizes the importance of collaboration and communication between development, operations, and other stakeholders. This is achieved through practices such as cross-functional teams, shared goals and responsibilities, and regular feedback loops, enabling faster problem resolution and continuous improvement. Furthermore, DevOps for Mainframes emphasizes the need for comprehensive monitoring and analytics capabilities. This enables teams to gain insights into the performance and health of mainframe applications and infrastructure, proactively detect and resolve issues, and optimize resource utilization. In conclusion, DevOps for Mainframes is a set of practices and principles aimed at improving the collaboration, efficiency, and agility of mainframe development and operations teams. By adopting CI/CD, IaC, collaboration, and monitoring practices, organizations can modernize mainframe software delivery processes and ensure the reliable and secure operation of their mainframe applications.

DevOps In Aerospace And Defense

DevOps in the aerospace and defense industry refers to the combination of cultural philosophies, practices, and tools that enable organizations to deliver software applications and systems faster, more reliably, and with improved efficiency. It aims to bring together the traditionally separate teams of developers and operations personnel to collaborate and work together throughout the entire software development lifecycle. In the aerospace and defense sector, DevOps focuses on achieving real-time visibility, seamless collaboration, and rapid deployment of software-related solutions. This approach helps organizations in this industry to address the unique challenges they face, such as strict regulatory compliance requirements, complex system architectures, and the need for high levels of security and reliability.

DevOps In Affordable And Clean Energy

DevOps in the context of affordable and clean energy refers to the application of DevOps principles and practices in the development, deployment, and operation of technological solutions that promote affordable and clean energy sources. DevOps, which stands for Development and Operations, is an approach to software development that emphasizes collaboration, communication, and automation between software developers and IT operations teams. It aims to streamline and automate the software delivery process, enabling faster and more frequent releases of high-quality software.

DevOps In Agriculture

DevOps in agriculture refers to the application of DevOps practices and principles to the agricultural industry. DevOps, a combination of development and operations, is a collaborative approach that aims to streamline processes, increase efficiency, and improve communication between software development teams and IT operations teams. In the context of agriculture, DevOps involves implementing and integrating tools, processes, and methodologies to optimize the development, deployment, and management of agricultural systems and applications. This includes the use of automation, continuous integration, and continuous delivery (CI/CD), as well as monitoring and feedback loops to ensure high-quality and reliable software solutions.

DevOps In Art And Culture

DevOps in art and culture refers to the application of DevOps principles and practices in the context of the art and cultural sector. DevOps, which stands for Development and Operations, is a set of practices aimed at improving collaboration, communication, and integration between software developers and IT operations teams. It involves the adoption of automation, continuous integration, continuous delivery, and other agile methodologies to streamline the software development and deployment processes. In the art and cultural sector, DevOps can be applied to various aspects, including the creation, curation, and dissemination of artistic and cultural content. It involves the use of technology and digital tools to enhance the efficiency and effectiveness of these processes. By adopting DevOps practices, art and cultural organizations can improve collaboration between artists, curators, producers, and other stakeholders involved in the creation and presentation of artistic works. This can lead to more efficient workflows, faster development cycles, and better decision-making. Furthermore, DevOps can help art and cultural organizations embrace digital transformation and leverage the latest technologies to enhance the artistic and cultural experiences they offer. This includes the use of data analytics, artificial intelligence, virtual reality, and other emerging technologies to create immersive and engaging experiences for audiences. Overall, DevOps in art and culture enables organizations to be more agile, responsive, and innovative in their approaches. It promotes the integration of technology with artistic and cultural practices, fostering creativity, experimentation, and collaboration.

DevOps In Clean Energy

DevOps in Clean Energy refers to the application of DevOps principles and practices in the context of the clean energy industry. DevOps is an approach that combines software development (Dev) and IT operations (Ops) to optimize and accelerate the delivery of software applications and services. The clean energy sector encompasses renewable energy sources such as solar, wind, hydroelectric, and geothermal power, as well as energy-efficient technologies and practices. The integration of DevOps in this industry aims to streamline and enhance the development, deployment, and operation of clean energy solutions.

DevOps In Clean Water Access

DevOps is a software development approach that emphasizes collaboration and communication between software developers and operations professionals. It aims to increase the efficiency, quality, and speed of software delivery by breaking down silos and integrating the development and operations teams. In the context of clean water access, DevOps can play a crucial role in ensuring the effective management and delivery of technology-enabled solutions for clean water access. This involves the application of DevOps principles and practices to develop, deploy, and maintain software systems that support the monitoring, treatment, and distribution of clean water.

DevOps In Climate Action

DevOps in Climate Action: DevOps in the context of climate action refers to the application of DevOps principles and practices in addressing and mitigating the environmental impacts of technology operations. DevOps, which stands for Development and Operations, is an approach that emphasizes collaboration, automation, and continuous improvement in the software development and deployment processes. It aims to streamline the development lifecycle by fostering better communication and integration between development teams (responsible for writing and testing code) and operations teams (responsible for deploying and maintaining applications). In the context of climate action, DevOps can play a significant role in reducing the carbon footprint and promoting sustainable practices in technology operations. Here are some key aspects of DevOps in climate action: 1. Efficiency and Optimization: DevOps practices focus on optimizing the efficiency of software development and deployment processes. By reducing waste, eliminating manual tasks, and implementing automation, DevOps helps to minimize energy consumption and resource usage in technology operations. This increased efficiency translates to reduced energy consumption, thereby contributing to climate action efforts. 2. Continuous Monitoring and Improvement: DevOps promotes the continuous monitoring of applications and infrastructure. This allows for the early detection of energy inefficiencies, excessive resource consumption, or unnecessary emissions. By identifying and addressing these issues promptly, DevOps enables organizations to continuously improve their technology operations and minimize their environmental impact. 3. Infrastructure as Code (IaC): DevOps encourages the use of Infrastructure as Code (IaC) practices, where the entire infrastructure configuration is defined and managed through code. By treating infrastructure as software, DevOps helps to minimize the physical hardware requirements, optimize resource allocation, and enable efficient scaling. This reduces the need for excessive hardware provisioning and results in reduced energy consumption and e-waste. 4. Cloud Computing and Virtualization: DevOps embraces cloud computing and virtualization technologies, which enable the efficient utilization of resources and optimize energy consumption. By leveraging these technologies, DevOps minimizes the need for physical servers and data centers, reducing energy consumption and environmental impact. Overall, DevOps in climate action focuses on leveraging the principles and practices of DevOps to promote sustainable and environmentally-friendly approaches in technology operations. By optimizing efficiency, continuously monitoring and improving, adopting IaC practices, and leveraging cloud computing and virtualization, DevOps contributes to climate action efforts by reducing the carbon footprint and promoting sustainable practices in the digital landscape.

DevOps In Decent Work And Economic Growth

DevOps, short for Development and Operations, is a framework that promotes collaboration and communication between software development teams and IT operations teams. It aims to automate and streamline the processes involved in building, testing, deploying, and maintaining software applications, with the ultimate goal of delivering high-quality products more efficiently. Within the context of Decent Work and Economic Growth, DevOps plays a crucial role in fostering innovation, productivity, and job creation in the technology industry. By breaking down traditional silos and promoting cross-functional collaboration, DevOps enables organizations to respond rapidly to changing market demands and deliver value to customers more effectively.

DevOps In Disaster Relief

DevOps in disaster relief refers to the application of DevOps principles and practices in the context of disaster response and recovery efforts. DevOps, a portmanteau of development and operations, is a collaborative approach to software development and delivery that aims to shorten the systems development life cycle and provide continuous delivery with high software quality. It emphasizes close collaboration between development and operations teams, as well as the use of automation and agile methodologies. In the realm of disaster relief, DevOps principles can be applied to enhance the efficiency and effectiveness of emergency response efforts. By applying DevOps practices, organizations involved in disaster relief can streamline their processes, improve coordination, and accelerate the delivery of essential services to affected areas. One key aspect of DevOps in disaster relief is the automation of processes and workflows. Automation tools and technologies can be used to automate routine tasks such as data collection, analysis, and reporting, allowing emergency responders to focus on more critical activities. This automation can significantly reduce response times and improve decision-making during a crisis. Another important aspect of DevOps in disaster relief is the use of agile methodologies. Agile principles, such as iterative and incremental development, can be applied to adapt to rapidly changing circumstances in disaster situations. By breaking down complex tasks into smaller, more manageable units, agile methodologies enable teams to respond quickly to evolving needs and make necessary adjustments to their plans. DevOps in disaster relief also emphasizes the importance of collaboration and communication. By fostering close collaboration between different stakeholders, such as emergency responders, government agencies, non-governmental organizations, and volunteers, DevOps practices can facilitate the sharing of information, resources, and expertise. This collaboration can lead to more efficient and coordinated response efforts, ultimately saving lives and minimizing the impact of disasters. In conclusion, DevOps in disaster relief is the application of DevOps principles and practices in the context of emergency response and recovery efforts. By leveraging automation, agile methodologies, and collaboration, organizations involved in disaster relief can enhance their capabilities to respond to crises more effectively and efficiently.

DevOps In Disaster Resilience

DevOps in Disaster Resilience is a practice that focuses on integrating the principles of DevOps with disaster resilience planning and implementation. It involves the use of DevOps methodologies and tools to enhance the ability of an organization to respond effectively to and recover from any type of disaster or disruption to its operations. The primary goal of DevOps in Disaster Resilience is to ensure continuous delivery and deployment of software and infrastructure changes, even in the face of unforeseen events or disasters. It aims to improve the resilience and stability of an organization's systems, enabling it to minimize downtime, recover quickly, and maintain business continuity. In the context of DevOps, disaster resilience refers to the ability to handle and mitigate the impact of various types of disasters, such as natural disasters, cyber attacks, system failures, or human errors. It involves proactive planning, risk assessment, and the implementation of measures to enhance system reliability, redundancy, and recovery capabilities. DevOps in Disaster Resilience involves several key practices and principles. Firstly, it emphasizes the use of infrastructure as code (IaC) and automation to create and manage systems that are easily replicable, scalable, and recoverable. This allows for rapid deployment and restoration of services in the event of a disaster. Another important aspect is the application of continuous monitoring and logging, which enables early detection and response to any anomalies or disruptions in system performance. Additionally, it involves the implementation of proper backup and disaster recovery strategies to ensure data and system availability under adverse conditions. DevOps in Disaster Resilience also encourages collaboration and communication between development, operations, and security teams to ensure that disaster resilience practices are integrated throughout the software development and deployment lifecycle. This includes incorporating security, compliance, and risk management into the DevOps process from the outset. In conclusion, DevOps in Disaster Resilience combines the principles of DevOps with disaster resilience planning and implementation to enhance an organization's ability to respond, recover, and maintain business continuity in the face of unexpected events or disasters. It involves the use of automation, infrastructure as code, continuous monitoring, and collaboration to create resilient systems that can withstand and quickly recover from any disruptions.

DevOps In Education Technology

DevOps in Education Technology refers to the application of DevOps principles and practices within the education technology field. DevOps is a software development methodology that emphasizes collaboration and communication between software developers and IT operations professionals. In the context of education technology, DevOps is used to streamline the development, deployment, and maintenance of technology solutions used in educational settings. It involves bringing together developers, system administrators, and other stakeholders to work collaboratively throughout the entire software development lifecycle, from planning and coding to testing and deployment. DevOps in education technology aims to improve the efficiency, reliability, and scalability of technology solutions used in education. By adopting DevOps practices, educational institutions and technology providers can accelerate the delivery of new features and updates, reduce downtime and service disruptions, and enhance the overall user experience for students, teachers, administrators, and other stakeholders. Key principles of DevOps, such as continuous integration, continuous delivery, and infrastructure as code, are particularly relevant in education technology. Continuous integration involves frequently merging code changes into a shared repository, allowing teams to detect and resolve conflicts early on. Continuous delivery enables the regular and automated deployment of software updates, ensuring that users have access to the latest features and fixes. Infrastructure as code allows the infrastructure supporting education technology solutions to be defined and managed programmatically, reducing manual errors and enabling consistent and reproducible environments. The adoption of DevOps in education technology also entails cultural and organizational changes. It requires fostering a collaborative and cross-functional culture, where developers and operations professionals work together closely and share responsibilities. Automation and agile practices are common in DevOps, with the aim of improving efficiency and responsiveness. Furthermore, the use of tools and technologies such as version control systems, continuous integration/delivery pipelines, and cloud computing platforms can greatly facilitate the implementation of DevOps practices in education technology.

DevOps In Education

DevOps in education refers to the application of DevOps principles and practices in the context of educational institutions. DevOps, which combines development (Dev) and operations (Ops), is an approach that emphasizes collaboration, communication, and integration between software developers and IT operations teams. This approach aims to streamline and automate the processes of software development, testing, deployment, and operations, enabling organizations to deliver high-quality software products more quickly and reliably. In the context of education, DevOps can be applied to various areas, including the development and maintenance of educational software applications, the management of IT infrastructure and systems, and the support of online learning platforms. By adopting DevOps practices, educational institutions can enhance the efficiency and effectiveness of their software development processes, improve the stability and availability of their systems, and provide a better user experience to students, faculty, and staff.

DevOps In Energy

DevOps in Energy refers to the application of the DevOps methodology within the specific context of the energy industry. DevOps is an approach to software development and IT operations that emphasizes collaboration, communication, and integration between development teams (Dev) and operations teams (Ops). It is a cultural shift that aims to break down silos and improve the efficiency and quality of software delivery. In the energy industry, DevOps focuses on applying these principles and practices to the development, deployment, and management of applications and systems related to energy generation, distribution, and consumption. This includes software used for monitoring and controlling power plants, managing smart grids, optimizing energy usage, and analyzing data to improve operational efficiency. DevOps in Energy is driven by the increasing digitalization and automation of processes in the energy sector. As energy companies adopt technologies such as Internet of Things (IoT), artificial intelligence (AI), and big data analytics, the need for efficient software delivery becomes crucial. DevOps enables energy companies to keep pace with these technological advancements and rapidly deliver reliable and secure software solutions. Key aspects of DevOps in Energy include continuous integration, continuous delivery, and continuous deployment (CI/CD), automation of infrastructure provisioning and configuration, and monitoring and observability of systems and applications. In the energy industry, these practices help ensure the smooth operation of critical infrastructure, minimize downtime, and enhance the overall reliability and resilience of energy systems. DevOps in Energy also involves close collaboration between software developers, operation engineers, and energy domain experts. This collaboration is necessary to understand the specific requirements and constraints of energy systems, ensure compliance with regulations and standards, and address the unique challenges of the industry, such as cybersecurity and safety concerns.

DevOps In Entertainment

DevOps in entertainment refers to the implementation of the principles and practices of DevOps specifically in the entertainment industry. DevOps is a set of practices that combines software development (Dev) and operations (Ops) to enable organizations to deliver applications and services at a high speed. It focuses on collaboration, automation, and measurement to improve the efficiency and effectiveness of the software development and deployment process. In the entertainment industry, DevOps plays a crucial role in the development and delivery of digital products and services, such as video games, streaming platforms, and mobile applications. By applying DevOps principles, organizations in the entertainment sector can streamline their software development lifecycle, enhance their product quality, and accelerate time-to-market. DevOps in entertainment involves multiple key components and practices. Firstly, it emphasizes the collaboration and communication between development teams and operations teams. By breaking down the silos between these two groups, organizations can promote better coordination, knowledge sharing, and innovation. This collaboration results in a more efficient and streamlined development process. Secondly, DevOps in entertainment relies heavily on automation. Automation tools and technologies enable organizations to automate repetitive tasks, such as code testing, integration, and deployment. This automation reduces the risk of human errors, increases efficiency, and allows for faster and more frequent releases. Measurement is another crucial aspect of DevOps in entertainment. Organizations need to continuously monitor and measure their software development and delivery process to identify bottlenecks, track performance, and make data-driven decisions. By collecting and analyzing data, organizations can optimize their workflows, identify areas for improvement, and drive continuous improvements. In summary, DevOps in entertainment refers to the application of DevOps principles and practices in the entertainment industry. It involves collaboration, automation, and measurement to improve the efficiency, quality, and speed of software development and delivery in the context of entertainment products and services.

DevOps In Environmental Conservation

DevOps in Environmental Conservation is a methodology that combines software development (Dev) and IT operations (Ops) principles to support and enhance the efforts of environmental conservation initiatives. It focuses on leveraging technology and automation to optimize processes, improve collaboration, and increase efficiency in the management of environmental conservation projects. The main objective of DevOps in Environmental Conservation is to bring together the various stakeholders, including developers, operations teams, and environmental experts, to work in synergy towards the common goal of preserving and protecting the environment. This approach allows for the seamless integration of software development and operations activities throughout the lifecycle of environmental conservation projects. By adopting DevOps practices, organizations involved in environmental conservation can streamline their processes, reduce redundancies, and eliminate inefficiencies. This can be achieved through the use of automated testing, continuous integration, and continuous deployment, which enable faster and more reliable delivery of software solutions and updates. Furthermore, DevOps in Environmental Conservation promotes a culture of collaboration and knowledge sharing among team members. It encourages the use of cross-functional teams, where developers, operations personnel, and environmental experts work closely together, breaking down silos and promoting effective communication. The use of infrastructure as code and configuration management tools also plays a crucial role in DevOps in Environmental Conservation. By treating infrastructure and environmental monitoring systems as code, changes and updates can be easily managed, tracked, and version controlled. This allows for rapid and controlled provisioning of resources, reducing the risk of errors and improving the overall reliability of the systems. In summary, DevOps in Environmental Conservation is a methodology that combines software development and operations principles with the objective of enhancing and optimizing environmental conservation efforts. By leveraging technology, automation, and collaboration, organizations can maximize their impact in preserving and protecting the environment.

DevOps In Finance

DevOps in finance refers to the application of DevOps principles and practices in the financial industry. DevOps is a software development approach that emphasizes collaboration, automation, and continuous delivery to improve the speed, quality, and reliability of software deployments. In the context of finance, DevOps aims to streamline and automate the software development and deployment processes to enable faster and more efficient delivery of financial applications and services. It involves close collaboration between software developers, operations teams, and other stakeholders to ensure that software applications are developed, tested, and deployed in a systematic and efficient manner. DevOps practices in the finance industry often include the use of agile development methodologies, continuous integration and delivery (CI/CD) pipelines, and infrastructure automation. Agile development methodologies, such as Scrum or Kanban, enable software development teams to deliver new features and updates in shorter development cycles, allowing financial institutions to respond to market changes more quickly. CI/CD pipelines automate the building, testing, and deployment of software applications, ensuring that updates and bug fixes can be released quickly and reliably. By automating these processes, financial institutions can reduce the risk of human errors and improve the overall speed and quality of software releases. Infrastructure automation, using tools like configuration management and infrastructure-as-code, allows financial organizations to provision and manage their IT infrastructure more efficiently. This enables faster and more consistent deployment of software applications and simplifies the process of scaling infrastructure as needed. Additionally, DevOps in finance promotes a culture of collaboration and shared responsibility among different teams involved in the software development and deployment lifecycle. This includes developers, operations engineers, security professionals, and compliance teams, all working together to ensure that software applications meet the regulatory and security requirements of the financial industry. In summary, DevOps in finance is the application of DevOps principles and practices to optimize software development and deployment processes in the financial industry. It enables financial organizations to deliver software applications and services faster, more reliably, and in a more collaborative and efficient manner.

DevOps In Financial Inclusion

DevOps in Financial Inclusion refers to the implementation of DevOps practices and principles in the context of promoting financial inclusion. Financial inclusion aims to provide individuals and communities with access to affordable and reliable financial products and services, such as banking, loans, insurance, and payment solutions. DevOps, on the other hand, is a set of practices and cultural mindset that combines development (Dev) and operations (Ops) teams to enhance collaboration, efficiency, and delivery of software applications. When applied to financial inclusion, DevOps can help streamline and accelerate the development and deployment of technology solutions that promote access to financial services, especially in underserved and marginalized populations. By adopting DevOps practices, financial institutions and organizations can improve their agility, scalability, and reliability, enabling them to deliver innovative and accessible financial solutions to a wider range of individuals and communities.

DevOps In Food Security

DevOps in the context of food security refers to the application of DevOps practices and principles to ensure the security of food-related systems and processes. It involves the collaboration and integration of development, operations, and security teams to create a secure and efficient food supply chain. DevOps in food security aims to address the various challenges and risks associated with the production, processing, packaging, and distribution of food products. It focuses on implementing security measures and best practices to protect the integrity and safety of food, as well as to prevent potential threats and vulnerabilities.

DevOps In Gaming

The term "DevOps in gaming" refers to the application of DevOps principles and practices in the development and operation of gaming software and infrastructure. DevOps, which is a combination of "development" and "operations," is a software development approach that aims to bridge the gap between software development and IT operations. In the context of gaming, DevOps is essential for effectively managing the complex and rapidly evolving nature of game development. It enables game development teams to streamline their processes, improve collaboration, and deliver high-quality games to players more efficiently.

DevOps In Gender Equality

DevOps in Gender Equality refers to the practice of implementing gender equality principles and promoting inclusivity within DevOps teams and practices. It involves creating an environment where people of all gender identities have equal opportunities, rights, and responsibilities. DevOps is a software development approach that combines software development and IT operations to increase collaboration and efficiency in delivering software. It emphasizes communication, automation, and measurement to achieve fast and reliable software releases. Gender equality in DevOps focuses on addressing the gender imbalances often seen in the tech industry and creating more diverse and inclusive teams.

DevOps In Global Health

DevOps in Global Health is a set of practices that combine software development (Dev) and information technology operations (Ops) within the context of global health initiatives. It focuses on streamlining the development, deployment, and maintenance of software solutions to address critical challenges in the field of global health. In this context, DevOps aims to enhance the efficiency, scalability, and reliability of software systems used in various aspects of global health, such as disease surveillance, healthcare delivery, data analysis, and resource allocation. It promotes collaboration and communication between software developers, quality assurance teams, system administrators, and other stakeholders involved in global health projects.

DevOps In Good Health And Well-Being

DevOps in the context of Good Health and Well-being refers to the implementation of DevOps practices and principles to improve the overall health and well-being of individuals and teams involved in the software development and operations processes. In the domain of software development and operations, the key objectives of DevOps are typically focused on enabling faster delivery of software products, improving the quality and stability of software systems, and enhancing collaboration and communication between development and operations teams. However, the implementation of DevOps principles can also have a positive impact on the health and well-being of individuals and teams involved in these processes. DevOps promotes a culture of collaboration, learning, and continuous improvement. By fostering effective collaboration between development and operations teams, DevOps helps to reduce silos, increase transparency, and promote shared responsibility. This collaborative culture can contribute to the well-being of individuals by encouraging teamwork, mutual support, and a sense of belonging. By breaking down barriers and promoting open communication, DevOps practices can also help to reduce stress and mitigate conflicts that can negatively impact the health and well-being of individuals. In addition, DevOps emphasizes the automation of manual and repetitive tasks. By automating these tasks, DevOps reduces the reliance on manual work, eliminating potential sources of stress and fatigue. This can not only improve productivity and efficiency but also contribute to the physical and mental well-being of individuals by reducing the risk of burnout. Furthermore, the iterative and incremental nature of DevOps practices encourages continuous learning and experimentation. This focus on continuous improvement can foster a growth mindset and promote professional development, which can contribute to the self-esteem and job satisfaction of individuals. By providing opportunities for learning and personal growth, DevOps can enhance the overall well-being and happiness of individuals involved in software development and operations.

DevOps In Government

DevOps in Government refers to the application of DevOps principles, practices, and tools in the context of government organizations. DevOps, which is a combination of "development" and "operations," is an approach that promotes collaboration, integration, and automation between software development teams and IT operations teams. DevOps in Government is focused on improving the efficiency, agility, and quality of government software development and delivery processes. It aims to align the priorities and goals of both development and operations teams, ensuring that software is developed and deployed in a timely and secure manner.

DevOps In Healthcare Innovation

DevOps in healthcare innovation refers to the application of DevOps principles and practices in the context of healthcare technology and innovation. DevOps is a set of software development and operations practices that aims to improve the efficiency, collaboration, and delivery speed of software development teams. In the healthcare industry, there is an increasing need for innovative solutions to improve patient care, enhance operational efficiency, and meet regulatory requirements. DevOps offers a systematic approach to overcome the challenges posed by complex software systems in the healthcare sector. DevOps in healthcare innovation emphasizes the integration of development, operations, and quality assurance functions to ensure the smooth and continuous delivery of software applications. It involves the use of automation, collaboration, and feedback loops to improve software quality, reduce time-to-market, and enhance the overall user experience. By adopting DevOps principles, healthcare organizations can establish a culture of collaboration and continuous improvement, enabling them to respond quickly to changing business needs and industry trends. The iterative and incremental nature of DevOps facilitates the rapid prototyping and validation of innovative solutions, helping healthcare organizations to stay ahead in a competitive market. In addition to software development and deployment, DevOps in healthcare innovation also encompasses infrastructure management, security, and compliance. It involves the use of infrastructure-as-code and configuration management tools to automate the provisioning, configuration, and deployment of infrastructure resources. Furthermore, DevOps in healthcare innovation promotes a rigorous approach to security and compliance by integrating security practices into the software development lifecycle. It emphasizes the need for proactive monitoring, vulnerability scanning, and continuous security testing to detect and address potential threats and vulnerabilities.

DevOps In Healthcare

DevOps in healthcare refers to the implementation of DevOps practices and principles in the healthcare industry. It involves the integration of development and operational teams, processes, and tools to optimize the delivery of healthcare services and products. DevOps in healthcare enables organizations to enhance efficiency, reduce errors, and improve patient care by fostering collaboration, automation, and continuous integration and delivery. It applies agile methodologies, automation, and feedback loops to streamline software development, testing, deployment, and monitoring in healthcare settings.

DevOps In Hospitality

DevOps in the hospitality sector refers to the implementation of DevOps practices and principles in the specific context of the hospitality industry. DevOps, as a methodology, aims to bridge the gap between software development and operations teams, fostering collaboration and enabling organizations to deliver high-quality applications and services more efficiently and rapidly. In the hospitality industry, DevOps focuses on streamlining and automating the software development and release processes associated with various hospitality services and systems. This includes but is not limited to the management of hotel reservations, online bookings, mobile applications, loyalty programs, and integrated payment systems. By adopting DevOps practices, hospitality organizations can improve the reliability, scalability, and security of their technology platforms, enhancing the overall guest experience. DevOps teams work closely with software developers, system administrators, network engineers, and other stakeholders to ensure smooth operations and seamless integration of new features or updates. Key elements of DevOps in the hospitality industry include continuous integration (CI), continuous delivery (CD), infrastructure as code (IaC), and automated testing. CI involves the frequent merging of code changes into a central repository, which is then automatically built, tested, and validated. CD extends CI by automating the deployment of applications to various environments, such as development, staging, and production. Infrastructure as code allows hospitality organizations to manage their IT infrastructure using version-controlled and scriptable configurations, reducing manual errors and enabling scalability. Automated testing ensures that software updates are thoroughly tested to detect and prevent issues before deployment. The benefits of implementing DevOps in the hospitality industry are significant. It enables organizations to rapidly respond to market demands and customer expectations. By reducing the time between development and deployment, DevOps allows organizations to deliver new features, updates, and improvements faster, gaining a competitive edge. Additionally, it improves collaboration between different teams and departments, breaking down silos and fostering an environment of shared responsibility and accountability. In summary, DevOps in the hospitality sector focuses on implementing DevOps practices and principles to streamline software development and operations processes, leading to improved guest experiences, increased efficiency, and faster innovation.

DevOps In Humanitarian Efforts

DevOps in humanitarian efforts refers to the implementation of DevOps practices and principles in the context of humanitarian and disaster response efforts. DevOps, which stands for Development and Operations, is an approach to software development and delivery that emphasizes collaboration, communication, automation, and continuous improvement. In the context of humanitarian efforts, DevOps aims to enhance the efficiency, speed, and effectiveness of relief operations through the application of agile and lean principles. It involves the integration of various teams and stakeholders involved in humanitarian response, including developers, operations staff, relief workers, volunteers, and local communities.

DevOps In Industry Innovation

DevOps is a methodology that combines software development (Dev) and IT operations (Ops) to improve the overall efficiency and effectiveness of software development and deployment processes. It is a collaborative approach that aims to bridge the gap between developers, who focus on creating and enhancing software, and operations teams, who are responsible for the stability, scalability, and availability of the software in production environments. The primary goal of DevOps is to enable organizations to deliver high-quality software products at a more rapid pace, while ensuring continuous integration, deployment, and delivery. It emphasizes automation, communication, and collaboration throughout the development lifecycle, helping teams to detect and fix issues early on, and enabling faster feedback loops. DevOps incorporates various practices and tools to streamline software development and operations, such as continuous integration (CI), continuous delivery (CD), infrastructure as code (IaC), and monitoring and observability. CI involves frequently integrating code changes into a shared repository, allowing teams to detect and address integration conflicts early. CD focuses on automating the deployment process, enabling teams to deliver changes to production environments more frequently and reliably. IaC involves managing infrastructure using code, which provides greater scalability, flexibility, and consistency. It allows teams to define and version control infrastructure as they would with software code, reducing the risk of configuration drift and enabling the replication of environments. Monitoring and observability ensure that teams have visibility into the performance and health of their systems, enabling them to proactively identify and address performance bottlenecks and potential issues. By adopting DevOps practices, organizations can accelerate software development cycles, improve collaboration and communication between teams, enhance system stability and reliability, and deliver value to customers more rapidly. It enables organizations to stay competitive in today's fast-paced and constantly evolving digital landscape, where innovation and time-to-market are key drivers of success. Overall, DevOps revolutionizes the way software is developed, deployed, and operated by promoting a culture of collaboration, automation, and continuous improvement. It empowers teams to deliver high-quality software products faster and more efficiently, while also ensuring the stability and reliability of the systems they operate.

DevOps In Life Below Water

DevOps in the context of Life Below Water refers to the application and adoption of DevOps principles and practices within organizations and initiatives focused on preserving and sustaining marine ecosystems and resources. DevOps, a combination of "development" and "operations," is an approach that promotes collaboration, integration, and automation between software development teams and IT operations teams. It aims to streamline the software delivery process, enhance deployment speed, and improve overall operational efficiency. When applied to the realm of Life Below Water, DevOps encompasses the utilization of these principles to address the challenges and complexities related to marine conservation and protection.

DevOps In Life On Land

DevOps in Life on Land is a methodology that focuses on the collaboration and communication between development teams and operations teams in order to streamline the process of deploying, testing, and releasing software applications. It aims to bridge the gap between the traditionally separate responsibilities of software development and operations by promoting a culture of continuous integration, delivery, and improvement. In the context of DevOps in Life on Land, the term "life on land" refers to the physical world outside of the digital realm. It encompasses various industries, such as agriculture, manufacturing, transportation, and many others, where software applications play a crucial role in improving efficiency, sustainability, and productivity.

DevOps In Manufacturing

DevOps in manufacturing refers to the adoption of DevOps practices and principles in the manufacturing industry to improve collaboration, efficiency, and quality in the production and delivery of goods. DevOps, a combination of development and operations, is an approach that emphasizes collaboration, communication, automation, and continuous integration and delivery. In the context of manufacturing, DevOps involves integrating and streamlining the software development, deployment, and operations processes with the production and supply chain management systems. It aims to bridge the gap between software development and the manufacturing process, enabling manufacturers to deliver products faster, more reliably, and with higher quality.

DevOps In No Poverty

DevOps in the context of No Poverty refers to the application of DevOps principles and practices to support efforts aimed at alleviating poverty and promoting sustainable development. DevOps, which is a combination of the words "development" and "operations," is a software development and delivery approach that emphasizes collaboration, communication, and automation between software development teams and IT operations teams. It aims to increase the efficiency, speed, and quality of software delivery, enabling organizations to respond more effectively to changing market needs.

DevOps In Nonprofits

DevOps in nonprofits refers to the application of DevOps principles and practices in the context of nonprofit organizations. DevOps is a software development methodology that combines software development (Dev) and IT operations (Ops) to facilitate collaboration, communication, and automation throughout the software development lifecycle. Nonprofit organizations, which operate with limited resources and often rely on volunteers, can benefit from adopting DevOps practices to enhance their software development processes and improve the delivery of digital services. By embracing DevOps, nonprofits can streamline their operations, enhance the efficiency of their software development teams, and ultimately maximize the impact of their technology initiatives.

DevOps In Partnerships For The Goals

DevOps in Partnerships for the Goals refers to the operational approach that integrates development and operations teams to collaboratively work towards achieving the Sustainable Development Goals (SDGs) set by the United Nations. DevOps is a set of practices that promotes collaboration, integration, automation, and communication between software development and IT operations teams, aiming to increase the efficiency and effectiveness of software delivery. In the context of Partnerships for the Goals, DevOps emphasizes the need for cross-functional collaboration and the alignment of technology initiatives with the SDGs. The SDGs encompass a broad range of goals, including eliminating poverty and hunger, promoting sustainable economic growth, reducing Inequality, ensuring access to quality education and healthcare, addressing climate change, and fostering peace and justice. DevOps teams can play a crucial role in supporting these goals by developing and delivering software solutions that address social, economic, and environmental challenges.

DevOps In Peace, Justice, And Strong Institutions

DevOps in the context of Peace, Justice, and Strong Institutions refers to the application of DevOps principles and practices to support and enhance the development, deployment, and operation of technology solutions in the pursuit of peace, justice, and strong institutions. DevOps is a collaborative approach that aims to bridge the gap between development and operations teams, enabling them to work together seamlessly and iteratively throughout the entire software development lifecycle. In the context of peace, justice, and strong institutions, DevOps can help streamline and optimize the delivery of technology solutions that empower organizations and governments to promote peace, justice, and strong institutions.

DevOps In Philanthropy

DevOps in philanthropy refers to the application of DevOps principles and practices in the context of nonprofit organizations and initiatives aimed at improving society and promoting social good. DevOps, a portmanteau of development (Dev) and operations (Ops), is an approach to software development and IT operations that emphasizes collaboration, communication, automation, and measurement. It aims to bridge the gap between software developers and IT operations teams, enabling the delivery of high-quality software products and services at a faster pace. In the context of philanthropy, DevOps can play a crucial role in enabling nonprofit organizations to more effectively deliver technology solutions that address social challenges. By adopting DevOps practices, such as continuous integration, continuous delivery, and infrastructure automation, philanthropic organizations can efficiently develop, deploy, and operate software systems that support their missions. The use of DevOps in philanthropy can bring several benefits. Firstly, it can enhance the speed and agility of technology development, allowing nonprofit organizations to iterate on their solutions quickly and respond to changing needs. This can be particularly important in disaster response scenarios or crisis situations where rapid deployment of technology solutions can save lives and improve outcomes. Secondly, DevOps can improve the reliability and stability of technology systems, reducing downtime and service disruptions. This is critical for nonprofit organizations that rely on technology to deliver their services, as any interruption can impact their ability to serve beneficiaries effectively. Furthermore, DevOps practices foster collaboration and communication between different teams within philanthropic organizations, including software developers, operations staff, and domain experts. This cross-functional collaboration enables a shared understanding of the challenges and requirements, leading to more effective solutions that address the unique needs of the targeted communities. In conclusion, DevOps in philanthropy refers to the adoption of DevOps principles and practices to enhance the development and delivery of technology solutions in nonprofit organizations. By leveraging automation, collaboration, and agility, DevOps can help philanthropic organizations create more impactful and resilient software systems that support their missions and serve the greater good.

DevOps In Quality Education

DevOps in Quality Education refers to the application of DevOps principles, practices, and tools in the field of education to achieve improved efficiency, collaboration, and quality in the delivery of educational services. In the context of DevOps, Quality Education can be defined as an approach that integrates the principles and practices of DevOps with educational processes, systems, and technologies. It focuses on fostering a culture of collaboration, automation, and continuous improvement to enhance the quality of education and learning outcomes.

DevOps In Reduced Inequalities

DevOps in the context of reducing inequalities is the practice of implementing and automating processes and technologies to bridge the gap between different individuals, teams, or organizations who are involved in software development and operations. It focuses on creating an inclusive and equitable environment where all individuals and teams have equal access to resources, opportunities, and decision-making power. In traditional software development and operations, there is often a division between developers and operations teams, leading to communication gaps, lack of collaboration, and unequal distribution of responsibilities. This can result in inequalities among team members, where certain individuals or teams may have more influence or control over the software development and deployment processes. DevOps aims to address these inequalities by fostering a culture of collaboration, transparency, and shared responsibility. It involves breaking down silos and encouraging cross-functional collaboration among developers, operations teams, and other stakeholders. This ensures that all individuals, regardless of their role or position, have equal opportunities to contribute and make decisions that impact the software development lifecycle. DevOps also emphasizes the use of automation and tooling to reduce inequalities caused by manual processes, bias, or human error. By automating repetitive tasks, such as building, testing, and deploying software, DevOps minimizes the dependency on specific individuals or teams, ensuring equal access to these processes for everyone involved. Moreover, DevOps promotes the use of metrics and data-driven decision-making to reduce inequalities stemming from biases or subjective judgments. By collecting and analyzing data on performance, efficiency, and quality, DevOps enables objective assessments and continuous improvement, ensuring fair and evidence-based evaluations of individuals or teams. In summary, DevOps in the context of reduced inequalities is the adoption of practices, processes, and technologies that promote collaboration, equity, and inclusivity among individuals and teams involved in software development and operations. It aims to eliminate communication gaps, unequal power dynamics, and biased decision-making, enabling equal access to resources, opportunities, and responsibilities.

DevOps In Regulated Industries Compliance

DevOps in regulated industries compliance refers to the application of DevOps practices and principles in industries that are subject to specific regulatory requirements and standards. In regulated industries, companies must comply with various regulations and guidelines to ensure the confidentiality, integrity, and availability of their systems and data. Compliance covers a wide range of areas, including data protection, privacy, financial reporting, healthcare, and more. DevOps, on the other hand, is an approach to software development and operations that emphasizes collaboration, automation, and continuous delivery. It aims to improve the speed, efficiency, and quality of software development and deployment. When applying DevOps in regulated industries, compliance with regulatory requirements becomes a critical aspect of the DevOps process. It involves integrating compliance considerations into each stage of the software development lifecycle, from planning and development to testing, deployment, and monitoring. DevOps teams in regulated industries must create and maintain a compliance environment that meets industry-specific regulations. This typically involves implementing controls and measures to ensure data protection, privacy, and security throughout the DevOps pipeline. Furthermore, DevOps practices must be adapted to accommodate compliance requirements. This includes enforcing segregation of duties, implementing secure coding practices, conducting regular security audits, and maintaining documentation that evidences compliance for auditing purposes. By integrating compliance into the DevOps process, companies in regulated industries can achieve faster and more efficient software development and deployment while maintaining compliance with applicable regulations and standards. This enables them to deliver high-quality software products and services to customers in a timely manner, while also meeting their legal and regulatory obligations.

DevOps In Regulated Industries

DevOps in regulated industries refers to the application of DevOps principles, practices, and methodologies in industries that are governed by strict regulations and compliance requirements. In regulated industries such as finance, healthcare, and government, organizations are compelled to adhere to specific standards and regulations to ensure data security, privacy, and compliance with industry-specific laws. These regulations often come from governing bodies such as regulatory agencies or industry-specific authorities. DevOps, which is a combination of development (Dev) and operations (Ops), is an approach that emphasizes collaboration, automation, and continuous integration and delivery. It aims to break down silos between development teams and operations teams, enabling faster and more efficient software development and deployment. In regulated industries, the implementation of DevOps requires additional considerations and adaptations to meet the stringent regulatory requirements. These industries often have strict compliance, security, privacy, and auditing standards that need to be integrated into the DevOps workflows and processes. DevOps practices in regulated industries often involve: - Ensuring compliance with regulatory standards and frameworks such as HIPAA (Health Insurance Portability and Accountability Act) in healthcare or PCI DSS (Payment Card Industry Data Security Standard) in finance. - Implementing security controls and measures throughout the software development lifecycle, including code reviews, vulnerability scans, and penetration testing. - Maintaining rigorous documentation, change management, and release management processes to ensure traceability and accountability. - Adhering to strict data privacy and protection protocols, including encryption, data segregation, and access controls. - Incorporating robust monitoring and logging mechanisms to detect and respond to any security incidents or breaches promptly. DevOps in regulated industries aims to strike a balance between agility and compliance. While regulatory requirements may introduce additional complexities and constraints, the principles of DevOps can still be applied to streamline and accelerate the software development and deployment processes within the boundaries of regulatory compliance.

DevOps In Renewable Energy

DevOps in renewable energy refers to the practice of applying DevOps principles and practices in the context of renewable energy projects and operations. DevOps, a combination of the words "development" and "operations," is an approach that promotes collaboration and integration between software development teams and IT operations teams. It aims to streamline and automate the processes of software development, testing, deployment, and operations to achieve faster and more reliable delivery of software applications. In the renewable energy sector, DevOps is becoming increasingly important due to the rapid growth and complexity of renewable energy systems and technologies. Renewable energy projects often involve a combination of software, hardware, and data analytics components, which need to work seamlessly together for optimal performance and efficiency. This requires close coordination and communication between the development teams responsible for building and maintaining the software systems, and the operations teams responsible for deploying, monitoring, and managing the renewable energy infrastructure.

DevOps In Responsible Consumption

DevOps in responsible consumption refers to the application of DevOps principles and practices in promoting responsible and sustainable consumption of resources within the software development lifecycle. It focuses on optimizing resource utilization, reducing waste, and minimizing environmental impact. In the context of DevOps, responsible consumption involves efficient and effective use of computing resources, such as servers, storage, and network infrastructure. This includes practices like infrastructure-as-code, where infrastructure and configuration are versioned and treated as code, enabling automated provisioning and configuration management. With infrastructure-as-code, resources can be easily scaled up or down based on demand, minimizing energy consumption and waste. Responsible consumption in DevOps also emphasizes the reduction of waste by streamlining processes and eliminating inefficiencies. Continuous integration and continuous deployment (CI/CD) pipelines automate the build, test, and deployment processes, ensuring that only high-quality and functional software is released. This eliminates waste in terms of time, effort, and resources that would have been spent on manual processes and rework due to errors or defects. Furthermore, responsible consumption in DevOps involves monitoring and optimizing the performance of applications and infrastructure to maximize resource utilization. Continuous monitoring and feedback loops provide insights into system performance, enabling proactive identification and resolution of bottlenecks and resource inefficiencies. This helps in optimizing the use of computing resources and reducing unnecessary consumption. DevOps teams also promote responsible consumption by adopting sustainable development practices, such as modular and reusable code. By designing and developing software components that can be easily reused across different projects, teams can reduce duplication of effort and resources. This approach reduces the environmental impact associated with the creation and maintenance of software systems. In summary, DevOps in responsible consumption focuses on optimizing resource utilization, reducing waste, and minimizing environmental impact within the software development lifecycle. It involves practices like infrastructure-as-code, CI/CD pipelines, continuous monitoring, and sustainable development to promote responsible and sustainable consumption of computing resources and minimize environmental footprint.

DevOps In Retail

DevOps in Retail refers to the implementation of DevOps principles and practices in the retail sector. DevOps is a set of cultural, organizational, and technical practices that aims to improve collaboration and communication between software development teams (Dev) and IT operations teams (Ops). DevOps in the retail industry involves streamlining and automating various IT processes to enhance the efficiency and effectiveness of retail operations. It focuses on bridging the gap between development and operations teams, ensuring faster delivery of software updates, and maintaining a high level of customer satisfaction.

DevOps In Social Impact

DevOps in the context of social impact refers to the application of DevOps practices and principles to address and solve social challenges, promote inclusion, and drive positive change in society. It involves utilizing the collaboration and automation aspects of DevOps to improve the delivery of services, programs, and initiatives that have a direct impact on individuals, communities, and the greater world. DevOps in social impact focuses on leveraging technology, agile methodologies, and cross-functional teams to deliver social-oriented projects efficiently and effectively. It aims to break down silos, foster collaboration, and facilitate continuous integration and delivery of solutions that address societal issues such as poverty, inequality, environmental sustainability, education, healthcare, and more. By adopting DevOps practices in the social impact sector, organizations can streamline processes, improve resource allocation, and maximize the impact of their initiatives. This includes leveraging cloud computing services, infrastructure as code, and automation tools to enable scalability, cost-efficiency, and rapid deployment of solutions. Furthermore, DevOps in social impact emphasizes the involvement and empowerment of stakeholders, beneficiaries, and end-users throughout the development and delivery process. This includes engaging with communities, conducting user research, and prioritizing inclusivity to ensure that solutions are designed and implemented in a manner that effectively addresses the needs and aspirations of the target audience. In summary, DevOps in social impact is about leveraging the principles and practices of DevOps in the context of social challenges and initiatives. It emphasizes collaboration, automation, efficiency, and inclusivity to drive positive change and improve the lives of individuals and communities.

DevOps In Space Exploration

DevOps in space exploration refers to the application of DevOps principles and practices in the context of space exploration missions. DevOps is a software development approach that emphasizes collaboration, communication, and integration between software developers and IT operations teams. It aims to break down the traditional silos between software development and operations, enabling faster and more efficient software delivery. When applied to space exploration, DevOps helps streamline the development and deployment of software systems that are critical for the success of space missions. This includes software for controlling spacecraft, collecting and analyzing data, and supporting various scientific experiments and research activities. The main goal of DevOps in space exploration is to ensure the timely and reliable delivery of high-quality software systems that can withstand the challenging and harsh conditions of space. This requires close collaboration between the software development teams, who are responsible for building and testing the software, and the operations teams, who are responsible for deploying and maintaining the software in space. DevOps principles, such as continuous integration and continuous delivery, play a crucial role in space exploration. Continuous integration involves regularly merging code changes from multiple developers into a shared repository, allowing for early detection of integration issues. Continuous delivery focuses on automating the deployment process, enabling frequent and incremental updates to the software systems in a controlled and reliable manner. By adopting DevOps practices, space agencies and organizations can accelerate the development and deployment of software for space missions. It helps in reducing the time required for software development, testing, and deployment, while improving the overall quality and reliability of the software systems. This is particularly important in space exploration, where missions often have tight schedules and require precise and accurate software systems to carry out complex tasks.

DevOps In Sports

DevOps in sports refers to the application of DevOps principles and practices in the realm of sports management and operations. DevOps, short for Development and Operations, is a collaboration and integration approach that aims to facilitate faster, more efficient, and more reliable software development and deployment processes. In the context of sports, DevOps involves the implementation of DevOps methodologies and tools to enhance various aspects of sports management and operations, including team performance analysis, player management, ticketing systems, stadium operations, and fan engagement.

DevOps In Sustainable Cities

DevOps in the context of sustainable cities refers to the application of DevOps principles and practices to the development, deployment, and management of software systems and infrastructure that enable and support sustainable urban environments. DevOps, which is a combination of development and operations, is a software development approach that focuses on collaboration, automation, and continuous delivery. It aims to shorten the software development lifecycle and increase the efficiency, reliability, and resilience of software systems. By applying DevOps practices in the development and deployment of software systems for sustainable cities, organizations can enhance the effectiveness and sustainability of urban infrastructure and services.

DevOps In Sustainable Development

DevOps in Sustainable Development refers to the integration of DevOps practices and principles into the sustainable development process. It involves adopting a holistic approach that combines software development, operations, and sustainability principles to create and maintain sustainable software solutions. DevOps is a set of practices that emphasizes collaboration, communication, and automation between software development teams and operations teams. It aims to improve the efficiency, reliability, and scalability of software development processes. Sustainable development, on the other hand, focuses on meeting the needs of the present without compromising the ability of future generations to meet their own needs. It addresses social, economic, and environmental aspects. When DevOps is applied in the context of sustainable development, it means that software development and deployment processes are designed and executed in a way that aligns with sustainability goals. This can include reducing the environmental impact of software development and operations, promoting social responsibility, and ensuring economic viability. Some of the key aspects of DevOps in Sustainable Development include: - Energy Efficiency: DevOps practices can help optimize software and infrastructure for energy efficiency, reducing the carbon footprint of software systems. - Resource Optimization: DevOps practices such as automation and continuous integration/continuous deployment (CI/CD) can help optimize resource utilization, minimizing waste. - Performance Optimization: DevOps practices can ensure that software systems perform optimally, minimizing resource usage and energy consumption. - Collaboration: DevOps encourages collaboration and communication between different teams involved in software development and operations, including stakeholders concerned with sustainability. - Monitoring and Feedback: DevOps promotes the use of monitoring and feedback mechanisms to identify and address sustainability-related issues and improve software performance. By integrating DevOps practices into sustainable development, organizations can create software solutions that not only meet their business needs but also contribute to a sustainable future. This approach aligns software development with sustainability goals, promoting responsible and efficient use of resources.

DevOps In Sustainable Partnerships

DevOps in sustainable partnerships refers to the practice of implementing DevOps principles and methodologies in long-term, stable, and mutually beneficial collaborations between different teams, departments, or organizations. In a DevOps context, sustainable partnerships focus on establishing and maintaining robust relationships that foster continuous collaboration, communication, and integration between development and operations teams. These partnerships aim to enhance software development and delivery processes, optimize efficiency, and drive value for all involved parties.

DevOps In Telecommunications

DevOps in Telecommunications refers to the application of DevOps principles and practices in the telecommunications industry. DevOps, which stands for Development and Operations, is a software development approach that combines software development (Dev) and IT operations (Ops) to enhance collaboration and improve the quality and speed of software delivery. In the telecommunications industry, which is responsible for managing complex network systems, maintaining high availability, and ensuring consistent service delivery, the implementation of DevOps practices can offer significant benefits. DevOps allows telecom companies to streamline their software development and deployment processes, enabling them to adapt quickly to changing customer demands and market trends. The key principles of DevOps, such as continuous integration, continuous delivery, and automation, can be applied in telecom organizations to achieve faster development cycles and more efficient operations. By automating repetitive tasks and eliminating manual interventions, telecom companies can reduce human errors and accelerate the release of new features and services. This can lead to improved customer satisfaction and a competitive edge in the market. In addition, the collaboration and communication fostered by DevOps practices can break down silos between development, operations, and other departments in telecommunication organizations. This helps create a culture of shared responsibility and promotes faster problem-solving and decision-making. By breaking down barriers and promoting cross-functional collaboration, telecom companies can achieve faster issue resolution, reduced downtime, and improved overall efficiency. Furthermore, the use of DevOps practices can enable telecom organizations to implement more robust and scalable infrastructure. By treating infrastructure as code and applying automation techniques, telecom companies can provision and configure network resources more efficiently, reducing the time and effort required for managing complex network environments. In summary, DevOps in Telecommunications refers to the application of DevOps principles and practices in the telecommunications industry to enhance collaboration, improve software delivery, and achieve faster development cycles. By embracing DevOps, telecom organizations can achieve improved customer satisfaction, faster problem resolution, and more efficient operations, ultimately gaining a competitive advantage in the industry.

DevOps In Transportation

DevOps in the transportation industry refers to the integration of development and operations practices to improve the efficiency, reliability, and agility of transportation system development and maintenance. Transportation involves various stakeholders, including manufacturers, logistics companies, regulatory bodies, and end-users, who rely on complex systems to ensure the smooth movement of goods and people. DevOps principles and practices can greatly benefit this industry by fostering collaboration, automation, and continuous improvement across the development, deployment, and operation phases.

DevOps In Wildlife Conservation

DevOps in Wildlife Conservation is the application of DevOps principles and practices to the field of wildlife conservation. DevOps, which stands for Development and Operations, is a collaborative approach to software development that emphasizes communication, integration, and automation between software developers and IT operations teams. It aims to shorten the systems development life cycle and provide continuous delivery with high software quality. In the context of wildlife conservation, DevOps can be applied to various aspects of conservation efforts, including data collection, analysis, and decision-making processes. By leveraging DevOps practices, conservation organizations can improve their efficiency, scalability, and effectiveness in their conservation initiatives. One key aspect of DevOps in wildlife conservation is the integration of technology and data management systems. Conservation organizations often collect vast amounts of data from various sources, such as tracking devices, remote sensing technologies, and crowd-sourced data. By applying DevOps principles, organizations can ensure that these disparate sources of data are integrated seamlessly and processed efficiently, enabling better decision making and effective conservation strategies. Another important aspect of DevOps in wildlife conservation is the automation of tasks and workflows. Conservation organizations often have limited resources and personnel, making it crucial to streamline processes and maximize operational efficiency. By automating repetitive and time-consuming tasks, such as data processing and analysis, organizations can free up resources and focus on more important conservation activities. Additionally, DevOps practices can enable collaboration and knowledge sharing among conservation professionals. By implementing DevOps tools and practices, organizations can create a culture of collaboration, where developers, operations teams, and domain experts work together to develop and deploy innovative solutions. This collaboration can lead to faster innovation, improved decision making, and more impactful conservation initiatives. In conclusion, DevOps in wildlife conservation is the application of DevOps principles and practices to the field of wildlife conservation. By leveraging technology, automation, and collaboration, conservation organizations can improve their efficiency, scalability, and effectiveness in their conservation efforts, ultimately leading to better wildlife management and preservation.

DevOps In Zero Hunger

DevOps in the context of Zero Hunger refers to the application of DevOps principles, practices, and methodologies to address and eradicate the global issue of hunger. It involves leveraging agile methodologies, collaboration, and automation techniques to optimize the efficiency and effectiveness of food production, distribution, and access systems. DevOps methodologies, originally developed in the software development and operations domain, emphasize the seamless integration of teams, continuous delivery, automation, and feedback loops. These principles can be adapted and applied to the complex challenge of ending hunger by creating a more efficient and sustainable food system.

DevSecOps Culture Promotion

DevSecOps Culture Promotion refers to the implementation of a set of practices, principles, and values within the DevOps framework that prioritize and integrate security measures throughout the software development and operations processes. It involves creating a collaborative environment where developers, operations teams, and security professionals work together seamlessly to ensure the security of the software being developed and deployed. In a DevSecOps Culture Promotion, security is not an afterthought or a separate phase in the development and deployment pipeline; it is embedded into every stage. This includes the design and architecture phase, the coding and testing phase, and the deployment and operations phase. The main objective of promoting a DevSecOps culture is to make security everyone's responsibility and to foster a mindset that prioritizes security from the start of the development process. By integrating security practices early on, vulnerabilities and risks can be identified and addressed in a timely manner, reducing the chances of security breaches or the release of insecure software. Key practices in DevSecOps Culture Promotion include: - Continuous security testing: Automated security testing tools are integrated into the DevOps pipeline to identify vulnerabilities and weaknesses in the software code or infrastructure. - Secure coding practices: Developers are trained to follow secure coding guidelines and best practices to minimize the introduction of vulnerabilities in the codebase. - Threat modeling: Security professionals collaborate with developers to identify potential threats and risks early in the development process, enabling proactive mitigation measures. - Security awareness and training: All stakeholders are provided with training and resources to enhance security awareness and understanding, enabling them to make informed decisions regarding security. By promoting a DevSecOps culture, organizations can ensure that security is not sacrificed for speed or agility. It enables the integration of security as an integral part of the software development and operations process, ultimately resulting in more secure and reliable software solutions.

DevSecOps Culture

DevSecOps culture refers to the integration of security practices into the DevOps methodology. It emphasizes the collaboration between development, operations, and security teams throughout the software development lifecycle to ensure the delivery of secure and reliable applications. In a DevSecOps culture, security is not seen as a separate step or responsibility but as an integral part of the development process. Traditionally, security has been treated as an afterthought, resulting in vulnerabilities and data breaches. However, by incorporating security practices from the early stages of development, DevSecOps aims to eliminate these risks and build robust and secure applications.

DevSecOps

DevSecOps is an extension of the DevOps methodology that incorporates security into the software development process. It aims to bridge the gap between development, operations, and security teams to enable the creation of secure and reliable software products. In the traditional software development lifecycle, security measures are often added as an afterthought, causing delays and leaving room for vulnerabilities. DevSecOps addresses this issue by encouraging the integration of security practices from the early stages of development. By incorporating security into the DevOps pipeline, organizations can build and deploy software that is inherently secure and compliant with industry standards.

Digital Forensics

Digital Forensics in the context of DevOps can be defined as the process of investigating and analyzing digital artifacts and evidence to uncover and understand potential security breaches, unauthorized activities, or malfunctions within a DevOps environment. DevOps is a software development methodology that combines software development (Dev) and IT operations (Ops) to improve collaboration, quality, and speed to deliver software applications. It involves the use of automated tools, continuous integration and delivery (CI/CD) pipelines, agile practices, and infrastructure as code (IaC) to enable faster and more efficient software development and deployment. Digital Forensics plays a crucial role in DevOps to ensure the security and integrity of software applications and infrastructure. It involves collecting, preserving, analyzing, and interpreting digital evidence to identify potential security incidents, detect vulnerabilities, and mitigate risks. Some key aspects of Digital Forensics in the context of DevOps include: 1. Incident Investigation: Digital Forensics helps in investigating security incidents, such as unauthorized access, data breaches, malware infections, or insider threats, within a DevOps environment. It involves identifying the root cause, analyzing the attack vectors, and determining the extent of the breach. 2. System and Network Analysis: Digital Forensics helps in analyzing systems, networks, and infrastructure components to detect any suspicious activities, vulnerabilities, or misconfigurations that could lead to security incidents. It involves examining log files, network traffic, system artifacts, and other digital traces to understand the state of the environment. 3. Evidence Collection and Preservation: Digital Forensics involves the proper collection, preservation, and documentation of digital evidence to ensure its admissibility and integrity. This includes capturing snapshots of systems or containers, creating forensic images, and maintaining a chain of custody for the evidence. 4. Malware Analysis: Digital Forensics helps in analyzing and understanding the behavior of malware within a DevOps environment. It involves extracting and examining malware samples, reverse engineering their code, and identifying their impact on the systems. 5. Security Monitoring: Digital Forensics supports proactive monitoring of the DevOps environment to identify potential security incidents or threats. It involves the use of security tools, anomaly detection techniques, and log analysis to detect any unusual activities or patterns that might indicate an ongoing attack. Overall, Digital

Forensics in the context of DevOps helps organizations in ensuring the security, compliance, and reliability of their software applications and infrastructure. It enables effective incident response, risk mitigation, and continuous improvement of security practices within the DevOps lifecycle.

Disaster Recovery Planning

Disaster recovery planning in the context of DevOps refers to the process of creating and implementing strategies and procedures to minimize the impact of potential disasters on the availability and functionality of an application or system. It involves the identification of potential risks, the development of recovery plans, and the implementation of measures to ensure the quick and efficient restoration of services in the event of a disaster or failure. The main goal of disaster recovery planning in DevOps is to reduce downtime and minimize the potential loss of data, revenue, and customer trust. It involves a combination of preventive, detective, and corrective measures to ensure the resilience and reliability of the application or system. One of the key aspects of disaster recovery planning is the identification and assessment of potential risks and vulnerabilities. This includes analyzing the impact of various events such as hardware or software failures, natural disasters, cybersecurity breaches, and human errors. By understanding the potential risks, organizations can develop appropriate contingency plans and implement necessary safeguards to mitigate the impact of these risks. Once the risks have been identified, organizations can develop recovery plans that outline the steps and procedures to be followed in the event of a disaster. These plans should include details on backup and recovery strategies, data replication and synchronization processes, and the allocation of resources required for recovery. The recovery plans should also consider the potential dependencies between different components or systems and ensure that adequate measures are in place to address these dependencies. In DevOps, disaster recovery planning is closely integrated with continuous delivery and continuous deployment practices. By automating the deployment process and using infrastructure-as-code principles, organizations can ensure that the recovery environment is consistent with the production environment. This allows for faster and more reliable recovery procedures, as well as the ability to test and validate the recovery processes on a regular basis. Overall, disaster recovery planning in DevOps is an essential part of ensuring the availability and reliability of applications and systems. By proactively identifying risks, developing recovery plans, and implementing preventive measures, organizations can minimize the impact of potential disasters and maintain their ability to deliver services to customers effectively.

Disaster Recovery Testing

Disaster Recovery Testing in the context of DevOps refers to the process of evaluating and validating the effectiveness of a disaster recovery strategy and plan. It involves simulating potential disasters or failures and examining how the system recovers and resumes normal operations. During disaster recovery testing, various scenarios are created, such as equipment failures, software glitches, natural disasters, or cyber-attacks. The purpose is to identify any vulnerabilities or weaknesses in the recovery plan and measure the system's ability to restore critical services and data in a timely manner. By conducting disaster recovery testing, DevOps teams can assess the overall resilience and reliability of their infrastructure, applications, and processes. It helps them identify areas that need improvement and implement necessary changes to enhance the system's ability to recover from unforeseen events. The testing process typically involves multiple stages: 1. Planning: This stage includes defining the objectives, scope, and methodology for testing. It involves identifying critical components and prioritizing them for testing. 2. Preparation: In this stage, the necessary resources, tools, and environments are set up to perform the tests. This may involve creating backups, configuring test environments, and establishing communication protocols. 3. Execution: During this stage, the defined scenarios are executed to simulate different disaster situations. The team closely monitors the system's responses, records the time taken to recover, and assesses the effectiveness of the recovery strategies in place. 4. Analysis: Once the testing is complete, the results are analyzed to identify any gaps or weaknesses. The team evaluates the recovery time objectives (RTO) and recovery point objectives (RPO) to determine if they meet the desired standards. 5. Documentation: Detailed documentation of the testing process, findings, and recommendations is created. This documentation serves as a reference for future improvements and as proof of compliance with disaster recovery regulations and requirements. Overall, disaster recovery testing is an essential part of the DevOps workflow as it ensures that the system can respond effectively to disruptions. It helps build confidence in the recovery plan and promotes a proactive approach towards maintaining business continuity in the face of potential disasters.

Distributed Tracing Tools Integration

Distributed Tracing Tools Integration in the context of DevOps refers to the process of seamlessly incorporating distributed tracing tools into a DevOps environment to enhance observability and troubleshooting capabilities. Distributed tracing is a technique used to monitor and investigate the flow of requests across multiple services or components in a distributed system. In a DevOps setting, where software development and operations are closely intertwined, distributed tracing tools integration plays a crucial role in ensuring the smooth operation and maintenance of complex distributed systems. These tools enable comprehensive visibility into the interactions between various microservices and components, allowing for effective identification and resolution of performance bottlenecks, latency issues, and errors.

Distributed Tracing Tools

Distributed Tracing Tools in the context of DevOps are software solutions that enable the monitoring and analysis of complex distributed systems. They provide a way to trace requests as they flow through various components and services of a distributed system, allowing for better visibility and understanding of system behavior. These tools capture and record information about each request made to the system, including details about the duration, latency, and any errors or exceptions encountered along the way. This information is then used to generate detailed trace logs, which can be used by DevOps teams to troubleshoot performance issues, identify bottlenecks, and optimize system performance.

Distributed Tracing

Distributed tracing is a DevOps practice that involves the capturing, analysis, and visualization of data about requests as they travel through a distributed system. It provides insights into the performance and behavior of the system by tracing individual requests across multiple services and components. In a distributed system, requests often traverse multiple services, each responsible for a specific task. As requests flow through these services, they may encounter issues such as latency, errors, or bottlenecks. Without distributed tracing, identifying the root cause of such issues can be challenging. Distributed tracing enables DevOps teams to understand the end-to-end journey of a request and identify where and why it may have encountered problems.

Diversity And Inclusion

Diversity and inclusion in the context of DevOps is the practice of creating an environment that values and encourages the participation of individuals from diverse backgrounds, perspectives, and experiences. It involves actively seeking out and incorporating diverse perspectives, ideas, and skills into the DevOps team and processes. Diversity refers to the representation, visibility, and inclusion of individuals from different demographics such as gender, race, ethnicity, age, sexual orientation, disability, and socioeconomic background. It recognizes that diverse teams bring a wider range of skills, ideas, and problem-solving approaches, leading to more innovative and effective solutions. Inclusion, on the other hand, refers to the intentional actions taken to ensure that diverse individuals feel valued, respected, and supported within the DevOps environment. It involves creating a culture of trust, psychological safety, and belonging, where everyone's ideas and contributions are welcomed and valued. By embracing diversity and inclusion practices, DevOps teams can benefit in several ways. Firstly, diverse teams are more likely to generate creative solutions and make better decisions because they approach problems from different perspectives and challenge conventional thinking. Secondly, inclusion fosters a sense of belonging and loyalty among team members, enhancing collaboration, engagement, and productivity. Thirdly, diversity and inclusion help organizations attract and retain top talent, as they signal a commitment to creating a fair and equitable workplace. To create a diverse and inclusive DevOps environment, organizations should foster open communication channels, encourage collaboration and teamwork, invest in diversity training and education, and implement inclusive policies and practices. It is essential to address unconscious biases and ensure equal opportunities for all team members. Additionally, creating diverse pipelines for talent acquisition and actively seeking candidates from underrepresented groups can help broaden the diversity within DevOps teams. In conclusion, diversity and inclusion in the context of DevOps is about recognizing the value of different perspectives and experiences, and actively fostering an environment where everyone's ideas and contributions are welcomed and valued. By embracing diversity and inclusion, organizations can enhance innovation, productivity, and overall team performance.

Documentation

Documentation in the context of DevOps refers to the systematic recording and organization of information, guidelines, procedures, and knowledge related to the development, deployment, and maintenance of software systems. It involves creating, curating, and updating a comprehensive set of documents that act as a reference for the various processes, configurations, codebases, and infrastructure involved in the DevOps lifecycle. The primary purpose of documentation in DevOps is to improve the efficiency and effectiveness of the development and operations teams by providing a standardized source of information. It serves as a valuable knowledge base that helps in knowledge transfer, collaboration, troubleshooting, and maintaining consistency across different stages of software development and deployment. DevOps documentation typically includes a variety of artifacts, such as architectural diagrams, project plans, installation guides, configuration instructions, runbooks, standard operating procedures (SOPs), code documentation, and user manuals. These documents capture essential details about the system architecture, software dependencies, deployment processes, configuration parameters, and operational best practices. Effective documentation in DevOps offers several benefits. Firstly, it promotes transparency and shared understanding by providing clear instructions and guidelines that enable team members to collaborate effectively. It reduces the reliance on tribal knowledge and minimizes the risk of information silos within an organization. Additionally, documentation improves the onboarding process for new team members by providing them with a structured and accessible source of information. It enhances the scalability of the DevOps practices by allowing for easy replication and adoption of successful processes, configurations, and strategies. Furthermore, documentation plays a crucial role in ensuring compliance and auditability. It allows organizations to track changes, maintain an audit trail of actions, and demonstrate adherence to security, compliance, and regulatory requirements. In summary, documentation in the context of DevOps is a systematic approach to creating, organizing, and curating information related to software development and operations. It acts as a central repository of knowledge, providing guidance, instructions, and best practices to enable successful collaboration, efficiency, scalability, and compliance within the DevOps lifecycle.

Drone

A drone, in the context of DevOps, refers to an automated system that is used to perform various tasks related to software development and operations. It is a combination of hardware and software that allows for efficient and seamless execution of DevOps processes. The hardware component of a drone typically consists of one or more physical devices, such as servers or computers, that are configured to perform specific actions. These devices are often connected to a central control system, which oversees the operation of the drone and ensures that all tasks are executed properly. The software component of a drone is responsible for controlling the hardware and executing the necessary actions. It may include specialized software tools and scripts that are designed to automate specific tasks, such as code deployment, infrastructure provisioning, or monitoring and logging. One of the key benefits of using drones in DevOps is the ability to automate repetitive and time-consuming tasks. By offloading these tasks to a drone, software development and operations teams can free up valuable time and resources, allowing them to focus on more important and strategic activities. Drones in DevOps can be used for a wide range of tasks, including continuous integration and deployment, environment setup and configuration, performance testing, and security scanning. They can also help with managing and monitoring infrastructure, automating workflows, and ensuring the smooth and efficient operation of various software systems. Overall, drones play a crucial role in modern DevOps practices by enabling automation, improving efficiency, and increasing reliability. They allow for faster and more accurate execution of tasks, reducing the risk of human error and enabling teams to deliver software at a faster pace.

Dynamic Application Security Testing (DAST)

Dynamic Application Security Testing (DAST) is a crucial component of the DevOps process that focuses on the assessment of the security of web applications through dynamic scanning and testing techniques. It is used to identify vulnerabilities and weaknesses in real-time, allowing for prompt action and mitigation. DAST plays a pivotal role in the dynamic and fast-paced DevOps environment, where frequent deployments and updates are the norm. By integrating DAST into the development cycle, organizations can proactively manage potential security risks and maintain the integrity of their web applications. During the DAST process, the application is systematically tested by simulating real-world attacks and malicious activities. The objective is to identify security gaps, such as injection flaws, cross-site scripting (XSS) vulnerabilities, insecure authentication mechanisms, and other common web application vulnerabilities. Unlike other security testing approaches, DAST takes a black-box perspective, meaning it doesn't require knowledge of the application's internal code or architecture. Instead, it focuses on the input and output of the application, inspecting the behavior and responses to different types of requests. DAST employs various scanning techniques, such as crawling, which explores all accessible links and pages of an application, and fuzzing, which sends unexpected or malformed data to identify potential vulnerabilities. It also analyzes the application's responses to different input, uncovering potential security weaknesses. By integrating DAST into a DevOps workflow, organizations gain the ability to detect vulnerabilities and security issues early on in the development cycle. This allows for rapid feedback, enabling developers to address these issues promptly and improve the application's overall security posture. Furthermore, DAST helps organizations meet compliance requirements and industry standards by identifying security gaps that could potentially lead to data breaches or other security incidents. It provides a valuable layer of defense to protect sensitive information and safeguard business-critical applications. In conclusion, DAST is a critical component of the DevOps process that enables organizations to identify and address security vulnerabilities in their web applications. By leveraging dynamic scanning and testing techniques, it helps ensure the integrity and security of applications, allowing for the delivery of secure and reliable software products.

Dynatrace

Dynatrace is a comprehensive observability platform that supports DevOps practices by providing real-time insights into the performance and availability of applications and infrastructure. With its intelligent monitoring capabilities, Dynatrace helps organizations streamline their DevOps processes by enabling continuous monitoring and feedback loops, ensuring faster time to resolution and improved application delivery.

ELK Stack (Elasticsearch, Logstash, Kibana)

The ELK Stack, consisting of Elasticsearch, Logstash, and Kibana, is a powerful combination of open-source tools that is widely used in the field of DevOps. This stack is designed to facilitate the collection, storage, and analysis of large volumes of data, specifically logs and other machine-generated data. Elasticsearch, the first component of the ELK Stack, is a distributed search and analytics engine built on top of Apache Lucene. It provides a scalable and highly available solution for indexing, searching, and analyzing data in real-time. Elasticsearch is capable of handling both structured and unstructured data, and its full-text search capabilities make it particularly useful for searching through large volumes of logs and records. Logstash, the second component, is an open-source data processing pipeline that allows for the ingestion and transformation of data from various sources. It provides a wide range of input and output plugins, enabling Logstash to collect logs from multiple sources, such as files, syslog, and databases. Logstash also offers filters that can be applied to the data to parse, enhance, and enrich it before sending it to Elasticsearch for indexing. Kibana, the third component, is a web-based data visualization platform that allows users to explore, analyze, and visualize data stored in Elasticsearch. It provides a user-friendly interface for creating and sharing dynamic dashboards, charts, and visualizations based on the indexed data. Kibana also offers various querying and filtering options, giving users the ability to drill down into the data and identify patterns, trends, and anomalies. Together, Elasticsearch, Logstash, and Kibana form a powerful and comprehensive stack for log management and data analysis. The combination of these tools enables DevOps teams to collect, store, search, and analyze large volumes of logs and machine-generated data in a scalable and efficient manner. By leveraging the capabilities of the ELK Stack, organizations can gain valuable insights, troubleshoot issues, identify performance bottlenecks, and make data-driven decisions to optimize their systems and applications.

Elasticity

Elasticity in the context of DevOps refers to the ability of a system or infrastructure to dynamically scale up or down in response to changing demands or conditions. It involves the flexibility and agility to efficiently allocate and manage resources, such as computing power, storage, and network bandwidth, based on the current workload and requirements. With the rapid advancement of technology and the growing complexity of applications and services, having an elastic infrastructure is crucial for organizations to ensure optimal performance, cost-efficiency, and customer satisfaction. Elasticity enables the system to adapt to fluctuations in demand, whether due to seasonal spikes, unexpected surges, or variable traffic patterns.

ElectricFlow

ElectricFlow is a comprehensive and powerful DevOps automation platform that streamlines and accelerates software delivery across diverse environments. With its robust set of features and capabilities, ElectricFlow empowers organizations to achieve continuous delivery, enabling faster and more reliable software releases. At its core, ElectricFlow provides a centralized platform for managing and orchestrating the entire software delivery pipeline. It enables collaboration and coordination between development, operations, and quality assurance teams, fostering a culture of cross-functional collaboration and automation in the software delivery process. ElectricFlow facilitates the continuous integration and continuous delivery (CI/CD) pipeline, automating the build, test, and deployment processes. It supports various deployment patterns, including rolling upgrades, canary deployments, and blue-green deployments, ensuring minimal downtime and risk-free releases. ElectricFlow also integrates with popular build, test, and infrastructure tools, providing out-of-the-box compatibility and flexibility for diverse technology stacks. One of the key features of ElectricFlow is its powerful release automation capabilities. It allows organizations to define and manage complex release pipelines, including multiple environments, dependencies, and approvals. ElectricFlow provides a visual and intuitive interface for creating and managing release templates, enabling organizations to standardize and enforce best practices. It also offers dashboards and reports to visualize and track release progress, enabling teams to identify bottlenecks and make data-driven decisions for improving the delivery process. Moreover, ElectricFlow promotes infrastructure as code (IaC) practices by offering support for provisioning and configuring infrastructure using declarative definitions. It integrates with popular infrastructure-as-code tools like Terraform and Ansible, enabling organizations to automate and manage their infrastructure deployments alongside the application deployments. In summary, ElectricFlow is a comprehensive DevOps automation platform that enables organizations to achieve continuous delivery through streamlined software delivery processes. It brings together development, operations, and quality assurance teams, automating build, test, and deployment processes while providing powerful release automation and infrastructure-as-code capabilities.

Empowerment

Empowerment in the context of DevOps refers to the approach of giving individuals and teams the autonomy, responsibility, and authority to make decisions and take ownership of the entire application lifecycle, from design and development to deployment and maintenance. In a traditional software development model, there is usually a clear separation of roles and responsibilities, with specialized teams handling specific aspects of the application lifecycle. This can lead to bottlenecks, lack of collaboration, and slower delivery times. The DevOps philosophy aims to break down these silos and empower individuals and teams to work together, collaborate, and take ownership of the entire process.

Enterprise Architecture

Enterprise architecture in the context of DevOps refers to the practice of designing and aligning the IT infrastructure, systems, processes, and information resources of an organization to support and enable the seamless integration and collaboration between development and operations teams. It involves the systematic approach of defining, analyzing, designing, and implementing the structure and components of an organization's IT ecosystem, ensuring that it meets the strategic goals and objectives of the business while facilitating the efficient and continuous delivery of software applications and services.

Error Monitoring Tools Implementation

Error monitoring tools implementation is the process of integrating and using software tools that allow for the proactive detection, monitoring, and analysis of errors or exceptions in the context of a DevOps environment. These tools provide developers, operations teams, and other stakeholders with the ability to identify, track, and resolve errors in real-time, aiding in the overall improvement of application performance, stability, and reliability. Implementing error monitoring tools in a DevOps workflow involves several key steps. First, organizations need to select and configure the appropriate error monitoring tool that aligns with their specific technical requirements and goals. This may involve evaluating different tools based on criteria such as scalability, integration capabilities, ease of use, and cost. Once the tool is selected, it is integrated into the DevOps pipeline, typically by leveraging APIs or SDKs provided by the tool. This allows for the seamless collection and transmission of error data from the application to the monitoring tool. The tool then analyzes this data, aggregating and presenting it in a user-friendly manner, highlighting critical errors and providing detailed information to aid in debugging and resolution efforts. One of the key benefits of error monitoring tools in a DevOps context is their ability to provide real-time notifications and alerts when errors occur. This allows development and operations teams to be promptly informed about critical issues, enabling them to act swiftly to address the errors and minimize their impact on the application and end-users. This proactive approach helps in reducing mean time to resolution (MTTR) and improving overall customer satisfaction. Additionally, error monitoring tools often provide advanced features such as error grouping and trend analysis. These features allow for the identification of patterns and trends in error occurrences, facilitating the detection of underlying root causes and enabling proactive measures to eliminate or mitigate recurring errors. This leads to more effective error handling and improved overall application quality and stability. In conclusion, error monitoring tools implementation in a DevOps environment is crucial for ensuring robust and reliable application performance. By integrating these tools into the workflow, organizations can proactively detect, monitor, and analyze errors, leading to faster resolution times, improved customer satisfaction, and enhanced overall application quality.

Error Monitoring Tools

Error monitoring tools are software solutions that are used in the DevOps context to identify, track, and analyze errors and exceptions that occur in the software development and deployment processes. These tools play a crucial role in improving the stability, reliability, and performance of software applications. With the increasing complexity of modern software systems, errors and exceptions are inevitable. These issues can affect the overall user experience, cause system crashes, and even lead to financial losses for organizations. Therefore, it is essential for DevOps teams to have robust error monitoring tools in place to promptly detect and address any issues that arise. Error monitoring tools provide real-time visibility into the errors and exceptions that occur within an application. They collect and aggregate log data, allowing DevOps teams to analyze and troubleshoot issues effectively. By continuously monitoring errors, these tools can help identify trends and patterns, enabling teams to proactively address potential problems and improve overall system performance. These tools offer various features to assist with error monitoring, such as error tracking, crash reporting, and alerting mechanisms. Error tracking allows teams to capture detailed information about each error, including its stack trace, affected users, and frequency of occurrence. Crash reporting provides insights into application crashes, enabling teams to understand the root causes and take appropriate actions to prevent further incidents. Alerting mechanisms notify teams about critical errors in real-time, ensuring that they are promptly addressed. Additionally, error monitoring tools often offer integrations with other DevOps tools, such as issue tracking systems and collaboration platforms. These integrations streamline the error resolution process by automatically creating tickets or notifying team members about errors, facilitating efficient collaboration and resolution. In conclusion, error monitoring tools are essential components of a DevOps strategy as they enable teams to proactively identify, track, and resolve errors and exceptions in software applications. By providing real-time visibility, detailed insights, and integration capabilities, these tools contribute to the overall stability, reliability, and performance of the applications.

Error Monitoring

Error Monitoring in the context of DevOps is the practice of continuously monitoring and analyzing software errors and exceptions that occur during the software development lifecycle. It involves the detection, tracking, and resolution of errors to improve the overall quality and reliability of the software application. DevOps teams use error monitoring tools and techniques to identify and troubleshoot errors promptly, ensuring that they do not impact the end user experience negatively. These tools help in identifying the root cause of errors, enabling quick and effective resolution.

Errorception

Errorception is a software tool commonly used in the DevOps environment to track and monitor JavaScript errors on web applications. It provides developers with a centralized platform to collect, analyze, and prioritize error reports, allowing them to identify and fix issues faster and improve the overall user experience. With Errorception, developers can gain valuable insights into the errors occurring in their applications in real-time. The tool captures and records information such as the stack trace, error message, user agent, and URL where the error occurred. This data is then analyzed and presented in a user-friendly interface, enabling developers to understand the root cause of the errors and take appropriate action to resolve them.

Evolvability

Evolvability is a concept in the context of DevOps that refers to the ability of a system or organization to adapt and respond to changes effectively and efficiently. It is the capacity to evolve and improve continuously based on the evolving needs and requirements of the users and the industry. In the DevOps context, evolvability involves several key aspects: - Flexibility: This involves the ability to make changes to the system or processes without compromising the overall stability or functionality. The system should be designed in a way that allows for easy updates, modifications, and enhancements. - Scalability: The system should be able to scale up or down as needed to accommodate changes in workload or demand. This includes the ability to add or remove resources, such as servers or storage, without causing disruptions or inefficiencies. - Automation: Evolvability is heavily dependent on automation. By automating repetitive and time-consuming tasks, organizations can free up resources and focus on innovation and improvement. Automation also allows for faster and more reliable deployments, reducing the time to release updates and new features. - Continuous Integration and Deployment: The ability to integrate changes frequently and deploy them quickly and reliably is essential for evolvability. Continuous integration ensures that changes made by multiple developers can be merged and tested together, while continuous deployment enables fast and automated delivery of changes to production environments. - Monitoring and Feedback: Evolvability is closely linked to the availability of real-time feedback and monitoring. By monitoring metrics, logs, and user feedback, organizations can quickly identify areas for improvement and take proactive measures to address issues or implement changes. Evolvability is a fundamental principle in DevOps, as it enables organizations to keep up with the rapidly changing technological and business landscape. By continuously evolving and adapting, organizations can stay competitive, deliver value to customers, and drive innovation.

Extreme Programming (XP)

Extreme Programming (XP) is an agile software development methodology that emphasizes the collaboration and communication of all stakeholders involved in a project. It focuses on delivering high-quality software quickly and continuously through a set of practices and principles. In the context of DevOps, Extreme Programming aligns with the core principles of this approach by advocating for constant collaboration, iterative development, and rapid feedback. It promotes the integration of development and operations teams, fostering a culture of shared responsibility and continuous improvement.

92

Fail Fast

Fail Fast is a principle commonly used in the context of DevOps, which refers to the approach of identifying and addressing failures or issues as quickly as possible in order to minimize their impact and improve overall system performance. By implementing the Fail Fast principle, DevOps teams aim to detect and rectify failures at the earliest stages of development and deployment, reducing the likelihood of larger-scale issues and the time required to resolve them. This approach encourages continuous monitoring, testing, and feedback loops to ensure that any potential problems are swiftly identified and addressed.

Failover Testing

Failover testing is a critical component of the DevOps process that ensures the availability and reliability of an application or system in the event of a failure or disruption. It involves testing the failover mechanisms and procedures in order to validate the system's ability to seamlessly switch to a backup or redundant system, minimizing or eliminating any downtime or impact on end users. The primary goal of failover testing is to simulate various failure scenarios and validate the failover mechanisms in place. This testing not only confirms the effectiveness of the failover process but also identifies any potential weaknesses, bottlenecks, or vulnerabilities that need to be addressed before they impact the system's availability or performance.

Fault Injection Testing Procedures

Fault Injection Testing is a software testing technique that involves intentionally introducing faults or failures into a system to assess its resilience and robustness. It is a crucial aspect of the DevOps approach, which emphasizes the seamless integration and collaboration between development and operations teams to enhance software quality and reliability. In the context of DevOps, fault injection testing is an essential practice to validate the system's behavior under abnormal or unexpected conditions. The goal is to expose potential weaknesses, vulnerabilities, or unforeseen failure scenarios that might arise in real-world production environments. By intentionally injecting faults, such as network delays, packet loss, hardware failures, or software bugs, organizations can evaluate their systems' ability to handle adversities and recover gracefully.

Fault Injection Testing

Fault injection testing is a technique used in the context of DevOps to identify and evaluate the resilience and robustness of a system by deliberately injecting faults or errors. It involves intentionally introducing failures or faults into a software or hardware system to observe how it behaves under abnormal or unexpected conditions. The objective of fault injection testing is to uncover potential vulnerabilities and weaknesses in a system, allowing DevOps teams to identify areas of improvement and make necessary fixes before deploying the system into production. By simulating various failure scenarios, fault injection testing helps determine how well a system can handle errors, exceptions, and unexpected behavior, enhancing its overall reliability and performance.

Fault Tolerance Engineering Strategies

Fault Tolerance Engineering Strategies refer to the practices and techniques implemented in a DevOps environment to ensure that systems and applications can continue to function and provide their intended services even in the presence of faults or failures. In DevOps, fault tolerance engineering focuses on designing, developing, and deploying systems that can recover from failures and continue operating with minimal disruptions. The goal is to minimize the impact of faults and failures on the availability, reliability, and performance of the system.

Fault Tolerance Engineering

Fault Tolerance Engineering in the context of DevOps refers to the process of designing and implementing systems that can continue to operate and provide reliable services, even in the presence of faults or failures. It involves the use of various techniques and strategies to minimize downtime, ensure availability, and maintain system functionality in the face of errors or disruptions. In a DevOps environment, where systems are constantly evolving and deploying changes, fault tolerance engineering becomes crucial to ensure the overall stability and reliability of the software delivery pipeline. It focuses on identifying and addressing potential points of failure, and implementing measures to mitigate their impact on the system.

Feature Branching

Feature branching is a software development practice that aims to improve collaboration and efficiency within a DevOps environment. It involves creating a separate branch, or copy, of the main codebase dedicated to the development of a specific feature or project. This allows developers to work on different features concurrently without impacting the stability of the main codebase. With feature branching, each new feature or project is assigned its own branch, which serves as an isolated workspace. Developers can make changes and experiment freely within their branch without worrying about conflicts or breaking the existing code. This promotes parallel development and helps teams work independently on different features without interfering with each other's progress.

Feature Flags

Feature Flags are a crucial component of DevOps methodology, serving as a powerful technique for mitigating risks and increasing flexibility during software development and deployment. These flags, also known as feature toggles or feature switches, enable developers to easily turn on or off specific functionalities or features in an application, allowing for seamless experimentation and control over the release process. With Feature Flags, developers can selectively enable or disable features in real-time without the need for code deployments, enabling teams to continuously deliver software updates while reducing the impact of potential bugs or issues. By decoupling feature rollout from code deployment, organizations can safely test and validate new functionalities on a subset of users or environments before making them available to the entire user base. These flags can be employed at various levels, such as the application level, specific user segments, geographic regions, or even individual users, enabling fine-grained control and personalized experiences. Feature Flags can be managed through a centralized dashboard or configuration file, facilitating easy feature management and support for A/B testing, phased rollouts, dark launches, and canary releases. In addition to feature availability control, Feature Flags offer additional benefits. They provide a clear separation between code deployment and feature activation, allowing for faster and more streamlined development cycles. They enable teams to iterate and gather feedback quickly, facilitating faster learning and decision-making. Moreover, Feature Flags enable teams to implement various release strategies, such as canary releases, blue-green deployments, or progressive rollouts, reducing the likelihood of errors or service disruptions. By leveraging Feature Flags, organizations can embrace continuous integration and continuous delivery (CI/CD) practices, promoting faster release cycles, reduced time-to-market, and improved user experiences. This DevOps practice enables organizations to respond to market demands swiftly and deliver value to users more efficiently.

Feature Toggles

Feature toggles, also known as feature flags, are a DevOps practice that allows teams to enable or disable specific features or parts of their software application during runtime. These toggles serve as a mechanism to control and manage the release of new functionality, bug fixes, or experiments without disrupting the overall user experience. By implementing feature toggles, organizations can decouple the process of deploying code from the process of releasing features. This separation enables teams to continuously deliver code to production while controlling when and to whom a specific feature is visible. Feature toggles also support the concept of dark launches, where new features are released to a subset of users or in a controlled environment to assess their impact and gather feedback.

FeatureToggle

A Feature Toggle, also known as a Feature Flag or Feature Switch, is a mechanism used in the context of DevOps to enable or disable certain features or functionalities in an application or system. It allows developers to control the activation and visibility of different features based on various conditions, such as user roles, environment settings, or specific criteria. The primary purpose of using Feature Toggles is to separate the process of deploying code changes from the process of releasing those changes to end users. By decoupling deployment and release, development teams can have more control and flexibility in managing new features and bug fixes.

Feedback Loops

A feedback loop in the context of DevOps refers to a continuous process that involves obtaining data, analyzing it, and using the insights gained from the analysis to make improvements in the software development and delivery process. It is a fundamental practice that helps teams in the DevOps culture to iterate and refine their work, aiming for better quality and efficiency. In a typical feedback loop, there are several key steps involved: Step 1: Collecting Data Teams gather data from various sources, such as user feedback, system logs, performance metrics, and testing results. This data provides insights into how the software is performing and where there might be areas for improvement. Step 2: Analyzing Data The collected data is then analyzed to identify patterns, trends, and areas of concern. This analysis helps teams understand the root causes of problems and determine the most effective solutions. Step 3: Identifying Improvements Based on the analysis, teams can identify areas for improvement in their processes, software architecture, infrastructure, or overall workflow. This step involves prioritizing these improvements based on their potential impact and feasibility. Step 4: Implementing Changes Teams implement the identified improvements through code changes, infrastructure modifications, or process adjustments. These changes can be small and frequent or larger and planned in iterations. Step 5: Monitoring and Testing After implementing the changes, teams monitor the system and collect new data to assess the impact of the improvements. Testing is conducted to validate the changes and ensure that they have not introduced any new issues. Step 6: Repeat The feedback loop is an ongoing process. Teams continuously repeat the above steps, collecting new data, analyzing it, and making further improvements. This iterative approach allows for a proactive and iterative development cycle. In DevOps, feedback loops play a vital role in promoting collaboration, learning, and a culture of continuous improvement. By embracing feedback loops, teams can identify bottlenecks, remove obstacles, and deliver higher quality software to their customers, ultimately driving business success.

Flagger

A flagger in the context of DevOps is a component or tool that is used to control and manage feature flagging in software development. Feature flagging, also known as feature toggling or feature flipping, is a technique used by DevOps teams to enable or disable certain features or functionalities of an application or system during runtime. The flagger acts as a switch that allows developers to turn specific features on or off without needing to modify or redeploy the entire software. This enables continuous delivery and allows for easy experimentation, A/B testing, and progressive rollouts. Flagger tools typically provide a simple and intuitive user interface, often integrated into the DevOps platform or CI/CD pipeline. This interface allows developers to define feature flags, set their status (i.e., enabled or disabled), and specify the conditions that determine when the flag should be activated or deactivated. Flagger tools also often offer advanced capabilities, such as targeting specific user groups or segments, enabling gradual rollout of features to control the rate of adoption, and collecting metrics and analytics on the usage and impact of different feature flags. By using flaggers, DevOps teams can easily control the release of new features, perform canary deployments to specific user groups, and quickly respond to issues or bugs by disabling certain functionality. This allows for more agile and efficient development processes, reduces the risk of introducing defects, and improves overall software quality. In summary, a flagger in the context of DevOps is a component or tool that enables feature flagging, providing developers with the ability to control and manage the activation and deactivation of specific features or functionalities in an application or system during runtime.

FlexDeploy

FlexDeploy is a powerful DevOps platform that automates the entire software development and delivery lifecycle. It provides a comprehensive set of tools and functionalities to streamline and accelerate the deployment process, allowing teams to deliver high-quality software applications in a faster, more efficient manner. FlexDeploy offers a single, centralized platform for managing the entire software development process, from code integration and building to testing, deployment, and release. It integrates seamlessly with popular DevOps tools and technologies, including version control systems, continuous integration servers, and testing frameworks, enabling teams to leverage their existing investments and infrastructure.

Fortify

Fortify is a software security product that is commonly used in the field of DevOps. It is designed to help developers identify and fix security vulnerabilities in their code during the software development lifecycle. Fortify provides a comprehensive set of static and dynamic analysis tools that can be integrated into the DevOps process to identify and mitigate potential security risks. One of the main features of Fortify is its ability to perform static code analysis. This involves scanning the source code of an application to identify potential security weaknesses, such as buffer overflows, SQL injection, and cross-site scripting vulnerabilities. Fortify's static code analysis tools can detect thousands of different security issues, helping developers identify and fix potential problems before the code is deployed to production. In addition to static code analysis, Fortify also offers dynamic analysis capabilities. This involves running the application and monitoring it for runtime security vulnerabilities. By analyzing the application's behavior during execution, Fortify can identify potential security risks that may not be apparent from static code analysis alone. Dynamic analysis can help identify issues such as insecure network communication, improper error handling, and access control vulnerabilities. Fortify integrates into the DevOps process by providing plugins and integrations for popular development environments and build systems. This allows developers to easily incorporate security testing into their existing workflows, without the need for significant changes to their processes. For example, Fortify integrates with popular development environments such as Visual Studio and Eclipse, as well as build systems such as Jenkins and TeamCity. Overall, Fortify is a valuable tool for DevOps teams looking to strengthen the security of their applications. By identifying and fixing security vulnerabilities early in the development process, Fortify helps developers reduce the risk of security breaches and ensure the confidentiality, integrity, and availability of their software.

GitLab CI/CD

GitLab CI/CD is a DevOps tool that stands for Continuous Integration and Continuous Deployment. It is an integral part of the GitLab platform, providing a robust and automated approach to software development and delivery. Continuous Integration refers to the practice of automatically integrating code changes from multiple developers into a shared repository, ensuring that the code works cohesively and without conflicts. GitLab CI/CD facilitates this process by automatically triggering builds and running tests whenever changes are pushed to the repository. This allows developers to identify and resolve conflicts or issues earlier in the development lifecycle, reducing the risk of introducing bugs into the codebase and improving overall code quality. Continuous Deployment, on the other hand, involves the automatic deployment of the application to the production environment once all tests have passed. GitLab CI/CD streamlines this process by providing a comprehensive pipeline configuration, allowing developers to define the stages and tasks required for deployment. This includes tasks such as building the application, running additional tests, and deploying the application to the production environment. By automating these steps, GitLab CI/CD enables faster and more reliable deployment, reducing the time and effort required for manual deployment processes. GitLab CI/CD is highly configurable and customizable, supporting a wide range of programming languages, frameworks, and deployment environments. It provides a simple and intuitive interface for defining pipelines and managing the entire CI/CD process. With its built-in visibility and monitoring features, GitLab CI/CD allows teams to track the progress of their pipelines, view logs, and gain insights into the performance and stability of their applications. Overall, GitLab CI/CD plays a crucial role in implementing DevOps practices, enabling teams to establish a consistent and efficient software development and delivery workflow. It helps streamline the integration and deployment processes, reduce errors, and provide faster feedback, ultimately improving collaboration, agility, and the overall quality of software development.

GitOps

GitOps is a modern approach to managing infrastructure and deploying applications in the context of DevOps. It is based on the principles of version control systems, specifically Git, and uses pull requests as the primary mechanism to manage and automate changes to infrastructure and application code. In GitOps, the entire infrastructure configuration, including infrastructure as code (IaC), application code, and deployment manifests, is stored in a Git repository. This repository serves as a single source of truth for the infrastructure and ensures that all changes are tracked and auditable. The GitOps workflow follows a declarative approach, where desired changes in the infrastructure are defined in the form of code changes. Pull requests are used to propose and review these changes before they are merged into the main branch. Once the changes are merged, GitOps tools automatically apply the changes to the actual infrastructure, ensuring that the desired state is always reflected. GitOps provides several benefits in the context of DevOps. It brings transparency and traceability to the infrastructure management process by leveraging the capabilities of Git. This enables teams to collaborate effectively and have a clear audit trail of all the changes made to the infrastructure. By using Git as the single source of truth, GitOps allows for versioning and rollback of infrastructure changes. If an issue arises, the infrastructure can be easily rolled back to a previous known-good state by reverting the changes in the Git repository. Furthermore, GitOps promotes the idea of immutable infrastructure, where the infrastructure is treated as code and can be tested, versioned, and deployed just like the application code. This ensures consistency and reproducibility in the deployment process, reducing the chances of configuration drift or manual errors. In conclusion, GitOps is a modern approach to managing infrastructure and deploying applications that leverages the power of Git and version control systems. It provides transparency, traceability, and rollback capabilities, bringing significant benefits to the DevOps workflow.

GoCD

GoCD is a continuous delivery tool that is specifically designed to help organizations implement and automate their DevOps practices. It provides a platform for managing and orchestrating the end-to-end software delivery process, ensuring smooth collaboration between development, operations, and quality assurance teams. With GoCD, organizations can take advantage of the continuous integration and continuous delivery principles of DevOps, enabling them to deliver high-quality software at a rapid pace. It offers a range of features that streamline the deployment pipeline, allowing teams to automate the build, test, and deployment process in a reliable and repeatable manner.

Golden Image

A Golden Image refers to a pre-configured and standardized template that contains the necessary software, settings, and configuration of an operating system or application. It is typically used in the context of DevOps, where it serves as a foundation for creating multiple identical instances or environments. In the DevOps workflow, the creation and deployment of software applications often involve the use of multiple environments, such as development, testing, staging, and production. These environments need to be consistent and reproducible to ensure that the application behaves consistently across different stages of the software development lifecycle. A Golden Image serves as a starting point for creating multiple instances or environments with identical configurations. It encapsulates all the required software dependencies, libraries, configurations, and settings, allowing for easy and consistent deployment across different environments. This template is usually built and maintained by the operations team or system administrators, who ensure that it adheres to the organization's standards and is kept up to date with the latest patches and updates. By using a Golden Image, organizations can achieve several benefits in their DevOps processes. Firstly, it eliminates the need for manual installation and configuration of software on each instance, as the template already contains all the necessary components. This saves time and reduces the likelihood of human error. Additionally, it promotes consistency and repeatability, as all instances created from the Golden Image will have the same configuration and software stack. Furthermore, a Golden Image enables rapid scalability and agility in development and deployment processes. By leveraging automation and orchestration tools, DevOps teams can easily spin up new instances or environments using the Golden Image, allowing them to quickly respond to changing business requirements and scale their applications as needed. In conclusion, a Golden Image is a pre-configured and standardized template that serves as a foundation for creating multiple instances or environments with identical configurations. It promotes consistency, repeatability, scalability, and agility in the DevOps workflow, facilitating efficient software development and deployment processes.

Grafana

Grafana is an open-source platform used in the field of DevOps. It provides a customizable and interactive dashboard for monitoring and visualizing data from various sources in real-time. The platform allows DevOps teams to gain insights into the performance and health of their systems, applications, and infrastructure. Grafana integrates with a wide range of data sources, including databases, cloud services, and monitoring tools. It collects and processes data from these sources and presents it in a visually appealing and easy-to-understand format. Users can create and customize dashboards to display metrics, logs, events, and alerts, which help in identifying and troubleshooting issues.

HashiCorp Vault

HashiCorp Vault is a secure secrets management tool used by DevOps teams to store, access, and manage sensitive information such as API keys, passwords, and certificates in a centralized and encrypted manner. It provides a reliable and robust solution for managing secrets in a distributed and dynamic infrastructure. With the increasing complexity of modern software systems and the need for secure and automated deployment, traditional methods of secrets management, such as storing credentials in configuration files or environment variables, have become inadequate and risky. Vault addresses these challenges by offering a secure and scalable platform that ensures secrets are safeguarded throughout their lifecycle.

Health Assessment

Health Assessment in the context of DevOps refers to the process of evaluating the overall health and performance of a DevOps environment or system. It is an essential practice that helps organizations identify any areas of improvement, assess risks, and make informed decisions to optimize the efficiency and effectiveness of their DevOps practices. The purpose of a DevOps health assessment is to provide a comprehensive evaluation of various aspects of the DevOps environment, including the infrastructure, tools, processes, and people involved. It involves analyzing metrics and indicators to gauge the performance and health of the system, identifying bottlenecks, vulnerabilities, and areas that require attention or enhancements.

Hybrid Cloud Deployment Approaches

Hybrid Cloud Deployment Approaches in the context of DevOps refer to the strategies and methods used to deploy applications and services that utilize both public and private cloud environments. It involves the combination of on-premises infrastructure and resources with cloud-based infrastructure and resources, resulting in a hybrid cloud architecture. There are two main approaches to hybrid cloud deployment: the Lift and Shift approach and the Modernize and Extend approach. The Lift and Shift approach involves migrating existing applications and workloads from on-premises infrastructure to the public cloud without making significant changes to the application architecture. It aims to quickly move applications to the cloud to take advantage of its scalability and flexibility without requiring extensive modifications. However, this approach may not fully leverage the benefits of cloud-native technologies and may result in suboptimal performance and resource utilization. The Modernize and Extend approach, on the other hand, focuses on modernizing and adapting applications to fully utilize cloud-native capabilities while extending existing on-premises infrastructure. This approach involves re-architecting applications to leverage cloud services, containers, and microservices. It allows for greater scalability, resilience, and flexibility, making it easier to adopt DevOps practices such as continuous integration and deployment. By modernizing applications, organizations can reduce technical debt, improve efficiency, and enable faster development and deployment cycles.

Hybrid Cloud Deployment

A hybrid cloud deployment, in the context of DevOps, refers to the use of both public and private cloud environments in a combined infrastructure. It allows organizations to leverage the benefits of both public and private clouds, while addressing the specific needs and requirements of their applications and workloads. In a hybrid cloud deployment, the public cloud is usually used for non-sensitive, less critical workloads that require scalable resources and on-demand availability. On the other hand, the private cloud is used for sensitive, critical workloads that require more control, security, and compliance. By adopting a hybrid cloud deployment, DevOps teams can take advantage of the flexibility, scalability, and cost-effectiveness of the public cloud, while also meeting the security, compliance, and control requirements of their organization. This enables seamless integration and collaboration between different development, testing, and production environments, resulting in improved agility and speed in delivering applications and services. DevOps teams can leverage the hybrid cloud environment to dynamically scale their application resources based on demand. They can provision additional compute, storage, or networking resources from the public cloud for peak periods, while utilizing the more cost-effective private cloud for regular workloads. This ensures optimal resource utilization and cost efficiency. Furthermore, the hybrid cloud deployment allows DevOps teams to easily migrate workloads between the public and private clouds, based on changing demands or requirements. This flexibility enables them to take advantage of the latest cloud technologies and services, while also maintaining control over sensitive data and critical applications. In summary, a hybrid cloud deployment in the context of DevOps combines the benefits of public and private clouds, allowing organizations to leverage on-demand scalability, cost efficiency, flexibility, and control. It enables seamless integration between different environments, empowers dynamic resource provisioning, and facilitates workload migration as needed.

ITIL (Information Technology Infrastructure Library)

ITIL (Information Technology Infrastructure Library) is a set of best practices for managing and delivering IT services. It provides a framework for aligning IT services with the needs of the business, focusing on delivering value to customers and improving overall service quality. In the context of DevOps, ITIL can play a crucial role in ensuring that the development and operations teams work together effectively to deliver high-quality software solutions. DevOps is a philosophy and set of practices that emphasizes collaboration, communication, and automation between software developers and IT operations professionals. It aims to enable continuous integration, continuous delivery, and continuous deployment of software changes. By incorporating ITIL principles into a DevOps environment, organizations can enhance the efficiency and reliability of their software development and delivery processes. ITIL provides a structured approach to managing IT services throughout their lifecycle, from design and transition to operation and improvement. This includes processes for incident management, problem management, change management, and service level management. When applied in a DevOps context, ITIL can help to identify and resolve issues more quickly, minimize the impact of changes, and maintain stable and secure IT environments. It promotes a proactive approach to service management, focusing on preventative measures and continuous improvement. This aligns well with the goals of DevOps, which strives for faster delivery, improved quality, and greater customer satisfaction.

Identity And Access Management (IAM)

Identity and Access Management (IAM) refers to the set of processes and technologies used to manage and control access to resources within a DevOps environment. It encompasses the administration of user identities, their authentication, and authorization to access various systems and services. In the context of DevOps, IAM plays a crucial role in ensuring the security and compliance of the software development and deployment lifecycle. It enables organizations to enforce granular controls over who can access specific resources and what actions they can perform, thereby reducing the risk of unauthorized access, data breaches, and insider threats.

Immutable Code

Immutable code is a fundamental principle in the context of DevOps that refers to a coding practice where code, once deployed, cannot be modified or changed. It ensures that the code remains unchanged throughout its lifecycle, regardless of any updates or changes made to the underlying infrastructure or configurations. Immutable code is a key concept behind the Infrastructure as Code (IaC) approach, where infrastructure is defined and managed through code. The immutable code approach brings several benefits to the DevOps process. Firstly, it improves maintainability and reliability by eliminating configuration drift and reducing the likelihood of human error. Since the code remains constant, there is no risk of unintentional

99

changes or discrepancies between different environments. This avoids potential issues that arise from manual intervention or ad hoc modifications to the code. Furthermore, the practice of immutable code promotes scalability and repeatability. With immutable code, it becomes easier to scale infrastructure and achieve consistent results across different deployments. It allows for faster and more efficient provisioning of resources, as the code can be replicated and reused without any modifications. This increases the automation potential and enables organizations to quickly adapt to changing business requirements or customer demands. Immutable code also enhances security and compliance aspects in the DevOps process. Since the code cannot be modified, it reduces the risk of unauthorized changes or vulnerabilities introduced through unauthorized access. It also simplifies the auditing and tracking of changes, as any modifications to the code would require a redeployment or a new version. This strengthens the overall compliance posture and provides better visibility into the state of the codebase.

Immutable Infrastructure Tools

Immutable Infrastructure refers to the concept of treating infrastructure as code and ensuring that it remains static, or immutable, once it is deployed. This approach is a fundamental principle in the context of DevOps, which aims to improve collaboration and efficiency in software development and deployment processes. Tools for managing immutable infrastructure provide organizations with the means to automate infrastructure provisioning and configuration, enabling them to easily create and deploy consistent environments. These tools help ensure that infrastructure remains consistent, reliable, and version-controlled throughout the entire development lifecycle.

Immutable Infrastructure

Immutable infrastructure, in the context of DevOps, refers to a system architecture approach wherein the infrastructure components, such as servers and networks, are created and deployed in an immutable manner. This means that once these components are deployed, they are never altered or updated; instead, any changes or updates require the creation of a new, completely independent instance. Immutable infrastructure is built around the principle of treating infrastructure as code, where infrastructure configurations are defined in code and managed through version control systems. This approach ensures that the infrastructure remains consistent, reproducible, and easily scalable. The key idea behind immutable infrastructure is that by treating infrastructure as code, organizations can achieve greater reliability, consistency, and efficiency in their operations. With immutable infrastructure, it becomes easier to automate tasks, such as provisioning and deploying infrastructure components, as well as rolling back changes if needed. Immutable infrastructure significantly reduces the risk of configuration drift, where infrastructure components diverge over time due to manual changes or updates. Since immutable infrastructure components are never updated in place, configuration drift becomes a non-issue, as any changes are introduced through new instances. Moreover, immutable infrastructure promotes the use of declarative infrastructure management tools, which define the desired state of infrastructure and automatically manage any changes required to achieve that state. These tools, such as Terraform or AWS CloudFormation, enable organizations to define infrastructure configurations using code, store them in version control, and apply them in a consistent and scalable manner. The benefits of immutable infrastructure extend beyond operational efficiency. By decoupling the infrastructure from the applications running on top of it, organizations can easily scale their applications by deploying additional instances of the infrastructure components. This allows for easier horizontal scaling, where more instances can be added to handle increased traffic or workload. In summary, immutable infrastructure is a DevOps approach that treats infrastructure components as code and deploys them in an immutable manner. By eliminating configuration drift and enabling automation, organizations can achieve greater reliability, consistency, and scalability in their operations.

Immutable Server

An immutable server is a concept in DevOps that refers to a server configuration that is treated as immutable or unchangeable after it is created. It follows the principle of not making any modifications or updates directly on the server itself, but instead creating a new server instance each time a change needs to be made. This approach offers several benefits in terms of stability, security, and scalability. By treating servers as immutable, organizations can ensure a more consistent and predictable environment. Since the server configuration is fixed and not subject to updates, there is a reduced risk of configuration drift, where servers gradually diverge from their intended state due to manual changes or software updates. This can result in inconsistencies and make troubleshooting and maintenance more challenging. Immutable servers also enhance security by reducing the attack surface. Since server instances are not modified directly, there is no opportunity for unauthorized changes or malicious actors to exploit vulnerabilities. In the event of a security threat, rolling back to a previous known good configuration is straightforward, as new instances can be created from a known baseline. Scalability is another advantage of immutable servers. They can easily be replicated and deployed across multiple environments, allowing for efficient horizontal scaling. The ability to quickly spin up new instances when needed and tear them down when they are no longer required enables organizations to respond to fluctuating demand and optimize resource allocation. In addition to these benefits, immutable servers also facilitate easy rollback and versioning. In case of issues or failures, it is simple to revert to a previous server version by deploying the corresponding image. This simplifies the troubleshooting process and minimizes downtime. In conclusion, the concept of immutable servers aligns with the principles of DevOps by promoting stability, security, scalability, and easy rollback. By adopting this approach, organizations can maintain a consistent and controlled infrastructure, reduce the risk of configuration errors, and enhance overall operational efficiency.

Immutable Servers

An immutable server, in the context of DevOps, refers to a server configuration that is created, deployed, and maintained in a manner that ensures it remains unchanged throughout its lifespan. This means that once the server is provisioned, no further modifications or updates are made to its configuration or installed software. Instead, any changes or updates are implemented by creating a new, updated server image and replacing the existing server with the new version. The concept of immutable servers aligns with the principles of infrastructure as code and embodies the "pets vs. cattle" mentality often found in modern DevOps practices. It emphasizes the importance of treating servers as disposable entities that can be easily replaced rather than fragile assets that require constant care and manual intervention.

Incident Command System (ICS) In DevOps Implementation

The Incident Command System (ICS) in DevOps implementation refers to a standardized management framework that facilitates effective coordination and communication during incidents or emergencies in the software development and operations process. DevOps is a set of practices that aims to bridge the gap between software development (Dev) and IT operations (Ops) by fostering collaboration, continuous integration and delivery, and automation. However, incidents are inevitable in any software development and operations environment, and they can disrupt normal operations, impact customers, and cause financial losses. Therefore, the implementation of ICS in DevOps becomes crucial to handle incidents in a structured and efficient manner. ICS provides a clearly-defined organizational structure and a set of standardized processes and procedures to manage incidents in the DevOps context. It establishes clear roles and responsibilities for each team member involved in the incident response. This ensures that everyone understands their tasks and can work cohesively towards resolving the incident. One of the key components of ICS in DevOps implementation is the Incident Commander. This individual, typically a senior member of the DevOps team, takes charge of the incident response and has the authority to make critical decisions. They prioritize tasks, allocate resources, and coordinate the efforts of different teams involved in the incident response. In addition, ICS establishes a clear communication structure in the DevOps environment. It ensures that all relevant stakeholders, both internal and external, are promptly informed about the incident and its progress. This improves transparency and helps manage expectations during an incident. The implementation of ICS in DevOps also emphasizes documentation and information management. All relevant information about the incident, including its timeline, actions taken, and lessons learned, is documented for future reference and continuous improvement. This documentation helps in analyzing incidents, identifying their root causes, and implementing preventive measures to avoid similar incidents in the future. In conclusion, the Incident Command System (ICS) in DevOps implementation provides a structured framework for managing incidents in software development and operations. It ensures effective coordination, communication, and decision-making during incidents, leading to faster resolution and improved operational resilience.

Incident Command System (ICS) In DevOps

The Incident Command System (ICS) in DevOps refers to a structured approach and set of guidelines that aims to effectively manage and respond to incidents, ensuring efficient and coordinated efforts from all team members involved. Adopting ICS in DevOps allows organizations to establish a clear chain of command, roles, and responsibilities during an incident, enabling teams to respond promptly and effectively. It ensures that all members involved in incident response are aligned in terms of goals, objectives, and communication, leading to better incident resolution and reduced downtime.

Incident Response Plan (IRP)

An Incident Response Plan (IRP) in the context of DevOps refers to a documented and structured approach that outlines the necessary steps to be taken by a DevOps team in response to any security incidents or breaches. It is a proactive strategy designed to minimize the impact of an incident and ensure a timely and effective response, with the ultimate goal of restoring normal operations as quickly as possible. The IRP serves as a guide for the entire incident response process, enabling the team to efficiently handle and manage incidents while adhering to established protocols. It provides a standardized framework that defines the roles, responsibilities, and actions that should be undertaken during each phase of incident response, including preparation, detection, containment, eradication, recovery, and post-incident analysis. First and foremost, the IRP focuses on prevention measures through robust security practices and procedures. This includes regularly assessing and identifying potential vulnerabilities in the DevOps system, implementing strong access controls, and continuously monitoring for any suspicious activity or signs of compromise. When an incident occurs, the IRP defines the necessary steps for detecting and analyzing the incident, as well as containing and eradicating the threat. This may involve isolating affected systems, conducting forensic investigations, and applying necessary patches or updates to mitigate the risk. Following containment, the IRP emphasizes the importance of restoring normal operations and recovering any lost or compromised data. This might involve restoring backups, rebuilding systems, or strengthening security measures to prevent future incidents. Once the incident has been resolved, a post-incident analysis is conducted to evaluate the incident response process and identify areas of improvement. Lessons learned from the analysis are used to update and refine the IRP for better preparedness in future incidents. In conclusion, an Incident Response Plan in the DevOps context is a critical component of ensuring the security and resilience of the system. By providing a clear roadmap for incident response, it enables the DevOps team to effectively handle and mitigate the impact of security incidents while working towards minimizing downtime and maintaining business continuity.

Incident Response Plan

An Incident Response Plan in the context of DevOps refers to a documented set of procedures and guidelines that outline the steps to be followed when responding to and managing security incidents or disruptions in a DevOps environment. It is a structured approach to handling incidents and minimizing their impact on the system and the business. In a DevOps setting, where continuous integration, continuous delivery, and continuous deployment are core principles, incidents can disrupt the smooth flow of development and deployment processes. An Incident Response Plan helps DevOps teams to efficiently and effectively address incidents, identify the root causes, mitigate risks, and restore normal operations as soon as possible. The Incident Response Plan typically includes predefined roles and responsibilities for incident management, communication protocols, escalation procedures, and step-by-step instructions for different types of incidents. These plans are proactive and are designed to ensure that the team reacts swiftly and consistently to incidents, rather than trying to figure out the response on the fly. Key components of an Incident Response Plan in a DevOps context often include: 1. Incident Identification and Reporting: Clear guidelines on how to identify and report incidents promptly. 2. Incident Categorization and Severity Assessment: Procedures to categorize and assess the severity of incidents based on predefined criteria. 3. Incident Response Team and Roles: Designation of specific roles and responsibilities for the Incident Response Team, defining who should be involved and their respective tasks. 4. Communication and Coordination:

Defined communication channels and protocols for relaying information to stakeholders, both internal and external, and coordinating the incident response efforts. 5. Incident Analysis and Investigation: Steps to investigate and analyze the incident to determine its root cause and potential impact. 6. Incident Resolution and Recovery: Procedures for containing the incident, implementing corrective actions, and restoring normal operations. 7. Post-Incident Review and Lessons Learned: A process to evaluate the effectiveness of the Incident Response Plan, identify areas of improvement, and capture lessons learned for future incidents. An Incident Response Plan is a critical component of a DevOps strategy as it helps minimize downtime, reduce the impact of incidents, and ensure the organization can quickly recover from disruptions. By having a well-defined plan in place, DevOps teams can respond to incidents promptly, maintain the trust of stakeholders, and ultimately deliver high-quality software products with minimal disruptions.

Incident Response

Incident Response in the context of DevOps refers to the process of identifying, analyzing, and mitigating incidents that occur during the development and operation of software systems. It involves a series of coordinated activities aimed at resolving incidents efficiently, minimizing their impact, and restoring normal operation as quickly as possible. The primary goal of incident response in DevOps is to ensure system availability, reliability, and performance, while maintaining rapid innovation and continuous delivery. It requires a collaborative approach, involving cross-functional teams that include developers, operations staff, security professionals, and other stakeholders.

Incremental Deployment

Incremental deployment in the context of DevOps refers to the practice of implementing changes and updates to a software system gradually, in a step-by-step manner. This approach aims to minimize risks and disruptions by breaking down large deployments into smaller, manageable increments. Each increment consists of a specific set of changes or updates that are tested, validated, and deployed independently, allowing for continuous integration and delivery.

Infrastructure Compliance Checks

Infrastructure compliance checks refer to the systematic evaluation and verification of infrastructure components to ensure that they adhere to established standards, regulations, and policies. In the context of DevOps, these checks are crucial for maintaining the integrity, reliability, and security of an organization's infrastructure. DevOps is an approach to software development that emphasizes collaboration, automation, and continuous delivery. It focuses on breaking down silos between development, operations, and other teams involved in the software development lifecycle. As a result, infrastructure compliance checks in the DevOps context encompass various aspects, including security, performance, scalability, maintainability, and adherence to best practices.

Infrastructure Compliance Tools Integration

Infrastructure compliance tools integration refers to the process of incorporating various compliance tools into the infrastructure as code (IaC) pipelines in a DevOps environment. These tools are designed to ensure that the infrastructure meets specified compliance standards and regulations. In a DevOps context, infrastructure compliance is crucial to maintain operational efficiency, reliability, and security. By integrating compliance tools into the IaC pipelines, organizations can automate compliance checks and validations, making the process more efficient and reliable.

Infrastructure Compliance Tools

Infrastructure compliance tools in the context of DevOps are software applications or services that are designed to help organizations ensure that their infrastructure adheres to a set of predefined compliance standards or regulations. These tools provide the necessary capabilities for monitoring, evaluating, and enforcing compliance requirements across the entire infrastructure stack, including hardware, operating systems, virtualization layers, networking, and applications. These tools often offer features such as automated scanning and auditing of infrastructure components to identify any non-compliant configurations or vulnerabilities. They can also generate reports and provide visibility into compliance status, enabling organizations to proactively address issues and maintain a secure and compliant infrastructure.

Infrastructure Monitoring Strategies

Infrastructure monitoring strategies refer to the processes and methods used to continuously monitor and manage the various components and systems that make up an organization's infrastructure. In the context of DevOps, infrastructure monitoring strategies are crucial in ensuring the reliable performance, availability, and security of the infrastructure that supports the development, deployment, and operation of software applications. DevOps is a software development approach that emphasizes collaboration, integration, and automation between software developers and IT operations teams. In a DevOps environment, infrastructure monitoring is essential to maintain the stability and reliability of the infrastructure that supports the deployment and operation of software applications. By proactively monitoring and detecting potential issues or performance bottlenecks in the infrastructure, organizations can prevent downtime, optimize resource utilization, and deliver better user experiences.

Infrastructure Monitoring Tools

Infrastructure monitoring tools refer to a set of software solutions used in the context of DevOps to continuously monitor and analyze the performance and status of an organization's infrastructure. This infrastructure includes servers, networks, databases, and any other technology components that make up the overall IT system. These tools play a crucial role in ensuring the availability, reliability, and performance of the infrastructure, allowing DevOps teams to proactively detect and resolve issues before they impact the end users. They provide real-time visibility into the various components of the infrastructure, collecting and aggregating data such as CPU usage, memory utilization, disk space, network traffic, and application performance metrics. The monitoring tools typically employ a combination of agents and sensors that are installed on the infrastructure components, enabling them to collect data and transmit it to a central monitoring system. The collected data is then processed and presented in a user-friendly interface, providing insights and alerts to the DevOps team. These tools facilitate the monitoring and management of infrastructure at scale, eliminating the need for manual monitoring and allowing for a proactive approach to addressing issues. They enable DevOps teams to identify trends and patterns, perform root cause analysis, and make informed decisions regarding capacity planning and resource allocation. Furthermore, infrastructure monitoring tools often offer features such as automated remediation, which can execute predefined actions or scripts in response to certain events or alerts. This helps to streamline the incident response process and reduce the time to resolution. In conclusion, infrastructure monitoring tools form an essential part of the DevOps toolchain, helping organizations maintain the health and performance of their infrastructure. By providing real-time visibility and actionable insights, they empower DevOps teams to effectively monitor, troubleshoot, and optimize their infrastructure, ultimately enhancing the overall reliability and availability of their applications and services.

Infrastructure Monitoring

Infrastructure monitoring in the context of DevOps refers to the process of continuously monitoring and collecting data about the health, performance, and availability of the underlying infrastructure that supports an application or system. This includes monitoring the servers, networks, databases, storage systems, and other components that make up the infrastructure. The goal of infrastructure monitoring is to ensure the smooth operation of the infrastructure and quickly identify and address any issues or potential bottlenecks that may impact the performance or availability of the application. By monitoring key performance indicators (KPIs) and metrics such as CPU usage, memory utilization, network latency, and disk space, DevOps teams can proactively detect and resolve issues before they escalate and impact end users. Infrastructure monitoring involves the use of monitoring tools and platforms that collect and analyze data from various sources within the infrastructure. These tools often provide real-time visibility into the health and performance of infrastructure components, allowing DevOps teams to monitor and respond to issues promptly. Alerts and notifications can be set up to automatically inform team members when predefined thresholds or anomalies are detected. Monitoring the infrastructure also plays a vital role in capacity planning and scalability. By analyzing historical data and trends, DevOps teams can make informed decisions about resource allocation, infrastructure scaling, and performance optimization. This proactive approach helps to ensure that the infrastructure can handle increasing workloads and maintain high availability. In summary, infrastructure monitoring is an essential practice in DevOps that involves continuously monitoring and collecting data about the performance and availability of the underlying infrastructure. It helps DevOps teams detect and resolve issues promptly, ensure optimal performance, and plan for future scaling and optimization efforts.

Infrastructure Optimization

Infrastructure Optimization is a fundamental concept in DevOps that focuses on improving the efficiency, reliability, and scalability of the underlying technology and systems infrastructure to support the rapid delivery of software applications. DevOps aims to bridge the gap between software development and operations teams to enable continuous integration, delivery, and deployment. Infrastructure Optimization plays a critical role in achieving these objectives by ensuring that the infrastructure is effectively managed, automated, and standardized.

Infrastructure Pipeline

An infrastructure pipeline in the context of DevOps refers to a set of automated processes and tools that are used to manage, provision, and maintain the infrastructure required for software development and deployment. In a DevOps environment, the infrastructure pipeline plays a crucial role in ensuring that developers can work efficiently by providing them with a reliable and consistent infrastructure to develop and test their code. It also enables the deployment of software applications to various environments, such as development, staging, and production, with minimal manual intervention. The infrastructure pipeline is typically composed of several stages or phases, each of which performs specific tasks and enforces certain rules or policies. These stages ensure that the infrastructure is provisioned correctly, that configuration is managed consistently, and that changes are tested and deployed in a controlled manner. Some common stages in an infrastructure pipeline include: 1. Infrastructure as Code (IaC): This stage involves defining and provisioning infrastructure resources, such as servers, networks, and databases, using code. Infrastructure as code allows for version control, repeatability, and automation of infrastructure provisioning. 2. Configuration Management: This stage focuses on managing and maintaining the desired state of the infrastructure configuration. It typically involves tools like Ansible, Puppet, or Chef to ensure consistent configurations across different environments. 3. Testing and Validation: This stage involves validating changes made to the infrastructure before deploying them to production. It may include different types of tests, such as unit, integration, and performance tests, to ensure the stability and reliability of the infrastructure. 4. Deployment: This stage automates the process of deploying software applications to different environments. It may involve strategies like blue-green deployment, canary releases, or rolling updates to minimize downtime and ensure smooth transitions between versions. By implementing an infrastructure pipeline, organizations can achieve better collaboration between development and operations teams, reduce manual errors, increase deployment speed, and improve overall software quality and reliability. It allows for continuous integration and delivery, enabling rapid and frequent releases of software applications while maintaining stability and scalability.

Infrastructure Provisioning Automation

Infrastructure provisioning automation refers to the process of automating the deployment and configuration of infrastructure resources through code, in order to support the needs of DevOps practices. DevOps is a collaboration between development and operations teams, aimed at enhancing the speed, efficiency, and reliability of software delivery. Traditionally, infrastructure provisioning has been a manual and time-consuming task, requiring significant coordination between different teams and departments. This approach can lead to various challenges such as human error, lack of consistency, and slow deployment cycles. Infrastructure provisioning automation seeks to address these challenges by leveraging code-based tools and frameworks.

Infrastructure Provisioning

Infrastructure provisioning in the context of DevOps refers to the process of setting up and managing the necessary hardware, software, and network resources required to support the development and deployment of software applications. It involves automating the provisioning of infrastructure resources, such as servers, storage, networking, and virtual machines, using code and configuration files, rather than manual configuration. The goal of infrastructure provisioning is to provide a consistent and reliable environment for software development and delivery, enabling teams to rapidly deploy and scale applications. It plays a crucial role in enabling the principles of DevOps, such as continuous integration, continuous delivery, and infrastructure as code.

Infrastructure Scaling

Infrastructure Scaling, in the context of DevOps, refers to the process of adjusting and expanding the underlying IT infrastructure to accommodate the changing demands of an application or system. It involves increasing or decreasing the resources, such as servers, storage, and network components, to ensure optimal performance, high availability, and scalability. Scaling infrastructure is a critical aspect of DevOps as it enables organizations to handle varying workloads, adapt to new business requirements, and deliver a seamless user experience. By scaling infrastructure, DevOps teams can effectively address the challenges posed by rapid growth, increased user traffic, or changing market conditions.

Infrastructure Testing

Infrastructure testing in the context of DevOps refers to the process of evaluating and verifying the underlying infrastructure components that support software applications. It involves testing the infrastructure elements such as servers, networks, databases, storage, and other IT resources to ensure they are functioning correctly and meet the performance, reliability, and scalability requirements of the software. This type of testing is crucial in the DevOps lifecycle as it helps identify and resolve any issues or vulnerabilities within the infrastructure that may affect the software's performance or stability. By thoroughly testing the infrastructure, organizations can mitigate risks and ensure the smooth functioning of their applications, minimizing the chances of downtime or service disruptions.

Infrastructure As Code (IaC) Adoption

Infrastructure as Code (IaC) is a critical concept in the field of DevOps that aims to bridge the gap between development and operations teams by treating infrastructure provisioning and management as code. It involves the automation of infrastructure deployment and configuration processes using version-controlled text files, allowing infrastructure to be maintained and managed in a repeatable, consistent, and efficient manner. With IaC, infrastructure components such as virtual machines, networks, storage, and security settings are defined and provisioned through the use of declarative or imperative code. This code is written in a human-readable language and can be easily shared, reviewed, and modified by development and operations teams. This approach enables organizations to apply proven software engineering practices, including version control, automated testing, and continuous integration, to their infrastructure provisioning processes.

Infrastructure As Code (IaC) Anti-Patterns

Infrastructure as Code (IaC) Anti-Patterns refer to common mistakes or faulty practices in implementing Infrastructure as Code in the context of DevOps. Infrastructure as Code is the practice of managing and provisioning infrastructure resources through machine-readable definition files, treating infrastructure configuration in the same way as application code. Anti-patterns in IaC can result in inefficiencies, flaws, or vulnerabilities in the infrastructure provisioning process, leading to issues such as inconsistent environments, slow deployment times, or high maintenance costs. It is important to identify and avoid these anti-patterns to ensure effective and efficient infrastructure management.

Infrastructure As Code (IaC) Automation

Infrastructure as Code (IaC) automation is a key concept in the DevOps methodology, which aims to bring together software development and IT operations to enable more efficient and reliable software delivery. In simple terms, IaC automation refers to the practice of managing and provisioning infrastructure resources using machine-readable, declarative code, rather than manual processes or traditional configuration methods. With IaC automation, infrastructure resources such as servers, networks, and storage are treated as code, allowing for consistent and repeatable provisioning and configuration. This code, often written using languages like YAML or JSON, is stored in version control systems and can be easily shared and collaborated upon by development and operations teams. By adopting IaC automation, organizations can benefit from several advantages. Firstly, it enables faster and more consistent infrastructure provisioning, eliminating the need for manual and error-prone configurations. This not only speeds up the software delivery process but also reduces the risk of misconfigurations, improving overall system stability and reliability. Secondly, IaC automation promotes the concept of infrastructure as a versioned and auditable artifact. By storing infrastructure code in version control, organizations can track and manage changes over time, facilitating better collaboration, and ensuring that deployments can be easily rolled back or replicated. This version control aspect also helps in enforcing compliance and security requirements, as infrastructure changes can be tracked and audited. Another advantage of IaC automation is the ability to treat infrastructure as disposable. With automation, infrastructure can be easily created and destroyed as needed, enabling a more agile and scalable approach. This aligns with the principles of cloud computing and allows organizations to dynamically adapt to changing business needs. In conclusion, IaC automation is a fundamental practice in the DevOps methodology that enables organizations to manage and provision infrastructure resources using code. By adopting IaC automation, organizations can achieve faster and more consistent provisioning, improved system stability and reliability, better collaboration and auditability, and increased agility and scalability.

Infrastructure As Code (IaC) Benefits

Infrastructure as Code (IaC) refers to the practice of managing and provisioning infrastructure resources using machine-readable scripts or configuration files. In the context of DevOps, IaC offers several benefits that contribute to the agility, scalability, and efficiency of software development and deployment processes. One of the key advantages of IaC is its ability to automate infrastructure provisioning, configuration, and management. By defining infrastructure requirements in code, DevOps teams can version control and automate the entire infrastructure lifecycle. This eliminates manual, error-prone processes and ensures consistent and reproducible deployments, reducing the risk of configuration drift and minimizing human error. IaC also promotes collaboration and transparency among development, operations, and security teams. With infrastructure defined as code, all stakeholders can contribute to the infrastructure's design, deployment, and maintenance. This collaborative approach ensures that infrastructure decisions are based on collective knowledge and expertise, leading to better designs and faster feedback loops. Another benefit of IaC is its support for infrastructure immutability. Through the use of declarative code, IaC enables the creation of disposable infrastructure, where changes are made by replacing existing resources rather than modifying them. This approach increases security and reduces the risk of configuration inconsistencies or conflicts, as infrastructure can be easily recreated from scratch whenever needed. IaC also helps in achieving infrastructure consistency across different environments. By defining infrastructure as code, DevOps teams can use the same scripts or configuration files to provision and configure infrastructure resources in development, testing, staging, and production environments. This reduces the likelihood of environment-specific issues and ensures that the infrastructure running in production closely matches the one used during development and testing. Lastly, IaC enables greater scalability and agility in software development and deployment. With automation and version control, teams can quickly spin up or tear down infrastructure resources as required by their applications. This allows for fast iteration and experimentation, accelerating the delivery of new features or improvements and enabling teams to react promptly to changing business requirements or user demands.

Infrastructure As Code (IaC) Best Practices Guides

Infrastructure as Code (IaC) is a set of practices that enables organizations to define and manage their infrastructure as software code. In the context of DevOps, IaC involves automating the provisioning, configuration, and management of infrastructure resources using code. In traditional infrastructure management approaches, infrastructure changes were made manually by system administrators. This process was time-consuming, error-prone, and lacked repeatability and scalability. With IaC, organizations can treat their infrastructure as a software-defined resource and apply software engineering principles to it. IaC best practices encompass several key principles. Firstly, infrastructure code should be version controlled using a code repository such as Git. This allows for collaboration, change tracking, and the ability to roll back changes if necessary. Additionally, code reviews and automated testing should be employed to ensure the quality and reliability of the infrastructure code. Another important best practice is to use declarative configuration languages, such as YAML or JSON, to describe the desired state of the infrastructure. Declarative languages enable easy reproducibility and idempotent infrastructure changes, meaning that the same code can be run repeatedly to achieve the desired state without causing conflicts or unexpected outcomes. Modularity and abstraction are also important principles in IaC. Infrastructure code should be organized into reusable modules that can be easily shared and combined to build complex infrastructure configurations. By abstracting infrastructure components into modules, code can be more maintainable and changes can be made in a more granular and targeted manner. Automated deployment pipelines are a crucial component of IaC. Continuous Integration and Continuous Deployment (CI/CD) pipelines enable frequent and reliable deployment of infrastructure changes. Automated tests, including infrastructure validation and integration tests, should be included in the pipeline to ensure the stability and correctness of the deployed infrastructure. IaC best practices also emphasize the use of configuration management tools such as Ansible, Puppet, or Chef. These tools enable the automated configuration and management of infrastructure resources, ensuring consistency and reducing manual effort. Overall, IaC best practices facilitate the adoption of DevOps principles by bringing the benefits of software engineering to infrastructure management. By treating infrastructure as code, organizations can achieve greater scalability, repeatability, and reliability in their infrastructure provisioning and management processes.

Infrastructure As Code (IaC) Best Practices

Infrastructure as Code (IaC) is a core practice in DevOps, which refers to the management of infrastructure resources through machine-readable configuration files or scripts. It automates the provisioning, configuration, and deployment of infrastructure components, such as virtual machines, networks, storage, and services. IaC treats infrastructure resources, including servers, databases, load balancers, and networking, as programmable objects. Instead of manually configuring and managing these resources, IaC allows teams to define and manage infrastructure using code, typically utilizing a declarative language.

Infrastructure As Code (IaC) Case Studies

Infrastructure as Code (IaC) is an approach used in DevOps to manage and automate the provisioning and configuration of infrastructure resources. It involves defining infrastructure resources, such as servers, networks, and storage, as code in a declarative language. This code is then used to create and configure the infrastructure, ensuring consistency and repeatability across different environments. IaC allows organizations to treat infrastructure as software, enabling developers and operations teams to collaborate more effectively and streamline the deployment process. By using code to provision and configure infrastructure, organizations can automate the entire lifecycle of infrastructure resources, from creation to deployment and scaling.

Infrastructure As Code (IaC) Challenges

Infrastructure as Code (IaC) is a core concept in the field of DevOps and refers to the practice of managing and provisioning infrastructure resources using machine-readable configuration files or scripts, rather than manual intervention or traditional methods. It involves treating infrastructure components, such as servers, networks, and storage, as code that can be version-controlled, tested, and deployed using the same principles and practices applied to software development. IaC brings several benefits to DevOps teams by enabling automation, consistency, and scalability. However, it also presents various challenges that organizations need to address in order to effectively implement and maintain their infrastructure. One of the major challenges of IaC is the complexity of defining infrastructure configurations in a way that is easily understandable and maintainable. Writing code that represents the desired state of the infrastructure requires a deep understanding of the underlying technologies and platforms. Additionally, the code needs to be robust and flexible enough to handle different deployment scenarios and adapt to changes in the environment. Another challenge is ensuring the reliability and stability of the infrastructure deployment process. As IaC involves automating the provisioning of resources, any errors or misconfigurations in the code can have far-reaching consequences, impacting the availability and performance of the infrastructure. Therefore, thorough testing and validation of IaC code is crucial to minimize the risk of failures and ensure smooth deployments. Managing infrastructure as code also requires careful consideration of security and compliance concerns. Configuration files and scripts can contain sensitive information, such as access credentials or network configurations, which need to be protected and properly managed. Organizations must implement secure practices for storing and handling infrastructure code, as well as establish mechanisms to monitor and enforce compliance with security policies. In conclusion, while Infrastructure as Code brings numerous advantages to DevOps teams, such as automation and scalability, it also introduces specific challenges that organizations need to overcome. Addressing these challenges requires expertise in writing and maintaining infrastructure code, thorough testing and validation processes, and robust security and compliance mechanisms.

Infrastructure As Code (IaC) Code Reviews Best Practices

Infrastructure as Code (IaC) is a key concept in the DevOps methodology, which aims to automate and streamline the deployment and management of infrastructure resources. It is the practice of defining and deploying IT infrastructure resources, such as virtual machines, networks, storage, and security settings, using code. IaC code reviews are an essential part of the DevOps process, ensuring that the infrastructure code adheres to best practices, is maintainable, and meets the required standards. These code reviews involve examining the code written to define the desired infrastructure state, identifying any issues or improvements, and providing feedback to the developers.

Infrastructure As Code (IaC) Code Reviews

Infrastructure as Code (IaC) code reviews are a crucial practice in the DevOps context, aimed at ensuring the quality and reliability of the infrastructure deployment scripts. IaC refers to the approach of managing and provisioning infrastructure resources using code, typically defined in declarative or imperative scripting languages. Code reviews in the context of IaC involve a systematic assessment of the infrastructure codebase by peers or experienced team members. The primary goal of these reviews is to identify potential issues, improve the overall code quality, and ensure that the infrastructure scripts align with established best practices.

Infrastructure As Code (IaC) Collaboration

Infrastructure as Code (IaC) Collaboration is a key aspect of DevOps that involves the use of code to manage and automate infrastructure provisioning and configuration. It is a practice that enables teams to work together on infrastructure-related tasks by treating infrastructure resources as code. In IaC Collaboration, infrastructure is defined and managed using code, typically written in a high-level programming language. This code is version-controlled and stored in a repository, allowing multiple team members to collaborate on it simultaneously. By using IaC Collaboration, teams can ensure consistency, traceability, and reproducibility of infrastructure configurations.

Infrastructure As Code (IaC) Compliance

Infrastructure as Code (IaC) Compliance refers to the practice of ensuring that the infrastructure deployed through automated provisioning tools or code is aligned with the predefined rules, regulations, and security standards set by the organization. It is a critical aspect of DevOps that focuses on managing and maintaining infrastructure configurations in a consistent, controlled, and auditable manner. In the context of DevOps, IaC Compliance emphasizes treating infrastructure as software code and applying the same rigorous practices of version control, testing, and automation to infrastructure deployments. By codifying infrastructure configurations, organizations can ensure that infrastructure provisioning is repeatable, consistent, and less error-prone. It enables organizations to achieve greater efficiency, scalability, and reliability in their infrastructure management.

Infrastructure As Code (IaC) Culture Promotion

Infrastructure as Code (IaC) culture promotion is an essential aspect of implementing DevOps practices within an organization. It refers to the promotion and adoption of a mindset and set of practices that treat infrastructure provisioning, management, and deployment as code. In the context of DevOps, IaC culture promotion involves shifting away from manual, error-prone, and time-consuming infrastructure management processes to a more automated, consistent, and scalable approach. It is about leveraging the principles of software development to manage infrastructure resources efficiently and effectively.

Infrastructure As Code (IaC) Culture

Infrastructure as Code (IaC) Culture is a fundamental principle in the context of DevOps that emphasizes the use of code to automate the provisioning, configuration, and management of infrastructure resources. It revolves around the idea of treating infrastructure and its configuration as software, enabling organizations to apply the same disciplined practices and methodologies used in software development to their infrastructure management processes. In an IaC Culture, infrastructure is defined and managed using high-level programming languages or configuration files that are version-controlled and can be executed programmatically. This approach brings numerous advantages, such as increased efficiency, consistency, scalability, and traceability, while reducing manual error-prone tasks and the risk of configuration drift. With IaC, engineers can define their infrastructure needs declaratively, specifying the desired state rather than the step-by-step process to achieve it. This allows for infrastructure to be treated as a code artifact, enabling reproducibility and fostering collaboration. The infrastructure code can be versioned, tested, and even be part of the continuous integration and delivery pipeline, providing agility and speed to infrastructure changes. Infrastructure as Code also promotes the principles of immutability, where infrastructure resources are treated as disposable and are replaced instead of being modified, and idempotency, ensuring that infrastructure can be repeatably deployed and configured without causing unintended side effects. Furthermore, an IaC Culture encourages the use of infrastructure configuration templates or modules that can be reused across different environments or projects. This enables teams to standardize and automate their infrastructure provisioning processes, reducing time and effort when setting up new environments or replicating existing ones. In conclusion, Infrastructure as Code (IaC) Culture is a DevOps principle that advocates for the use of code to automate the management of infrastructure resources. By treating infrastructure as software, organizations can achieve greater efficiency, consistency, scalability, and collaboration in their infrastructure management processes.

Infrastructure As Code (IaC) Deployment

Infrastructure as Code (IaC) is a fundamental principle of DevOps that involves using code to automate the deployment, provisioning, and management of infrastructure resources in a repeatable, reliable, and scalable manner. In the context of DevOps, IaC brings together the practices of software development and infrastructure management. It allows teams to define and configure infrastructure resources using code, treating infrastructure as if it were software. This approach offers several benefits, including improved efficiency, increased agility, and reduced risk of errors or inconsistencies. The deployment of infrastructure resources typically involves various steps such as setting up servers, configuring networking, installing software, and managing security. In a traditional setup, these tasks are often performed manually, which can be time-consuming, error-prone, and difficult to reproduce consistently. IaC addresses these challenges by abstracting the infrastructure components into code and automating their deployment and configuration. With IaC, infrastructure configurations are expressed in a high-level, human-readable language, such as YAML or JSON. These configuration files describe the desired state of the infrastructure, specifying the resources and their properties. Infrastructure platforms, such as AWS CloudFormation or Terraform, interpret these configuration files and automatically provision the required resources accordingly. By treating infrastructure as code, organizations can benefit from the same principles that have revolutionized software development. They can version control their infrastructure configurations, enabling better collaboration and traceability. They can leverage Continuous Integration and Continuous Delivery (CI/CD) pipelines to automate and expedite the deployment process. They can also enforce consistency and standardization across different environments, allowing for easier testing, staging, and production deployments. IaC promotes the concept of "immutable infrastructure," where changes to infrastructure are achieved by creating new instances rather

110

than modifying existing ones. This approach ensures a predictable and reliable deployment process and enables quick rollbacks in case of issues. It also promotes infrastructure scalability, as new instances can be quickly provisioned or retired as needed, based on code-driven configuration. In conclusion, Infrastructure as Code (IaC) is a key practice in DevOps that involves using code to deploy, provision, and manage infrastructure resources. It enables automation, repeatability, scalability, and standardization, bringing the benefits of software development to infrastructure management.

Infrastructure As Code (IaC) Documentation

Infrastructure as Code (IaC) is a fundamental concept in the field of DevOps that refers to the process of managing and provisioning infrastructure resources using machine-readable definition files. It involves treating infrastructure configurations, deployments, and updates as code, enabling automation, repeatability, and collaboration throughout the software development lifecycle. With IaC, infrastructure components such as servers, networks, and databases are defined and controlled through code, typically using a declarative language or configuration management tool. This allows infrastructure systems to be easily versioned, automated, and tested, ensuring consistent and reliable deployments. By representing infrastructure as code, teams can efficiently manage complex infrastructures, achieve scalability, and rapidly respond to changing business requirements.

Infrastructure As Code (IaC) Frameworks

Infrastructure as Code (IaC) frameworks refer to the set of tools, practices, and processes used in the context of DevOps to automate the management and provisioning of infrastructure resources through code. This approach provides teams with the ability to define, configure, and manage infrastructure resources using code files, such as YAML or JSON, which can be version controlled, shared, and automated. The key principles behind IaC frameworks are to eliminate manual processes, increase efficiency, and ensure consistency in infrastructure management. By treating infrastructure as code, organizations can apply the same practices and discipline they use for their application code to the management of infrastructure resources. These frameworks typically provide a way to define infrastructure resources, such as virtual machines, storage systems, networks, and security rules, using a declarative or imperative language. Declarative languages, like YAML or JSON, allow users to describe the desired state of the infrastructure and let the framework handle the provisioning and configuration. On the other hand, imperative languages, like Python or PowerShell, provide a more procedural approach, allowing users to specify the exact steps needed to achieve the desired infrastructure state. One of the key benefits of using IaC frameworks is the ability to easily reproduce and version infrastructure. Instead of manually configuring each component, infrastructure can be defined in code files, which can be stored in a version control system. This enables teams to track changes, collaborate, and roll back to a previous state if necessary. Furthermore, IaC frameworks promote collaboration and consistency. Infrastructure code can be shared among team members, ensuring everyone is working from the same version. This reduces the risk of configuration drift and inconsistencies between development, testing, and production environments. In conclusion, IaC frameworks are essential tools in the DevOps ecosystem that enable organizations to treat infrastructure as code. By automating the management and provisioning of infrastructure resources, teams can achieve greater efficiency, consistency, and collaboration in their deployments.

Infrastructure As Code (IaC) Governance Frameworks

Infrastructure as Code (IaC) Governance Frameworks in the context of DevOps refer to a set of established practices, processes, and guidelines that enable organizations to effectively manage and control the deployment and management of infrastructure through automation. These frameworks ensure that the infrastructure provisioning, configuration, and management are treated as code, enabling repeatability, consistency, scalability, and versioning. IaC Governance Frameworks are designed to address the challenges associated with managing infrastructure manually, as well as to mitigate the risks and complexities that arise from ad-hoc deployments and configurations. By applying these frameworks, organizations can enforce standardization, governance, and compliance across their infrastructure and application deployments.

111

Infrastructure As Code (IaC) Governance

Infrastructure as Code (IaC) Governance refers to the set of practices and processes implemented in the context of DevOps to establish control and ensure compliance throughout the lifecycle of infrastructure deployment and management using the principles of Infrastructure as Code. DevOps is an approach that combines development and operations teams to create a more efficient and reliable software delivery pipeline. Infrastructure as Code, on the other hand, is a practice in which infrastructure configuration and provisioning is managed through machine-readable definition files, instead of manual processes. IaC Governance aims to address the challenges associated with rapidly changing infrastructure and the risk of configuration drift, where changes made manually to infrastructure components can lead to inconsistencies and potential disruptions. By applying governance practices to IaC, organizations can ensure accountability, maintain regulatory compliance, enforce security policies, and achieve consistency in infrastructure deployment and management. The key components of IaC Governance include: 1. Policy Definition and Enforcement: Organizations establish a set of rules, policies, and guidelines that govern the deployment and management of infrastructure using IaC. These policies can cover security, compliance, cost optimization, and operational best practices. They are enforced through continuous integration and deployment pipelines, code reviews, and automated testing. 2. Version Control and Change Management: IaC code is treated as a valuable asset and managed in a version control system. Changes to infrastructure configuration are tracked, reviewed, and documented. This enables better collaboration, facilitates auditing, and provides the ability to rollback or revert changes when necessary. 3. Testing and Validation: IaC code undergoes testing and validation processes to ensure that it meets the quality requirements and adheres to the defined policies. This includes static analysis, linting, and automated testing of infrastructure deployment to catch errors, vulnerabilities, and misconfigurations during the development stage. 4. Infrastructure Compliance and Security: IaC Governance establishes controls and mechanisms to ensure that infrastructure deployments meet regulatory and security standards. This includes vulnerability scanning, security audits, access controls, encryption, and compliance checks. By implementing IaC Governance in the context of DevOps, organizations can improve the reliability, repeatability, and scalability of their infrastructure deployments. It fosters collaboration, reduces manual effort, and increases agility in adapting to changing business needs. Furthermore, it provides a holistic view of infrastructural changes, enhancing visibility and traceability for auditing and troubleshooting purposes.

Infrastructure As Code (IaC) Linting

Infrastructure as Code (IaC) Linting refers to the process of analyzing and validating infrastructure code to ensure its adherence to best practices, standards, and policies. It is an integral part of the DevOps culture and aims to improve the quality, reliability, and security of infrastructure deployments. In the context of DevOps, where teams strive for automation, repeatability, and scalability, IaC Linting plays a crucial role in maintaining the integrity of infrastructure code and preventing common errors and vulnerabilities. By utilizing linters, which are static analysis tools, developers can identify and rectify potential issues early in the development lifecycle, thereby minimizing the chances of costly failures or downtime in production.

Infrastructure As Code (IaC) Patterns

Infrastructure as Code (IaC) is an approach in the field of DevOps that allows for the management and provisioning of infrastructure resources through the use of machine-readable configuration files. It involves treating infrastructure as if it were software, enabling automated and repeatable processes for infrastructure management, deployment, and scaling. IaC Patterns refer to reusable solutions or design patterns that can be applied to infrastructure code to address common challenges and improve the efficiency, reliability, and maintainability of infrastructure management. These patterns are based on best practices and lessons learned from real-world scenarios, providing guidance on how to structure and organize infrastructure code in a scalable and manageable manner.

Infrastructure As Code (IaC) Principles

Infrastructure as Code (IaC) is a fundamental principle in the field of DevOps, where the process of managing and provisioning infrastructure resources is treated as code. In this context, code refers to a set of declarative configuration files that describe the desired state of the infrastructure. IaC brings the benefits of automation, agility, and consistency to infrastructure management. By defining infrastructure as code, organizations can adopt the same practices and tools used in software development to manage their infrastructure. This means that infrastructure components, such as servers, networks, and databases, can be versioned, managed, and deployed in a similar manner to software applications. There are several key principles that govern the practice of Infrastructure as Code: 1. Declarative Configuration: Infrastructure is defined using configuration files that describe the desired state of the infrastructure. These files specify what resources should be provisioned, their configuration settings, and any dependencies between them. The underlying infrastructure automation tools interpret these configuration files and ensure that the desired state is achieved. 2. Version Control: Infrastructure code is treated like any other code and should be version controlled. This enables teams to track changes, collaborate effectively, and roll back to previous versions if necessary. Version control provides visibility into the history and evolution of infrastructure configurations, making it easier to troubleshoot issues and maintain a reliable infrastructure. 3. Automation: Infrastructure provisioning and management tasks should be automated using tools and frameworks. Automation eliminates manual processes and reduces human error, ensuring consistent and repeatable outcomes. Automated workflows enable teams to provision infrastructure on-demand, scale resources up or down, and easily replicate environments across development, testing, and production stages. 4. Testing and Validation: Infrastructure code should undergo testing and validation to ensure correctness and reliability. By employing automated testing techniques, organizations can detect configuration errors, resource conflicts, and security vulnerabilities early in the development process. Testing infrastructure code helps mitigate risks and improves the overall quality of the infrastructure. In conclusion, Infrastructure as Code encompasses the practices and principles that enable organizations to manage and provision infrastructure resources through declarative configuration files. By treating infrastructure as code, DevOps teams can leverage automation, version control, and testing to optimize the management of infrastructure components and ensure consistency and reliability across the software delivery pipeline.

Infrastructure As Code (IaC) Refactoring Techniques

Infrastructure as Code (IaC) refers to the practice of managing and provisioning infrastructure resources using machine-readable configuration files instead of manual processes. In the context of DevOps, IaC plays a crucial role in automating the deployment and management of infrastructure, enabling organizations to adopt a more agile and scalable approach. IaC refactoring techniques focus on improving the quality, efficiency, and maintainability of infrastructure configuration code. Refactoring refers to the process of restructuring code without changing its external behavior, aiming to enhance readability, performance, and flexibility.

Infrastructure As Code (IaC) Refactoring

Infrastructure as Code (IaC) is a fundamental practice in the field of DevOps that involves managing and provisioning infrastructure resources programmatically using code, rather than manually configuring them. It is an approach that brings the principles of software development to infrastructure, enabling organizations to treat infrastructure as a versionable and maintainable asset. In the context of DevOps, IaC involves writing infrastructure configurations as code, usually in a declarative language or a domain-specific language (DSL). This code describes the desired state of infrastructure resources, including servers, networks, databases, and more. By defining infrastructure as code, teams can automate the provisioning, deployment, and management of their infrastructure, ensuring consistency, reliability, and scalability. Refactoring, in the context of IaC, refers to the iterative process of improving the design, structure, and efficiency of infrastructure code without changing its external behavior. It involves analyzing the existing code, identifying areas of improvement, and making changes to enhance readability, modularity, and performance. Refactoring helps eliminate technical debt, reduces complexity, and improves maintainability of infrastructure code. The goal of IaC refactoring is to create infrastructure code that is easier to understand, test, and modify. By following best practices, such as modularization, encapsulation, and separation of concerns, teams can create reusable and scalable infrastructure code. Refactoring also allows teams to align infrastructure code with coding standards and design principles, making it consistent with the rest of their codebase.

113

Furthermore, refactoring IaC also involves incorporating feedback loops and iterations. Continuous integration and continuous delivery (CI/CD) pipelines can automatically trigger code analysis, testing, and validation of infrastructure code. By integrating refactoring into their CI/CD process, teams can detect and fix issues in infrastructure code early in the development lifecycle, reducing the risk of deployment failures and improving overall reliability.

Infrastructure As Code (IaC) Repositories

Infrastructure as Code (IaC) Repositories refer to version-controlled repositories that contain all the configuration files, scripts, and other artifacts necessary to automatically provision and manage infrastructure resources in a consistent and repeatable manner. As a fundamental practice in DevOps, IaC enables developers and operations teams to define and manage infrastructure resources using code, rather than manually configuring them. IaC repositories serve as a single source of truth for the entire infrastructure lifecycle, allowing teams to collaborate, track changes, and automate the deployment and management of infrastructure services.

Infrastructure As Code (IaC) Security Practices Enhancement

Infrastructure as Code (IaC) Security Practices Enhancement refers to the implementation of measures and processes aimed at strengthening the security of infrastructure provisioning and management through code in the context of DevOps. It involves adopting security practices and frameworks to safeguard the infrastructure-as-code artifacts, configuration management files, and deployment scripts used in the automation of infrastructure provisioning and management. DevOps is a software development approach that emphasizes collaboration, integration, and automation between development and operations teams. Infrastructure as Code is a key practice in DevOps that involves representing infrastructure elements, such as servers, networks, and storage, as code artifacts. These code artifacts are version-controlled, maintainable, and can be deployed and managed programmatically. The enhancement of security practices in Infrastructure as Code is crucial to protect infrastructure resources from vulnerabilities, unauthorized access, data breaches, and other security threats. It ensures that the entire lifecycle of infrastructure provisioning, configuration, and deployment is performed securely and efficiently. Some of the key practices for enhancing IaC security include: - Implementing code reviews and security testing to identify and address vulnerabilities in infrastructure code, such as hardcoded credentials or insecure configurations. - Utilizing secure coding practices, such as input validation and output encoding, to prevent common security vulnerabilities like SQL injections or cross-site scripting. - Adopting role-based access control (RBAC) and least privilege principles to restrict access to infrastructure code and sensitive resources, ensuring that only authorized personnel can make changes. - Regularly updating and patching infrastructure components and dependencies to address any known security vulnerabilities. - Implementing security monitoring and logging to detect and respond to potential security incidents in the infrastructure. By enhancing IaC security practices, organizations can significantly reduce the risk of security breaches in their infrastructure provisioning and management processes. It ensures that security considerations are integrated into the DevOps workflow and enables organizations to respond quickly to emerging threats.

Infrastructure As Code (IaC) Security Practices

Infrastructure as Code (IaC) Security Practices in the context of DevOps refers to the set of principles and techniques used to ensure the security and integrity of infrastructure configurations and deployments that are managed and controlled through code. IaC is an approach that enables the automatic provisioning and management of infrastructure resources through machine-readable definitions specified in code. This code is typically version-controlled and stored in a repository, allowing for collaboration, auditability, and reproducibility of infrastructure changes. By treating infrastructure as code, organizations can achieve greater speed, agility, and scalability in deploying and managing their systems. IaC security practices focus on mitigating risks and securing the entire lifecycle of infrastructure deployments. These practices encompass various security controls and measures throughout the development, testing, and deployment processes: 1. Secure coding practices: Following secure coding practices helps ensure that the infrastructure code itself is free from vulnerabilities and follows best practices. This includes proper input validation, output encoding, and protection against common security flaws such as injection attacks and cross-site scripting. 2. Code review and testing: Performing regular code reviews and automated testing of infrastructure code is crucial to identify and address any security vulnerabilities or weaknesses. This process helps validate the correctness, integrity, and security of the infrastructure code before it is deployed. 3. Secrets management: Effective management of secrets, such as passwords, API keys, and database credentials, is essential to prevent unauthorized access and potential data breaches. IaC security practices emphasize the use of secure storage and encryption mechanisms for storing and retrieving sensitive information. 4. Least privilege principle: Adhering to the principle of least privilege ensures that infrastructure resources and services are granted only the minimum permissions necessary to perform their intended functions. This reduces the attack surface and helps prevent unauthorized actions on the infrastructure. 5. Automated compliance checks: Regularly performing automated compliance checks against predefined security policies helps organizations maintain a secure and compliant infrastructure. These checks can detect and remediate any deviations from security standards and ensure ongoing adherence to security requirements. By incorporating these IaC security practices into the DevOps workflow, organizations can significantly improve the security posture of their infrastructure deployments. This not only helps identify and address potential security issues early on but also promotes a culture of security awareness and responsibility among development and operations teams.

Infrastructure As Code (IaC) Security

Infrastructure as Code (IaC) Security is the practice of implementing security measures throughout the lifecycle of infrastructure code in the context of DevOps. In a DevOps environment, where infrastructure is provisioned and managed through code, IaC security focuses on ensuring the confidentiality, integrity, and availability of the infrastructure code and the resulting infrastructure itself. At its core, IaC security aims to address potential vulnerabilities and mitigate risks associated with the adoption of IaC practices. It involves policies, processes, and tools that are integrated into the software development lifecycle (SDLC) to identify, prevent, and remediate security issues in infrastructure code. By implementing security measures from the initial stages of development, IaC security enables organizations to proactively address security concerns and enhance the overall security posture.

Infrastructure As Code (IaC) Templates Best Practices

Infrastructure as Code (IaC) templates are best practices in the context of DevOps that enable the management and provisioning of infrastructure resources through code. This approach promotes automation, scalability, and consistency by treating infrastructure as software-defined resources. With IaC templates, infrastructure resources such as virtual machines, networks, storage, and configurations are described and defined in code, rather than being manually configured. These templates, written in a declarative language, allow for the repeatable and version-controlled creation and modification of infrastructure resources.

Infrastructure As Code (IaC) Templates

Infrastructure as Code (IaC) templates refer to a key component of the DevOps approach that involves using machine-readable files to define and manage IT infrastructure. These files contain code that describes the desired state of the infrastructure, and automation tools then interpret and execute this code to provision and configure the necessary resources. IaC templates provide a structured and repeatable way to define infrastructure configurations, making it possible to version control and collaborate on infrastructure changes. This approach takes inspiration from software development practices, treating infrastructure as if it were code. By defining infrastructure configurations in code, teams can leverage familiar software development tools and practices, such as version control systems, continuous integration/continuous deployment pipelines, and automated testing frameworks.

Infrastructure As Code (IaC) Testing Frameworks

Infrastructure as Code (IaC) Testing Frameworks are tools and frameworks designed to support the automation and testing of infrastructure code in the context of DevOps practices. With the rise of cloud computing and the adoption of infrastructure automation tools like Ansible, Terraform, and CloudFormation, testing infrastructure code has become an essential part of the software delivery pipeline. IaC Testing Frameworks help ensure the correctness, reliability, and security of infrastructure code by providing a set of pre-built tests, test capabilities, and best practices. These frameworks enable teams to write tests for infrastructure code, execute them automatically, and obtain detailed reports and feedback on the test results. By including IaC testing in the development and deployment process, organizations can catch and address issues earlier in the development lifecycle, reducing the risk of misconfigurations, downtime, and security vulnerabilities in production environments. Some key features of IaC Testing Frameworks include: - Test Definition: These frameworks provide a way to define tests in a declarative manner. Teams can write tests using a domain-specific language or a configuration file, specifying the desired state of the infrastructure and the corresponding assertions to validate its correctness. - Test Execution: IaC Testing Frameworks enable the automated execution of tests against infrastructure code. When integrated into the continuous integration/continuous deployment (CI/CD) pipeline, tests can be triggered automatically on each code change or deployment, ensuring that every change is thoroughly tested. - Test Orchestration: These frameworks facilitate the organization and execution of tests, allowing teams to group tests based on different criteria such as target environments, modules, or infrastructure components. They provide features like parallel execution, test distribution, and reporting to increase efficiency and provide detailed insights into the state of the infrastructure. - Integration with CI/CD Tools: IaC Testing Frameworks seamlessly integrate with popular CI/CD tools like Jenkins, GitLab CI, and Azure DevOps, enabling teams to incorporate infrastructure tests into their existing automation and deployment workflows. In summary, IaC Testing Frameworks play a crucial role in ensuring the quality and reliability of infrastructure code in DevOps environments. By automating the testing process, these frameworks help teams catch issues early, enforce best practices, and avoid costly mistakes in production environments.

Infrastructure As Code (IaC) Testing

Infrastructure as Code (IaC) Testing is a fundamental component of the DevOps approach that involves the verification and validation of infrastructure code to ensure its quality, reliability, and compliance with desired configuration and functionality requirements. Essentially, IaC testing focuses on evaluating the code that defines and manages infrastructure, such as servers, networks, and storage, as code. In the context of DevOps, IaC testing plays a crucial role in enabling organizations to treat infrastructure code with the same level of rigor and discipline as application code. By adopting testing practices for infrastructure code, teams can gain increased confidence in their deployments and enforce consistency and predictability throughout the infrastructure lifecycle.

Infrastructure As Code (IaC) Tools

Infrastructure as Code (IaC) tools are technology solutions used in the practice of DevOps to automate the process of managing and provisioning infrastructure resources. IaC refers to the approach of defining and deploying infrastructure resources, such as virtual machines, networks, and storage, through machine-readable configuration files, rather than manually configuring them through traditional methods. These tools enable organizations to treat infrastructure as code, allowing for the application of software development practices, such as version control, automated testing, and continuous integration, to infrastructure provisioning and management. By treating infrastructure as code, organizations can increase their agility, flexibility, and scalability, while reducing the risk and complexity associated with manual changes to infrastructure resources.

Infrastructure As Code (IaC) Validation

Infrastructure as Code (IaC) validation is a vital practice in the context of DevOps that involves verifying and ensuring the correctness, consistency, and reliability of the infrastructure code used for automating the deployment and management of infrastructure. In simpler terms, it refers to the process of validating the code used to define and configure the infrastructure resources, such as servers, networks, and storage, as part of the software development lifecycle. With the rise of cloud computing and the increasing adoption of DevOps principles, IaC has emerged as a fundamental approach to provisioning and managing infrastructure. It shifts the traditional manual and error-prone practices towards treating infrastructure configurations as code, allowing them to be versioned, tested, and deployed alongside application code. IaC validation plays a crucial role in this paradigm by guaranteeing that the infrastructure code is accurate, consistent, and aligns with the desired state of the infrastructure. During IaC validation, various techniques and tools are employed to validate the infrastructure code against a set of predefined rules or best practices. These rules can be defined based on industry standards, compliance requirements, or internal organizational policies. By validating the code, potential issues, such as security vulnerabilities, performance bottlenecks, or architectural flaws, can be identified early in the development process, ultimately reducing the risk of failures and downtime in production environments. In addition to rule-based validation, IaC validation can also involve testing the infrastructure code using continuous integration and testing frameworks. This ensures that changes to the infrastructure code are thoroughly tested before being merged into the main codebase, preventing any regressions or unintended consequences. Automated testing of the infrastructure code helps foster a culture of quality and reliability, preventing human errors and enabling faster and more frequent deployments. Overall, IaC validation is an essential component of the DevOps mindset and practices, promoting reliability, scalability, and agility in infrastructure management. It enables teams to treat infrastructure configurations as code, providing the ability to version, reuse, and automate the provisioning and management of infrastructure resources. By validating the infrastructure code, organizations can ensure that their infrastructure deployments are repeatable, consistent, and free from misconfigurations, thereby enhancing the overall resilience and stability of their systems.

Infrastructure As Code (IaC) Versioning

Infrastructure as Code (IaC) Versioning is a key practice in the context of DevOps that enables teams to manage and control the configuration and deployment of infrastructure resources in an automated and consistent manner. It involves using version control systems to track and manage changes to infrastructure code, allowing for collaborative development, testing, and deployment of infrastructure resources. IaC Versioning provides several benefits to DevOps teams. Firstly, it allows teams to treat infrastructure code just like any other software code, applying the same principles and practices for version control, including branching, merging, and rollbacks. This improves traceability and accountability, as changes can be attributed to specific individuals or teams, and issues can be tracked and resolved efficiently. Furthermore, IaC Versioning promotes experimentation and innovation, as it enables teams to easily iterate and test different infrastructure configurations. With version control, it becomes possible to spin up multiple environments, such as development, staging, and production, with different infrastructure code versions, facilitating parallel development and testing. This reduces the risk of introducing breaking changes to production environments, as changes can be thoroughly tested and validated beforehand. IaC Versioning also enhances collaboration among team members, as it provides a centralized repository for infrastructure code, making it easier to share, review, and contribute to the codebase. By leveraging pull requests and code review processes, teams can ensure that changes are thoroughly reviewed and approved before being merged into the main codebase. This improves code quality and helps catch potential issues or misconfigurations before they impact the infrastructure. In summary, Infrastructure as Code (IaC) Versioning is a fundamental practice in DevOps that allows teams to manage and control the configuration and deployment of infrastructure resources using version control systems. It brings benefits such as traceability, accountability, experimentation, innovation, and collaboration, ultimately leading to more efficient and reliable infrastructure management.

Infrastructure As Code (IaC)

Infrastructure as Code (IaC) is a practice in the field of DevOps that involves managing and provisioning computer infrastructure through machine-readable definition files rather than manual configuration. It brings together principles from software development and infrastructure management to streamline the deployment and management of infrastructure resources. In the traditional approach, infrastructure setup and configuration were often manually performed by system administrators, leading to inconsistencies, human errors, and slower processes. IaC addresses these challenges by treating infrastructure as code, allowing it to be version-controlled, tested, and deployed in a similar way to software applications.

Infrastructure As Data

Infrastructure as Data in the context of DevOps refers to the practice of representing the entire infrastructure of an application or system as programmable data. This approach allows for the automation and management of infrastructure through the use of code, providing increased scalability, agility, and reliability. Traditionally, infrastructure management involved manual processes and configurations that were prone to errors and inconsistencies. With the rise of DevOps, Infrastructure as Data has emerged as a fundamental principle to achieve the desired levels of efficiency and control in the infrastructure management process.

Infrastructure As A Service (IaaS) Security

Infrastructure as a Service (IaaS) security in the context of DevOps refers to the practices and measures taken to protect the underlying infrastructure that supports the deployment and operation of applications in a cloud environment. It involves implementing security controls, protocols, and procedures to safeguard the infrastructure from unauthorized access, data breaches, and other potential security threats. DevOps, which combines development and operations, aims to streamline software development and deployment through automation and collaboration. In this context, IaaS security is crucial to ensure the protection and integrity of the infrastructure components that support the DevOps processes.

Innovation

In the context of DevOps, innovation refers to the process of implementing new and creative ideas, technologies, or approaches to improve the efficiency, effectiveness, and agility of software development and operations processes. Innovation in DevOps is driven by the desire to continuously enhance collaboration, communication, and integration between development and operations teams. It involves the exploration and adoption of emerging tools, methodologies, and techniques that enable faster delivery of high-quality software products, while also ensuring stability, scalability, and security.

Istio

Istio is an open-source service mesh platform that provides a set of integrated features for running, managing, and securing microservices-based applications. It is designed to enhance the capabilities of the underlying microservices architecture by offering advanced traffic management, observability, and security functionalities. In the context of DevOps, Istio serves as a critical component for organizations aiming to build and maintain highly resilient and scalable applications. It simplifies the complexity of managing microservices by providing a unified control plane for traffic routing, load balancing, and service discovery. With Istio, DevOps teams can implement sophisticated traffic management techniques such as intelligent routing based on service-level objectives and canary deployments. These features enable gradual rollouts of new versions, A/B testing, and automatic fallbacks in case of failures, all while minimizing the impact on end users. Furthermore, Istio enhances the observability of microservices applications by collecting telemetry data on service behavior, allowing DevOps teams to gain insights into various metrics such as latency, error rates, and request volumes. It provides a centralized dashboard for monitoring and troubleshooting, enabling quick identification and resolution of issues. From a security perspective, Istio offers powerful features for enforcing authentication, authorization, and encryption within the service mesh. It provides mutual TLS (Transport Layer Security) between services to ensure secure communication. It also facilitates the implementation of fine-grained access control policies, allowing DevOps teams to easily define and enforce restrictions on service-to-service communication. In summary, Istio serves as a crucial tool in the DevOps toolbox, enabling efficient management and operation of microservices-based applications. It empowers organizations to improve the resilience, scalability, and security of their applications, ultimately leading to better user experiences and faster delivery of software.

JFrog Xray

JFrog Xray is a comprehensive vulnerability and compliance scanning tool that integrates seamlessly into the DevOps pipeline. It provides continuous scanning of all artifacts and components across the extensive DevOps ecosystem, including container images, libraries, and even code dependencies. By analyzing the entire software stack, JFrog Xray helps organizations identify potential security vulnerabilities, license violations, and other compliance issues. With its powerful scanning capabilities, JFrog Xray detects known security vulnerabilities by leveraging comprehensive vulnerability databases such as the National Vulnerability Database (NVD), as well as proprietary databases. It also identifies license violations by comparing the components used in the software against a comprehensive license database. This ensures that organizations are aware of any potential legal risks associated with the licenses of their software components.

Jenkins Pipeline

Jenkins Pipeline is a declarative method for defining continuous integration and delivery (CI/CD) pipelines in a DevOps environment. As a code-based approach, it allows teams to create, visualize, and manage their entire software delivery process as code. With Jenkins Pipeline, developers can define the different stages, tasks, and steps involved in the software delivery process using a domain-specific language (DSL). This DSL provides a set of building blocks, called "steps," that can be used to perform various actions such as building code, running tests, deploying applications, and more. By defining pipelines as code, Jenkins Pipeline enables teams to version control and treat their delivery process with the same rigor as their application code. This brings benefits such as reproducibility, traceability, and the ability to review and collaborate on the pipeline definition itself. Jenkins Pipeline allows for the creation of both linear and parallel pipelines, giving teams the flexibility to design their delivery process according to their requirements. It supports conditional execution, allowing certain stages or steps to be skipped based on specific conditions. It also offers advanced features like parallelization, allowing multiple tasks to be executed concurrently to minimize overall pipeline execution time. Another key feature of Jenkins Pipeline is its integration with other DevOps tools and technologies. Through plugins and integrations, Jenkins Pipeline can interact with source code repositories, issue tracking systems, artifact repositories, testing frameworks, and deployment tools. This makes it a central hub for managing the entire delivery lifecycle. In conclusion, Jenkins Pipeline provides a powerful and flexible way to define, visualize, and manage CI/CD pipelines in a DevOps environment. By treating the delivery process as code, teams can automate and standardize their software delivery, increasing efficiency, reliability, and collaboration among team members.

Jenkins X

Jenkins X is a cloud-native, open-source automation tool that facilitates continuous integration and continuous deployment (CI/CD) within the DevOps framework. It is designed to streamline the software development life cycle (SDLC) by automating the processes involved in building, testing, and deploying applications. As a CI/CD tool, Jenkins X focuses on providing efficient and reliable automation for software development teams. It enables developers to integrate their code changes into a shared repository, where automated tests and builds are triggered. This allows for early detection of bugs, improved code quality, and faster application delivery.

Jira

Jira is a comprehensive project management tool widely used in the field of DevOps. It serves as a centralized platform for planning, tracking, and releasing software projects, allowing teams to effectively collaborate and manage their work. With Jira, DevOps teams can create and organize tasks, known as issues, to represent work items such as features, bugs, or improvements. These issues can be assigned, tracked, and prioritized, providing a clear view of the project's progress and status. Jira's flexible customization options allow teams to adapt the tool to their specific workflows and processes.

KPI Alignment

KPI Alignment, in the context of DevOps, refers to the process of establishing and aligning key performance indicators (KPIs) with the goals and objectives of a DevOps initiative. This involves defining and measuring the metrics that are most relevant to the success of the DevOps strategy, and ensuring that they are in line with the overall business objectives. The first step in KPI Alignment is to clearly define the goals and objectives of the DevOps initiative. This includes identifying the specific outcomes that are expected to be achieved through the implementation of DevOps practices, such as improved software delivery speed, increased reliability, and enhanced customer satisfaction. Once the goals and objectives are established, the next step is to identify the KPIs that will be used to measure progress towards these objectives. These KPIs should be relevant, measurable, and aligned with the overall business strategy. For example, if the goal is to reduce software deployment time, a relevant KPI could be the average time it takes to deploy a new feature or update. After identifying the KPIs, it is important to establish a baseline or benchmark for each metric. This baseline will serve as a point of reference for measuring future performance and improvement. It is also important to regularly track and analyze the metrics to monitor progress and identify areas for improvement. One of the key benefits of KPI Alignment in DevOps is that it provides a clear and objective way to measure the success of the initiative. By defining and tracking relevant KPIs, organizations can assess the impact of their DevOps practices and identify opportunities for optimization and improvement. In conclusion, KPI Alignment in DevOps involves defining and aligning key performance indicators with the goals and objectives of a DevOps initiative. It is an essential step in measuring the success of the initiative and identifying areas for improvement. By regularly tracking and analyzing relevant metrics, organizations can optimize their DevOps practices and drive continuous improvement in software delivery and customer satisfaction.

Kanban

Kanban is a visual project management method that focuses on continuous delivery and optimization in the context of DevOps. It is designed to improve workflow efficiency and collaboration by enabling teams to visualize their work, limit work in progress (WIP), and optimize the flow of work through the system. In DevOps, Kanban provides a framework for managing software development and delivery by promoting transparency, efficiency, and flexibility. The method originated from the manufacturing sector and has been tailored for use in software development and IT operations.

Katalon Studio

Katalon Studio is an integrated development environment (IDE) designed specifically for implementing and automating testing activities in the context of DevOps. It provides a comprehensive set of tools and features to support the entire software testing process, from test case creation to execution, reporting, and analysis. Katalon Studio promotes collaboration and integration between development and operations teams by offering seamless integration with popular DevOps tools and platforms, such as Jenkins, Git, JIRA, and Docker. This enables organizations to adopt and embrace a continuous testing approach within their DevOps pipelines.

Keel

DevOps is a software development methodology that aims to bridge the communication and collaboration gap between development teams and operation teams in order to enhance the delivery of software applications. It focuses on automating the software development lifecycle, from planning and development to testing, deployment, and monitoring. Keel is a DevOps tool that facilitates the continuous deployment and release management of software applications. It enables teams to automate and streamline the process of releasing new features, updates, and bug fixes to production systems.

Key Performance Indicators (KPIs)

Key Performance Indicators (KPIs) in the context of DevOps refer to quantifiable measures used to evaluate the success of operational activities and the overall performance of the DevOps process. These indicators are crucial for assessing the efficiency, effectiveness, and quality of the software delivery pipeline, as well as the collaboration and alignment between development and operations teams. KPIs provide valuable insights into the performance of various components within the DevOps environment, enabling organizations to identify areas of improvement, optimize processes, and drive continuous improvement. These indicators are typically established based on specific objectives and goals, aligning with the organization's overall strategic objectives.

Knowledge Base

DevOps is a set of practices and cultural beliefs aimed at unifying software development (Dev) and IT operations (Ops) teams to enable faster and more reliable software delivery. It focuses on breaking down silos and fostering collaboration between development and operations, with the goal of creating a culture of shared responsibility and continuous improvement. At its core, DevOps aims to streamline the software development lifecycle by promoting automation, collaboration, and feedback loops. It emphasizes the use of infrastructure as code, allowing teams to provision and manage infrastructure resources programmatically. This ensures consistency and repeatability, reducing the risk of errors caused by manual configurations. DevOps also encourages the use of continuous integration and continuous delivery (CI/CD) practices. CI involves regularly integrating code changes into a shared repository, allowing for automated testing and early detection of issues. CD extends this by automating the release and deployment of software to production environments, enabling rapid and frequent delivery of new features and bug fixes. One of the key principles of DevOps is the concept of "shifting left" – moving tasks traditionally performed later in the development process to earlier stages. This includes promoting a shift in mindset towards taking proactive measures to prevent issues, rather than just reacting to them. By involving operations teams earlier in the development process, potential deployment and operational issues can be identified and addressed earlier, reducing the time and effort required for remediation. In addition to technical practices, DevOps also emphasizes a cultural shift towards collaboration and shared ownership. Development and operations teams work together closely, with a focus on communication and shared goals. This enables faster feedback cycles and more efficient resolution of issues, fostering a culture of learning and continuous improvement. In summary, DevOps is a set of practices and cultural beliefs that aim to enable faster and more reliable software delivery by unifying development and operations teams. By promoting automation, collaboration, and proactive measures, DevOps helps streamline the software development lifecycle and create a culture of shared responsibility and continuous improvement.

Knowledge Sharing

Knowledge sharing in the context of DevOps refers to the process of disseminating information, best practices, lessons learned, and expertise among team members within a DevOps environment. It involves creating a culture of collaboration, communication, and continuous learning within the organization. Effective knowledge sharing in DevOps is crucial for several reasons. First, it helps teams to work more efficiently by avoiding duplication of efforts and leveraging the expertise of others. DevOps practitioners can learn from their colleagues' successes and failures, which can inform their decision-making and enable them to make more informed choices. Additionally, it enables teams to adapt and stay updated with emerging trends, technologies, and industry standards in order to drive continuous improvement and innovation.

Kong

Kong is an open-source cloud-native API gateway that acts as an intermediary between clients and microservices. It enables organizations to manage, secure, and distribute APIs efficiently, promoting the principles and practices of DevOps. By helping to streamline the development and deployment process, Kong contributes to the seamless integration and continuous delivery of software applications. As a key component of the DevOps approach, Kong facilitates the collaboration and communication between development (Dev) and operations (Ops) teams by providing a centralized platform for managing APIs. It allows developers to create, publish, and update APIs swiftly without disrupting the underlying microservices. With Kong, operations teams can enforce security measures, such as authentication and authorization, and ensure high availability and reliability by implementing rate limiting, caching, and health checks. Kong supports various features that align with the DevOps principles, including automation, scalability, and flexibility. Through its comprehensive set of plugins, Kong enables developers to automate tasks and integrate with other tools like monitoring and analytics solutions. Additionally, Kong's horizontal scalability ensures that as the application's demands increase, the API gateway can handle the additional traffic efficiently. Its pluggable architecture allows organizations to customize and extend its functionality according to their specific requirements. By adopting Kong in a DevOps environment, organizations can enhance their software delivery processes. Kong promotes continuous integration and continuous deployment by enabling teams to iterate quickly on API design and implementation. It allows for seamless integration with existing DevOps tools, such as CI/CD pipelines and container orchestration platforms. With its robust performance, scalability, and extensibility, Kong provides a reliable foundation for teams to accelerate their software development lifecycle and deliver exceptional digital experiences to end-users.

Kubeflow

Kubeflow is an open-source machine learning (ML) platform that aims to simplify the deployment and management of ML workflows on Kubernetes, a popular container orchestration system widely used in the field of software development and DevOps. It provides a comprehensive set of tools and components specifically designed for ML tasks, allowing developers and data scientists to build, deploy, and scale ML models efficiently in a distributed environment. With Kubeflow, DevOps teams can leverage the power of Kubernetes to create reproducible ML pipelines that automate the entire ML workflow, from data preprocessing and model training to serving predictions and monitoring performance. It offers a unified interface and a set of optimized frameworks and libraries, such as TensorFlow, PyTorch, and Apache Spark, that enable developers to easily develop and experiment with ML models using their preferred programming languages and tools.

Kubernetes Operators

Kubernetes Operators are software extensions that automate the management and operation of applications on Kubernetes clusters. They were introduced by the CoreOS team, now part of Red Hat, to provide a way to package, deploy, and manage complex applications using Kubernetes primitives. Operators are designed to simplify the deployment and management of stateful applications, such as databases, message queues, and monitoring tools, on Kubernetes. They encapsulate the operational knowledge required to run these applications, enabling developers and operators to focus on higher-level tasks. An Operator embodies the domain-specific knowledge and best practices for a particular application or service. It leverages Kubernetes' declarative model to define how the application should behave and provides the necessary automation to ensure that the desired state is achieved and maintained. Operators extend Kubernetes' native API by introducing custom resources that represent the application or service being managed. These custom resources define the desired state of the application and any additional configuration or policies. The Operator then continuously monitors the cluster, reconciles the current state with the desired state, and takes actions to bring the application into the desired state. Operators typically include several key components: - Custom Resource Definition (CRD): Defines the custom resource that represents the application or service being managed. - Controller: Monitors the cluster for changes to the custom resource and performs reconciliation to ensure the desired state is achieved. - Operator Lifecycle Manager (OLM): Manages the installation, upgrade, and removal of Operators within a cluster. By leveraging Operators, development and operations teams can automate the management of their applications in a Kubernetes-native way. Operators provide a higher level of abstraction, simplifying complex tasks and reducing the risk of human error. They enable organizations to scale and operate their applications more efficiently, while staying aligned with the principles and practices of DevOps.

Latency Monitoring

Latency Monitoring, in the context of DevOps, refers to the practice of continuously monitoring and measuring the time it takes for data to travel from a source to its destination. It involves analyzing the delays or latencies in the network or infrastructure components, including hardware, software, and services. Latency, in simple terms, is the time delay that occurs during data transmission or communication. In the world of DevOps, where rapid software development and deployment are essential, latency monitoring plays a crucial role in ensuring optimal performance and identifying any bottlenecks or issues that may impact the user experience.

Latency Testing Strategies

Latency testing is a key practice in the field of DevOps that involves measuring the delay or response time between sending a request and receiving a response in a system. It focuses on assessing the performance of a software application or network infrastructure by determining the amount of time it takes for data to travel from one point to another. The main objective of latency testing is to identify and analyze any bottlenecks or delays in the system, which may impact its overall performance and user experience. By measuring the latency, DevOps teams can gain valuable insights into how different components of the system interact and contribute to the overall response time.

Latency Testing

Latency testing in the context of DevOps refers to the process of measuring the time delay or latency between two systems or components of a software application. It helps identify any potential performance bottlenecks and ensures that the system meets the required response time and throughput expectations. During latency testing, specialized tools and techniques are used to simulate real-world scenarios and measure the latency between different components of the software stack, such as servers, networks, databases, and external services. The objective is to identify areas where latency is unexpectedly high and optimize them for better performance.

LaunchControl

LaunchControl is a DevOps tool that enables the efficient management, deployment, and monitoring of software applications across various platforms and environments. It provides a centralized platform for automating and coordinating the deployment processes, ensuring seamless integration and delivery of software projects. LaunchControl allows DevOps teams to define and organize their deployment workflows efficiently. It facilitates the automation of tasks such as building, testing, packaging, and deploying software applications to different environments, including development, staging, and production. By streamlining the deployment processes, LaunchControl reduces the potential for human error and improves the overall reliability of software releases.

LaunchDarkly

LaunchDarkly is a feature management platform that enables software development teams to implement feature flags and manage feature rollouts effectively. In the context of DevOps, LaunchDarkly plays a crucial role in the continuous delivery and deployment process. By using LaunchDarkly, DevOps teams can easily toggle features on or off at any time, without the need for code deployments or configuration changes. This feature flagging capability allows teams to decouple feature releases from software deployments, resulting in a more flexible and controlled deployment process.

Lead Time

Lead time is a concept in the context of DevOps that refers to the amount of time it takes to complete a process, from the initial request to the final delivery. It measures the elapsed time between the identification of a requirement or a change and the successful deployment of the corresponding feature or functionality. In a DevOps environment, lead time is a critical metric as it directly impacts the speed and efficiency of software delivery. By reducing lead time, organizations can shorten the time it takes to deliver value to their customers, increase customer satisfaction, and maintain a competitive edge in the market.

Lean Portfolio Management

Lean Portfolio Management in the context of DevOps refers to the practice of applying lean principles and practices to manage and prioritize the portfolio of projects and initiatives within an organization that are aligned with DevOps practices. Traditional portfolio management approaches often rely on a waterfall approach where projects are defined and planned upfront, with limited flexibility to adapt to changing requirements and priorities. However, DevOps emphasizes an iterative and flexible approach to software development and delivery, requiring a different approach to portfolio management.

Lean

Lean is a methodology that focuses on the elimination of waste and the continuous improvement of processes. In the context of DevOps, it is applied to streamline software development and delivery by minimizing inefficiencies and maximizing value to the end-users. DevOps is a set of practices that emphasizes collaboration, communication, and integration between development and operations teams to enable the rapid and reliable delivery of software. By incorporating Lean principles, DevOps seeks to identify and eliminate waste, such as unnecessary manual tasks, delays, defects, and rework, in the software delivery process.

Learning Culture

Learning Culture in the context of DevOps refers to an environment where individuals and teams are encouraged to continuously acquire new knowledge, develop their skills, and share their learnings with others. It is a mindset that values learning as a key aspect of personal and professional growth. In a DevOps environment, a learning culture is vital for fostering collaboration, innovation, and continuous improvement. It promotes the idea that learning is not limited to a specific project or task but is a continuous process that should be embedded in every aspect of work. It encourages individuals to embrace challenges, experiment with new ideas, and learn from failures.

Learning From Failure

Learning from Failure in the context of DevOps refers to the practice of actively seeking and analyzing failures or mistakes that occur during the software development and operations processes, with the objective of identifying the root causes, understanding the underlying issues, and implementing improvements to prevent similar failures in the future. This approach recognizes that failures are inevitable in complex systems and can provide valuable insights for continuous improvement. By embracing failure as an opportunity for learning and growth, DevOps teams can foster a culture of resilience, innovation, and adaptability.

Least Privilege Access

Least Privilege Access refers to the principle of limiting user access rights to only those necessary to perform their specific tasks and responsibilities within a DevOps environment. This approach aims to minimize the potential damage that can be caused by unauthorized access or misuse of privileges. By implementing the least privilege access model, organizations can reduce the risk of data breaches, system vulnerabilities, and the potential for insider threats. DevOps teams can assign access rights based on the principle of least privilege, ensuring that individuals are granted only the permissions required to perform their duties effectively.

Legacy Modernization

Legacy modernization refers to the process of updating and transforming outdated software systems or applications into more efficient and adaptable ones, in the context of DevOps. It involves a comprehensive overhaul and reengineering of legacy systems, enabling them to be more compatible with modern technologies, improve performance, enhance scalability, and seamlessly integrate with cloud environments. Legacy systems are often characterized by their outdated programming languages, architectures, and infrastructures that make it challenging to meet the dynamic demands of the digital era. These systems, built on older technologies, may not be able to effectively handle the increased volumes of data, complicated workflows, and evolving user expectations. DevOps, on the other hand, is a software development approach that emphasizes collaboration, integration, and automation between development and operations teams with the goal of achieving continuous delivery and improvement. It focuses on streamlining and accelerating the software development lifecycle through practices such as continuous integration, continuous delivery, and infrastructure as code. When applying DevOps principles to legacy modernization, organizations aim to transform their outdated systems into more agile, scalable, and adaptable ones that seamlessly integrate with modern DevOps pipelines. This involves breaking down monolithic architectures into microservices-based architectures, containerizing applications for easier deployment and management, automating testing and deployment processes, and adopting cloud-native technologies. The modernization process often involves conducting a thorough analysis of the existing legacy system, identifying pain points and areas for improvement, and defining a clear roadmap for the transformation journey. It requires collaboration between development, operations, and business teams to ensure that the modernized system aligns with the organization's strategic goals and meets the requirements of different stakeholders. In conclusion, legacy modernization in the context of DevOps refers to the comprehensive process of updating and transforming outdated software systems into more agile, scalable, and efficient ones that seamlessly integrate with modern DevOps practices. It aims to bring the benefits of DevOps, such as continuous integration, delivery, and improvement, to legacy applications, enabling organizations to keep pace with the rapidly evolving technological landscape.

Legacy System Integration Challenges

Legacy system integration challenges refer to the obstacles and difficulties faced when incorporating or connecting legacy systems with newer technologies, methods, or platforms as part of the DevOps process. One of the main challenges in integrating legacy systems into a DevOps environment is the lack of compatibility between the old and new systems. Legacy systems are often built on outdated technologies, programming languages, or architectures that may not align with modern DevOps practices. This can make it difficult to seamlessly integrate these systems into a DevOps pipeline without causing disruptions or bottlenecks. Another challenge is the complexity of legacy systems. Over time, these systems tend to accumulate layers of customizations, integrations, and specific business logic, making them complex and hard to understand or modify. DevOps practices emphasize automation, traceability, and continuous delivery, but legacy systems may lack the necessary automation capabilities and documentation, making it challenging to streamline the integration process. One specific challenge is the integration of legacy systems with version control systems. While modern systems typically rely on Git or other distributed version control systems, legacy systems may use older, proprietary version control mechanisms or no version control at all. This can lead to difficulties in tracking changes, managing conflicts, or rolling back changes, impeding the benefits of version control and hindering the overall DevOps workflow. Security is another significant concern when integrating legacy systems. These systems might have vulnerabilities or weaknesses that were acceptable in the past but could pose risks in a DevOps context. Ensuring the security of the entire pipeline, from development to deployment, becomes crucial when integrating legacy systems, as any security breach could have severe consequences. Lastly, cultural and organizational challenges can arise when integrating legacy systems into a DevOps environment. Resistance to change, differing mindset or priorities between different teams, and incompatible processes or policies can hinder the smooth integration of legacy systems. It requires collaboration, communication, and alignment between various stakeholders, including developers, operations, QA, and business teams. In summary, legacy system integration challenges in the context of DevOps encompass compatibility issues, complexity, version control integration, security risks, as well as cultural and organizational obstacles. Addressing these challenges requires careful planning, automation, documentation, and collaboration to ensure the successful integration of legacy systems into the DevOps pipeline.

Legacy System Integration

Legacy system integration in the context of DevOps refers to the process of incorporating older, existing systems or applications into a modern continuous integration and delivery (CI/CD) pipeline. It involves connecting and automating the deployment, testing, and release processes of these legacy systems, enabling them to be integrated seamlessly with newer technologies and workflows. Legacy systems often pose challenges in a DevOps environment due to their outdated architecture, lack of documentation, and resistance to change. They may have been developed using different technologies, programming languages, and methodologies, making their integration with modern CI/CD pipelines complex and time-consuming. However, integrating legacy systems into the development and release processes is crucial to ensure a continuous delivery of value to end-users and to avoid disruptions caused by manual interventions or siloed processes.

Linkerd

Linkerd is a service mesh for cloud-native applications, designed to provide the infrastructure necessary for building, deploying, and managing microservices. It is an open-source project developed specifically to enhance the reliability, observability, and security of communication between different components of a distributed system. Within the context of DevOps, Linkerd plays a pivotal role in promoting collaborative and efficient development and operations practices. By providing a transparent layer of abstraction between services, it enables developers to focus on building and deploying individual microservices without concerning themselves with the intricacies of underlying network communication. At the same time, operations teams can gain comprehensive visibility into the flow of data and dependencies, facilitating troubleshooting, performance optimization, and capacity planning. One of the key features of Linkerd is its automatic instrumentation of service-to-service communication. It seamlessly injects itself as a proxy into the network traffic, allowing it to collect rich telemetry data without requiring any code changes within the individual services. This not only simplifies the integration process but also enables fine-grained visibility into latency, error rates, and other metrics, helping teams identify and resolve issues quickly. Another important aspect of Linkerd is its ability to provide advanced traffic management capabilities. It supports intelligent load balancing, enabling the fine-tuning of traffic distribution across different instances of a service based on user-defined rules and policies. This can improve application performance, increase resilience by easily implementing circuit-breaking or rate limiting mechanisms, and enable canary deployments for gradual rollouts of new features or updates. Furthermore, Linkerd offers powerful security features to safeguard the communication within a microservices architecture. It supports mutual Transport Layer Security (mTLS) authentication, encrypting traffic between services to protect against unauthorized access or eavesdropping. It also integrates with external systems, such as certificate authorities, to simplify key and certificate management. In summary, Linkerd is a service mesh that enhances the overall DevOps practices by providing necessary infrastructure and capabilities for building, deploying, and managing microservices. It improves reliability, observability, and security of service-to-service communication, empowering developers to focus on their core tasks while enabling operations teams to gain deep insights and control over the distributed systems.

Load Testing

Load testing is a fundamental practice in the context of DevOps that aims to evaluate the performance and behavior of a system or application under specific conditions, determining its ability to handle a predefined workload and sustain its expected performance levels. Conducted throughout the software development lifecycle, load testing enables organizations to identify and address potential performance bottlenecks or issues before deploying their applications, thereby enhancing the overall quality and reliability of the system. Load testing involves simulating realistic user loads and scenarios to measure how a system or application responds to varying levels of traffic and usage. By subjecting the system to various stress points, load testing helps to determine its breaking point and understand its behavior under peak loads, ensuring that the infrastructure and architecture can handle the expected user load without compromising performance or stability.

Log Aggregation

Log aggregation is a crucial practice in the field of DevOps that involves consolidating and analyzing logs from various sources within a distributed system. It aims to provide a centralized view of logs, making it easier to identify and debug system issues, monitor performance, and gain insights for optimizing the system's behavior. By gathering logs from multiple sources, log aggregation enables DevOps teams to have a comprehensive understanding of the system's state and behavior. Different components of a distributed system, such as applications, servers, databases, and networking devices, generate their own logs containing valuable information about their activities. Log aggregation collects these logs into a single system, facilitating efficient analysis and troubleshooting. The process of log aggregation typically involves collecting logs in real-time from diverse sources through various mechanisms such as log shippers or agents. These mechanisms forward the logs to a centralized log storage or processing system. The logs are usually organized based on timestamps and other relevant metadata, allowing easy exploration and analysis. Log aggregation provides several benefits for DevOps teams. It simplifies the process of debugging issues and identifying root causes by providing a unified view of logs from different system components. DevOps professionals can search, filter, and correlate logs, enabling them to quickly grasp the context and dependencies of events. Moreover, log aggregation enables proactive monitoring and alerting. By continuously analyzing logs, anomalies and patterns can be detected, triggering alerts for potential issues. This helps in identifying and resolving problems before they impact the system's stability or performance. Additionally, log aggregation plays a vital role in system optimization. By analyzing logs, DevOps teams can uncover performance bottlenecks, identify inefficient processes, and make data-driven decisions to improve the system's overall performance and efficiency. In conclusion, log aggregation is a fundamental practice in the DevOps domain that involves collecting and analyzing logs from various sources within a distributed system. It provides a centralized view of logs, aiding in troubleshooting, monitoring, and optimizing system behavior.

Log Analysis

Log analysis in the context of DevOps refers to the process of examining and interpreting log files generated by software applications or systems. These log files contain valuable information about activities and events occurring within the software or system, helping DevOps teams gain insights, troubleshoot issues, and improve performance and reliability. Log analysis plays a crucial role in the DevOps lifecycle, enabling teams to monitor and understand the behavior of their applications and infrastructure. By analyzing logs, DevOps professionals can detect and diagnose problems, identify patterns, and make data-driven decisions to optimize their systems.

Log Management

Log management, in the context of DevOps, refers to the practice of collecting, analyzing, and monitoring logs generated by various systems and applications within an organization's infrastructure. It involves the systematic collection of log data, analysis of the data to identify patterns and anomalies, and the implementation of proactive measures to address potential issues. Effective log management is crucial for ensuring the availability, performance, and security of an organization's IT environment. By centralizing logs from multiple sources, such as servers, applications, network devices, and security systems, organizations can gain valuable insights into the overall health and operations of their systems.

LogRocket

LogRocket is a powerful tool used in the context of DevOps to monitor, log, and analyze user sessions in web applications and help developers identify and troubleshoot issues more efficiently. DevOps refers to the practice of combining software development (Dev) and operations (Ops) to improve collaboration and streamline the software development lifecycle. It aims to automate and optimize processes, enhance communication, and increase efficiency in delivering software applications. In this context, LogRocket plays a critical role by providing real-time insights into user sessions. It captures everything that happens in a web application, including network requests, console logs, JavaScript errors, and user interactions. This comprehensive recording allows developers to replay and visualize sessions, gaining a deeper understanding of how users interact with the application. By utilizing LogRocket, DevOps teams can identify and reproduce bugs more effectively. Instead of relying on vague descriptions from users, developers can review exact user interactions, network activity, and JavaScript errors that occurred during the session. This level of specificity reduces the time and effort required to diagnose and resolve issues. LogRocket also promotes collaboration within DevOps teams. Developers can share recorded sessions with team members or stakeholders, allowing everyone to see the issue firsthand. With a detailed understanding of user behavior, various team members can work together to diagnose and troubleshoot problems more efficiently. Furthermore, LogRocket integrates seamlessly with other DevOps tools and workflows. It provides integrations with popular ticketing systems, collaboration tools, and monitoring platforms. This integration ensures that recorded sessions are easily accessible within existing workflows, enhancing the overall efficiency of the development process. In summary, LogRocket is a valuable tool in the realm of DevOps. It enables developers to monitor and analyze user sessions, aiding in bug identification and resolution. By capturing and replaying sessions, LogRocket facilitates collaboration and streamlines the troubleshooting process. Integrated with other DevOps tools, LogRocket enhances the overall efficiency of the software development lifecycle.

Machine Learning In DevOps Use Cases

Machine Learning in DevOps refers to the use of machine learning techniques and algorithms to enhance and streamline the practices and processes involved in DevOps. DevOps is an approach that combines software development (Dev) and IT operations (Ops) to enable organizations to deliver applications and services at high velocity. Machine learning in DevOps leverages the power of data analysis and predictive modeling to drive automation, optimize resource allocation, and improve overall system performance. One use case of machine learning in DevOps is the prediction and prevention of system failures. By analyzing historical data related to system performance, machine learning algorithms can learn to identify patterns and anomalies that precede system failures. This enables proactive identification and mitigation of potential issues, reducing downtime and enhancing the reliability of the system.

Machine Learning In DevOps

Machine Learning in DevOps refers to the application of machine learning techniques and algorithms to optimize and improve the efficiency and effectiveness of DevOps processes. DevOps, a combination of development and operations, focuses on integrating software development and IT operations to achieve faster and more reliable software delivery. The use of machine learning in DevOps allows organizations to gain valuable insights from data generated by various software development and operational activities. It enables the automation and optimization of different DevOps tasks, leading to increased efficiency, enhanced collaboration, and improved software delivery cycles. One key area where machine learning can be applied in DevOps is in the prediction and prevention of software failures and performance issues. By analyzing historical data and patterns, machine learning models can identify potential bottlenecks, bugs, or infrastructure problems. This enables proactive measures to be taken to prevent these issues, resulting in a more stable and reliable software environment. Another important aspect is the intelligent allocation of resources in DevOps environments. Machine learning models can analyze various factors such as workload, resource utilization, and performance metrics to identify optimal resource allocation strategies. This helps in achieving cost savings, maintaining system performance, and meeting service level agreements. Furthermore, machine learning can assist in automating and optimizing continuous integration and continuous deployment (CI/CD) pipelines. By analyzing data from different stages of the CI/CD pipeline, machine learning algorithms can identify areas where improvements can be made, such as code quality, test coverage, or deployment efficiency. This helps in reducing manual effort, increasing release frequency, and improving overall software quality. In conclusion, machine learning in DevOps offers organizations a powerful set of tools and techniques to enhance software development and operational processes. By leveraging machine learning algorithms, organizations can achieve faster, more efficient, and higher quality software delivery, leading to increased customer satisfaction and competitive advantage.

Mean Time Between Failures (MTBF)

Mean Time Between Failures (MTBF) is a crucial metric in the context of DevOps that quantifies the reliability and resilience of a system or a component within a system. It refers to the average time elapsed between one failure event and the next failure event, and it is often expressed in hours or any other relevant time unit. MTBF provides valuable insights into the operational efficiency of a system by measuring the average time it can perform its intended functions without experiencing any failures. It is a key performance indicator (KPI) that helps DevOps teams evaluate the robustness and availability of their systems, enabling them to proactively identify and address potential weaknesses and vulnerabilities. Calculating MTBF involves analyzing historical data on system failures and the corresponding downtimes. By dividing the total operating time by the number of failures, one can derive the average time between failures. This metric is particularly useful in predicting the performance and reliability of systems when used in conjunction with other metrics such as Mean Time to Repair (MTTR) and Availability. MTBF is widely used in the design and maintenance of highly reliable and fault-tolerant systems. It allows DevOps teams to optimize their strategies for maintenance, upgrade, and recovery. By monitoring MTBF, teams can track the effectiveness of their efforts in reducing potential failures and minimizing downtime. Furthermore, it aids in determining the necessity for system improvements, implementing redundancy measures, or replacing faulty components, all of which contribute to achieving higher system availability and uninterrupted service. It is important to note that while MTBF plays a critical role in evaluating system reliability, it does not take into account the severity or impact of failures. Additionally, MTBF should be interpreted with caution as it is influenced by external factors such as environmental conditions, usage patterns, and maintenance practices. In conclusion, MTBF is a fundamental metric within the DevOps landscape that provides insights into the reliability and availability of systems. By analyzing

MTBF along with other relevant metrics, DevOps teams can continuously enhance the performance and resilience of their systems through effective maintenance and optimization practices.

Mean Time To Recovery (MTTR)

Mean Time to Recovery (MTTR) is a key performance metric used in the context of DevOps to measure the average time it takes for a system or application to recover from an incident or failure. It is an important indicator of the reliability and resilience of a system, as well as the efficiency of the incident response process. MTTR is calculated by summing up the total downtime caused by incidents and dividing it by the number of incidents that occurred within a specific time period. The result is the average time it takes to resolve and recover from an incident. This metric is usually measured in hours or minutes.

Measurement

Measurement in the context of DevOps refers to the process of collecting and analyzing data to understand the performance, stability, and efficiency of software development and deployment practices. It involves the systematic monitoring and evaluation of various metrics and key performance indicators (KPIs) to gain insights into the effectiveness of specific processes and make data-driven decisions to drive continuous improvement. Measurement is essential in DevOps as it allows organizations to identify areas of improvement, track progress towards goals, and quantify the impact of changes implemented in the software development lifecycle. By measuring various aspects of the DevOps process, teams can identify bottlenecks, inefficiencies, and areas for optimization, leading to faster and more reliable software delivery.

Micro Frontends Communication Patterns

Micro Frontends Communication Patterns in the context of DevOps refers to the practices and techniques used to enable efficient communication and coordination between different micro frontends in a distributed system. Micro frontends are independently deployable and scalable front-end components or applications that work together to create a cohesive user interface. There are several communication patterns that can be used to facilitate the interaction between micro frontends, ensuring seamless collaboration and continuous delivery. One commonly used pattern is the API Gateway pattern, where a centralized gateway acts as a proxy between the micro frontends and the backend services. This pattern simplifies communication by providing a single entry point for the micro frontends to access data and services from various backend systems. Another communication pattern is known as the Event Bus pattern, where micro frontends communicate with each other through events. In this pattern, each micro frontend can publish events to the event bus, and other micro frontends can subscribe to specific events of interest. This decoupled communication mechanism allows for flexibility and scalability, as changes in one micro frontend do not impact the others. The Shared State pattern is another approach to communication between micro frontends. In this pattern, a shared state container, such as Redux or MobX, is used to manage and synchronize state across multiple micro frontends. This enables consistent data sharing and helps maintain a coherent user experience. A variant of the Shared State pattern is the Micro Frontend Shell pattern, where a shell application provides a consistent layout and navigation across the micro frontends. The shell application acts as a container for the individual micro frontends and manages the shared state between them. Overall, these communication patterns play a crucial role in the successful implementation of micro frontends in a DevOps environment. They provide mechanisms for efficient collaboration, seamless integration, and continuous delivery, ultimately enabling teams to work independently and deliver high-quality user experiences.

Micro Frontends Communication

Micro Frontends Communication refers to the mechanism or process through which individual micro frontends communicate and interact with each other in a DevOps environment. It involves the exchange of data, events, and messages between different micro frontends, enabling them to work together cohesively as a single application. This communication is crucial for the seamless integration and coordination of diverse frontends, allowing for efficient development, deployment, and maintenance processes within a DevOps context. In a DevOps setup, where teams work collaboratively on different parts of an application, micro frontends provide a modular approach to frontend development. Instead of having a monolithic frontend, the application is broken down into smaller, independent frontends, each responsible for a specific functionality or feature. This division allows teams to work autonomously and deploy changes to their respective micro frontends without impacting the entire application. However, for the application to function as a cohesive whole, these individual micro frontends need to communicate and share information with each other. There are various ways in which micro frontends can communicate: A common approach is through the use of events, where micro frontends emit and listen for events to exchange data and trigger actions. This event-based communication allows for loosely coupled frontends, as they don't need to be aware of each other's internal implementation details. Instead, they only need to understand the events and data formats they exchange. Another method of communication is through a centralized state management system. This involves maintaining a shared state that can be accessed and modified by different micro frontends. By synchronizing their state with this centralized system, micro frontends can communicate and stay in sync with each other, ensuring consistent data across the application.

Micro Frontends Deployment Strategies

Micro Frontends Deployment Strategies in the context of DevOps refer to the different approaches and techniques used for deploying and managing micro frontends, which are independent and self-contained parts of a front-end application. One deployment strategy is the Single-SPA approach, where all the micro frontends are bundled and deployed as a single application. This strategy simplifies the deployment process as the entire application is deployed in one go. However, it may pose challenges in terms of versioning, as all the micro frontends need to be in sync to ensure compatibility and prevent any conflicts.

Micro Frontends Deployment

A micro frontends deployment refers to the practice of deploying and managing front-end applications as separate, independently deployable units, each responsible for a specific feature or functionality. This approach allows development teams to work in isolation, enabling faster development cycles and promoting scalability and maintainability. In a micro frontends architecture, the front-end codebase is divided into smaller, self-contained units, often referred to as micro frontends. Each micro frontend represents a specific part or module of the overall front-end application, such as a login component, a shopping cart module, or a user profile section. With micro frontends, each team can develop and release their micro frontend independently, using their preferred technology stack, programming language, or framework. This decoupling of the front-end codebase enables teams to adopt different technologies and experiment with new features without affecting the overall stability and performance of the application. DevOps plays a crucial role in facilitating the deployment and management of micro frontends. Continuous integration and continuous deployment (CI/CD) pipelines are set up to automate the build, test, and deployment processes of each micro frontend. This automation ensures that changes and updates made to individual micro frontends can be deployed quickly and reliably to production. Additionally, DevOps practices such as infrastructure as code, containerization, and orchestration are used to efficiently manage the deployment of micro frontends. By using containerization technologies like Docker and container orchestration platforms like Kubernetes, teams can encapsulate and deploy their micro frontends as isolated, lightweight units that can be easily scaled up or down based on demand. In conclusion, micro frontends deployment in the context of DevOps refers to the practice of deploying front-end applications as independent units, allowing teams to work autonomously and enabling faster development cycles, scalability, and maintainability. By leveraging DevOps practices and technologies, teams can automate the deployment and management processes of micro frontends, ensuring reliable and efficient delivery of updates to production environments.

Micro Frontends Frameworks

A micro frontend framework refers to a development approach where frontend applications are broken down into smaller and more manageable pieces, allowing independent teams to work on different parts of the frontend simultaneously. In the context of DevOps, micro frontend frameworks enable efficient collaboration and streamlined deployment processes. By dividing a monolithic frontend application into smaller micro frontends, development teams can focus on specific functionality or features. Each micro frontend can be developed and deployed independently, reducing bottlenecks that often occur when multiple teams are working on a single monolithic frontend. This allows for faster development cycles and more efficient use of resources.

Micro Frontends Scalability Solutions

Micro Frontends Scalability Solutions in the context of DevOps refer to the methodologies, practices, and approaches used to enhance the scalability of micro frontend architectures. Micro frontend architecture is an architectural pattern where front-end applications are divided into smaller, loosely-coupled, and independent components, facilitating easier development, maintenance, and deployment. Scalability in micro frontend architectures poses challenges due to the distributed nature of the components. As the number of micro frontends increases, managing their scalability becomes crucial to ensure optimal performance and efficiency. Therefore, various solutions have emerged to address these challenges and enhance scalability. One common solution is to utilize containerization technologies like Docker. Containers allow packaging micro frontends along with their dependencies, making it easier to deploy and scale them in a consistent manner across different environments. By leveraging container orchestration platforms such as Kubernetes, DevOps teams can automate the deployment, scaling, and management of micro frontends, ensuring efficient resource utilization and scalability. Another solution is to implement a service mesh architecture. Service mesh provides a dedicated infrastructure layer for managing communication between micro frontends. It offers features like load balancing, traffic routing, and service discovery, enabling seamless scalability without affecting the overall application. With a service mesh in place, DevOps teams can easily add or remove micro frontends, scale them horizontally, and dynamically manage traffic flow, leading to enhanced scalability. Additionally, employing serverless computing can also contribute to scalability in micro frontend architectures. With serverless, the infrastructure and scaling aspects are abstracted away, allowing micro frontends to automatically scale based on demand. DevOps teams can leverage serverless platforms like AWS Lambda or Azure Functions to build and deploy micro frontends, enabling efficient scalability without worrying about infrastructure management. Furthermore, adopting a reactive programming model can enhance scalability in micro frontend architectures. By designing micro frontends to be event-driven and reactive, DevOps teams can easily scale individual components based on specific events or changes. This approach promotes loose coupling, enhances responsiveness, and allows for independent scaling of micro frontends as per requirements. In conclusion, micro frontend scalability solutions in DevOps encompass leveraging containerization, service mesh, serverless computing, and reactive programming to enable efficient scaling of micro frontends. These solutions address the challenges associated with scaling distributed front-end components and provide DevOps teams with flexibility, control, and performance optimization.

Micro Frontends Scalability

Micro Frontends Scalability refers to the ability of a system or application built using micro frontend architecture to handle increasing demands and workload by effectively distributing the frontend responsibilities across multiple independent and autonomous teams, enabling them to work in parallel and scale the application horizontally. In the context of DevOps, micro frontends scalability is achieved through the use of decoupled and modular frontend components that can be developed, deployed, and scaled independently. This approach allows teams to work on smaller and more focused portions of the application, reducing dependencies and enabling faster development and deployment cycles.

Micro Frontends Security Measures

Micro Frontends Security Measures are the practices and techniques implemented in the context of DevOps to ensure the security of micro frontends, which are independently deployable frontend components of a web application. These measures are essential in order to protect the integrity, confidentiality, and availability of data and services provided by the micro frontends. In a micro frontend architecture, multiple frontend teams are responsible for separate micro frontends, which are composed together to create the final user interface. This decentralization introduces additional security challenges compared to monolithic frontend architectures. Therefore, various security measures are employed to address these challenges and mitigate potential risks.

Micro Frontends Security

Micro frontends are a software development approach that breaks down a user interface (UI) into smaller, autonomous and loosely-coupled components. In the context of DevOps, micro frontends allow multiple development teams to work on different parts of an application's UI independently, enabling faster development, deployment, and release cycles. However, the use of micro frontends brings about unique security challenges that need to be addressed within a DevOps environment. As each component of the UI may be developed and deployed by different teams, it is crucial to ensure the security of the entire application.

Micro Frontends Testing Approaches

Micro Frontends Testing Approaches refers to the various strategies and methods employed in the context of DevOps to ensure the efficient and effective testing of micro frontends.In a DevOps environment, micro frontends are small, self-contained frontend modules that are developed and deployed independently of each other. These modules can range from UI components, widgets, or even entire frontend applications. The main goal of micro frontends is to enable teams to work independently and deliver features quickly to end-users without dependencies or bottlenecks.

Micro Frontends Testing

Micro Frontends Testing, in the context of DevOps, refers to the process of verifying and validating the functionality, quality, and performance of micro frontends, which are independent, self-contained user interface components that are developed and deployed separately. Testing micro frontends is essential to ensure that these components work as intended and provide a seamless user experience. It involves a combination of different testing techniques and methodologies, such as unit testing, integration testing, end-to-end testing, and performance testing. Unit testing focuses on testing individual micro frontend components in isolation to verify the correctness of their functionality. It typically involves writing and executing test cases for each component to validate its behavior and ensure that it meets the specified requirements. Integration testing is performed to ensure that all the micro frontends, when combined together, work correctly and seamlessly. It involves testing the interactions and dependencies between different micro frontends to ensure that they integrate correctly and communicate effectively with each other. End-to-end testing checks the overall functionality of the application by simulating real user interactions across multiple micro frontends. It aims to validate the entire user journey and ensure that all the micro frontends work together in harmony. Performance testing focuses on assessing the performance and scalability of micro frontends under different load conditions. It involves testing the response time, throughput, and resource utilization of the micro frontends to ensure that they can handle the expected user load without any performance degradation. In addition to these testing techniques, DevOps practices emphasize the use of automation and continuous testing to ensure the timely and efficient testing of micro frontends. This involves setting up test automation frameworks, integrating them with the CI/CD pipeline, and running automated tests on each code change to catch any potential issues early in the development process. Overall, micro frontends testing plays a crucial role in ensuring the quality, reliability, and performance of applications that are built using a micro frontend architecture. It enables organizations to deliver user-centric, robust, and scalable applications by identifying and fixing issues early in the software development lifecycle, leading to faster time-to-market and increased customer satisfaction. End

Micro Frontends

Micro Frontends is a software development architectural pattern where frontend applications are split into multiple smaller and independent parts, called micro frontends. Each micro frontend represents a specific feature or functionality of the overall application and is developed and deployed separately. This approach follows the principles of microservices and allows teams to work independently, delivering their features faster and more efficiently. The main goal of using micro frontends is to overcome the limitations of monolithic frontend applications where all the

132

features are tightly coupled and any change or update requires the whole application to be redeployed. With micro frontends, teams can develop and deploy their parts independently, avoiding the need for coordination between teams and minimizing the impact of one team's changes on others.

Microservices Architecture

A microservices architecture is a software development approach that structures an application as a collection of small, loosely coupled services, each serving a specific business capability. These services are built and deployed independently, enabling teams to work on different services simultaneously. It promotes the use of DevOps practices to improve agility, scalability, and resilience of the overall system. In a microservices architecture, each service is responsible for a single, self-contained functionality and can communicate with other services through well-defined APIs, typically using lightweight protocols like HTTP or messaging systems. This decoupling of services allows for independent scaling, deployment, and maintenance of each service, resulting in increased flexibility and quicker time-to-market for new features.

Mobile Application Security Testing (Mobile AST)

Mobile Application Security Testing (Mobile AST) in the context of DevOps is the process of assessing and evaluating the security of mobile applications, with the goal of identifying vulnerabilities and weaknesses that could be exploited by malicious actors. It involves a comprehensive examination of the application's code, configuration, and behavior to uncover any potential security flaws. The main objective of Mobile AST is to proactively detect security vulnerabilities in mobile applications before they are exploited by attackers. By integrating this testing into the DevOps workflow, organizations can identify and address security issues early in the software development life cycle, reducing the risk of compromises and ensuring that their applications meet the necessary security standards.

Monday.Com

Monday.com is a collaborative work management platform that is widely used in the context of DevOps. DevOps is a software development methodology that combines software development (Dev) and IT operations (Ops) to improve collaboration, communication, and efficiency within the development and operations teams. Monday.com provides a centralized workspace for DevOps teams to manage their projects, tasks, and processes. It allows teams to streamline their workflows, track progress, and collaborate in real-time. The platform offers a range of features and tools that support various aspects of the DevOps lifecycle, including planning, development, testing, deployment, monitoring, and incident management.

Monitoring

Monitoring in the context of DevOps refers to the practice of continuously observing and collecting data from various sources within a system or application to ensure its optimal performance and availability. It involves the systematic examination of metrics, logs, and alerts to gain insights into the health, efficiency, and reliability of the software development and deployment processes. Monitoring plays a crucial role in DevOps as it provides real-time visibility into the different components of a system, including servers, networks, databases, applications, and infrastructure. By monitoring these elements, DevOps teams can identify and resolve issues proactively, minimizing downtime, improving system performance, and enhancing the overall user experience. Monitoring involves the use of specialized tools and technologies that enable the collection, aggregation, analysis, and visualization of data. These tools can track various metrics such as response time, CPU usage, memory utilization, network traffic, error rates, and throughput. They can also monitor logs and events for anomalies and patterns that may indicate potential problems or security breaches. DevOps monitoring follows several key principles to ensure its effectiveness. These include: 1. Proactive Monitoring: Actively monitoring systems and applications to identify and resolve issues before they become critical. 2. End-to-End Visibility: Monitoring the entire software delivery pipeline, including development, testing, deployment, and production environments. 3. Automation: Utilizing automated monitoring tools and processes to streamline data collection, analysis, and reporting, reducing the manual effort required. 4. Scalability: Designing monitoring systems that can handle the increasing

133

complexities and volumes of data as the system or application grows. 5. Alerting and Notifications: Setting up thresholds and notifications to alert DevOps teams about abnormal or critical metrics, allowing them to take immediate action. 6. Continuous Improvement: Regularly reviewing and refining monitoring strategies and techniques to adapt to evolving requirements and technologies. In conclusion, monitoring in the context of DevOps involves continuous observation, data collection, and analysis of various system components to ensure optimal performance and availability. By following key principles such as proactive monitoring, end-to-end visibility, automation, scalability, alerting, and continuous improvement, DevOps teams can effectively monitor their systems and applications, enabling efficient problem detection and resolution.

Monolith Decomposition

Monolith decomposition is a software development approach in the context of DevOps where a monolithic application is divided into smaller, more manageable services or components that can be developed, deployed, and scaled independently. It involves breaking down a large, complex application into smaller, loosely coupled parts, allowing for more efficient development, deployment, and maintenance. In a monolithic architecture, different functionalities of an application are tightly integrated into a single codebase and deployed as a single unit. This can make it difficult to make changes, add new features, and scale the application, as any modifications or updates require the entire application to be redeployed. This lack of flexibility can hinder agility in development and deployment processes. Monolith decomposition addresses these challenges by breaking down the monolithic application into smaller, self-contained services or components, often referred to as microservices. Each microservice is focused on a specific functionality or business capability and can be developed and deployed independently. This allows for faster development cycles and more frequent, targeted deployments. Decomposing a monolith involves identifying the different functionalities or modules within the application and separating them into separate services. Communication between these services is facilitated through APIs or message queues. Each service can be developed by a separate team using different technologies and can scale independently based on the specific requirements. Monolith decomposition enables a more modular and scalable architecture that aligns with the principles of DevOps. It allows for faster development cycles, easier maintenance, and improved scalability. Additionally, it enables organizations to adopt modern technologies and practices, such as containerization and orchestration, which further enhance the flexibility and agility of the application.

Monolithic To Microservices Transition

A monolithic to microservices transition refers to the process of transforming a monolithic application architecture into a microservices architecture in the context of DevOps. Monolithic applications are characterized by a single, large codebase where all components of the application are tightly coupled together. This architecture pattern can make it challenging to scale and deploy the application efficiently, as any changes or updates to the system require redeployment of the entire application. On the other hand, microservices architecture is an approach that breaks down an application into smaller, loosely coupled services, each responsible for a specific business capability. Each service operates independently and can be developed, deployed, and scaled separately. This modular structure allows for greater agility, resilience, and scalability of the system. The transition from a monolithic architecture to microservices involves several steps. It often starts with identifying the boundaries and functionalities of the existing monolith and mapping them into separate microservices. This process involves analyzing the dependencies, defining the communication mechanisms, and ensuring data consistency between services. Once the services are identified, they can be developed and deployed independently. This enables teams to adopt agile and iterative development practices, with each service having its own deployment pipeline and release cycle. DevOps practices such as continuous integration, continuous delivery, and automated testing play a crucial role in ensuring the successful transition. The transition also requires establishing effective communication and coordination mechanisms between services. API gateways, service discovery, and event-driven architectures are commonly used to enable seamless interaction and integration between microservices. Monitoring and observability are critical during the transition process to ensure the overall health and performance of the system. Logging, metrics, and distributed tracing help identify issues, troubleshoot problems, and optimize the performance of individual services. Ultimately, the monolithic to microservices transition enables organizations to achieve greater scalability, resilience, and flexibility in their applications. It allows for more efficient development and deployment cycles, facilitating the implementation of DevOps practices and fostering a culture of continuous improvement and innovation.

MuleSoft

MuleSoft is a leading software company that provides a platform for building application networks, enabling organizations to connect data, devices, and applications across different technologies and environments. In the context of DevOps, MuleSoft plays a crucial role in the integration and automation of processes, facilitating efficient communication and collaboration between development and operations teams. DevOps is a collaborative approach to software development that combines development (Dev) and operations (Ops) teams to improve the speed, quality, and reliability of software delivery. It emphasizes communication, collaboration, and integration between these traditionally siloed teams to streamline the entire software development lifecycle. MuleSoft's platform offers a range of tools and services that align with DevOps principles and practices. It allows organizations to connect various systems and applications seamlessly, automate processes, and ensure reliable delivery of software solutions. Through its integration capabilities, MuleSoft enables teams to easily share data, services, and applications, fostering effective communication and collaboration between different stakeholders involved in the software delivery process. One key aspect of DevOps is continuous integration and continuous delivery (CI/CD), which aims to automate the build, testing, and deployment of software solutions. MuleSoft's platform supports CI/CD practices by providing automated integration and deployment capabilities. It allows developers to easily build, test, and deploy applications, ensuring faster and more efficient delivery of software solutions. Furthermore, MuleSoft's platform enables organizations to adopt agile development methodologies, another key component of DevOps. It allows teams to rapidly iterate, experiment, and adapt to changing requirements by providing a flexible and scalable environment for building and deploying applications. In summary, MuleSoft's platform plays a vital role in enabling organizations to implement DevOps practices, fostering collaboration, integration, automation, and agility. By utilizing MuleSoft's tools and services, organizations can streamline their software development and delivery processes, enhance communication and collaboration between teams, and ensure the efficient and reliable delivery of applications in a fast-paced and dynamic business environment.

Multi-Cloud Deployment

Multi-cloud deployment, in the context of DevOps, refers to the strategy of leveraging multiple cloud service providers to provision and manage various components of an application or system. It involves distributing workloads, storage, and resources across different cloud environments, such as Amazon Web Services (AWS), Microsoft Azure, and Google Cloud Platform (GCP), among others. Organizations adopt multi-cloud deployment to enhance the reliability, scalability, and flexibility of their applications or systems. By diversifying their cloud infrastructure, they can mitigate risks associated with vendor lock-in, single point of failure, and service outages. Additionally, it allows them to take advantage of the unique features, pricing models, and geographic locations offered by different cloud providers. In a multi-cloud deployment, various cloud resources are connected and integrated using DevOps practices and tools. This enables seamless collaboration, continuous integration and deployment, and efficient management of the entire application lifecycle across different cloud environments. DevOps teams utilize automation, infrastructure as code, and containerization technologies to facilitate the deployment and orchestration of workloads across multiple clouds. They streamline and standardize the configuration, monitoring, and management of cloud resources, regardless of the underlying cloud infrastructure. Multi-cloud deployment necessitates a comprehensive and well-defined cloud strategy that aligns with the organization's goals and requirements. It involves careful planning, workload allocation, and data management to optimize performance, cost, and security across different cloud environments. By adopting a multi-cloud approach, organizations can avoid vendor lock-in and achieve greater flexibility in choosing the most suitable cloud services for their specific needs. It allows them to leverage the strengths of different cloud providers, optimize costs, and enhance the overall resilience and availability of their applications or systems.

Multi-Cloud Strategy Formulation

A Multi-Cloud Strategy in the context of DevOps refers to the adoption of multiple cloud service providers and platforms for hosting, managing, and delivering software applications and services. It involves the deliberate choice and deployment of multiple cloud environments to leverage the unique features, capabilities, and strengths of each provider to achieve specific technical, operational, and business objectives. Organizations implementing a Multi-Cloud Strategy aim to avoid vendor lock-in, increase resilience, improve performance, optimize costs, and enhance flexibility and agility in deploying and scaling their applications. By diversifying their cloud hosting infrastructure, they can leverage the strengths of different cloud providers, such as their regional coverage, performance capabilities, compliance certifications, and cost models. A Multi-Cloud Strategy allows organizations to distribute their workloads across multiple cloud providers and avoid reliance on a single cloud platform. This distribution of workloads helps in achieving high availability and fault tolerance, as applications can be deployed across geographically diverse regions and can be easily migrated or scaled based on varying demands or market conditions. Implementing a Multi-Cloud Strategy also helps in mitigating risks associated with data sovereignty, regulatory compliance, and vendor-specific vulnerabilities. It allows organizations to choose the most suitable cloud provider for storing sensitive data or to comply with specific regulations and requirements of different geographic regions. Furthermore, a Multi-Cloud Strategy promotes flexibility and reduces dependency on a single cloud provider's service catalog. Developers and operations teams can leverage a variety of cloud-native tools, services, and APIs offered by different providers to build, deploy, manage, and monitor applications. This flexibility enables organizations to choose the most suitable components and services for their specific application requirements, rather than being limited to the offerings of a single provider. In summary, a Multi-Cloud Strategy in the context of DevOps allows organizations to harness the benefits of multiple cloud providers, enabling them to optimize costs, increase resilience, improve performance, and enhance flexibility in deploying and managing their applications and services.

Multi-Cloud Strategy

A multi-cloud strategy in the context of DevOps refers to the practice of using multiple cloud service providers to deploy and manage different components of an application or system. Instead of relying on a single cloud provider, organizations adopt a multi-cloud approach to take advantage of the unique offerings and capabilities of each provider, while mitigating risks and avoiding vendor lock-in. With a multi-cloud strategy, DevOps teams have the flexibility to choose the most suitable cloud services for different aspects of their application architecture, such as compute, storage, network, databases, and specialized services like machine learning or analytics. This approach enables them to optimize costs, performance, reliability, and security based on specific requirements and constraints. Organizations that embrace a multi-cloud strategy can leverage the strengths of different cloud providers to achieve various benefits. For example, they can distribute workloads across multiple clouds to minimize the impact of downtime or service disruptions. By avoiding a single point of failure, they enhance availability and resilience. Another advantage is the ability to avoid vendor lock-in. By using multiple cloud providers, organizations can prevent dependency on a single vendor's infrastructure, tools, and services. This flexibility allows them to avoid technology silos and switch providers if necessary, to take advantage of better pricing, features, or security options. Additionally, a multi-cloud strategy enables organizations to optimize costs by selecting the most cost-effective services from various providers. By analyzing the pricing models, organizations can choose providers that offer the best fit for specific workloads, resulting in potential cost savings. However, implementing a multi-cloud strategy requires careful planning, as it adds complexity to the DevOps workflow. Teams need to ensure compatibility and interoperability between different cloud services, maintain consistent operational processes, and overcome challenges such as data migration, security management, and monitoring. They must also invest in automation and orchestration tools to facilitate the deployment and management of applications across multiple clouds. In conclusion, a multi-cloud strategy in DevOps allows organizations to maximize the benefits of different cloud providers, minimizing risks and avoiding vendor lock-in. It provides flexibility, scalability, and cost optimization by leveraging the strengths of multiple cloud services while ensuring interoperability and consistent operations.

Multi-Factor Authentication (MFA)

Multi-Factor Authentication (MFA) is a security mechanism that requires multiple forms of identification from a user in order to grant access to a system or application. In the context of DevOps, MFA plays a crucial role in enhancing the security of the development and deployment process. MFA involves the use of at least two different factors for authentication. These factors typically fall into three categories: 1. Something the user knows, such as a password or a PIN. 2. Something the user has, such as a physical token or a mobile device. 3. Something the user is, such as biometric data like fingerprints or voice recognition. By combining these different factors, MFA strengthens the security of a system by adding an extra layer of protection. This additional layer makes it more difficult for attackers to gain unauthorized access, even if they manage to obtain one factor of authentication. In the context of DevOps, MFA is implemented to safeguard critical infrastructure and sensitive data throughout the development and deployment lifecycle. It helps to mitigate risks associated with unauthorized access, data breaches, and other security threats. When using MFA in a DevOps environment, developers and operations teams are required to go through the multi-factor authentication process before accessing and making changes to production systems or sensitive resources. This ensures that only authorized individuals can perform actions that can impact the stability and security of the application or infrastructure. Some common MFA methods used in DevOps include: - One-time passwords (OTP) generated through secure mobile apps or physical tokens - Time-based One-time passwords (TOTP) that change at fixed time intervals - Biometric authentication, utilized through fingerprint or facial recognition - Smart cards or USB keys that store digital certificates In summary, Multi-Factor Authentication (MFA) in DevOps involves the use of multiple identification factors to enhance the security of system access and protect sensitive data. By requiring users to provide multiple forms of authentication, MFA adds an extra layer of protection and helps minimize the risk of unauthorized access and security breaches.

Nessus

Nessus is a widely used vulnerability assessment tool that helps organizations identify and address potential security risks within their IT infrastructure. As a vital component of DevOps practices, Nessus assists teams in ensuring the security of their software and systems throughout the development process. By conducting comprehensive scans and evaluations, it helps to identify vulnerabilities, misconfigurations, and weaknesses that can pose a threat to the overall integrity of the infrastructure.

NeuraLegion

NeuraLegion, in the context of DevOps, is a cybersecurity platform that specifically focuses on application security testing. It provides a comprehensive suite of automated tools and services that help organizations identify and mitigate potential vulnerabilities in their software applications. The primary goal of DevOps is to streamline the software development and deployment processes, allowing organizations to deliver applications more quickly and efficiently. However, an often overlooked aspect of this process is ensuring the security of these applications. NeuraLegion plays a crucial role in the DevOps lifecycle by providing developers and operations teams with the necessary resources to address application security concerns.

New Relic

New Relic is a comprehensive software analytics platform that enables DevOps teams to monitor, troubleshoot, and optimize their applications and infrastructure in real-time. It provides end-to-end visibility into the performance and health of an application stack, allowing DevOps teams to identify and resolve issues quickly, improve overall system performance, and optimize user experience. With New Relic, DevOps teams can gain insights into various aspects of their application stack, including application performance, server performance, database performance, and network performance. The platform collects and aggregates data from various sources, such as application logs, server metrics, and user interactions, and provides a unified view of the entire application ecosystem. This enables DevOps teams to understand the impact of different components on the overall performance and take proactive measures to address any issues.

Nexus Lifecycle

Nexus Lifecycle is a software supply chain management tool that integrates with existing DevOps workflows to provide visibility and control over the open source components used in software development. It helps organizations identify vulnerabilities, enforce policies, and remediate risks throughout the software development lifecycle. With Nexus Lifecycle, organizations can automatically scan and analyze their software projects for open source components and their associated dependencies. The tool maintains a comprehensive database of open source components, including information about known vulnerabilities and licensing restrictions. By integrating with existing DevOps tools and workflows, Nexus Lifecycle provides real-time feedback during the software development process. As developers add or update open source components, the tool alerts them to any known vulnerabilities or policy violations. This allows developers to make informed decisions about the components they use and helps them avoid introducing potential security risks into their codebase. Additionally, Nexus Lifecycle enables organizations to enforce policies and standards for open source component usage. Administrators can define policies based on factors such as vulnerability severity, licensing restrictions, and component age. The tool can then automatically block the use of components that violate these policies, reducing the risk of using insecure or non-compliant software. Furthermore, Nexus Lifecycle supports the remediation of vulnerabilities and risks. It provides information on available updates and patches for vulnerable components, enabling organizations to quickly address any issues. The tool also offers guidance on alternate components that can be used as replacements, ensuring that development can continue with minimal disruption. In summary, Nexus Lifecycle is a software supply chain management tool that integrates with DevOps workflows to provide visibility and control over open source components. It helps organizations identify vulnerabilities, enforce policies, and remediate risks, enabling them to develop secure and compliant software.

Notion

Notion is a concept in the context of DevOps that refers to the integration and coordination of development and operations teams to streamline the software development and deployment process. In the DevOps philosophy, Notion emphasizes collaboration and communication between development and operations teams to achieve a number of key goals. These goals include faster time-to-market, increased deployment frequency, and improved reliability and stability of software systems. Notion brings together a set of practices, tools, and cultural values to enable the smooth functioning of DevOps. It involves the breaking down of silos between different teams and promoting a shared responsibility for software development and operations. One of the main principles of Notion is the automation of repetitive tasks. By automating processes such as testing, building, and deployment, development and operations teams can save time and effort, reduce the risk of human errors, and ensure consistency and reliability in the software development lifecycle. Another important aspect of Notion is the adoption of Agile methodologies and practices. Agile methodologies emphasize iterative development, continuous integration, and continuous delivery, which align well with the objectives of DevOps. By using Agile approaches, teams can quickly respond to changing requirements and customer feedback, leading to faster delivery of value. Furthermore, Notion encourages the use of monitoring and feedback loops to ensure continuous improvement. By actively monitoring software systems in production, teams can identify issues and bottlenecks early on and take corrective actions. Feedback loops enable teams to learn from failures and optimize their processes to deliver better software in subsequent iterations. In summary, Notion is a fundamental concept in DevOps that encompasses collaboration, automation, Agile methodologies, and continuous improvement. By embracing Notion, organizations can achieve faster time-to-market, increased deployment frequency, and improved software reliability and stability.

Observability Platforms Selection

Observability platforms, in the context of DevOps, refer to tools or solutions that provide comprehensive visibility into the performance, health, and behavior of software systems or applications. These platforms facilitate the monitoring, troubleshooting, and optimization of complex, distributed systems to ensure efficient and reliable operations. Observability platforms are designed to collect and analyze various data sources, such as metrics, logs, traces, and events, from different components within a system. By aggregating and correlating this data, these platforms enable DevOps teams to gain insights into the system's behavior, identify anomalies or issues, and make informed decisions to improve performance, reliability, and overall user experience.

Observability Platforms

Observability platforms refer to the tools and systems utilized in the field of DevOps to gain visibility and insights into complex software systems. These platforms provide a comprehensive view of the distributed and interconnected components of a system, allowing DevOps teams to monitor, analyze, and troubleshoot any issues that may arise. In a DevOps environment, observability is crucial for maintaining and improving system performance, reliability, and scalability. It is the ability to understand and measure the internal state of a system by analyzing its external outputs, such as logs, metrics, and traces. Traditional monitoring approaches typically focus on collecting metrics and alerts, but observability platforms go beyond that by providing a more holistic view of the system and its behavior. Observability platforms enable DevOps teams to monitor the health and performance of their systems in real-time. They collect and analyze various types of data, including logs, metrics, and traces, to identify patterns, anomalies, and potential bottlenecks. By visualizing this data in a user-friendly and intuitive format, observability platforms empower teams to detect and resolve issues before they impact the end-users. These platforms often provide features such as automated alerting, anomaly detection, and correlation analysis to help DevOps teams identify and respond to issues proactively. They also facilitate collaboration and knowledge sharing among team members by providing a centralized repository of system information and historical data. Observability platforms contribute to the overall DevOps objectives of continuous integration, delivery, and improvement. By providing real-time insights into the system's behavior, they enable teams to optimize performance, enhance security, and streamline troubleshooting processes. They also facilitate the identification of potential areas for improvement and inform decision-making regarding system architecture, resource allocation, and deployment strategies.

Observability

Observability in the context of DevOps refers to the ability to gain insights into the internal state and behavior of a system by collecting and analyzing relevant data. It is a fundamental aspect of managing and maintaining complex software systems in order to ensure their availability, performance, and reliability. By implementing observability practices, organizations can proactively monitor and troubleshoot their systems, detect and diagnose issues, and make informed decisions to optimize performance and resource allocation. This helps to reduce downtime, improve service quality, and enhance overall system resilience.

Octopus Deploy

Octopus Deploy is a DevOps tool that enables organizations to automate and streamline their application deployment processes. Specifically designed for Microsoft .NET applications, it provides a centralized platform for managing the deployment of software across various environments, such as development, testing, and production. With Octopus Deploy, DevOps teams can simplify the deployment of applications by eliminating manual processes and reducing the potential for human error. It offers a user-friendly interface that allows developers and operations personnel to define the deployment steps, configure variables, and manage the release lifecycle. One of the key features of Octopus Deploy is its ability to support complex deployment workflows. It allows teams to define deployment targets, which can be servers, virtual machines, or cloud resources. By specifying the order of deployment steps and defining dependencies between them, teams can ensure that their applications are deployed consistently and reliably across different environments. Octopus Deploy also simplifies the management of configuration settings for applications. It provides a mechanism for storing and encrypting sensitive data, such as connection strings or API keys, and allows for the easy promotion of configuration settings between environments. Additionally, Octopus Deploy integrates with popular DevOps tools, such as Jenkins, TeamCity, and Azure DevOps, enabling seamless automation and integration of the deployment process. It supports version control systems, allowing teams to track changes to their deployment configurations and rollback to previous versions if needed. In conclusion, Octopus Deploy is a powerful DevOps tool that helps organizations automate and streamline their application deployment processes. By providing a centralized platform for managing deployments, supporting complex workflows, and integrating with other tools, it enables teams to deliver software more efficiently and reliably.

Operational Intelligence Platforms Utilization

Operational Intelligence Platforms (OIPs) play a crucial role in the context of DevOps by providing real-time visibility and analysis of operational data from various sources. These platforms enable organizations to monitor and manage their IT infrastructure, applications, and services to ensure smooth operations and quick resolution of issues. DevOps is an approach that combines software development and IT operations to foster collaborative and efficient processes for delivering reliable software and services. In this context, OIPs act as the central nervous system, collecting and analyzing operational data from diverse systems, tools, and applications. Through their advanced analytics capabilities, these platforms provide insights into the performance, availability, and utilization of resources, helping organizations make informed decisions and take proactive actions to optimize their DevOps workflows. OIPs collect data from various sources, including logs, metrics, events, and traces, and consolidate them into a unified view. By correlating and analyzing these data points, the platforms identify patterns, anomalies, and trends that may impact the operations and performance of the software delivery pipeline. This enables DevOps teams to quickly identify and resolve bottlenecks, performance issues, and errors, ensuring efficient delivery of high-quality software. The real-time monitoring capabilities of OIPs enable organizations to track the health and availability of critical applications and services. By setting up customizable dashboards, DevOps teams can visualize key performance indicators, status updates, and alerts related to their infrastructure and applications. These platforms provide drill-down capabilities, allowing teams to deep dive into specific components or areas of concern for detailed analysis. OIPs also facilitate the automation of operational tasks, allowing organizations to streamline their DevOps processes. By integrating with other tools and systems, these platforms enable automated remediation actions and proactive notifications. This reduces the manual effort required for issue resolution and frees up resources for more strategic tasks. In conclusion, Operational Intelligence Platforms (OIPs) are essential in the context of DevOps as they provide real-time visibility, analysis, and automation capabilities for efficient software delivery. These platforms enable organizations to monitor their IT infrastructure, applications, and services, identify and resolve issues promptly, and optimize their DevOps workflows for improved collaboration and productivity.

Operational Intelligence Platforms

Operational Intelligence Platforms in the context of DevOps are software tools or systems that provide real-time monitoring, analysis, and visualization of data generated from various IT operations and applications. These platforms collect and process large volumes of operational data from sources such as logs, metrics, events, and traces, enabling organizations to gain insights, make informed decisions, and take actions to optimize their IT operations and performance. Operational Intelligence Platforms combine elements of data collection, data processing, and data visualization to provide a comprehensive understanding of an organization's IT infrastructure, applications, and services. They enable organizations to proactively detect and resolve issues, improve system performance, enhance security, and ensure compliance with operational and business requirements. These platforms typically feature advanced analytics capabilities, including real-time analytics, machine learning, pattern recognition, and anomaly detection. They can identify trends, patterns, and anomalies in the operational data, helping organizations to predict and prevent potential issues before they impact the system or end-users. Operational Intelligence Platforms play a crucial role in DevOps practices by providing teams with a holistic view of their IT environments, facilitating collaboration, and enabling continuous improvement. They allow teams to monitor the performance of their applications, infrastructure, and services in real-time, gather metrics to measure key performance indicators, and identify areas for optimization and automation. With the help of these platforms, DevOps teams can monitor the effectiveness of their deployments, track the impact of changes, and quickly identify the root cause of any incidents or failures. They provide dashboards, reports, and alerts that enable teams to react promptly, make data-driven decisions, and ensure the stability and reliability of their systems.

Operational Intelligence

Operational Intelligence refers to the practice of gathering and analyzing real-time data from various sources within the IT infrastructure to gain meaningful insights into the performance, health, and efficiency of software development and deployment processes in a DevOps environment. It involves the continuous monitoring of all stages of the software development lifecycle, including planning, coding, testing, and deployment, to identify issues, bottlenecks, and opportunities for improvement. By leveraging real-time data and analytics, operational intelligence enables organizations to make informed decisions, optimize workflows, and enhance overall operational efficiency.

Orchestration Tools

Orchestration tools, in the context of DevOps, refer to a set of software solutions that automate and manage the deployment, coordination, and configuration of diverse software applications and infrastructure resources within an IT environment. These tools are primarily responsible for streamlining and optimizing the entire software delivery process, ensuring efficient collaboration, scalability, and reliability. Orchestration tools play a crucial role in bridging the gap between development and operations teams, as they enable organizations to automate and manage the deployment and integration of applications, services, and infrastructure components. They provide a centralized platform to define, deploy, and control the interdependencies between various system components, facilitating faster and more reliable delivery of software solutions.

OverOps

OverOps is a software tool that plays a vital role in the context of DevOps. Its primary objective is to improve the efficiency and reliability of software development and operations processes. Specifically, OverOps helps in identifying and resolving code errors and exceptions quickly and efficiently, thereby reducing downtime and enhancing the overall quality of software products and services. By integrating with existing DevOps workflows, OverOps provides real-time visibility into production code. It continuously monitors the application stack and identifies critical errors as they occur. OverOps captures the complete state of each error, including the variable state, input values, and relevant application logs. This detailed information helps development and operations teams identify the root cause of the issue quickly and eliminate it before it impacts end-users, thus improving application availability and stability. OverOps works by intercepting exceptions and errors across the entire application, regardless of whether they are handled or not, and logs them with complete contextual information. It provides automatic detection and analysis of code quality and stability issues, highlighting problematic sections of code and presenting the relevant details to the developers. This allows developers to proactively address potential bugs, performance bottlenecks, and system failures by providing them with the necessary information to reproduce and debug the issue efficiently. The seamless integration of OverOps into existing DevOps processes ensures that it becomes an integral part of continuous integration and continuous delivery (CI/CD) pipelines. It enables developers and operations teams to collaborate effectively, promoting a culture of transparency, accountability, and rapid application development. With OverOps, organizations can reduce the time spent on troubleshooting, increase the deployment frequency, and enhance the user experience by delivering more stable and reliable software in a shorter amount of time.

Patch Management

Patch management, in the context of DevOps, refers to the process of systematically managing and applying software patches to the systems, applications, and infrastructure within an organization's IT environment. As organizations strive to embrace a continuous delivery model, where software updates are released frequently and seamlessly, patch management becomes a critical aspect of maintaining the security, stability, and performance of the systems. It involves identifying, testing, and deploying patches to address vulnerabilities, fix bugs, and enhance functionality.

Performance Chaos Engineering Scenarios

Performance Chaos Engineering is a practice carried out in the context of DevOps to proactively identify and address system performance issues. It involves intentionally injecting disruptive events or conditions into a system to observe and study its behavior under stress. By simulating realistic scenarios that can potentially impact performance, organizations can gain valuable insights into the system's robustness and develop contingency plans to mitigate or prevent performance-related problems. Performance Chaos Engineering aims to validate the system's ability to handle fluctuations in workload, failures of individual components, network delays, or other adverse conditions. It provides a controlled environment to test the performance and reliability of a system, facilitating the identification of bottlenecks, weak points, or unexpected dependencies that can impact performance under real-world conditions. To carry out Performance Chaos Engineering, teams must design and execute various scenarios. These scenarios can include sudden increases in user traffic, overloaded databases, network failures, component failures, or resource exhaustion. By measuring and analyzing system performance during these scenarios, organizations can evaluate the system's resilience, identify potential performance optimization opportunities, and make data-driven decisions to enhance overall system performance. The results obtained from Performance Chaos Engineering can be used to implement specific improvements to the system design, such as optimizing resource allocation, enhancing fault tolerance mechanisms, or improving network configurations. Additionally, it allows organizations to validate and refine their performance monitoring and alerting mechanisms, leading to quicker detection and response times for performance issues. By conducting Performance Chaos Engineering tests regularly, organizations can increase their system's overall performance, reliability, and scalability. It assists in proactively identifying and addressing potential issues before they impact end-users, minimizing downtime, and ensuring a seamless user experience. Moreover, Performance Chaos Engineering encourages cross-functional collaboration within DevOps teams, promotes knowledge sharing, and facilitates continuous improvement efforts. In conclusion, Performance Chaos Engineering is a valuable technique in the DevOps context as it allows organizations to proactively assess system performance under various stressful scenarios. By intentionally creating disruptions within a controlled environment, teams can gather valuable insights, optimize system performance, and enhance overall system reliability and scalability.

Performance Chaos Engineering

Performance Chaos Engineering is a practice within the DevOps domain that aims to improve the overall performance and resilience of a system or application through controlled and deliberate experiments. It involves injecting various performance-related failures, such as high CPU usage, network latency, or disk IO congestion, into a system to uncover vulnerabilities and weaknesses. This approach is inspired by Chaos Engineering, which focuses on injecting failures into a system to test its resilience and identify potential failure points. Performance Chaos Engineering takes this concept a step further by specifically targeting performance and scalability aspects of the system.

Performance Metrics

Performance metrics are quantitative measurements and analyses that assess the performance and effectiveness of a DevOps system or process. These metrics provide valuable insights into the system's efficiency, reliability, scalability, and overall performance, helping organizations identify areas of improvement and make data-driven decisions to optimize their DevOps practices. Performance metrics in the context of DevOps can be categorized into various dimensions, such as: 1. Deployment Metrics: These metrics assess the speed and frequency at which deployments are made in the DevOps environment. Some commonly used deployment metrics include deployment frequency, lead time for changes, change failure rate, and mean time to recover (MTTR) from failures. These metrics help measure the agility and reliability of the deployment process, facilitating continuous delivery and quick response to failures. 2. Infrastructure Metrics: Infrastructure metrics evaluate the performance and capacity of the underlying infrastructure that supports the DevOps system. These metrics include server availability, resource utilization, response time, and throughput. Monitoring these metrics enables organizations to ensure sufficient capacity and scalability to meet the demands of the software delivery pipeline. 3. Application Metrics: Application metrics focus on the performance and behavior of the software application itself. These metrics include response time, error rate, throughput, and resource consumption. By monitoring these metrics, organizations can identify and resolve performance bottlenecks, optimize resource allocation, and enhance the overall user experience. 4. Quality Metrics: Quality metrics assess the reliability and stability of the software being developed and deployed. These metrics include defect density, mean time between failures (MTBF), test coverage, and customer satisfaction. By tracking these metrics, organizations can ensure the delivery of high-quality software, minimize defects, and enhance customer satisfaction. 5. Business Metrics: Business metrics tie the performance of the DevOps system to the organization's overall business goals and objectives. These metrics include revenue generated, customer acquisition, customer retention, and time to market. Monitoring these metrics helps align the DevOps practices with business outcomes, fostering innovation and competitive advantage.

Performance Testing Tools

Performance testing tools are software applications that are used in the context of DevOps to assess the performance, stability, and scalability of an application or system under specific workloads and conditions. These tools enable DevOps teams to evaluate the system's behavior, identify bottlenecks, and measure key performance indicators (KPIs), such as response time, throughput, and resource utilization. With the increasing complexity of modern software systems and the growing demands from end-users, performance testing has become an integral part of the software development lifecycle. By simulating real-world scenarios and stress testing the application, performance testing tools help DevOps teams to uncover performance issues and ensure that the system meets its performance requirements.

Performance Testing

Performance testing in the context of DevOps refers to the systematic process of evaluating the speed, stability, and scalability of a software application under different workload conditions. It involves measuring and analyzing various performance attributes, such as response time, throughput, resource utilization, and reliability, to ensure that the application meets the performance requirements and can handle the expected user load. Performance testing is an integral part of the DevOps lifecycle, as it helps identify performance bottlenecks, scalability issues, and other performance-related problems early in the development cycle. By conducting performance tests, DevOps teams can optimize the application's performance, improve user experience, and ensure its stability even under high load conditions.

Platform As A Service (PaaS) Security

Platform as a Service (PaaS) Security is a concept in the context of DevOps that focuses on ensuring the protection and security of the underlying platform and infrastructure provided by a PaaS provider. PaaS is a cloud computing model that allows developers to efficiently build, deploy, and manage applications without the need to manage the underlying hardware or software infrastructure. In the realm of DevOps, where speed and collaboration are key, PaaS offers a streamlined and automated solution for application development, testing, and deployment. However, this convenience and agility also introduce potential security risks that need to be addressed and mitigated. The primary goal of PaaS security is to protect the platform infrastructure from unauthorized access, data breaches, and other security threats. This involves implementing robust access controls, authentication mechanisms, and encryption protocols to safeguard sensitive data and resources. PaaS security encompasses a range of best practices and measures, including: 1. Identity and Access Management (IAM): Implementing strong authentication and authorization mechanisms to ensure that only authorized individuals and systems have access to the platform and its resources. This involves the use of multi-factor authentication, role-based access control (RBAC), and fine-grained access controls. 2. Data Protection: Encrypting sensitive data both at rest and in transit to prevent unauthorized access and data breaches. This includes the use of encryption algorithms, secure transmission protocols (such as HTTPS), and secure storage mechanisms. 3. Vulnerability Management: Regularly scanning the platform infrastructure for vulnerabilities and implementing patches and updates to address any identified security weaknesses. This includes ensuring that the underlying infrastructure and software components are up to date and properly configured. 4. Audit and Monitoring: Implementing comprehensive logging and monitoring mechanisms to detect and respond to security incidents and breaches. This involves collecting and analyzing log data, setting up alerts and notifications, and conducting regular security audits and assessments. In conclusion, PaaS security in the context of DevOps is focused on safeguarding the platform infrastructure provided by a PaaS provider. By implementing robust access controls, data protection measures, vulnerability management, and audit and monitoring processes, organizations can ensure the security and integrity of their applications and data in the PaaS environment.

Plutora

Plutora is a DevOps platform that enables organizations to streamline and optimize their software delivery processes. It provides a centralized hub that brings together various tools and teams involved in the software development lifecycle, facilitating collaboration, automation, and transparency. With Plutora, organizations can effectively plan, track, and manage their software releases from end to end. It offers a holistic view of the entire release pipeline, allowing teams to identify bottlenecks, resolve conflicts, and ensure smooth coordination between different stakeholders. One of the key features of Plutora is its Release Manager, which enables teams to manage and orchestrate multiple releases simultaneously. It provides a visual timeline that shows the status of each release, including milestones, dependencies, and risks. This allows teams to prioritize and allocate resources effectively, ensuring that releases are delivered on time and with high quality. Plutora also offers a Test Environment Manager, which helps teams optimize their testing processes. It provides a centralized platform to request, provision, and manage testing environments, reducing lead time and improving efficiency. It also allows teams to track and monitor the usage of testing environments, ensuring optimal resource utilization. In addition, Plutora provides a Deployment Manager that facilitates the automation of deployment tasks. It allows teams to define and execute deployment plans, automate rollbacks, and monitor the status of deployments in real time. This helps organizations achieve faster and more reliable deployments, reducing errors and risks. Overall, Plutora enables organizations to adopt a more collaborative and streamlined approach to DevOps. By providing a centralized platform that brings together various teams and tools, it helps organizations improve their software delivery processes, reduce time-to-market, and enhance overall quality and efficiency.

Polyglot Programming

Polyglot Programming is a software development approach that involves writing code in multiple programming languages and using multiple programming paradigms within the same project. In the context of DevOps, Polyglot Programming refers to the practice of using different programming languages and tools across various stages of the development, deployment, and operation processes. This approach promotes flexibility and enables teams to leverage the strengths of different languages and tools to solve specific problems or to achieve specific goals. Polyglot Programming in DevOps allows organizations to choose the best language and tool for each stage of the software development lifecycle. For example, a team may use a dynamically typed language like Python for scripting and automation tasks, as it offers concise and expressive syntax. They may choose a statically typed language like Java for backend development, as it provides robustness and performance. Additionally, they may use a configuration management tool, such as Chef or Puppet, which are designed to manage infrastructure as code. Each of these tools and languages serves different purposes and allows the team to work efficiently and effectively. One of the key advantages of Polyglot Programming in DevOps is the ability to leverage existing skills and knowledge within the team. Different team members may have expertise in different languages, and by allowing them to use their preferred language, organizations can maximize their productivity and enable them to contribute their best work. Moreover, Polyglot Programming encourages learning and growth within the team, as individuals can explore and expand their knowledge in new languages and paradigms. Another benefit of Polyglot Programming in DevOps is improved productivity and maintainability. By using the right language and tool for each task, teams can optimize their workflow and reduce development time. Furthermore, by leveraging the strengths of each language, they can write cleaner and more maintainable code. For example, using a language-specific framework or library can simplify development and reduce the likelihood of introducing errors. This ultimately leads to higher quality software and more efficient operations. In summary, Polyglot Programming in the context of DevOps is the practice of using multiple programming languages and tools for different stages of the software development lifecycle. It promotes flexibility, leverages existing skills, and improves productivity and maintainability. By embracing Polyglot Programming, organizations can maximize their resources and deliver high-quality software more efficiently.

Post-Incident Analysis

A Post-Incident Analysis is a systematic examination and evaluation process performed by a DevOps team after an incident has occurred in order to identify the root cause, understand the impact, and prevent similar incidents from happening in the future. During a Post-Incident Analysis, the team analyzes the entire incident lifecycle, starting from the initial detection and response through to the resolution and recovery. The analysis involves a deep dive into the incident, looking at various aspects such as the timeline of events, actions taken, and communication between team members. The primary goal is to gain a comprehensive understanding of the incident and its impact on the system, as well as to learn from the experience to improve future incident response and prevention strategies. The first step in a Post-Incident Analysis is to gather relevant data and evidence related to the incident. This may include logs, monitoring data, incident reports, and any documentation or artifacts produced during the incident response process. The team then analyzes this data to identify the factors that contributed to the incident, such as system failures, software bugs, or human errors. By identifying the root cause, the team can focus on addressing the underlying issue rather than just treating the symptoms. Once the root cause is determined, the team evaluates the impact of the incident on the system, customers, and business operations. This analysis helps in understanding the severity of the incident and its consequences. It also helps in prioritizing the necessary corrective actions and determining the level of urgency in implementing them. In addition to identifying the root cause and assessing the impact, a Post-Incident Analysis examines the effectiveness of the incident response process. The team evaluates the decisions made, actions taken, and communication among team members to identify areas of improvement. This involves considering factors such as incident detection processes, response time, incident escalation procedures, and collaboration between different teams or stakeholders. The team may also review the incident management tools and technologies used to identify any gaps or limitations that need to be addressed. Based on the findings of the analysis, the team develops a set of recommendations and action items to prevent similar incidents in the future. These recommendations may include implementing system improvements, updating processes and procedures, enhancing monitoring and alerting capabilities, conducting training or knowledge sharing sessions, and refining incident response playbooks. The recommendations are aimed at building resilience, reducing the likelihood of incidents, and minimizing the impact when incidents do occur.

Post-Incident Review

A Post-Incident Review, in the context of DevOps, refers to the process of evaluating and analyzing incidents that have occurred in a production environment. It is a practice aimed at improving the overall system reliability and minimizing the likelihood of similar incidents in the future. During a Post-Incident Review, the focus is not only on identifying the root cause of the incident but also on understanding the contributing factors, the impact it had on the system, and the effectiveness of the response and resolution procedures. The review involves a collaborative effort, involving various stakeholders such as developers, operations teams, and customer support.

Proactive Problem Management

Proactive Problem Management is a crucial aspect of the DevOps methodology that focuses on identifying and resolving potential issues before they can impact the production environment. It involves a systematic approach to problem-solving that aims to detect, analyze, and mitigate problems before they cause substantial disruptions or downtime. In the DevOps context, proactive problem management plays a vital role in reducing the mean time to detect and resolve incidents, improving system reliability, and enhancing overall customer experience. By taking a proactive approach to problem management, organizations can effectively manage risks, minimize the impact of incidents, and maintain efficient operations.

Problem Solving

Problem solving in the context of DevOps refers to the process of identifying and resolving issues and challenges that arise in the development and operations of software systems. It involves a systematic approach to analyzing problems, identifying their root causes, and implementing appropriate solutions in order to improve the overall reliability, efficiency, and quality of software delivery and operations. Problem solving in DevOps typically involves collaboration and communication between various teams, including developers, operations personnel, quality assurance engineers, and other stakeholders. It requires a holistic understanding of the software development lifecycle and the interdependencies between different stages, such as planning, coding, testing, deployment, and monitoring.

Product Ownership

Product Ownership is a key role in the DevOps process that is responsible for maximizing the value of the product being developed by effectively managing and prioritizing the product backlog. It involves taking ownership of the product vision, understanding customer needs, and collaborating with various stakeholders to ensure successful delivery. The Product Owner is the bridge between the business, development, and operations teams, ensuring that the product meets the needs of the customers and aligns with the overall business objectives. They are responsible for defining and communicating the product vision, goals, and requirements to the development team. The Product Owner is the primary person responsible for managing the product backlog, which is a prioritized list of features, enhancements, and bug fixes. They work closely with the development team to clarify requirements, answer questions, and provide guidance throughout the development process. One of the key responsibilities of the Product Owner is to prioritize items in the product backlog based on business value and customer needs. They continuously evaluate and reassess the backlog to ensure that the most valuable and critical features are developed first. Another important aspect of Product Ownership is stakeholder management. The Product Owner collaborates with various stakeholders, including customers, business stakeholders, and development team members, to gather requirements, seek feedback, and ensure that the product meets their needs and expectations. The Product Owner also plays a crucial role in ensuring the quality and usability of the product. They work closely with the development team to define the acceptance criteria for each feature and perform acceptance testing to ensure that the features meet the requirements and are ready for release. In summary, Product Ownership in the context of DevOps involves taking ownership of the product vision, managing the product backlog, prioritizing items based on business value, collaborating with stakeholders, and ensuring the quality and usability of the product.

Prometheus

Prometheus is an open-source monitoring and alerting solution designed for DevOps teams to gain insights into the performance and health of their systems and applications. It is part of the Cloud Native Computing Foundation (CNCF) ecosystem and is widely used in the DevOps community.Prometheus follows a pull-based model where it collects and stores time-series data from various targets such as servers, applications, containers, and other sources. It uses the Prometheus Query Language (PromQL) to query and analyze this data, enabling users to create custom metrics and alerts based on specific thresholds or patterns.

Provisioning Tools

Provisioning tools in the context of DevOps refer to software or frameworks that automate the process of setting up and configuring infrastructure resources, such as servers, networks, storage, and applications, to support the development and deployment of software applications. These tools play a crucial role in enabling the principles of infrastructure as code, efficient resource management, and rapid deployment in DevOps practices. The primary objective of provisioning tools is to streamline and simplify the process of provisioning and managing infrastructure resources, reducing manual effort and minimizing errors. These tools allow DevOps teams to define infrastructure requirements in code, which can be version-controlled, reviewed, and automated, enabling repeatability, consistency, and scalability. Provisioning tools typically provide a declarative approach to infrastructure provisioning, where desired configurations are described in a configuration file or script. They then automate the provisioning process by interfacing with the underlying infrastructure providers, such as cloud platforms or virtualization technologies, to create resources, configure them, and install necessary software packages. Some of the popular provisioning tools used in DevOps include: Terraform: A widely adopted open-source tool that allows infrastructure to be defined using a declarative language. It supports multiple cloud platforms and providers, enabling the creation and management of resources such as virtual machines, networking, and storage. Ansible: A powerful automation tool that uses a simple YAML-based language to describe infrastructure configurations. It can connect to remote hosts and provision them by executing predefined tasks or playbooks. Chef: A configuration management tool that uses a domain-specific language (DSL) to define

146

infrastructure as code. It enables the creation of recipes and cookbooks to manage infrastructure configurations and automate the installation and management of software packages. Puppet: Another popular configuration management tool that uses its own declarative language to manage infrastructure configurations. It provides a centralized approach to infrastructure management and allows for the automation of software deployment, compliance checking, and system monitoring. These provisioning tools offer a wide range of features and integrations, empowering DevOps teams to create, manage, and scale infrastructure resources efficiently and reliably. By automating the process of provisioning, these tools contribute to the agility and speed of software delivery, reducing time-to-market and enabling organizations to respond rapidly to changing business requirements.

Public Key Infrastructure (PKI)

Public Key Infrastructure (PKI) is a framework used in the context of DevOps to secure digital communications and ensure the authenticity, integrity, and confidentiality of information exchanged between different entities within the system. PKI consists of a set of policies, procedures, and technologies that enable the creation, distribution, and management of cryptographic keys, digital certificates, and other security artifacts. The main components of PKI include: 1. Certificate Authority (CA): The CA is a trusted third-party entity responsible for issuing digital certificates that bind a public key to an entity's identity. The CA validates the identity of the entity, signs the digital certificate with its private key, and provides a means for others to verify the integrity and authenticity of the certificate. 2. Public and Private Key Pair: PKI utilizes asymmetric encryption, which involves the use of a public key to encrypt data and a corresponding private key to decrypt it. The public key is widely distributed while the private key remains securely held by the entity. This key pair ensures encryption, decryption, and authentication processes within the system. 3. Certificate Repository: A certificate repository is a centralized or distributed database that stores and manages digital certificates. It allows entities to retrieve and verify the certificates of other entities involved in digital transactions, ensuring the trustworthiness of their public keys. PKI in DevOps enables secure authentication, data integrity, and confidentiality by facilitating the following processes: - Authentication: PKI allows DevOps teams to verify the identities of individuals or systems before granting access. Digital certificates, issued by trusted CAs, establish the trustworthiness of an entity's identity through the verification of their public key. - Encryption and Data Integrity: PKI uses asymmetric encryption to protect sensitive data during transmission. The sender uses the recipient's public key to encrypt the data, ensuring that only the recipient with the corresponding private key can decrypt and access the information. Additionally, digital signatures created using private keys provide data integrity by allowing recipients to verify that the data has not been tampered with. - Secure Communication: PKI provides a secure framework for communication channels. By encrypting data with public keys and verifying digital certificates, DevOps can establish secure connections between different entities, such as servers, services, and infrastructure components.

Puppet

Puppet is a configuration management tool widely used in the field of DevOps. It is designed to automate the provisioning, configuration, and management of software and systems across multiple platforms and environments. With Puppet, organizations can define and enforce desired states for their infrastructure, ensuring consistency and reducing manual effort. At its core, Puppet operates based on a client-server architecture. The Puppet master, installed on a centralized server, acts as the control plane, managing the configuration information and policies. The Puppet agent, installed on individual nodes or servers, connects to the Puppet master to fetch and apply the desired configurations. Puppet leverages a declarative language, known as the Puppet Domain Specific Language (DSL), to describe the desired state of resources and the relationships between them. These resources can include files, packages, services, and more. Through a combination of modules and manifests, Puppet enables administrators to define how the resources should be configured and maintained. One of the key advantages of Puppet is its ability to ensure consistency and repeatability. By defining the desired state of infrastructure in code, organizations can easily make changes and reproduce the exact configurations across different environments. Puppet facilitates the management of complex systems at scale, helping organizations achieve infrastructure as code and accelerate their DevOps practices. Furthermore, Puppet provides a robust ecosystem of modules and a vibrant community, which contribute to a vast collection of pre-built configurations that can be reused and shared. This allows organizations to leverage existing knowledge and best practices, saving time and effort in configuration management. In summary, Puppet is a powerful tool used in DevOps to automate the configuration and management of software and systems. It enables organizations to define and enforce desired states, ensure consistency, and accelerate infrastructure as code practices. With its declarative language and extensive ecosystem, Puppet simplifies the management of complex systems at scale.

Qualys

Qualys is a cloud-based security and compliance platform that helps organizations streamline and automate their DevOps processes. DevOps is a software development approach that combines software development (Dev) and IT operations (Ops) to shorten the systems development life cycle and deliver software quickly and efficiently. It involves collaboration, communication, and integration between software developers and IT operations teams to automate and monitor the entire software delivery process.

RapidDeploy

RapidDeploy is a DevOps tool that enables organizations to automate and streamline the process of deploying software applications and infrastructure changes. It focuses on facilitating rapid and consistent deployment of code, ensuring that teams can deliver updates and new features to production environments quickly and efficiently. RapidDeploy utilizes various automation techniques, such as Continuous Integration and Continuous Deployment (CI/CD) pipelines, to drive the deployment process. It helps teams automate tasks like code compilation, testing, packaging, and deployment, eliminating manual errors and reducing the time required for each deployment cycle. With RapidDeploy, developers can push code changes to repositories, triggering a series of predefined actions that are necessary for deployment. These actions often include code validation, building binaries, running tests, and deploying the updated code to the target environment. RapidDeploy provides a centralized dashboard where developers can monitor the deployment progress, view logs, and manage any issues that may arise during the process. The tool also supports collaboration and visibility across teams by providing a shared platform for developers, quality assurance personnel, and operations teams. This allows for seamless communication, version control, and coordination between different stakeholders involved in the deployment process. RapidDeploy is designed to be flexible, enabling organizations to customize and tailor their deployment workflows to suit their specific requirements. It supports a wide range of deployment targets, including on-premises servers, virtual machines, cloud-based infrastructure, and containerized environments. In summary, RapidDeploy is a DevOps tool that simplifies and automates the deployment of software applications and infrastructure changes. By automating the deployment process, it helps organizations improve software delivery speed, reduce manual errors, and enhance collaboration across teams.

Raygun

Raygun is a DevOps tool that is designed to monitor and optimize software applications. It helps developers and operations teams to identify and resolve software errors and performance issues quickly and efficiently. Using a variety of modules and features, Raygun collects and analyzes data from software applications in real-time. It tracks errors, logs, and user interactions, providing deep insights into the performance and functionality of the application. With this information, teams can prioritize and address software issues promptly.

Real User Monitoring (RUM) Tools Configuration

Real User Monitoring (RUM) is a key component of modern DevOps practices that focuses on measuring the performance and user experience of applications in real-time. RUM tools provide valuable insights into the actual experience of end users by capturing data about their interactions with web or mobile applications. This allows organizations to proactively identify and address performance issues that impact user satisfaction and business outcomes. The configuration of RUM tools involves setting up and customizing the monitoring solution to collect and analyze data from various sources, such as web browsers or mobile devices. This process typically involves the following steps: 1. Instrumentation: RUM tools require the installation of

JavaScript tags or SDKs in the application's code base. These tags or SDKs are responsible for capturing user interactions, such as page load times, network requests, and user input. The configuration process involves integrating these tracking mechanisms into the application's code and ensuring they are deployed correctly across all relevant pages or screens. 2. Data Collection: Once the RUM tool is instrumented, it starts collecting data about user interactions and performance metrics. This data is typically sent to a centralized monitoring platform or dashboard where it can be analyzed and visualized. The configuration process includes defining which data points to collect, such as page load times, error rates, or user interactions, based on the specific monitoring objectives and requirements. 3. Filtering and Aggregation: RUM tools often generate a significant amount of data, especially for high-traffic applications. To avoid overwhelming the monitoring system and to focus on relevant insights, it is important to configure filters and aggregation rules. These rules determine which data points to keep, discard, or aggregate. For example, filtering out automated bot traffic or grouping similar user interactions together can help to reduce noise and provide a clearer picture of real user behavior. 4. Visualization and Alerting: The final configuration step involves visualizing the collected data and setting up alerting mechanisms to notify teams about performance anomalies or user experience issues. RUM tools typically offer dashboards, charts, and reports that allow DevOps teams to monitor key performance indicators (KPIs) in real-time. By configuring alerts based on predefined thresholds or patterns, teams can receive proactive notifications when issues arise and quickly respond to ensure optimal user experience.

Real User Monitoring (RUM) Tools

Real User Monitoring (RUM) tools, in the context of DevOps, are software solutions that track and analyze the performance of an application or website from the perspective of real users. These tools provide insights into the end-user experience, helping organizations identify and address performance issues, optimize user interactions, and ultimately improve customer satisfaction. RUM tools collect data by monitoring the actual interactions between end-users and the application or website. This data includes metrics such as page load time, response time, error rates, and user interactions like clicks and scrolls. By capturing this information, RUM tools provide a real-time view of how users are experiencing the application, allowing DevOps teams to pinpoint areas of improvement and identify bottlenecks.

Real User Monitoring (RUM)

Real User Monitoring (RUM) in the context of DevOps refers to the practice of collecting data and insights on how end users interact with a software application in real time. It involves the measurement and analysis of user behavior, performance, and overall user experience, with the goal of identifying and resolving issues that impact user satisfaction. RUM works by capturing and analyzing data from actual user interactions with an application, including page load times, transaction speed, and error rates. This data is collected through various instrumentation techniques, such as JavaScript tags inserted into website code or hooks embedded within native mobile applications. This allows DevOps teams to gain visibility into the performance of their applications from the user's perspective.

Redmine

Redmine is an open-source project management and issue tracking tool that plays a crucial role in the DevOps landscape. It provides a comprehensive and centralized platform for teams to plan, track, and collaborate on software development projects, integrating various aspects of project management, version control, and communication. By adopting Redmine as part of their DevOps practices, organizations can streamline their project management workflows, enhance team collaboration, and ensure effective communication. Redmine offers a multitude of features and functionalities that facilitate continuous integration, continuous delivery, and continuous deployment, essential components of the DevOps methodology.

Reinforcement Learning For Automation Applications

Reinforcement Learning (RL) is a subfield of Artificial Intelligence (AI) that focuses on enabling agents to learn from their interactions with an environment in order to make optimal decisions. In the context of DevOps, RL can be applied to automate various tasks and processes by training agents to make intelligent decisions based on feedback received from the environment. DevOps is a software development approach that emphasizes collaboration, integration, and automation between software development and IT operations teams. It aims to increase the speed, efficiency, and reliability of software delivery by implementing continuous integration, continuous delivery, and agile practices. Reinforcement Learning for automation applications in the field of DevOps involves training agents to perform tasks such as infrastructure provisioning, deployment, monitoring, and incident response. The RL agents learn from the feedback received from the environment, which can include metrics such as response times, error rates, and resource utilization. For example, an RL agent can be trained to automatically scale up or down the infrastructure based on the current demand. The agent interacts with the environment, collects feedback in the form of performance metrics, and learns to make decisions on when and how to scale the infrastructure to optimize performance and cost. Another example is training an RL agent to automate incident response. The agent interacts with the monitoring system, detects anomalies or issues, and takes appropriate actions to resolve or mitigate them. The agent learns from the feedback received during these interactions and improves its decision-making abilities over time. By using RL for automation in DevOps, organizations can achieve increased efficiency, reduced manual efforts, and improved reliability of their software delivery processes. RL agents can adapt to evolving environments, handle complex decision-making scenarios, and continuously optimize system performance based on real-time feedback. This can lead to faster delivery cycles, higher availability, and better resource utilization.

Reinforcement Learning For Automation

Reinforcement Learning for Automation in the context of DevOps refers to the application of machine learning techniques to automate and optimize the deployment, management, and operation of software systems in the DevOps lifecycle. It involves using the concept of reinforcement learning to enable systems to learn and make intelligent decisions based on their interactions with the environment. Reinforcement learning is a branch of machine learning that focuses on using an agent to learn from its environment through trial and error, aiming to maximize a reward signal. In the case of automation in DevOps, the agent can be a software system or tool that interacts with the various components and processes involved in the DevOps pipeline. The automation process begins with the agent's observation of the environment, which includes monitoring the current state of the software system, infrastructure, and deployment pipeline. The agent uses this information to make decisions and take actions accordingly. These actions can include deploying new code, scaling resources, configuring infrastructure, or triggering tests and monitoring processes. As the agent performs actions, it receives feedback in the form of rewards or penalties. Rewards can be positive when the system achieves its intended objectives, such as successfully deploying a new feature or meeting defined service level agreement targets. Penalties, on the other hand, are given when the system fails to meet these objectives, such as encountering errors or performance issues. The reinforcement learning algorithm learns from these rewards and penalties to update its decision-making policies and improve its future actions. Over time, the system becomes more intelligent and efficient in handling the automation tasks, ultimately leading to optimized deployment cycles, improved resource management, and enhanced overall performance of the software system in the DevOps environment.

Release Automation

Release Automation, in the context of DevOps, refers to the process of automating and streamlining the deployment of software releases. It involves automating various tasks involved in releasing software, such as packaging, testing, and deploying, to ensure a smooth and efficient release process. The goal of release automation is to reduce human error, accelerate the release process, increase efficiency, and improve the quality of software releases. By automating repetitive and time-consuming tasks, it enables organizations to release software more frequently and consistently, while minimizing the risk of errors and downtime.

Release Candidate

A Release Candidate, in the context of DevOps, refers to a version of software or an application that is considered to be stable and ready for deployment. It is the last stage before the final release to production. Release Candidates are extensively tested in various environments to ensure that all the intended features and functionalities are working as expected and that there are no critical bugs or issues. This includes performing rigorous testing, such as functional testing, integration testing, performance testing, and security testing, among others.

Release Coordinator

A Release Coordinator in the context of DevOps is a crucial role responsible for coordinating and managing the release process of software applications. This role acts as a bridge between development and operations teams, ensuring smooth and efficient deployment of software releases. The primary objective of a Release Coordinator is to plan, coordinate, and track the release activities throughout the software development lifecycle. They collaborate closely with various stakeholders, including development teams, QA teams, operations teams, and project managers, to ensure timely and successful software releases.

Release Orchestration

Release Orchestration in the context of DevOps refers to the process of managing and coordinating the deployment and release of software applications within an organization. It involves automating and streamlining the various tasks and activities involved in the release process, such as building, testing, packaging, and deploying software. The goal of release orchestration is to ensure that software releases are planned, coordinated, and executed seamlessly, with minimal disruption to the production environment and end-users. It provides a structured and standardized approach to managing the release process, allowing organizations to deliver software updates and features to their customers in a timely and efficient manner.

Release Pipeline

A Release Pipeline, in the context of DevOps, refers to an automated process that allows for the seamless release and deployment of software applications or updates across multiple environments. It is a core component of the DevOps philosophy and is aimed at achieving continuous integration and delivery. The release pipeline encompasses various stages, starting from the development phase and ending with the deployment of the software into production. Each stage within the pipeline is designed to ensure that every update or release is thoroughly tested, validated, and seamlessly integrated with the existing codebase and infrastructure. Typically, a release pipeline includes stages such as code compilation, unit testing, integration testing, acceptance testing, deployment to staging environments, and finally, production deployment. Each stage incorporates automation, which minimizes human error and accelerates the release process, ultimately leading to faster feedback cycles and higher software quality. Continuous integration plays a crucial role in the release pipeline, as it involves merging all code changes from various developers multiple times a day. This process ensures that the changes are continuously integrated, tested, and validated against a predefined set of tests and quality standards. In case any issues or defects are identified during the integration phase, they can be quickly resolved within the pipeline before they impact the production environment. Another significant aspect of the release pipeline is continuous delivery, which involves automating the deployment process to ensure that software updates are consistently and reliably delivered to different environments, such as staging and production. By automating the deployment, organizations can eliminate the manual steps required for each release, reducing the risk of errors and enabling frequent deployments. In summary, a release pipeline in DevOps is an automated and standardized process that enables seamless and efficient software release and deployment. It incorporates continuous integration and delivery practices to ensure that software updates are thoroughly tested and seamlessly integrated with existing codebase and infrastructure before being deployed into production environments.

Release Train

A Release Train is a concept in DevOps that refers to a structured approach for delivering software updates and enhancements to end users. It involves organizing and coordinating multiple teams and their work on different features or components of a software product. At its core, a Release Train is a project management framework that enables efficient collaboration and synchronization across teams, ensuring that the various pieces of software being developed are integrated and deployed together. It aims to minimize conflicts and delays caused by dependencies between different features or components, allowing for a more streamlined and predictable release process.

Resilience

Resilience in the context of DevOps refers to the ability of a system or application to withstand and recover from failures, disruptions, or errors without compromising its functionality or user experience. It involves implementing measures and practices that ensure the system remains operational and responsive even in the face of unforeseen challenges. This resilience is achieved through various strategies and techniques, such as redundancy, fault tolerance, and rapid recovery. Redundancy involves having multiple instances or components of a system in place, so that if one fails, the others can seamlessly take over and continue providing service. Fault tolerance focuses on designing systems that can detect and handle errors or failures gracefully, with minimal impact on users or services. Rapid recovery involves implementing quick and efficient processes to recover from failures and restore normal operations as soon as possible. Resilience is a crucial aspect of DevOps because it helps ensure the continuous delivery and availability of software applications, even in dynamic and unpredictable environments. By building resilient systems, organizations can minimize downtime, avoid data loss, and maintain a high level of customer satisfaction. One approach to achieving resilience in DevOps is through automated monitoring and alerting. By continuously monitoring the performance and health of systems, organizations can proactively identify potential issues before they escalate into major problems. Alerts can be configured to notify relevant stakeholders, enabling them to take immediate action and implement remedial measures. This proactive approach helps prevent failures or disruptions from impacting users or services. Another key aspect of resilience is the ability to roll back or roll forward changes in a controlled and efficient manner. This involves implementing robust version control systems and configuration management practices, allowing organizations to easily revert to a previous working state if a change introduces unexpected issues. Conversely, the ability to roll forward involves applying updates or fixes quickly and safely, without causing any adverse effects on the system.

Resource Exhaustion Testing Techniques

Resource exhaustion testing is a critical practice in the field of DevOps that involves systematically evaluating an application or system's ability to handle excessive loads that could potentially lead to performance degradation or failure. It focuses on identifying and mitigating potential bottlenecks or shortcomings in the system's resources, such as CPU, memory, network, and disk space. This testing technique aims to simulate real-world scenarios where the system is subjected to an overwhelming amount of concurrent users, requests, or data processing. By doing so, it helps assess the system's capacity and scalability, ensuring it can efficiently handle the expected workload and beyond.

Resource Exhaustion Testing

Resource Exhaustion Testing is a type of testing performed in the DevOps context to evaluate the behavior and performance of a system under excessive resource consumption. It involves stressing the system beyond its normal capacity limits to identify potential bottlenecks and areas of weakness. This testing technique aims to ensure that the system can handle a high load and does not collapse or become unresponsive when subjected to peak or heavy usage scenarios. By simulating extreme conditions, such as a sudden surge in user activity or an unusually high volume of data, Resource Exhaustion Testing evaluates the system's ability to maintain stability, responsiveness, and availability.

Risk Management

Risk Management in the context of DevOps can be defined as the systematic process of identifying, assessing, and minimizing risks that may arise during the development, deployment, and operation of software applications. DevOps is a software development approach that emphasizes collaboration, integration, and automation between development and operations teams. It aims to deliver software applications quickly and efficiently, while ensuring high quality and reliability.

Role-Based Access Control (RBAC)

Role-Based Access Control (RBAC) is a security principle in the context of DevOps that provides a systematic and structured approach to managing access control permissions within an organization's infrastructure. It enables organizations to define roles based on job responsibilities and allocate access privileges accordingly.RBAC operates on the principle of least privilege, ensuring that individuals are granted the necessary permissions to perform their assigned tasks but no more. This approach minimizes the risk of unauthorized access or misuse of sensitive information and resources.RBAC consists of several components that work together to enforce access control policies. These components include roles, permissions, and users.A role defines a set of responsibilities or job functions within an organization. Roles can be assigned to individuals or groups, and each role is associated with a specific set of permissions. Permissions define the actions or operations that a role is allowed to perform, such as read, write, or execute. Users are individuals or groups who are assigned one or more roles based on their job functions.RBAC uses a hierarchical structure to manage access control. The roles are organized in a hierarchical manner, with higher-level roles inheriting permissions from lower-level roles. This hierarchical structure enables more efficient management of permissions and simplifies the process of granting or revoking access.RBAC provides a centralized and standardized approach to access control, making it easier to enforce security policies and ensure compliance. It offers several benefits in the context of DevOps, including increased efficiency, improved security, and better accountability.By implementing RBAC, organizations can streamline access management processes, reduce administrative overhead, and mitigate the risk of unauthorized access. DevOps teams can focus on their specific roles and responsibilities without having to worry about managing access permissions, promoting collaboration and productivity.In conclusion, Role-Based Access Control (RBAC) is a security principle in DevOps that organizes access control permissions into roles based on job responsibilities. RBAC promotes the principle of least privilege and ensures efficient access management, improved security, and better accountability.

Roles

Roles in the context of DevOps refer to the specific responsibilities and functions that individuals or teams undertake within an organization to support the development and operations of software products. These roles are crucial for achieving the goals of DevOps, which include faster delivery of software, improved collaboration, and continuous improvement. In a typical DevOps setup, there are several key roles that contribute to the overall success of the software development and deployment processes. One of the primary roles is that of the DevOps Engineer. DevOps Engineers are responsible for establishing and maintaining the tools and infrastructure necessary for continuous integration, continuous delivery, and continuous deployment. They work closely with development teams, operations teams, and other stakeholders to streamline the software development lifecycle and ensure efficient and reliable deployment of software. Another important role in DevOps is the Software Developer. Software Developers are responsible for writing and testing code, building software components, and troubleshooting issues that arise during the development process. They work closely with DevOps Engineers to ensure that the code integrates seamlessly into the overall system, and that it meets the requirements of the product and the organization. Additionally, there is the Operations Engineer role in DevOps. Operations Engineers focus on ensuring the stability and performance of the systems and applications. They monitor the infrastructure, troubleshoot issues, and optimize performance to ensure smooth operations. They collaborate with the DevOps Engineers and Software Developers to ensure that the software is delivered and deployed in a reliable and efficient manner. Other roles in DevOps include the Quality Assurance Engineer, who is responsible for testing and ensuring the quality of the software, and the Release Manager, who oversees the release process and coordinates with different teams to ensure smooth and efficient deployment of software updates and releases.

Rollbar

Rollbar is a DevOps tool that helps teams identify, diagnose, and resolve errors and issues in their software applications. It is a cloud-based error monitoring and logging solution that provides real-time visibility into the health and performance of applications across different environments and platforms. With Rollbar, developers can easily track and analyze errors, exceptions, and other issues that occur in their code. It automatically collects and aggregates error data from multiple sources, including server-side, client-side, and mobile applications. This allows developers to quickly identify and prioritize the most critical issues impacting their application's performance and user experience. Rollbar provides a range of features and functionalities that empower DevOps teams to streamline their error resolution process. It offers customizable alerting and notification capabilities, ensuring that developers are immediately informed about critical errors or issues that require attention. It also integrates with popular collaboration tools, such as Slack and JIRA, facilitating seamless communication and workflow management among team members. In addition to error monitoring, Rollbar also offers comprehensive logging and debugging capabilities. It allows developers to capture and analyze application logs, track user interactions, and trace code execution to identify the root cause of issues. This helps in reducing the time and effort required to resolve errors, leading to faster application performance improvements and enhanced user satisfaction. Rollbar's intuitive interface and powerful reporting tools enable developers to gain deep insights into their application's performance and error trends. It provides detailed dashboards, visualizations, and analytics that help in identifying patterns, hotspots, and areas for optimization. These insights empower DevOps teams to proactively detect and fix issues before they impact the end users, resulting in higher application reliability and stability.

Rollout.Io

Rollout.io is a DevOps tool that enables seamless feature releases and controlled feature rollbacks for mobile applications. It allows development teams to safely deploy and manage new features in real-time, without requiring users to update or reinstall the app. By leveraging Rollout.io, DevOps teams can reduce the risk associated with feature releases and ensure a positive user experience. Rollout.io follows a feature flagging approach, where developers can wrap new features into flags that can be toggled on and off remotely. This enables them to release new functionality gradually, to a small subset of users or to specific target audiences, before rolling it out to all users. This gradual rollout approach minimizes the impact of any potential bugs or performance issues, as developers can monitor the new features in real-time and disable them if necessary. Moreover, Rollout.io provides a feature rollback mechanism that allows DevOps teams to quickly revert to a previous version of the application if any issues arise after a feature release. This feature is particularly useful in cases where a released feature negatively affects the user experience or causes critical errors. By rapidly rolling back to a stable version, the impact on users can be minimized while the underlying issues are addressed. Rollout.io integrates seamlessly with popular mobile development frameworks and Continuous Integration/Continuous Deployment (CI/CD) tools, making it easy to incorporate into existing DevOps workflows. It provides detailed analytics and insights into feature usage, allowing development teams to make data-driven decisions about feature releases and rollbacks. In summary, Rollout.io is a powerful DevOps tool for managing feature releases and rollbacks in mobile applications. It enables development teams to release new features in a controlled and gradual manner, reducing the risk associated with feature deployments. With features like remote flag toggling and quick rollbacks, Rollout.io empowers DevOps teams to ensure a positive user experience and maintain application stability.

Root Cause Analysis (RCA)

Root Cause Analysis (RCA) is a systematic problem-solving technique used in the context of DevOps to identify and understand the underlying causes of incidents or issues that occur in the development and operations process. It aims to address the root causes of problems rather than just treating the symptoms. RCA involves a thorough investigation and analysis of the incident to determine the contributing factors and primary cause. It goes beyond simple problem resolution and focuses on preventing future occurrences by implementing effective countermeasures.

Root Cause Analysis

Root Cause Analysis (RCA) in the context of DevOps refers to a systematic approach to identifying and addressing the underlying causes of incidents, problems, or failures in software development and operations. It involves the use of various tools, techniques, and methodologies to analyze and investigate the root causes, with the ultimate goal of improving the overall system reliability and performance. RCA is an essential practice within the DevOps culture as it

154

promotes a proactive and continuous improvement mindset. By understanding and addressing the root causes, organizations can prevent recurring incidents, reduce downtime, and enhance the quality and stability of their software systems.

Rundeck

Rundeck is a powerful open-source automation tool that is specifically designed for infrastructure operations and deployments in the context of DevOps. It provides a centralized platform for managing and executing workflows, jobs, and tasks across a variety of systems and environments. With Rundeck, DevOps teams can easily automate routine operational activities such as provisioning and configuring resources, executing scripts and commands, and coordinating complex workflows. It offers a user-friendly web-based interface that allows users to define and schedule jobs, monitor their execution, and view detailed logs and reports.

SRE Playbooks Development

SRE Playbooks Development in the context of DevOps refers to the process of creating standardized and repeatable sets of instructions and best practices for handling common incidents and tasks in a Site Reliability Engineering (SRE) environment. Playbooks serve as a guide for SRE teams to respond to incidents, troubleshoot issues, and perform routine maintenance and operations tasks efficiently and effectively. The primary goal of developing SRE playbooks is to establish a shared understanding and response plan for various scenarios that can occur in a production environment. Playbooks outline step-by-step instructions, known as runbooks, that SRE teams can follow to mitigate issues and restore services quickly and reliably. These runbooks capture the collective knowledge and expertise of the SRE team and promote collaboration and consistency in incident response. Playbooks typically cover a wide range of scenarios, such as system failures, performance degradation, security incidents, and infrastructure changes. They may also include playbooks for common tasks like deploying new services, scaling resources, conducting post-incident reviews, and implementing proactive monitoring and alerting mechanisms. SRE playbooks prioritize automation and self-service wherever possible, enabling SRE teams to execute necessary actions with minimal manual intervention. They often integrate with existing monitoring and observability tools, chat platforms, and incident management systems to streamline incident response workflows. Regular review and iteration of SRE playbooks are crucial to ensure accuracy, relevance, and effectiveness. As the technology landscape evolves, playbooks need to be updated to reflect changing best practices, emerging threats, and enhancements in tooling and automation capabilities. In conclusion, SRE playbooks development is a critical DevOps practice that promotes consistency, reliability, and efficiency in incident response and operational tasks. By documenting and standardizing the knowledge and procedures required to manage various scenarios, SRE playbooks empower SRE teams to handle incidents proactively and maintain high system reliability.

SRE Playbooks

SRE Playbooks refer to a set of predefined and documented procedures, guidelines, and best practices that are employed by Site Reliability Engineers (SREs) in the context of DevOps. These playbooks aim to provide a standardized approach for handling various operational tasks and incidents. They serve as a knowledge repository and offer step-by-step instructions for different scenarios, ensuring consistent and efficient management of systems and services. The primary purpose of SRE Playbooks is to facilitate incident response, troubleshooting, and problem resolution. By documenting proven solutions and procedures, SRE teams can reduce downtime, mitigate risks, and establish a shared understanding of how to handle specific incidents. Playbooks also promote collaboration among team members, enabling them to work together effectively and ensure continuity of operations. These playbooks typically cover a wide range of operational areas, including system monitoring and alerting, capacity planning, deployment processes, incident management, post-incident reviews, and disaster recovery. They offer detailed instructions, tools, and methodologies to follow when encountering routine tasks and complex issues. Furthermore, SRE Playbooks are regularly reviewed and updated to incorporate new learnings and changes in the system architecture. This ensures that the playbooks remain relevant and effective, adapting to the evolving needs and challenges of the DevOps environment. In summary, SRE Playbooks are essential resources for SRE teams in

DevOps. They provide a standardized framework for handling operational tasks, incidents, and problems. By documenting best practices and procedures, these playbooks facilitate efficient incident response, minimize downtime, and promote collaboration among team members.

SaltStack

SaltStack is a powerful configuration management tool commonly used in the context of DevOps. It helps automate the deployment and management of complex infrastructure and application environments. As a configuration management tool, SaltStack provides a platform for defining and enforcing the desired state of systems and applications. It allows DevOps teams to declaratively specify the configuration settings for the various components of an environment, such as operating systems, network devices, databases, web servers, and applications. These configurations are written in a human-readable language, making it easy for teams to manage and version control their infrastructure code. SaltStack operates using a client-server architecture, with the Salt master serving as the central control point and the Salt minions as the managed nodes. The Salt master communicates with the Salt minions over secure channels, ensuring the integrity and confidentiality of the configuration data exchanged between them. The Salt minions can be installed on a variety of systems, including physical servers, virtual machines, and containers, allowing for a flexible and scalable deployment model. One of the key features of SaltStack is its ability to perform remote execution on a large number of systems simultaneously. This allows DevOps teams to execute commands and run scripts on multiple systems in parallel, greatly speeding up routine tasks such as software installation, patching, and system updates. SaltStack also supports orchestration, which enables the coordination and sequencing of complex tasks across multiple systems, ensuring consistency and reliability in the deployment process. Additionally, SaltStack provides a sophisticated event-driven architecture, allowing for real-time monitoring and reactive responses to system events. This enables DevOps teams to build intelligent, self-healing infrastructure that can automatically adapt to changing conditions and resolve issues without manual intervention. The event-driven nature of SaltStack also facilitates integration with other tools in the DevOps toolchain, enabling seamless communication and collaboration between different systems and processes.

Scalability

Scalability in the context of DevOps refers to the capability of a system, software application, or infrastructure to handle an increasing workload without experiencing performance degradation or requiring extensive modifications. It is a crucial aspect of DevOps as it ensures that the system can effectively handle growth and meet the demands of users and applications. Scalability aims to achieve optimal performance by efficiently utilizing resources, such as computing power, memory, storage, and network bandwidth. It involves designing and implementing systems that can adapt and scale seamlessly, both vertically (scaling up) and horizontally (scaling out), to accommodate changes in workload and user traffic.

Scrum

Scrum is a framework used in the context of DevOps to facilitate the effective and efficient delivery of software products. It is based on an iterative and incremental approach that allows cross-functional teams to collaborate and deliver high-quality software in a timely manner. In Scrum, the work is organized into short cycles known as sprints, typically lasting between one and four weeks. Each sprint begins with a planning meeting, where the team determines the scope of work to be completed during that sprint. The team then executes the work in a series of daily meetings called daily scrums, where they discuss progress, challenges, and plans for the day. At the end of each sprint, a review meeting takes place to showcase the completed work to stakeholders, gather feedback, and make any necessary adjustments. This allows for continuous improvement and adaptation throughout the development process. Scrum also includes other key components, such as the product backlog, which is a prioritized list of features and requirements. The product owner is responsible for managing the backlog and ensuring that the team is working on the most valuable and relevant items. Additionally, the scrum master acts as a facilitator, ensuring that the team follows the Scrum framework and removing any impediments that may hinder progress. By using Scrum in the context of DevOps, organizations can benefit from increased collaboration, transparency, and flexibility. The iterative nature of Scrum allows for frequent feedback and adjustments, resulting in quicker and more accurate delivery of software products. It also promotes self-organization and empowerment within the team, leading to improved productivity and satisfaction. In conclusion, Scrum is a powerful framework that enables teams to effectively manage software development projects in the context of DevOps. Its iterative and incremental approach, combined with cross-functional collaboration, facilitates the delivery of high-quality software in a timely and efficient manner.

Secret Encryption

Secret Encryption in the context of DevOps refers to the process of encoding sensitive information or data using cryptographic algorithms to protect it from unauthorized access or disclosure. It is an essential component in ensuring the security and confidentiality of data in DevOps environments.Secret Encryption involves transforming plaintext, which is the original form of the data, into ciphertext, which is the encrypted form of the data. The ciphertext can only be decrypted back into plaintext using a secret key or password, known only to authorized individuals or systems.One of the key objectives of DevOps is to automate processes and enable efficient collaboration between development and operations teams. However, this automation and collaboration often require the sharing of sensitive information such as API keys, passwords, and configuration data. Secret Encryption plays a crucial role in securing this sensitive information.By encrypting sensitive data, organizations can prevent unauthorized access and mitigate the risk of data breaches or leaks. In DevOps environments, secret encryption enables secure storage and transmission of secrets, ensuring that only authorized systems or individuals can access the encrypted data.Secret Encryption algorithms leverage cryptographic techniques such as symmetric encryption or asymmetric encryption. Symmetric encryption uses a single shared secret key for both encryption and decryption, making it efficient for encrypting and decrypting large amounts of data. Asymmetric encryption, on the other hand, uses a pair of public and private keys, where the public key is used for encryption and the private key is used for decryption.In addition to encryption, secret management is also crucial in DevOps environments. Secret management refers to the secure storage, distribution, rotation, and revocation of secrets. Organizations often utilize secret management tools or services to automate the lifecycle of secrets, including their encryption and decryption processes.Overall, Secret Encryption is a fundamental practice in DevOps to protect sensitive information, ensuring the security and integrity of data in automated and collaborative environments.+

Secret Management

Secret management in the context of DevOps refers to the practice of securely storing and handling sensitive information, such as passwords, API keys, database credentials, and other confidential data that is required for applications to function properly. It involves implementing processes, tools, and techniques to protect this sensitive information from unauthorized access and ensure that it is only accessible to authorized personnel or systems. Secrets are critical components of modern software systems and their security is of utmost importance. Effective secret management practices aim to minimize the risk of data breaches, unauthorized access, and other security vulnerabilities that can result in significant consequences, such as compromised customer data, financial losses, reputational damage, and regulatory compliance issues. In a DevOps environment, where applications are frequently deployed and updated, secret management becomes even more crucial. The dynamic nature of DevOps, with its automation and continuous integration/continuous deployment (CI/CD) pipelines, requires a robust approach to secret management that ensures secrets can be securely shared across different stages of the software development lifecycle. Key principles of effective secret management in DevOps include: 1. Confidentiality: Secrets should be stored in an encrypted format and kept confidential from unauthorized parties. Strong encryption algorithms and secure key management practices should be employed to protect the secrets at rest and in transit. 2. Access control: Only authorized individuals or systems should have access to the secrets. Access control mechanisms, such as role-based access control (RBAC) and multi-factor authentication (MFA), should be implemented to limit access to secrets based on defined roles and responsibilities. 3. Auditing and monitoring: Logging, auditing, and monitoring mechanisms should be in place to track and detect any unauthorized access or usage of secrets. This helps in identifying and addressing security incidents promptly. 4. Rotation and revocation: Secrets should be regularly rotated to minimize the impact of potential breaches. When a secret is compromised or no longer needed, it should be promptly revoked and replaced with a new secret. By following these principles and utilizing secret management tools and technologies,

157

organizations can ensure the confidentiality, integrity, and availability of their secrets, thereby reducing the risk of security incidents and strengthening the overall security posture of their DevOps environments.

Secret Rotation

Secret Rotation in the context of DevOps refers to the process of regularly changing and updating sensitive information or credentials that are used by applications and systems to authenticate and access secure resources. These secrets can include passwords, security tokens, encryption keys, API keys, database credentials, and other forms of sensitive data. The purpose of secret rotation is to enhance the security of systems and prevent unauthorized access in case the secrets become compromised or exposed. By regularly changing the secrets, the potential window of opportunity for attackers to use stolen or leaked credentials is reduced, mitigating the risk of unauthorized breaches.

Secure Access Service Edge (SASE)

Secure Access Service Edge (SASE) is a concept that combines network security and wide-area networking (WAN) capabilities into a single cloud-based service. It aims to provide organizations with a secure and reliable way to connect users and devices to both cloud and on-premises resources. In the context of DevOps, SASE plays a crucial role in enabling secure and reliable communication between different components of an organization's infrastructure. By offering integrated security and networking services in the cloud, SASE eliminates the need for separate networking and security appliances, simplifying the infrastructure deployment and management processes for DevOps teams.

Security Automation

Security automation in the context of DevOps refers to the process of integrating security measures and practices into the automated workflows and pipelines of software development, deployment, and operations. It involves the automation of security scanning, testing, monitoring, and remediation activities to identify and address vulnerabilities, threats, and risks in the software development lifecycle. By incorporating security automation, organizations can ensure that security is not treated as an afterthought but becomes an integral part of the DevOps process. It allows for the early detection and mitigation of security vulnerabilities, reducing the time and effort required for manual security reviews and audits. This helps in accelerating the software delivery process while ensuring that security remains a top priority. In the DevOps context, security automation is mainly achieved through the use of various tools, technologies, and practices. These include: 1. Continuous Integration and Continuous Deployment (CI/CD) pipelines, where security checks and tests are integrated into the automated build, test, and deployment processes. These pipelines ensure that security measures are applied consistently across different stages, from source code management to production deployment. 2. Static Application Security Testing (SAST) and Dynamic Application Security Testing (DAST) tools, which automatically scan the source code and running applications for potential security vulnerabilities and weaknesses. These tools provide developers and operators with valuable insights into potential security issues and suggest remediation actions. 3. Security Orchestration, Automation, and Response (SOAR) platforms, which help automate security incident response and enable quick and effective remediation of security events. These platforms integrate with various security tools and systems to automate the detection, analysis, and response to security incidents in real-time. Overall, security automation in DevOps aims to enable proactive and continuous security measures throughout the software development lifecycle. By integrating security into the automated processes, organizations can achieve faster, more reliable software delivery while maintaining robust security posture and reducing the overall risk of security breaches.

Security Champions In DevOps Advocacy

A Security Champion in the context of DevOps is an individual who advocates for and promotes security principles, practices, and requirements throughout the development and operations process. They are responsible for ensuring that security is integrated seamlessly into the DevOps workflow, addressing any vulnerabilities and mitigating risks associated with deploying software in a fast-paced, iterative environment. The Security Champion takes a proactive approach to security, collaborating closely with development, operations, and security teams to identify potential threats and implement measures to protect sensitive data, systems, and infrastructure. They act as the bridge between these different teams, fostering communication and knowledge sharing to create a culture of security awareness and understanding.

Security Champions In DevOps

A Security Champion in the context of DevOps is an individual who serves as a key advocate for security principles, practices, and processes within a DevOps team or organization. They are responsible for ensuring that security is integrated into all stages of the software development lifecycle, from design and coding to deployment and operations. The Security Champion works closely with cross-functional teams, including developers, operations engineers, and quality assurance professionals, to identify and address security vulnerabilities and risks. They act as a bridge between security specialists and the development team, helping to translate security requirements into actionable tasks and providing guidance on best practices. Key responsibilities of a Security Champion include: - Promoting a security-aware culture within the DevOps team, fostering a proactive approach to identifying and addressing security issues. - Reviewing and providing feedback on security-related design documents, architectural decisions, and code changes. - Conducting security assessments, such as code reviews and vulnerability scans, to identify potential weaknesses in applications and infrastructure. - Collaborating with developers to implement secure coding practices, such as input validation, output encoding, and access control. - Working with operations engineers to ensure that security controls, such as access management and logging, are in place and functioning effectively. - Staying up to date with the latest security threats and industry best practices, and sharing this knowledge with the DevOps team. By having a dedicated Security Champion within the DevOps team, organizations can proactively address security concerns and ensure that security is an integral part of the development process. This helps to reduce the risk of security incidents and vulnerabilities in software applications and infrastructure, ultimately enhancing the overall security posture of the organization.

Security Champions

A Security Champion, in the context of DevOps, refers to an individual or a team member who takes on the responsibility of driving security practices and fostering a security-first mindset within an organization's development and operations teams. They serve as a bridge between the security team and the software development team, ensuring that security concerns are addressed early in the development process and that secure coding practices are implemented throughout the software development lifecycle. Security Champions play a crucial role in promoting security awareness, education, and collaboration within DevOps teams. They work closely with developers, system administrators, and other stakeholders to identify potential security risks, provide guidance on secure coding practices and architectural decisions, and help prioritize security-related tasks. By taking an active role in code reviews, threat modeling, and security testing, they help to identify and mitigate vulnerabilities before they can be exploited.

Security Chaos Engineering Practices

Security Chaos Engineering Practices refer to the application of chaos engineering principles and practices in the context of security within a DevOps environment. Chaos engineering is a discipline that aims to test and improve the resilience and robustness of systems by intentionally injecting failures and disruptions to identify and address weaknesses before they become major incidents. In the realm of security, chaos engineering practices focus on proactively testing and assessing the effectiveness and responsiveness of security measures in place. By simulating real-world attack scenarios and malicious activities, security chaos engineering aims to identify vulnerabilities, weaknesses, and potential blind spots in the security infrastructure of an organization. DevOps, on the other hand, is an approach to software development and operations that emphasizes collaboration, automation, continuous integration, and continuous delivery. In this context, security chaos engineering practices are integrated into the DevOps pipeline to ensure that security concerns are addressed throughout the software development lifecycle. The key principles of security chaos engineering include: - Identifying critical security controls and systems: Understanding the key security controls and systems that protect the organization's assets and sensitive data. This includes identifying security devices, firewalls, access controls, intrusion detection systems, and other security components. - Defining realistic threat scenarios: Creating and simulating realistic attack scenarios that emulate the techniques, methods, and tools used by potential attackers. This involves considering internal and external threats, such as physical access breaches, social engineering attacks, malware, or network-based attacks. - Implementing controlled chaos experiments: Conducting controlled experiments by intentionally introducing failures, disruptions, or security breaches into the system to evaluate the effectiveness of security controls and the organization's response capabilities. These experiments can include scenarios like DDoS attacks, data breaches, user identity theft, or privilege escalation. - Monitoring and analyzing the impact: Continuously monitoring and analyzing the impact of chaos experiments on the system, including how security controls respond and how well the organization's incident response processes are functioning. This helps in identifying weaknesses in the security infrastructure and processes, allowing for improvements and remediation. By integrating security chaos engineering practices into the DevOps pipeline, organizations can identify and address security vulnerabilities and weaknesses proactively. This helps in building a more resilient and secure software ecosystem that can better withstand real-world threats and attacks.

Security Chaos Engineering

Security Chaos Engineering is a practice in the field of DevOps that focuses on intentionally introducing security vulnerabilities and weaknesses into a system or application to test its resilience against security threats. It is a proactive approach that aims to identify and address potential security vulnerabilities early in the development process, rather than waiting for them to be discovered during production. Similar to Chaos Engineering, which involves intentionally injecting failures and faults into a system to test its resilience and ability to handle unexpected events, Security Chaos Engineering takes this concept a step further by specifically targeting security aspects of the system. By deliberately introducing security vulnerabilities, such as weak authentication mechanisms, SQL injection, or cross-site scripting, Security Chaos Engineering helps uncover potential weaknesses and allows for the development of strategies to address them.

Security Incident Response Automation Tools

A security incident response automation tool in the context of DevOps is a software tool that is designed to automate and streamline the process of responding to security incidents within a DevOps environment. These tools are specifically developed to integrate with the various DevOps tools and processes, such as version control systems, continuous integration/continuous deployment (CI/CD) pipelines, configuration management tools, and monitoring systems, among others.

Security Incident Response Automation

The term "Security Incident Response Automation" refers to the process of automating the management and response to security incidents within the context of DevOps. It involves the use of tools, technologies, and methodologies to streamline the identification, analysis, and resolution of security incidents in order to minimize the impact on the system's availability, integrity, and confidentiality. DevOps is a collaborative approach that emphasizes the integration of development, operations, and security teams to deliver software more quickly and reliably. In this context, Security Incident Response Automation is a crucial component that ensures the security of the software development and deployment process. It allows organizations to detect, contain, and remediate security incidents promptly and efficiently, reducing the overall risk posture.

Security Information Exchange (SIE) Strategies

Security Information Exchange (SIE) strategies are a set of practices and approaches implemented in the context of DevOps to enhance the secure exchange of information between teams, systems, and applications. These strategies aim to promote collaboration, communication, and transparency while ensuring the protection of sensitive data and mitigating potential security risks. In the DevOps methodology, software development and IT operations teams work together to deliver high-quality applications and services at a faster pace. However, the rapid development and deployment cycles in DevOps can pose challenges to maintaining robust security practices. SIE strategies help bridge this gap by integrating security measures and information sharing into the DevOps workflow. One key aspect of SIE strategies is the implementation of secure communication channels between teams and systems. This involves enforcing secure protocols, such as encrypted connections, to protect sensitive data in transit. Additionally, secure authentication methods, such as strong passwords or multifactor authentication, may be utilized to ensure authorized access to critical information. Regular and timely sharing of security-related information is another crucial element of SIE strategies. This can involve sharing threat intelligence, security incidents, vulnerabilities, and other relevant information across teams involved in the DevOps process. By promoting a culture of information exchange, teams can collectively address security issues more effectively and reduce the time required to identify and remediate potential risks. Implementing security controls and measures at various stages of the DevOps pipeline is essential for a robust SIE approach. This can include automated security tests, vulnerability scanning, code analysis, and security audits, among others. By integrating security practices into the development, testing, and deployment processes, potential vulnerabilities can be identified and addressed early, reducing the likelihood of security breaches or incidents in production. Overall, Security Information Exchange (SIE) strategies play a critical role in ensuring the security and integrity of DevOps processes. By promoting secure communication, information sharing, and implementing security controls, these strategies enable organizations to maintain a DevOps workflow that is both efficient and secure.

Security Information Exchange (SIE) Tools

Security Information Exchange (SIE) Tools in the context of DevOps can be defined as software or platforms used to facilitate the exchange of security information among different systems, teams, and stakeholders involved in the software development and deployment process. These tools play a crucial role in DevOps by enabling the timely and efficient sharing of security-related insights, vulnerabilities, threats, and mitigation strategies. They help to establish a collaborative and transparent approach to security, promoting a proactive stance in addressing potential risks and ensuring the protection of software and infrastructure.

Security Information Exchange (SIE)

A Security Information Exchange (SIE), in the context of DevOps, refers to a platform or system that facilitates the sharing of security-related information among various stakeholders involved in the software development and operations process. The goal of a SIE is to improve the overall security posture of an organization by enabling effective collaboration, coordination, and communication regarding security incidents, threats, vulnerabilities, and best practices. This exchange of information helps DevOps teams to quickly identify and respond to security issues, mitigate potential risks, and enhance the security of the software deployment pipeline.

Security Information And Event Management (SIEM)

Security Information and Event Management (SIEM) is a comprehensive approach to managing security incidents and events in the context of DevOps. It involves the collection, analysis, and correlation of data from various sources to enable effective monitoring and identification of potential security threats and breaches. SIEM tools help organizations gain real-time visibility into their IT infrastructure, including logs, events, and network traffic. By centralizing and analyzing this information, SIEM systems provide valuable insights into security incidents, aiding in the timely detection and response to potential threats.

Security Orchestration, Automation, And Response (SOAR)

Security Orchestration, Automation, and Response (SOAR) is a systematic approach that combines people, processes, and technology in order to enhance and streamline the security incident response process in the context of DevOps. It integrates security tools, workflows, and procedures to provide a unified and cohesive security infrastructure. In the DevOps landscape, where continuous integration and continuous deployment (CI/CD) pipelines are crucial for rapid application development and delivery, security is often an overlooked aspect. SOAR bridges the gap between DevOps and security, ensuring that security is embedded into the development and deployment processes. By leveraging automation and orchestration capabilities, SOAR enables organizations to identify and respond to security incidents more effectively and efficiently. It automates routine security tasks, such as threat detection, incident triage, and response coordination, freeing up security teams to focus on more complex and critical issues. SOAR also facilitates collaboration and communication between different teams involved in the incident response process. It provides a centralized platform where security analysts, developers, operations teams, and other key stakeholders can work together, share information, and coordinate their actions. Furthermore, SOAR incorporates intelligent decision-making capabilities, using machine learning and artificial intelligence algorithms to analyze and prioritize security events. This helps in reducing false positives, improving detection accuracy, and enabling faster response to high-priority threats. Overall, in the context of DevOps, SOAR brings efficiency, agility, and scalability to the security incident response process. It enhances the security posture of organizations by ensuring that security is an integral part of the software development lifecycle, rather than an afterthought. By automating routine tasks, facilitating collaboration, and enabling intelligent decision-making, SOAR enables organizations to effectively manage and mitigate security risks in a DevOps environment.

Security Practices

Security Practices in the context of DevOps refer to the set of guidelines, policies, and procedures put in place to protect the confidentiality, integrity, and availability of software and systems throughout the software development and deployment lifecycle. These practices encompass various measures and controls that aim to minimize security risks, vulnerabilities, and threats, allowing organizations to deliver secure and high-quality software continuously.

Security Scanning Tools

Security scanning tools in the context of DevOps refer to software tools that are used to identify and detect security vulnerabilities and weaknesses in applications, networks, and systems. These tools play a crucial role in ensuring that DevOps teams can proactively address and mitigate potential security risks throughout the software development lifecycle. By conducting automated scans and analyses, security scanning tools help identify vulnerabilities such as software flaws, misconfigurations, weak authentication mechanisms, and other potential security loopholes. They use various techniques such as vulnerability scanning, static code analysis, dynamic application security testing (DAST), and interactive application security testing (IAST) to uncover potential security weaknesses.

Security Testing

Security testing in the context of DevOps refers to the process of evaluating and validating the security mechanisms and protocols implemented within an application or system during its development and deployment lifecycle. It aims to identify and address vulnerabilities and weaknesses that could potentially expose the application or system to security breaches or threats. This type of testing involves conducting a series of tests, assessments, and audits to assess the effectiveness of security measures and controls. It helps in identifying security gaps, misconfigurations, coding flaws, and potential entry points that could be exploited by malicious actors or cybercriminals.

Security Vulnerability Scanners Utilization

Security Vulnerability Scanners are tools utilized in the context of DevOps to identify and assess potential weaknesses and vulnerabilities within software applications, systems, networks, or infrastructure. These scanners aim to proactively detect security flaws that could be exploited by malicious actors, enabling organizations to prioritize and address these vulnerabilities to reduce the risk of unauthorized access, data breaches, or other security incidents. As a key component of a DevOps security strategy, vulnerability scanners automate the process of identifying security weaknesses, minimizing the manual effort involved in traditional manual code reviews and security audits. These scanners usually employ a combination of automated techniques, such as static analysis, dynamic testing, and pattern matching, to comprehensively evaluate the security posture of an environment.

Security Vulnerability Scanners

A security vulnerability scanner is a tool used in the context of DevOps to identify potential weaknesses or vulnerabilities in software or systems. It is designed to assess the security posture of an application or infrastructure by scanning for known vulnerabilities and providing insights on potential attack vectors or weaknesses that could be exploited by malicious actors. The scanner follows a systematic approach to identify security vulnerabilities by scanning the target system or application for known vulnerabilities or misconfigurations. It typically uses a database or repository of known vulnerabilities, which is continuously updated to include the latest threats and weaknesses. The scanner applies various techniques and checks to identify vulnerabilities, such as analyzing configuration files, examining network communication, or performing code analysis. Once the scan is complete, the security vulnerability scanner provides a detailed report that highlights the identified vulnerabilities and their severity levels. This report serves as a valuable resource for DevOps teams to prioritize and address the vulnerabilities in a systematic manner. The severity levels help prioritize the vulnerabilities based on their potential impact, allowing teams to focus on the most critical ones first. By using security vulnerability scanners as part of the DevOps process, organizations can proactively identify and mitigate potential security risks. Integrating vulnerability scanning into the CI/CD pipeline enables continuous monitoring and detection of vulnerabilities throughout the software development lifecycle. This allows for early identification and remediation of vulnerabilities, reducing the risk of exploitation and potential damage to systems and data. In summary, security vulnerability scanners play a crucial role in the context of DevOps by identifying potential weaknesses or vulnerabilities in software or systems. They help organizations enhance their security posture by proactively identifying and addressing vulnerabilities, reducing the risk of security breaches or attacks.

Security As Code

Security as Code, in the context of DevOps, refers to the practice of integrating security measures and controls into the development and deployment process of software. It involves the automation and continuous integration of security tasks, policies, and practices within the DevOps workflow, treating them as code. This approach aims to make security an integral part of the software development lifecycle (SDLC) rather than an afterthought or separate process. By treating security as code, organizations can leverage the same principles and practices they use for developing and deploying software to ensure that security measures are consistently applied, tested, and enforced throughout the entire development process. It promotes the idea of "shifting left" security, where security considerations are introduced early in the development cycle, reducing the risk of vulnerabilities and making the development process more secure by design.

Selenium

Selenium is a widely-used open-source framework that automates web browsers for testing and other purposes in the DevOps context. Specifically, Selenium provides a suite of tools and libraries that enable software teams to automate the testing and verification of web applications. With Selenium, developers and QA engineers can write scripts and tests in various programming languages, such as Java, Python, C#, and Ruby, to simulate user interactions with web browsers and validate the behavior of web applications.

Self-Healing Systems Implementation

Self-Healing Systems Implementation refers to the process of implementing automated mechanisms and practices within the DevOps framework to allow the system to detect, diagnose, and resolve issues and failures without human intervention. This approach aims to minimize downtime, optimize system performance, and maintain high availability, reliability, and quality of software delivery. In a DevOps environment, self-healing systems implementation involves several key components: 1. Proactive Monitoring: Continuous monitoring of the system, infrastructure, and applications is essential to detect anomalies, deviations, and failure patterns. This includes monitoring of metrics such as CPU usage, memory utilization, network latency, and response time. By leveraging machine learning and anomaly detection algorithms, systems can learn normal behavior patterns and raise alerts when deviations are detected. 2. Alerting

163

and Notifications: Once anomalies or failures are detected, the system should trigger appropriate alerts and notifications to inform the relevant teams or stakeholders. These alerts can be sent through various communication channels such as email, messaging platforms, or dashboards. Clear and concise alert messages should provide essential details for effective troubleshooting. 3. Automated Incident Response: Upon receiving alerts, the self-healing system should automatically attempt to diagnose the root cause of the issue. This can involve running predefined scripts or commands to gather additional data or perform preliminary troubleshooting steps. The system should also prioritize incidents based on severity and impact to allocate resources efficiently. 4. Remediation and Recovery: Once the root cause is identified or inferred, the self-healing system should perform automated actions to resolve the issue or mitigate its impact. This can include restarting services, reallocating resources, or triggering other remediation steps. Additionally, the system should maintain a log or audit trail of all performed actions for future analysis and improvement. The implementation of self-healing systems reduces the manual effort required to identify and resolve issues, enabling businesses to achieve faster incident resolution and improved system reliability. It also enhances scalability by automatically adjusting resources based on demand patterns and optimizing system performance. With self-healing systems in place, DevOps teams can focus their efforts on more strategic and value-added tasks, leading to higher productivity and improved customer satisfaction.

Self-Healing Systems

A self-healing system in the context of DevOps refers to a software architecture or infrastructure that has the ability to automatically detect, diagnose, and resolve issues without human intervention. This concept aligns with the principles of automation and continuous improvement in order to achieve reliable and resilient systems. Self-healing systems aim to minimize downtime, reduce the impact of failures, and improve overall system availability. These systems employ a combination of monitoring, alerting, and automated recovery mechanisms to achieve their objectives.

Semaphore

A semaphore is a synchronization construct used in DevOps to control access to a shared resource or a critical section of code in a concurrent environment. It acts as a signaling mechanism to coordinate the execution of multiple processes or threads running concurrently. The semaphore maintains a count, known as its value or the number of available resources, which indicates the current state of the shared resource.

Sentry

Sentry is a platform that provides real-time error tracking and monitoring to help improve the stability and reliability of software applications in a DevOps environment. It captures and aggregates errors and exceptions that occur in the codebase, allowing developers to quickly identify and resolve issues. With Sentry, teams can proactively monitor their applications and receive instant alerts whenever errors or performance issues arise. It provides detailed insights into the root cause of errors, including stack traces, code context, and environment data, helping developers troubleshoot and fix problems more efficiently.

Serverless API Gateway Configuration

A serverless API Gateway configuration is a DevOps practice that involves the setup and management of an API Gateway without the need for traditional server provisioning and management. The term "serverless" refers to the abstraction of servers away from the developers, allowing them to focus solely on writing code and not worry about server infrastructure. In a serverless architecture, the API Gateway acts as a middleman between clients (such as mobile apps or web browsers) and server-side functions or services. It serves as an entry point for incoming requests, provides authentication and authorization mechanisms, and routes requests to the appropriate backend services or lambda functions.

Serverless API Gateway

A Serverless API Gateway is a cloud service that acts as a front door for managing and routing

API requests across different microservices and serverless functions. It enables developers to build, publish, monitor, and secure APIs without the need to manage infrastructure or servers. Serverless API Gateway automates the process of handling incoming API requests and routes them to the appropriate backend service endpoints based on the defined configurations. It acts as a communication layer between the clients and the backend services, ensuring that requests are properly authenticated, authorized, and routed to the correct destination.

Serverless Architecture

Serverless architecture is a software design pattern in the context of DevOps that allows developers to focus on code development and business logic without having to manage the underlying infrastructure. In this architecture, applications are built and deployed as small, independent functions, which are executed in response to specific events or triggers. These functions are stateless and short-lived, meaning that they don't maintain a persistent connection to resources or store data between invocations. With serverless architecture, developers don't need to worry about provisioning and managing servers, as the cloud provider takes care of scaling and managing the infrastructure based on demand. This enables developers to focus more on writing code and delivering value to their customers, without being burdened by the complexities of traditional server-based architectures.

Serverless Authentication And Authorization

Serverless authentication and authorization is a DevOps practice that involves securing access to serverless applications and resources. In the context of DevOps, serverless authentication refers to the process of verifying the identity of users or systems that attempt to access serverless resources. This authentication is typically done using credentials, such as usernames and passwords, API keys, or JSON Web Tokens (JWTs). By authenticating users and systems, serverless authentication ensures that only authorized entities can access the relevant resources. Serverless authorization, on the other hand, is the process of granting or denying access to specific serverless resources based on authenticated user attributes or other factors. It involves defining granular access control policies that determine who can perform certain operations, such as reading, writing, or modifying data stored in a serverless database. Authorization ensures that even authenticated entities can only access the resources they are authorized to use, enforcing the principle of least privilege.

Serverless CI/CD Pipelines

A serverless CI/CD pipeline is a continuous integration and continuous deployment process that uses a serverless architecture to automate the building, testing, and deployment of software applications. In the context of DevOps, serverless CI/CD pipelines enable developers and operations teams to streamline and accelerate the delivery cycle of software updates and new features. Traditionally, CI/CD pipelines require the setup and maintenance of infrastructure, such as servers and virtual machines, to execute the various stages of the pipeline. However, with serverless architecture, developers can leverage cloud computing platforms to offload the responsibility of infrastructure management. A serverless CI/CD pipeline typically consists of several stages, including: 1. Source code management: Developers commit their code changes to a version control repository, such as Git, which serves as the single source of truth for the application code. 2. Build and test automation: The pipeline automatically pulls the latest code changes from the repository, compiles the code, runs automated tests to ensure code quality and integrity, and generates artifacts. 3. Artifact storage: The generated artifacts, such as compiled code or Docker images, are stored in a secure and accessible location. 4. Deployment automation: The pipeline automates the deployment of the artifacts to the target environment, such as a staging or production environment, using serverless computing resources. 5. Continuous monitoring: The pipeline integrates monitoring and logging tools to track the performance and stability of the deployed application in real-time. Serverless CI/CD pipelines offer several benefits for DevOps teams. Firstly, it reduces the need for infrastructure management, as the serverless architecture handles scalability, elasticity, and availability. This allows teams to focus more on developing and releasing high-quality software. Secondly, serverless pipelines enable faster delivery cycles, as code changes can be built, tested, and deployed automatically, removing manual, error-prone processes. Finally, serverless CI/CD pipelines offer cost efficiency, as they dynamically scale resources based on demand, reducing infrastructure costs.

Serverless Cold Starts

Serverless cold starts refers to the delay experienced when a serverless function is invoked for the first time or after a period of inactivity. In the context of DevOps, serverless cold starts can impact the performance and responsiveness of applications that rely on serverless architecture. When a serverless function is invoked, the underlying cloud provider needs to provision resources and allocate infrastructure to handle the request. This process takes time and can result in a delay in the execution of the function. Cold starts occur when the function has been idle for a certain period or when it is invoked for the very first time. This delay can have implications for the overall user experience and the scalability of the application. One of the main reasons behind serverless cold starts is the concept of "scaling to zero" that many cloud providers adopt to optimize resource allocation and cost. Scaling to zero means that when a function is not in use, the cloud provider will deallocate the resources associated with it to minimize costs. When a new request arrives, the provider needs to spin up the required resources again, leading to a delay. Serverless cold starts can have a significant impact on applications that have strict latency or real-time processing requirements. The delay introduced by cold starts can result in increased response times and performance degradation. To mitigate this, various strategies can be employed, such as pre-warming functions by sending periodic requests or using different deployment architectures that minimize cold starts, such as keeping functions warm by invoking them periodically.

Serverless Compliance And Auditing

Serverless compliance and auditing in the context of DevOps refers to the processes, practices, and tools used to ensure that serverless applications and their associated infrastructure comply with relevant regulations, policies, and security standards. It involves implementing measures to assess and validate the compliance of serverless systems, as well as establishing controls to monitor and enforce compliance on an ongoing basis.Compliance and auditing are crucial aspects of DevOps because they help organizations meet legal and regulatory requirements, protect sensitive data, and maintain the integrity, availability, and confidentiality of their serverless environments.

Serverless Computing

Serverless computing is a cloud computing execution model that allows developers to build and run applications without the need to manage servers or infrastructure. In the context of DevOps, serverless computing is a paradigm that enables automated deployment, scaling, and management of applications by abstracting away the underlying infrastructure. By eliminating the need for server management, serverless computing simplifies the development and deployment processes, allowing DevOps teams to focus on the application logic rather than infrastructure concerns. In this model, developers can write code in the form of event-driven functions or microservices, which are executed in response to specific events or triggers. One of the main advantages of serverless computing in DevOps is the ability to scale applications automatically in response to changes in demand. With traditional servers, scaling requires manual intervention and provisioning of additional resources. In contrast, serverless platforms, such as AWS Lambda or Azure Functions, automatically scale the number of function instances based on the incoming workload, ensuring optimal performance and cost-efficiency. Another benefit of serverless computing for DevOps is the pay-per-use pricing model. With serverless platforms, organizations only pay for the actual execution time of functions or the number of resources consumed. This pricing model provides cost savings, especially for applications with intermittent or unpredictable workloads. In addition to scalability and cost-efficiency, serverless computing also offers improved availability and fault tolerance. Serverless platforms typically provide built-in redundancy and fault isolation mechanisms, ensuring that functions are executed reliably. This resilience is crucial for maintaining the availability of applications, especially during peak traffic periods or in the event of server failures. In summary, serverless computing in the context of DevOps is a cloud execution model that allows developers to build and deploy applications without the need to manage servers or infrastructure. It simplifies the development and deployment process, provides automatic scaling and cost savings, and offers improved availability and fault tolerance. By leveraging serverless platforms, DevOps teams can

166

streamline their workflows and focus on delivering high-quality applications.

Serverless Containers

Serverless Containers refers to the combination of serverless computing and containerization to enable developers to run applications in an efficient and scalable manner, without the need to manage underlying infrastructure. Serverless computing allows developers to focus on writing code without the hassle of provisioning, managing, and scaling servers. It abstracts away the server infrastructure, automatically and dynamically allocating resources as needed. This serverless model is event-driven, meaning that functions are triggered by specific events and only run when necessary. This approach offers various benefits, including cost savings as resources are only consumed when code is executed, automatic scaling to handle fluctuating workloads, and simplified deployment and management tasks. Containerization, on the other hand, provides a lightweight and portable way to package and isolate applications and their dependencies. Containers encapsulate the application and its dependencies into a single executable package, ensuring consistency and simplifying deployment across different environments. Containers are highly scalable, efficient, and enable applications to run consistently across different platforms. When combined, serverless computing and containers create a powerful and flexible environment for running applications. Serverless containers offer the benefits of both models, allowing developers to run code in a containerized environment without worrying about managing the underlying infrastructure. Developers can focus on writing code, while the serverless platform takes care of automatically scaling the containers based on demand. In the context of DevOps, serverless containers enable organizations to adopt a more agile and efficient approach to software development and deployment. Developers can package their applications into containers and deploy them in a serverless environment, taking advantage of the scalability and cost savings offered by serverless computing. DevOps teams can leverage automation and infrastructure-as-code practices to seamlessly deploy and manage serverless containers, reducing the operational overhead and allowing for faster and more reliable deployments. Overall, serverless containers provide a powerful combination of serverless computing and containerization, enabling developers and DevOps teams to build and deploy applications in a more efficient, scalable, and flexible manner.

Serverless Cost Management

Serverless cost management, in the context of DevOps, refers to the process of effectively monitoring and controlling expenses associated with serverless computing architectures. Serverless computing, a cloud computing model, allows developers to run applications and execute code without needing to provision or manage the underlying infrastructure. While serverless computing offers numerous benefits, such as scalability and reduced operational tasks, it also introduces new cost considerations that need to be managed efficiently. Effective serverless cost management involves several key strategies and practices. Firstly, it requires monitoring and analyzing the usage patterns of the serverless functions or services. This helps identify any inefficiencies, unused resources, or over-provisioned functions that may contribute to unnecessary costs. By continuously tracking resource utilization, organizations can make informed decisions on optimizing the allocation of serverless resources. Additionally, visibility into the usage patterns can enable teams to identify potential cost-saving opportunities, such as rightsizing functions or leveraging cost-effective service tiers. Furthermore, serverless cost management involves setting appropriate budgets and thresholds to maintain control over spending. By defining budget limits and implementing automated alerts, organizations can be promptly notified when costs approach or exceed defined thresholds. This proactive approach allows for timely intervention and adjustments to prevent unexpected financial burdens. Another critical aspect of serverless cost management is optimizing the performance and efficiency of serverless functions. Fine-tuning the code and architecture of serverless functions can minimize execution time and resource consumption, resulting in cost savings. Furthermore, leveraging techniques such as caching, queuing, and intelligent load balancing can improve efficiency and reduce the overall usage of serverless resources. In summary, serverless cost management in DevOps involves monitoring resource utilization, setting budgets and thresholds, optimizing serverless function performance, and constant analysis of cost-saving opportunities. By implementing these practices, organizations can harness the benefits of serverless computing while avoiding unnecessary costs and maintaining control over their cloud expenses.

167

Serverless Data Processing

Serverless data processing refers to the practice of executing data processing tasks without the need for dedicated servers or infrastructure management. It is a cloud computing model that enables developers to focus on writing and deploying code without the overhead of provisioning or maintaining servers. In the context of DevOps, serverless data processing allows for the automation of data pipelines and workflows. It involves the use of cloud services, such as AWS Lambda or Azure Functions, to execute code in response to specific events or triggers. This approach eliminates the need to manually provision and configure servers, resulting in increased flexibility, scalability, and cost efficiency.

Serverless Data Storage

Serverless data storage refers to a cloud computing architecture that allows the storage and retrieval of data without the need for managing the underlying server infrastructure. It enables developers to focus on writing code and designing applications without worrying about provisioning, scaling, or managing servers. In the context of DevOps, serverless data storage offers several advantages. First and foremost, it eliminates the need for capacity planning and provisioning of servers, as the cloud provider takes care of maintaining and scaling the infrastructure automatically. This allows DevOps teams to focus on the business logic and application development rather than spending time and effort on server management and maintenance tasks. Serverless data storage also provides a higher level of scalability and availability. With traditional server-based architectures, scaling up or down requires manual intervention, which can be time-consuming and error-prone. In contrast, serverless architectures provide an elastic scalability model, where resources are automatically allocated based on demand. This ensures that applications can handle varying workloads efficiently, without interruptions or performance bottlenecks. Additionally, serverless data storage offers cost optimization benefits. Rather than paying for idle server capacity, organizations only pay for the actual resources consumed. This makes serverless architectures more cost-effective, especially for applications with unpredictable or fluctuating workloads. It also simplifies cost management and budgeting for DevOps teams, as they only need to monitor and optimize resource utilization, rather than dealing with complex server cost calculations. Furthermore, serverless data storage promotes agility and faster time-to-market. Developers can quickly prototype, build, and deploy applications without the need to set up and configure servers. This enables them to iterate and release new features or updates more rapidly, resulting in shorter development cycles and improved competitiveness in the market. In conclusion, serverless data storage is a cloud computing paradigm that allows developers to store and retrieve data without managing servers. In the DevOps context, it offers benefits such as reduced server management overhead, automatic scalability, cost optimization, and increased agility and speed of application development.

Serverless Database

A serverless database is a database management system that does not require the use of a dedicated server or infrastructure to run. It is designed to provide a scalable and flexible solution to manage and store data without the need for server management and maintenance. In the context of DevOps, a serverless database can be seen as a way to simplify the deployment and management of databases in cloud-native environments. Traditionally, managing databases required provisioning and managing dedicated servers, ensuring high availability, and handling various infrastructure-related tasks. This often involved significant overhead and operational complexity for DevOps teams. Serverless databases, on the other hand, abstract away much of the underlying infrastructure management and provide automated scaling and performance optimizations. By leveraging cloud services and technologies, serverless databases enable DevOps teams to focus more on application development and less on infrastructure management. With a serverless database, developers can simply define the required resources and the database service takes care of scaling, replication, and other backend tasks automatically. Serverless databases also offer pay-as-you-go pricing models, meaning that users only pay for the resources actually consumed. This can be advantageous for DevOps teams as it helps optimize costs and eliminates the need for capacity planning and overprovisioning. Furthermore, serverless databases often provide built-in functionality for automatic backups, disaster recovery, and data replication, ensuring high availability and data durability. This enables DevOps teams to have peace of mind knowing that their data is safe and protected. In conclusion, a serverless database in the context of DevOps is a database management system that eliminates the need for server management and provides automated scaling and performance optimization. It enables DevOps teams to focus more on application development and reduces the operational complexity associated with traditional database management.

Serverless Deployment Strategies

A serverless deployment strategy is a method of deploying applications and services in a cloud environment without the need for managing or provisioning servers. It is a key concept in DevOps, which focuses on automating and improving the collaboration between development and operations teams. By leveraging serverless architecture, organizations can achieve a more efficient and scalable deployment process. In a serverless deployment strategy, developers write code snippets or functions, which are then deployed as individual units of execution, known as serverless functions or function-as-a-service (FaaS). These functions are managed and executed by a cloud provider, such as Amazon Web Services (AWS) Lambda or Microsoft Azure Functions, without the need for the developer to explicitly manage the infrastructure. By adopting a serverless deployment strategy, organizations can benefit from several advantages. Firstly, it eliminates the need for managing and scaling servers, as the cloud provider handles the infrastructure for execution. This enables developers to focus solely on writing code and delivering features, rather than worrying about managing servers. Secondly, serverless deployment allows for automatic scaling and high availability. With traditional server-based deployment models, organizations need to provision and manage servers based on anticipated traffic. In contrast, serverless environments automatically scale up or down based on demand, ensuring efficient resource utilization and cost savings. Additionally, serverless deployment strategies enable organizations to reduce time to market and accelerate the development process. With functions deployed individually, organizations can quickly iterate and update specific features without having to deploy and test an entire application. This flexibility allows for faster development cycles and faster delivery of new features and updates to end-users. In summary, a serverless deployment strategy in the context of DevOps is an approach that involves deploying applications and services in a cloud environment without the need for managing servers. It leverages function-as-a-service (FaaS) platforms to execute code snippets, providing benefits such as simplified infrastructure management, automatic scaling, high availability, and faster development cycles.

Serverless Error Handling

Serverless Error Handling refers to the strategic approach of identifying, managing, and resolving errors or exceptions that occur within a serverless architecture or application. In the context of DevOps, it involves implementing effective methods and practices to handle errors encountered during the execution of serverless functions or services. This process plays a crucial role in ensuring the seamless operation and optimal performance of serverless applications. When errors occur within a serverless architecture, they can disrupt the functionality of the application, lead to degraded performance, or even result in complete service outage. Therefore, it is essential to implement a robust error handling mechanism to detect, diagnose, and resolve errors promptly.

Serverless Framework

The Serverless Framework is a powerful and widely-used tool in the DevOps world that allows developers to build and deploy applications without worrying about server management. It simplifies the process of creating and managing serverless functions, making it easier for teams to develop, test, and deploy their code. Serverless computing, also known as Function-as-a-Service (FaaS), is a cloud computing model where cloud providers manage the infrastructure and automatically allocate resources based on the application's needs. With Serverless Framework, developers can write their application logic as small, independent functions that are triggered by events, such as an HTTP request or a database update. This "function-as-a-service" approach allows for efficient resource utilization and eliminates the need to provision and manage servers. The Serverless Framework abstracts away the complexity of managing servers and infrastructure, providing a higher level of abstraction for developers. It allows them to focus on writing quality code and building scalable applications instead of worrying about server provisioning, scaling, and maintenance. Using the Serverless Framework, developers can define their application's infrastructure and configuration using a simple configuration file, typically written in YAML. This file specifies the functions, events, and resources needed for the application. The Serverless Framework then translates this configuration into the necessary cloud provider-specific configurations and automates the deployment of the application. In addition to deployment automation, the Serverless Framework offers other features to simplify the development process. It supports local development and testing of functions, allowing developers to iterate on their code quickly. It also integrates with popular development tools and services, such as version control systems, continuous integration and deployment platforms, and monitoring solutions. Overall, the Serverless Framework provides a seamless experience for developers to build and deploy serverless applications. It enables teams to embrace the advantages of serverless computing, such as scalability, cost-efficiency, and reduced operational overhead, while streamlining the development and deployment process.

Serverless Frameworks

A serverless framework is a software framework that allows developers to build and deploy applications without having to manage the underlying infrastructure. In the context of DevOps, serverless frameworks facilitate the implementation of a serverless architecture, where the responsibility for managing and scaling servers is offloaded to the cloud provider.Serverless frameworks provide an abstraction layer that automates the deployment, scaling, and management of serverless applications. They enable developers to focus on writing code and implementing business logic, without having to worry about provisioning servers, configuring load balancers, or managing databases.

Serverless Function Versioning

Serverless function versioning is a DevOps practice that involves creating and managing different versions of serverless functions, which are small modular units of code that are executed in response to specific events. These functions are typically used in cloud computing environments, where they allow developers to write code without the need to provision or manage servers. Versioning serverless functions is essential for several reasons. Firstly, it allows developers to make changes to their code without affecting the stability or functionality of existing applications. By creating different versions of a serverless function, developers can test new features or bug fixes without impacting the production environment. This promotes a safer and more controlled deployment process, as it reduces the risk of introducing unintended errors or breaking existing functionality.

Serverless Functions

Serverless functions, in the context of DevOps, refer to small units of code that are executed in a cloud environment without the need to provision or manage servers. They are event-driven and automatically triggered by specific events, such as HTTP requests, database changes, or file uploads. These functions are typically written in a specific programming language, such as JavaScript, Python, or Go, and are bundled into standalone units of code known as function packages or artifacts. The cloud provider takes care of the infrastructure required to run the code, automatically scaling it up or down based on demand.

Serverless Integration Patterns

Serverless integration patterns, in the context of DevOps, refer to the strategies and approaches used to seamlessly connect and integrate various serverless components or services within a larger system or infrastructure. Serverless architecture has gained popularity in modern application development due to its scalability, cost-effectiveness, and ease of maintenance. However, as applications become more complex and rely on a combination of serverless services, integrating these components effectively becomes crucial for overall system functionality and performance.

Serverless Logs

Serverless Logs refer to the log files generated by applications running in a serverless environment. In the context of DevOps, serverless logs are essential for monitoring, troubleshooting, and optimizing the performance of serverless applications. In a typical serverless architecture, applications are composed of small, self-contained functions that are executed in response to specific events. These functions run on cloud infrastructure provided by a managed service, such as AWS Lambda or Google Cloud Functions, without the need for provisioning or managing servers. As these functions execute, they generate log data that captures important information about their execution, including errors, warnings, and performance metrics. Serverless logs play a crucial role in DevOps practices, providing valuable insights into the overall health and behavior of serverless applications. DevOps teams can leverage these logs to gain visibility into the execution flow, identify and debug issues, and optimize the performance of their applications. By analyzing serverless logs, DevOps professionals can track the execution of functions, pinpoint errors or bottlenecks, and gather performance data. They can identify patterns of slow response times or high error rates, helping them to identify and resolve performance issues. Moreover, serverless logs can provide useful information for capacity planning, security audits, and compliance requirements. Monitoring serverless logs is typically achieved by integrating with a logging service or central log management system, such as Amazon CloudWatch Logs, Azure Monitor Logs, or Google Cloud Logging. These services collect and aggregate logs from multiple functions and provide search, filtering, and visualization capabilities for efficient log exploration and analysis. In summary, serverless logs are the log files generated by functions running in a serverless environment. DevOps teams rely on these logs to monitor, troubleshoot, and optimize serverless applications, enabling them to ensure the reliability, performance, and overall success of their applications.

Serverless Monitoring And Alerts

Serverless monitoring and alerts in the context of DevOps refer to the process of collecting and analyzing data from serverless applications to ensure their availability, performance, and overall health. Serverless computing is a cloud computing model that allows developers to build and run applications without the need to manage or provision servers. Monitoring and alerting in a serverless environment is essential to ensure that applications are running smoothly, identify and troubleshoot issues, and proactively respond to potential problems. Monitoring in a serverless environment involves collecting and analyzing various metrics and logs from the different components of a serverless application. This can include metrics related to function invocations, resource utilization, error rates, and latency. By monitoring these metrics, DevOps teams can get a comprehensive understanding of the application's behavior and performance, enabling them to identify potential bottlenecks or areas for optimization. Monitoring can also help detect and mitigate issues such as outages, performance degradation, or resource constraints. Alerting is an integral part of serverless monitoring, as it enables DevOps teams to be immediately notified of critical issues or abnormal behavior in the application. Alerts can be set up based on predefined thresholds or specific conditions, such as a sudden spike in error rates or a significant increase in latency. When an alert is triggered, notifications are sent to the appropriate team members, allowing them to quickly respond and resolve the issue before it impacts the application's performance or availability. In addition to proactive monitoring and alerting, serverless monitoring and alerts also help with capacity planning and cost optimization. By analyzing usage patterns and resource consumption, DevOps teams can make informed decisions regarding the allocation and scaling of resources, ensuring optimal performance and cost efficiency. This allows organizations to effectively manage their serverless deployments and allocate resources according to actual demand, avoiding underutilization or unnecessary costs.

Serverless Monitoring

Serverless monitoring, in the context of DevOps, refers to the practice of overseeing and analyzing the performance and availability of serverless applications. Serverless computing allows developers to focus solely on writing code, without having to manage the underlying infrastructure or servers. As a result, monitoring serverless applications requires a different approach compared to traditional application monitoring. Serverless monitoring tools aim to provide insights into the health, performance, and usage of serverless applications. These tools collect and analyze data from various sources, including logs, metrics, and tracing. They help identify issues, track down bottlenecks, and optimize the overall performance of serverless functions.

Serverless Multi-Region Deployment

A serverless multi-region deployment is a methodology in the context of DevOps that involves deploying an application across multiple regions without the need for managing traditional server infrastructure. It leverages the capabilities of cloud computing to distribute the application across different regions, providing improved availability, scalability, and fault tolerance. This approach is based on the principles of serverless computing, where developers focus on writing and deploying code without having to provision and manage servers. In a multi-region deployment, the application is broken down into smaller functional components or microservices, each running independently and independently scalable, within a serverless architecture.

Serverless Observability

Serverless observability is a concept in the field of DevOps that refers to the ability to effectively monitor and gain insights into the performance and behavior of serverless architectures. In a serverless computing environment, applications are built and run on cloud platforms, where the underlying infrastructure and scaling capabilities are managed by the cloud provider. This allows developers to focus solely on writing code and not worry about infrastructure management. However, with the distributed and event-driven nature of serverless architectures, it becomes crucial to have visibility into the various components and functions of the application to ensure optimal performance, identify issues, and troubleshoot problems. Serverless observability encompasses different monitoring and logging techniques that enable DevOps teams to gather data, gain visibility, and analyze the behavior of serverless applications.

Serverless Orchestration

Serverless orchestration is a concept in the context of DevOps that refers to the coordination and management of serverless functions or services within an application or system. These serverless functions are pieces of code that run in a cloud environment, allowing developers to focus solely on writing the code and leaving the underlying infrastructure management to the cloud provider. Orchestration is the process of ensuring that different serverless functions or services work together harmoniously to accomplish a specific task or business requirement. It involves defining the sequence of execution, managing the flow of data, and handling any dependencies or interactions between the different functions or services. In a serverless architecture, each function or service performs a specific task, such as processing data, performing calculations, or interacting with external systems. Orchestrating these functions allows developers to create complex workflows by chaining and coordinating the execution of multiple functions. Serverless orchestration plays a crucial role in the development and deployment of applications in a DevOps environment. It enables developers to break down applications into smaller, more manageable pieces of code, known as microservices, which can be deployed and scaled independently. This modular approach enhances agility, as developers can make changes to individual functions without affecting the entire application. Furthermore, serverless orchestration promotes automation and enables developers to define workflows using configuration files or code, eliminating the need for manual intervention. This automation simplifies the deployment and operational management of serverless applications, making it easier to test, troubleshoot, and update them. In summary, serverless orchestration is the coordination and management of serverless functions or services within an application or system. It enables developers to create complex workflows, break down applications into smaller pieces, automate deployment and operational management, and enhance agility in the development process.

Serverless Performance Optimization

Serverless Performance Optimization in the context of DevOps refers to the practice of fine-tuning and enhancing the performance of serverless applications. Serverless architecture, also known as Function as a Service (FaaS), allows developers to focus on writing code without the need to manage servers or infrastructure. However, to ensure optimal performance and efficiency, it is crucial to optimize various aspects of serverless applications, including code, configurations, and dependencies. Serverless Performance Optimization involves several key activities. Firstly, developers need to analyze and refactor their code to eliminate any unnecessary or redundant operations. This includes reducing the size of functions, minimizing the number of external API calls, and optimizing resource utilization. By optimizing the code, developers can improve the overall execution speed and reduce latency in serverless applications. Secondly, fine-tuning the configurations and settings of serverless applications is essential for achieving optimal performance. Developers need to configure the appropriate amount of memory and CPU resources for each function to ensure efficient execution. Additionally, optimizing the networking configurations, such as adjusting timeouts and increasing concurrent request limits, can further enhance the performance of serverless applications. Thirdly, managing dependencies efficiently is crucial in serverless performance optimization. Developers should review the dependencies of their functions and ensure they only include necessary libraries and packages. Reducing unnecessary dependencies can significantly improve the cold-start time and reduce the overall resource consumption of serverless functions. In order to optimize the performance of serverless applications, monitoring and performance testing are also essential. Developers should implement robust monitoring systems to track the performance metrics and identify potential bottlenecks. Performance testing, including load testing and stress testing, can help identify the limitations and scalability of serverless applications, allowing developers to make necessary optimizations. In summary, Serverless Performance Optimization in the context of DevOps is the practice of analyzing, optimizing, and fine-tuning various aspects of serverless applications, including code, configurations, dependencies, and monitoring. By implementing these optimization techniques, developers can enhance the performance, efficiency, and scalability of serverless applications, ultimately providing a better user experience.

Serverless Pricing Models

A serverless pricing model is a cost structure used in the context of DevOps for hosting applications and executing code in a serverless computing environment. Serverless computing, also known as Function as a Service (FaaS), allows developers to write and deploy code without the need to provision or manage servers. Instead, the cloud provider takes care of all the underlying infrastructure and automatically scales the resources based on demand. Serverless pricing models typically involve charging users based on the number of function invocations, execution duration, and resource consumption. This pay-as-you-go approach offers more flexibility and cost-effectiveness compared to traditional server-based models since users only pay for the actual usage of their functions rather than for allocated server resources that may remain idle.

Serverless Providers

Serverless providers are cloud service providers that offer serverless computing platforms as a service. Serverless computing, also known as Function as a Service (FaaS), is a cloud computing execution model where the cloud provider manages the infrastructure and automatically provisions, scales, and manages the servers required to run the application code. In this model, developers only need to focus on writing and deploying the code, and the serverless provider takes care of the rest. These serverless providers offer a range of services and features that enable developers to build and deploy applications without the need to worry about managing servers or infrastructure. The applications are broken down into small, independent functions that are triggered by events, such as HTTP requests or changes to data in a database. With serverless computing, developers can easily scale their applications based on demand, as the cloud provider automatically allocates and releases resources as needed.

Serverless Queues And Event Streams

Serverless Queues and Event Streams are key components in the world of DevOps that enable seamless communication and data flow between different services and applications without the need for traditional servers. These technologies play a crucial role in building scalable, resilient, and flexible architectures by decoupling components and providing efficient ways to handle asynchronous communication and event-driven workflows. A Serverless Queue is a messaging service that acts as a buffer or intermediary between producers and consumers. It allows the exchange of messages in a reliable and scalable manner, where producers publish messages to the queue, and consumers retrieve and process them. Queue-based communication enables loose coupling between services, as producers and consumers do not need to be aware of each other's existence or state, leading to better maintenance and scalability. Serverless Queues also provide additional features like message ordering, prioritization, and dead-letter queues to handle exceptional scenarios. On the other hand, Event Streams are a mechanism to capture and distribute events that occur within a system. Events are messages that represent significant occurrences or changes in an application or service. Event Streams enable the implementation of event-driven architectures, where different components react to events and trigger actions based on those events. This approach reduces tight dependencies between services and promotes flexibility, scalability, and responsiveness. By utilizing Event Streams, applications can process and react to events in real-time, enabling near-instantaneous communication and seamless integration of services.

Serverless Resource Scaling

Serverless resource scaling refers to the process of automatically adjusting the allocated resources for serverless functions or applications based on the current demand or workload. In the context of DevOps, serverless resource scaling plays a crucial role in optimizing the performance, cost, and reliability of serverless applications. Traditionally, in a non-serverless environment, developers need to manually provision and manage the resources required to support their applications. This often results in over-provisioning, where resources are underutilized during periods of low demand, leading to unnecessary costs. Conversely, during periods of high demand, the lack of sufficient resources may result in performance issues or service outages. With serverless computing, the cloud provider takes care of the underlying infrastructure, allowing developers to focus on writing code and delivering value to their users. Serverless resource scaling enables automatic provisioning and deprovisioning of resources based on the current workload, leading to optimal utilization of computing resources and cost efficiency. There are two types of scaling in serverless computing: horizontal scaling and vertical scaling. Horizontal scaling involves adding or removing instances of a serverless function to handle fluctuating workloads. This allows the application to scale out and meet increased demand efficiently. Vertical scaling, on the other hand, involves adjusting the allocated resources within a single instance of a serverless function. It allows the application to scale up or down based on the current workload, optimizing the utilization of CPU, memory, and other resources. Serverless resource scaling is achieved through the use of autoscaling policies and triggers. Autoscaling policies define the rules for scaling and can be based on metrics such as CPU utilization, request rate, or queue length. Triggers, such as API calls or scheduled events, can also be used to initiate scaling actions. When the defined thresholds are exceeded, the autoscaling mechanism will automatically provision or deprovision resources, ensuring the application can handle the workload efficiently. In conclusion, serverless resource scaling is a vital aspect of DevOps in serverless computing. It allows for automatic provisioning and deprovisioning of resources, ensuring optimal performance, cost efficiency, and reliability of serverless applications.

Serverless Security Best Practices Enhancement

Serverless security best practices refer to a set of guidelines and techniques aimed at enhancing the security of serverless applications in the context of DevOps. Serverless architecture is a cloud computing model where the infrastructure provider manages the server and the execution environment, allowing developers to focus mainly on writing code to handle the business logic. DevOps, on the other hand, is a collaborative approach that combines software development (Dev) and IT operations (Ops) to improve the efficiency and speed of delivering applications and services. With the rise of serverless computing, it is essential to implement robust security measures to protect serverless applications from potential threats and vulnerabilities. These best practices involve various aspects of the development and deployment process, ensuring the confidentiality, integrity, and availability of serverless applications.

Serverless Security Best Practices

Serverless security best practices refer to the guidelines and strategies that organizations should follow to ensure the secure development and deployment of serverless applications in the context of DevOps. Serverless computing is a cloud computing model where users can run functions or applications without managing the infrastructure. This model eliminates the need for traditional servers and accelerates the development and deployment processes. However, it also introduces a unique set of security challenges that need to be addressed. The following are some serverless security best practices in the context of DevOps: Avoid storing sensitive information in function code or environment variables: Storing sensitive information such as API keys or database credentials directly in function code or environment variables increases the risk of exposure. Instead, use secure storage solutions such as key management services or secret management tools to store and retrieve sensitive information. Follow the principle of least privilege: Implement strict access controls and only grant necessary permissions to functions and related resources. Limit access based on the principle of least privilege, ensuring that each function has only the permissions required to fulfill its intended purpose. Regularly review and update permissions to prevent unauthorized access. Implement strong authentication and authorization mechanisms: Utilize robust authentication and authorization mechanisms to validate the identity of users or systems and control access to serverless functions and associated resources. Implement multi-factor authentication, role-based access control, and fine-grained access controls to ensure secure access. Enable logging and monitoring: Implement comprehensive logging and monitoring mechanisms to capture and analyze system and application logs. Monitor for suspicious activities, such as unauthorized access attempts or unexpected behavior. Regularly review logs and respond to security incidents promptly. Implement secure communication: Encrypt data in transit using secure communication protocols such as HTTPS. Securely transmit sensitive information between serverless functions and other systems or services. Implement encryption at rest to safeguard data stored in databases or storage systems. Regularly update dependencies and libraries: Keep serverless functions up to date by monitoring and updating dependencies and libraries to their latest versions. Vulnerabilities in outdated libraries can expose functions to security risks. Regularly check for security updates and patches and apply them promptly. Conduct regular security assessments and testing: Perform security assessments and penetration testing of serverless functions and associated resources. Identify and mitigate vulnerabilities and weaknesses in the system. Implement secure coding practices and perform code reviews to identify and fix potential security issues. By following these serverless security best practices, organizations can ensure the secure development and deployment of serverless applications in the context of DevOps, reducing the risk of data breaches and unauthorized access.

Serverless Security

Serverless security in the context of DevOps refers to the measures and practices that ensure the protection of serverless applications and the data they handle within the cloud environment. Serverless computing, commonly known as Function as a Service (FaaS), is a cloud computing model where the cloud provider manages the infrastructure and automatically scales the resources based on the demand. In this model, developers can focus solely on writing and deploying individual functions without the need to worry about servers or their maintenance. Ensuring security in a serverless environment requires a multilayered approach, as the responsibilities for security are distributed between the cloud provider and the application developers. The cloud provider is responsible for securing the underlying infrastructure, including managing authentication, authorization, and encryption protocols. On the other hand, developers have the responsibility of securing their code and configuring the application appropriately to mitigate potential vulnerabilities. One of the key aspects of serverless security is enforcing proper identity and access management (IAM) controls. This involves implementing strong authentication mechanisms, such as multi-factor authentication (MFA), and granular access control to restrict access to sensitive resources. Role-based access control (RBAC) should be used to assign the least privileges necessary for each function or user, minimizing the potential impact of a potential compromise. Another critical aspect of serverless security is ensuring the confidentiality and integrity of the data being processed by the serverless functions. This can be achieved through the use of encryption techniques, both in transit and at rest. Transport Layer Security (TLS) should be used to secure communication between functions and other services, while encryption at rest should be implemented for data stored within the cloud provider's infrastructure. Furthermore, serverless security involves implementing proper monitoring and logging mechanisms to detect potential security incidents and enable timely response. Real-time monitoring and analysis of logs and events generated by serverless functions can help identify and respond to suspicious activities or unauthorized access attempts. Additionally, regular vulnerability scanning and penetration testing should be conducted to identify and address any potential weaknesses in the application's code or configuration.

Serverless Testing Frameworks

A serverless testing framework is a set of tools and practices designed to test and evaluate the functionality, performance, and reliability of serverless applications in a DevOps environment. It provides a way for developers and operations teams to automate the testing process, ensuring the application is functioning as expected and delivering value to end-users. In a DevOps context, serverless testing frameworks enable teams to adopt a continuous testing approach, where tests are automated and integrated into the deployment pipeline. This allows for frequent and consistent testing throughout the development lifecycle, reducing the risk of bugs and issues being introduced into production. Serverless testing frameworks typically offer a range of features and capabilities to support DevOps practices. These may include: 1. Mocking and stubbing: The ability to simulate the behavior of external dependencies and services, allowing developers to test their code in isolation. This is especially important in serverless applications, where functions often rely on external services such as databases or APIs. 2. Integration with deployment tools: Integration with CI/CD tools, such as Jenkins or GitHub Actions, enabling tests to be automatically triggered as part of the deployment process. This ensures that new features and updates are thoroughly tested before being released. 3. Performance and scalability testing: The ability to simulate high loads and monitor the performance of serverless applications under different conditions. This helps identify any bottlenecks or performance issues that may impact the application's ability to handle real-world traffic. 4. Fault injection: The ability to intentionally introduce failures and errors into the application, allowing teams to test its resilience and ability to recover. This is particularly important in serverless architectures, where functions are often distributed and can fail independently. 5. Reporting and analysis: A comprehensive reporting mechanism that provides insights into test results, including detailed logs and metrics. This enables teams to quickly identify and resolve any issues that arise during testing. Overall, a serverless testing framework plays a crucial role in enabling teams to develop and deploy reliable serverless applications in a DevOps environment. By automating and integrating testing into the development process, teams can ensure that their applications meet the highest standards of quality and performance.

Serverless Testing

Serverless testing refers to the process of testing software applications that are built using serverless architecture in the context of DevOps. Serverless architecture, also known as Function as a Service (FaaS), allows developers to focus on writing code without worrying about managing servers or infrastructure. In this approach, applications are broken down into small, independent functions that can be executed in response to triggers or events. These functions are typically hosted and managed by a cloud provider, such as Amazon Web Services (AWS) Lambda or Microsoft Azure Functions. In a DevOps environment, serverless testing plays a crucial role in ensuring the quality and reliability of software applications. It involves the verification and validation of individual functions as well as the overall application to ensure that they meet the desired functional and non-functional requirements. Serverless testing encompasses various types of testing, including unit testing, integration testing, performance testing, and security testing.

Serverless Triggers

Serverless triggers refer to the events that initiate the execution of serverless functions or workflows in a DevOps environment. These triggers can range from various sources such as databases, file uploads, message queues, or even scheduled tasks. By defining these triggers, developers can ensure that their serverless functions are automatically invoked whenever specific events or conditions occur. In the context of DevOps, serverless triggers play a crucial role in enabling continuous integration and delivery (CI/CD) pipelines. They allow developers to trigger the execution of serverless functions as part of their automated deployment processes, ensuring seamless integration with other components of the application stack. A typical example of a serverless trigger is a webhook. A webhook is an HTTP callback that occurs when a specific event takes place. For instance, when a code repository receives new commits, it can trigger a webhook to notify a serverless function responsible for running automated tests or initiating a deployment pipeline. This webhook acts as a trigger, initiating the execution of the serverless function in response to the event. Serverless triggers can also be event-driven, meaning they respond to events within the application or external systems. For instance, a serverless function can be triggered by the creation of a new record in a database, the arrival of a message in a queue, or the upload of a file to cloud storage. These triggers provide a way to execute serverless functions in real-time, responding to changes or events as they occur. By leveraging serverless triggers, DevOps teams can build highly scalable and responsive applications. As serverless architectures abstract away the underlying infrastructure, it becomes easier to scale up or down based on the incoming triggers. This enables efficient resource utilization and cost optimization while maintaining responsiveness to events.

Serverless Vendor Lock-In Mitigation

Serverless vendor lock-in mitigation in the context of DevOps refers to strategies and techniques used to minimize the dependency and potential disadvantages associated with using a specific serverless provider's platform or ecosystem. As DevOps teams adopt serverless computing for building and deploying applications, they often rely on a specific vendor's serverless platform, which might offer unique features, tools, and integrations. However, this can create a potential risk of vendor lock-in, where migrating to another serverless provider becomes challenging, costly, or even impractical. One approach to mitigate serverless vendor lock-in is through the use of abstraction layers and standardization. By abstracting away provider-specific details and relying on industry-standard interfaces and frameworks, DevOps teams can reduce the impact of switching serverless providers. Technologies like AWS Lambda Functions, Azure Functions, or Google Cloud Functions can be used interchangeably, as they all conform to the same serverless computing concept. Furthermore, adopting serverless architectures that follow the principles of loose coupling and microservices can help mitigate vendor lock-in. By decomposing applications into smaller, independently deployable functions or services, the impact of transitioning to a different serverless provider can be minimized. Each function or service can encapsulate a specific business capability, making it easier to rewrite or reimplement when changing serverless providers. Using infrastructure as code (IaC) practices and tools, such as AWS CloudFormation or Terraform, can also aid in mitigating serverless vendor lock-in. By defining serverless infrastructure configuration and deployment processes in a declarative format, the infrastructure becomes more portable. DevOps teams can then use the same IaC templates with different serverless providers, minimizing the effort required to switch platforms.

Service Catalog

A service catalog is a centralized and standardized collection of the various services that an organization offers to its customers or end users. In the context of DevOps, a service catalog serves as a crucial component for facilitating self-service and automation. It provides a structured approach for organizing and categorizing different services, allowing users to easily discover and request the specific services they need without relying on manual intervention from IT or operations teams. By enabling self-service capabilities, a service catalog empowers development and operations teams to access and consume the necessary resources and tools for their projects, reducing dependency on traditional service request processes.

Service Discovery

Service discovery in the context of DevOps refers to the process of automatically and dynamically finding and configuring services within a distributed infrastructure. It is a critical component in modern application development and deployment, particularly in microservices architectures. Traditionally, in monolithic applications, services are tightly coupled and can easily discover each other through direct method calls or configuration files. However, in a distributed environment with numerous services that may be running on different machines or containers, manual configuration and tracking of service locations becomes impractical and error-prone. Service discovery addresses this challenge by providing a mechanism for services to register and discover each other dynamically. It enables services to be loosely coupled and independently deployable, allowing for greater scalability and flexibility. There are several approaches to service discovery, with the most common being a centralized service registry. In this model, services register themselves with a central registry, typically through an API, providing information such as their location and available endpoints. Other services can then query the registry to discover and connect to the required services. This approach decouples service configuration from deployment, making it easier to add or remove services without impacting the overall system. Another approach is peer-to-peer service discovery, where services communicate directly with each other to discover and establish connections. This eliminates the need for a central registry and can be beneficial in highly dynamic or decentralized environments. Service discovery also includes features such as service health checks, load balancing, and automatic service reconfiguration. Health checks ensure that only healthy services are discovered and utilized, while load balancing distributes requests evenly across available instances of a service. Automatic reconfiguration handles scenarios where services may change their location or endpoints, ensuring other services can still discover and connect to them without manual intervention. In summary, service discovery is a crucial aspect of DevOps, enabling dynamic and scalable deployment of services in a distributed environment. It eliminates the need for manual configuration and promotes loosely coupled architectures, enhancing flexibility and agility in application development and deployment processes.

Service Level Objectives (SLOs) Management Strategies

Service Level Objectives (SLOs) management encompasses the strategies and practices employed within a DevOps environment to define, track, measure, and optimize the performance of services provided to users. SLOs serve as the agreed-upon targets or goals that organizations set in order to ensure the reliability, availability, and performance of their services, while allowing for continuous improvement and aligning with user expectations. In a DevOps context, SLOs are critical for establishing a common understanding between development, operations, and business teams regarding the desired level of service quality, as well as to set proper expectations with users. SLOs also facilitate collaboration and shared responsibility among cross-functional teams, providing a framework to drive continuous improvement and deliver value. Effective SLO management requires a well-defined process that spans the entire service lifecycle, incorporating the following key strategies: 1. SLO Definition: This involves identifying and defining the critical metrics that will be used to measure the performance and reliability of a service. SLOs should be precise, measurable, and achievable, reflecting the needs and priorities of users and the business. 2. Monitoring and Alerting: Proactive monitoring is essential for tracking the performance of services and ensuring that they meet the defined SLOs. Monitoring tools and techniques should be integrated into the DevOps pipeline, providing real-time visibility into service health and triggering alerts when thresholds are breached. 3. Measurement and Reporting: Accurate and reliable measurement of service performance against the defined SLOs is crucial for identifying areas of improvement and facilitating data-driven decision-making. Regular reporting and analysis of performance metrics help in identifying trends, spotting bottlenecks, and making informed decisions for optimization. 4. Incident Management: SLOs play a pivotal role in incident management by providing a baseline for prioritizing and triaging issues. When incidents occur, teams can quickly assess the impact on SLOs and allocate resources accordingly, aiming to minimize the impact and restore the service within the defined SLOs. 5. Continuous Improvement: SLOs should not be static, but rather evolve with changing business needs and user expectations. With a culture of continuous improvement, teams regularly review and reassess their SLOs, leveraging data and insights to refine targets, optimize services, and enhance the overall user experience.

Service Level Objectives (SLOs) Management

Service Level Objectives (SLOs) management is a critical aspect of DevOps that involves setting, monitoring, and governing performance goals for a particular service or system. SLOs serve as a means to define the performance expectations and requirements for a service, ensuring that it meets the needs of its users and stakeholders. SLOs are typically defined in quantifiable terms, such as response time, availability, or error rates, and are often accompanied by an associated Service Level Agreement (SLA) that outlines the consequences of not meeting these objectives. They provide a way to measure and track the performance of a service, allowing stakeholders to assess its reliability, scalability, and overall quality. The process of managing SLOs starts with the identification and prioritization of key performance indicators (KPIs) that align with the goals of the service. KPIs could be related to the response time, throughput, error rates, or any other metric that is crucial to the success of the service. Once the KPIs are identified, specific targets or thresholds are set for each metric to represent the desired level of performance. Monitoring tools and systems are then implemented to collect data and measure the actual performance of the service against the defined SLOs. This data is analyzed to identify trends, patterns, and potential areas for improvement. In the context of DevOps, automated monitoring and alerting systems are typically utilized to provide real-time visibility into the service's performance, allowing teams to proactively address any issues that may arise. Regular reviews and evaluations of service performance are conducted to ensure that the SLOs remain relevant and reflect the evolving needs of the users and the business. Whenever SLOs are not met, the cause of the failure is investigated, and remedial actions are taken to resolve the underlying issues. This iterative process of monitoring, analysis, and improvement ensures that the service continues to meet or exceed the defined objectives. In summary, SLO management is an integral part of the DevOps lifecycle, guiding the design, development, and operation of services. By defining quantifiable performance objectives and continuously monitoring and improving performance against these objectives, organizations can ensure that their services meet the needs of their users while maintaining a high level of reliability, availability, and quality.

Service Mesh

A Service Mesh is a dedicated infrastructure layer that enables communication between services in a distributed system. It provides a centralized management and control plane for handling service-to-service communication, including service discovery, load balancing, encryption, and observability. In the context of DevOps, a Service Mesh plays a crucial role in enabling teams to build, deploy, and operate microservices-based applications with increased reliability, scalability, and security. It abstracts the complexity of network communication from individual services, allowing developers to focus on business logic rather than dealing with low-level networking concerns.

Shift-Left Security

Shift-Left Security in the context of DevOps refers to the approach of integrating security practices and considerations into the software development process from its earliest stages. Traditionally, security is often an afterthought in the software development lifecycle, addressed only towards the end of the process or during deployment. However, this reactive approach can result in significant vulnerabilities and delays in addressing security issues. Shift-Left Security aims to address these challenges by shifting the focus on security to the left side of the development lifecycle. This means incorporating security practices early on, during the design and development phases, to proactively identify and mitigate vulnerabilities. By integrating security measures throughout the development process, organizations can reduce the risk of potential security breaches and ensure that security becomes an integral part of software development. One of the key principles behind Shift-Left Security is that security is not solely the responsibility of a dedicated security team. Instead, it is a shared responsibility among all members of the development team. This means that developers, testers, and operations personnel all take active roles in identifying potential security risks and implementing measures to address them. Collaboration and communication among team members are crucial to ensure that security considerations are properly integrated from the start. Shift-Left Security also emphasizes the use of automation and tooling to support security practices throughout the development process. Automated security scanning, static code analysis, and vulnerability assessments are examples of tools that can help identify potential security risks early on. By integrating these tools into the development pipeline, organizations can detect and remediate vulnerabilities more efficiently and effectively. Overall, Shift-Left Security is a proactive and collaborative approach that aims to minimize security risks by integrating security practices into the early stages of the software development lifecycle. By doing so, organizations can build more secure and resilient applications while reducing the burden and costs associated with addressing security issues later in the development process.

Shippable

Shippable in the context of DevOps refers to a continuous delivery platform that helps automate the software development cycle, allowing teams to rapidly and reliably ship code. Shippable provides a comprehensive set of tools and capabilities that support the DevOps principles of collaboration, automation, and continuous integration/continuous delivery (CI/CD). It enables teams to achieve desired levels of agility, speed, and quality in the software development and deployment process. The platform offers a range of features aimed at streamlining and simplifying the end-to-end software delivery pipeline. It provides robust support for source code management, enabling version control and collaboration among team members. Shippable integrates with popular repository hosting services, such as GitHub and Bitbucket, allowing developers to easily manage their codebase. Shippable also offers powerful build automation capabilities, allowing teams to define and execute build workflows. It supports various build systems and languages, allowing developers to build applications written in different programming languages and frameworks. The platform automatically manages the build infrastructure, scaling as needed to accommodate varying workloads. One of the key strengths of Shippable is its focus on continuous integration and continuous delivery (CI/CD). It enables automated testing, validation, and deployment of software artifacts, ensuring the continuous delivery of high-quality code. Shippable integrates with popular testing frameworks, enabling teams to define and execute automated tests as part of their CI/CD process. Furthermore, Shippable provides comprehensive deployment automation capabilities. It supports deployment to multiple environments, allowing teams to easily promote code changes from development to staging to production. The platform simplifies the process of deploying applications to various cloud platforms, such as Amazon Web Services (AWS) and Microsoft Azure. In summary, Shippable is a DevOps platform that helps organizations streamline and automate their software development and delivery process. It enables collaboration, automation, and continuous integration/continuous delivery, allowing teams to ship code faster, more reliably, and with higher quality.

Single Sign-On (SSO)

Single Sign-On (SSO) in the context of DevOps is a method of authentication that allows users to access multiple systems and applications with just one set of credentials. It eliminates the need for users to remember and manage multiple usernames and passwords, which can reduce the risk of security breaches due to weak or compromised credentials. With SSO, users authenticate themselves once, usually through a central authentication server or service, and obtain a token or ticket that grants them access to various systems and applications within the organization. This token is typically valid for a specified period, after which the user may need to authenticate again. The benefits of implementing SSO in a DevOps environment are numerous. Firstly, it simplifies user access by providing a seamless and consistent login experience across different applications and systems. This can improve productivity and user satisfaction, as users do not have to go through the hassle of remembering and entering multiple credentials. Secondly, SSO enhances security by reducing the risk of password-related vulnerabilities. With SSO, users are encouraged to create strong, complex passwords since they only need to remember one. This mitigates the chances of weak passwords being used across multiple systems and applications. Furthermore, SSO allows for better control and management of user access. For example, when an employee leaves the organization, revoking access to all systems and applications can be done centrally, ensuring that there are no lingering access rights that could pose a security risk. It also simplifies the onboarding and offboarding processes, as user accounts can be provisioned or deprovisioned in one central location. In conclusion, Single Sign-On in the context of DevOps is a powerful authentication method that simplifies user access, enhances security, and provides efficient management of user accounts and access rights. By implementing SSO, organizations can streamline their authentication processes, reduce the risk of password-related security breaches, and improve user productivity and satisfaction.

Site Reliability Engineering (SRE) Practices Adoption

Site Reliability Engineering (SRE) practices adoption, in the context of DevOps, refers to the incorporation of SRE principles and methodologies into the processes and operations of an organization to enhance the reliability, scalability, and efficiency of their software systems. SRE practices aim to bridge the gap between software development and operations teams by merging their responsibilities and goals. It emphasizes the importance of automation, monitoring, and proactive problem-solving to achieve high availability and reliability of the system. SRE teams work closely with software engineers to design, build, and maintain highly scalable and reliable systems, reducing the burden on traditional operations teams while fostering collaboration and shared ownership of services.

Site Reliability Engineering (SRE) Practices

Site Reliability Engineering (SRE) is a set of practices and principles utilized in the context of

DevOps aiming to ensure the reliability, scalability, and efficiency of software systems and services. SRE integrates software engineering and operational expertise to bridge the gap between development and operations teams, fostering collaboration, and ensuring the continuous improvement of systems. As a discipline, SRE focuses on building and maintaining highly reliable systems by applying software engineering principles such as automation, monitoring, and fault tolerance. SRE practitioners work closely with development teams to understand the architecture and requirements of the software system, ensuring its reliability from the design phase onwards. The key practices associated with SRE include: 1. Service Level Objectives (SLOs): SRE establishes measurable objectives for system performance and availability, defining the desired level of service that the system should provide to its users. SLOs often include metrics such as uptime percentage, response time, and error rates. 2. Error Budgets: SRE also introduces the concept of error budgets, which quantifies the allowable amount of system errors or downtime within a specific time frame. Error budgets enable teams to balance innovation and reliability, allowing for a certain degree of risk-taking while ensuring a high-quality user experience. 3. Monitoring and Alerting: SRE emphasizes the need for effective monitoring and alerting systems, enabling proactive identification and resolution of issues. Monitoring tools provide real-time insights into system performance, while well-defined alerting mechanisms notify teams about anomalies or thresholds breaches. 4. Incident Management: SRE advocates for a structured incident management framework, including clear roles, responsibilities, and processes. It emphasizes the importance of a blameless post-mortem culture, where incidents are analyzed to identify root causes and prevent them from recurring in the future. 5. Automation: SRE encourages the automation of repetitive tasks and processes, enabling teams to scale and manage complex systems efficiently. By automating tasks such as deployment, provisioning, and testing, SRE minimizes the risk of human error and improves overall system reliability. In summary, SRE practices aim to ensure the reliability and scalability of software systems by integrating engineering and operational expertise. By aligning SLOs, error budgets, monitoring, incident management, and automation, SRE enables development and operations teams to build and maintain highly reliable systems in the fast-paced world of DevOps.

Site Reliability Engineering (SRE)

Site Reliability Engineering (SRE) is a discipline within the DevOps framework that focuses on applying software engineering principles to operations tasks in order to improve the reliability and performance of software systems. SRE aims to bridge the gap between development and operations teams, ensuring that software deployments are efficient, scalable, and resilient. In the context of DevOps, SRE is responsible for monitoring and managing the health, performance, and availability of software systems. It involves designing and implementing systems that can handle high traffic and uptime demands, while also troubleshooting and resolving issues to minimize system downtime and user impact.

Snyk

Snyk is a DevOps tool that provides fast and automated security testing for open source libraries and container images. It helps developers identify and fix vulnerabilities in their applications early in the development lifecycle, minimizing the risk of security breaches. As a DevOps tool, Snyk integrates seamlessly with popular CI/CD platforms, such as Jenkins and GitHub Actions, and can be easily incorporated into existing workflows. It scans project dependencies, including libraries and frameworks, and identifies any known vulnerabilities or license compliance issues. Snyk also analyzes container images to detect potential vulnerabilities or configuration weaknesses. One of the key features of Snyk is its ability to provide actionable remediation advice. When a vulnerability is detected, Snyk not only highlights the issue but also suggests specific steps to resolve it, such as upgrading to a patched version or applying a configuration change. This helps developers quickly address security issues without disrupting their development process. Snyk also offers continuous monitoring capabilities, allowing teams to stay updated on the security posture of their projects over time. By regularly scanning and analyzing dependencies and container images, Snyk provides insights into any newly discovered vulnerabilities and tracks the progress of remediation efforts. In addition to its analysis capabilities, Snyk also supports policy enforcement. Organizations can define custom security policies that align with their specific requirements and industry standards. Snyk enforces these policies during scans and provides visibility into any violations, enabling teams to ensure compliance and maintain good security hygiene across all projects. Overall, Snyk is a powerful DevOps tool that combines security testing, vulnerability management, and policy enforcement in an automated and easy-to-use manner. By integrating Snyk into the development pipeline, organizations can proactively identify and address security vulnerabilities, reducing the risk of potential breaches and ensuring the overall integrity of their software applications.

Software Composition Analysis (SCA)

Software Composition Analysis (SCA) is a key practice in the context of DevOps that involves evaluating and managing the open source and third-party software components used in a software application. It is a proactive approach that helps in identifying vulnerabilities, licensing issues, and potential security risks associated with these components. SCA is an essential part of the software development lifecycle (SDLC) within the DevOps methodology, where speed and agility are crucial. With the increasing adoption of open source components in modern software development, it has become imperative to have a systematic and automated process to analyze and monitor these components. SCA enables organizations to ensure the use of secure and compliant software components while minimizing the risk of security breaches and legal liabilities.

Software Composition Analysis

Software Composition Analysis (SCA) is a critical DevOps practice that involves the automated identification and analysis of software components and their dependencies in order to effectively manage open source and third-party code within an organization's application portfolio. Through SCA, software development and DevOps teams gain insights into the composition of their applications, identifying the specific components used and the vulnerabilities or license compliance issues associated with them. By understanding and managing their software supply chain, organizations can mitigate security risks, ensure license compliance, and improve overall software quality.

Software As A Service (SaaS) Security

Software as a Service (SaaS) Security in the context of DevOps refers to the measures and practices implemented to protect SaaS applications in a DevOps environment. DevOps is an approach that combines software development and IT operations to enable the continuous delivery and deployment of software. SaaS, on the other hand, is a software delivery model where applications are hosted by a service provider and made available to customers over the internet. SaaS Security in a DevOps context involves ensuring the confidentiality, integrity, and availability of SaaS applications throughout the software development lifecycle. It encompasses a range of security considerations, including data protection, user authentication, access control, network security, and compliance.

SonarQube

SonarQube is a static code analysis tool that helps in identifying and fixing code quality issues in software development projects. In the context of DevOps, it plays a vital role in ensuring continuous integration and delivery by automating the code review process and providing actionable insights for effective decision making. With its comprehensive set of rules and guidelines, SonarQube analyses the source code, detects coding issues, and measures adherence to coding standards. It covers various aspects of code quality, including code duplication, complexity, potential bugs, vulnerability, and more. By highlighting these issues early on in the development cycle, SonarQube helps in reducing technical debt and improving the overall reliability, maintainability, and security of the software.

Spinnaker (CD Tool)

Spinnaker is a continuous delivery (CD) tool that plays a vital role in automating the software release process within the DevOps methodology. It is designed to facilitate the rapid and reliable delivery of applications and updates, allowing organizations to release software at a faster pace while maintaining stability and quality in their deployments. With its sophisticated set of features and integrations, Spinnaker provides a unified platform for managing the CD pipeline, from building and testing to deploying and monitoring applications across various cloud environments, including Kubernetes, Amazon Web Services (AWS), Microsoft Azure, and Google Cloud Platform (GCP).

Spinnaker

Spinnaker is an open-source, multi-cloud continuous delivery platform that is specifically designed for scaling applications in the context of DevOps. It aims to simplify the process of deploying software across multiple cloud providers or on-premises environments in a consistent and reliable manner. Spinnaker provides a unified interface to define, automate, and manage the deployment pipelines for applications, regardless of the target infrastructure. It allows teams to define their delivery workflows as a series of stages, each of which represents a distinct step in the deployment process. These stages can include building, testing, and deploying code, as well as executing custom scripts or other actions. One of the key features of Spinnaker is its ability to abstract away the differences between various cloud providers, allowing teams to deploy their applications to multiple environments with minimal effort. It supports a wide range of cloud platforms, including Amazon Web Services (AWS), Google Cloud Platform (GCP), Microsoft Azure, and Kubernetes, among others. Spinnaker employs a flexible and customizable deployment strategy called "bake and deploy" to ensure consistent and repeatable deployments. This strategy involves baking an immutable machine image, which encapsulates the application and its dependencies, and then deploying this image to the target environment. By using immutable images, Spinnaker eliminates many of the common issues associated with traditional deployment approaches, such as configuration drift and inconsistent environments. Furthermore, Spinnaker includes advanced deployment strategies, such as canary deployments and blue/green deployments, which allow teams to roll out new versions of their applications gradually or in a zero-downtime manner. These strategies enable teams to minimize the impact of potential issues or regressions by gradually shifting traffic to the new version and verifying its performance and stability before fully transitioning. In summary, Spinnaker is a powerful DevOps tool that simplifies and automates the deployment process across multiple cloud providers or environments. Its flexibility, scalability, and support for advanced deployment strategies make it an ideal choice for organizations looking to streamline their software delivery pipelines.

Split.io

Split.io is a feature experimentation and release management platform that enables teams to implement feature flags and manage their release process. Within the context of DevOps, Split.io provides a powerful solution for implementing continuous delivery practices and achieving faster, more efficient software releases. Feature experimentation is a critical element of modern software development, allowing teams to quickly test and validate new features before rolling them out to all users. Split.io enables teams to easily define and manage feature flags, which are simple Boolean variables that determine whether a feature is enabled or disabled for specific users or user groups. This allows teams to gradually roll out new features to a small subset of users, gather feedback, and make data-driven decisions on whether to fully release the feature. By using Split.io, teams can decouple deployment from release, allowing for greater control and flexibility in the release process. This decoupling is achieved through the use of feature flags, which can be updated in real-time without requiring code deployments. This means that teams can instantly turn on or off features, or change their behavior, without impacting the underlying codebase. This enables teams to easily experiment with different feature configurations, rollback changes if necessary, and reduce the risk of breaking the production environment. Furthermore, Split.io provides a comprehensive suite of analytics and monitoring tools that enable teams to gain insights into how features are performing. Teams can easily track and analyze key metrics, such as adoption rates, error rates, and conversion rates, and use this data to make informed decisions on feature improvements or adjustments. In summary, Split.io is a feature experimentation and release management platform that empowers DevOps teams to implement continuous delivery practices and achieve faster, more efficient software releases. By using feature flags and decoupling deployment from release, teams can gradually roll out features, gather feedback, and make data-driven decisions. Additionally, Split.io provides analytics and monitoring tools to track feature performance and drive further improvements.

Splunk

Splunk is a software platform that is used in the context of DevOps to collect, analyze, and visualize machine-generated data. It provides a centralized and real-time monitoring solution for IT infrastructure and applications, allowing teams to gain deep insights and make data-driven decisions. With Splunk, DevOps teams can aggregate data from various sources such as logs, metrics, and events, regardless of format or location. It supports both structured and unstructured data, allowing for flexibility in data analysis. By indexing and storing the collected data, Splunk enables fast and efficient searching and correlation of information, helping to identify trends, troubleshoot issues, and gain operational visibility.

Static Analysis Security Testing (SAST)

Static Analysis Security Testing (SAST) is a software testing technique used in the context of DevOps to identify security vulnerabilities in code during the development phase. It is a form of white-box testing that analyzes the source code or compiled code without executing it. SAST works by scanning the code for known patterns and identifying potential security risks such as buffer overflows, SQL injection, cross-site scripting (XSS), and other code vulnerabilities. It analyzes the code structure, syntax, and data flow to detect potential security flaws that could be exploited by attackers.

Static Code Analysis

Static Code Analysis is a process used in DevOps to analyze source code without executing it. It involves the examination of code at rest, looking for potential errors, vulnerabilities, or compliance violations. This analysis is performed by a specialized tool or application that scans the code and identifies issues through various methods and algorithms. The purpose of Static Code Analysis in the context of DevOps is to identify and rectify code quality issues early in the development cycle. It helps developers improve the overall quality and maintainability of their code, reducing the chances of introducing bugs or security vulnerabilities into the software. By detecting issues before the code is deployed, it prevents them from becoming more complex and costly to fix in later stages of the development process.

Stress Testing

Stress testing is a critical component of the DevOps process aimed at evaluating the performance and stability of a system under extreme and demanding conditions. It involves subjecting a software application, website, or infrastructure to high levels of stress by simulating heavy traffic loads, excessive data volumes, or resource limitations, in order to measure its overall reliability, scalability, and robustness. The objective of stress testing is to identify and uncover any potential weaknesses or bottlenecks in the system that may affect its performance or cause failures when it is subject to high loads. By intentionally overwhelming the system, stress testing helps to determine its breaking point and understand its behavior in challenging scenarios, enabling organizations to optimize and fine-tune their systems accordingly.

Structure

DevOps is a collaborative approach to software development and delivery that emphasizes the integration and communication between development and operations teams. It aims to streamline the software development lifecycle, improve the agility and quality of software releases, and enhance collaboration and efficiency within an organization. DevOps focuses on breaking down silos and fostering a culture of collaboration and shared responsibility between development, operations, and other stakeholders involved in the delivery process. It involves the adoption of a set of practices, tools, and mindset that enable teams to automate and optimize the entire software development process, from code creation to deployment and maintenance.

Synthetic Monitoring Tools Deployment

Synthetic monitoring tools deployment in the context of DevOps refers to the process of implementing and configuring synthetic monitoring tools or software within the DevOps infrastructure to proactively monitor the performance and availability of applications and services. Synthetic monitoring tools simulate user interactions and transactions, such as accessing web pages, performing specific actions, or initiating transactions, to monitor the behavior and performance of applications. These tools are deployed in multiple stages of the

DevOps lifecycle, including development, testing, staging, and production environments, to identify and address any performance or availability issues before they impact end users. The deployment process involves several steps, which may vary depending on the specific synthetic monitoring tool being deployed and the DevOps environment. Firstly, the appropriate synthetic monitoring tool needs to be selected based on the specific requirements and objectives of the DevOps team. Once selected, the tool is installed and configured to align with the DevOps infrastructure and the applications or services that need to be monitored. The configuration of the synthetic monitoring tool includes defining the various monitors and checks that need to be performed, such as URL monitoring, transaction monitoring, or API monitoring. Parameters such as frequency of monitoring, geographic locations, and expected response times are also set during the configuration process. After the deployment and configuration, the synthetic monitoring tool starts executing synthetic transactions or interactions based on the predefined criteria. These transactions can be scheduled periodically or triggered based on specific events or conditions. The tool captures and analyzes the responses and performance metrics, such as response time, availability, and error rates, to provide insights into the performance and availability of the applications or services being monitored. The results and data collected from the synthetic monitoring tool are then used by the DevOps team to identify any bottlenecks, performance issues, or potential improvements in the applications. This allows the team to proactively address any issues and optimize the performance and availability of the applications or services, enhancing the overall user experience and minimizing downtime or disruptions.

Synthetic Monitoring Tools

Synthetic monitoring tools in the context of DevOps refer to software or services that simulate user interactions with applications or systems to monitor their performance and functionality. These tools typically run automated tests on a regular basis from different geographic locations to mimic real user behavior and provide insights into the application's availability, response time, and uptime. By using synthetic monitoring tools, DevOps teams can proactively identify performance issues, bottlenecks, and downtime before they impact end-users. These tools help measure and monitor key performance indicators (KPIs) such as server response time, page load time, DNS resolution time, and transaction success rate to ensure optimal user experience.

Synthetic Monitoring

Synthetic monitoring is a type of monitoring strategy used in the context of DevOps to simulate user interactions and test the performance of digital products and services. It involves the creation of artificial transactions or user journeys that mimic real user interactions with the system. These synthetic transactions are typically scripted and executed at regular intervals to provide continuous monitoring and feedback on the health and reliability of the system. The objective of synthetic monitoring is to proactively identify performance issues, such as slow response times, errors, and downtime, before they impact real users. By simulating user interactions from different locations and devices, synthetic monitoring helps to ensure that the system is functioning optimally from the end-user's perspective.

Sysdig

Sysdig is a powerful monitoring and troubleshooting platform designed specifically for DevOps teams. It provides comprehensive visibility into containerized environments, allowing for efficient monitoring, troubleshooting, and security analysis.With Sysdig, DevOps teams can gain real-time insights into how their applications and infrastructure are behaving, enabling them to quickly identify and address performance issues, vulnerabilities, and compliance violations.

Taiga

Taiga is an open-source project management tool specifically designed for the implementation of DevOps practices within an organization. It provides teams with a collaborative platform for planning, tracking, and managing their software development and delivery processes. As a DevOps tool, Taiga offers a range of features that facilitate the integration of development and operations activities, enabling the efficient deployment of software products. Its core functionality includes project boards, task management, and issue tracking, allowing teams to streamline their workflows and ensure smoother project execution.

TeamCity

TeamCity is a popular Continuous Integration (CI) and Continuous Deployment (CD) tool that plays a crucial role in the DevOps process. As a CI/CD tool, TeamCity is designed to automate the build, test, and deployment processes of software development projects. It helps to ensure that changes to the codebase are verified and integrated regularly, reducing the risk of integration issues and enabling teams to deliver high-quality software at a faster pace.

Telemetry

Telemetry in the context of DevOps refers to the process of collecting and analyzing data from various systems and applications to gain insights and improve decision-making for operational efficiency and enhanced user experience. DevOps teams heavily rely on telemetry data to effectively monitor, measure, and optimize the performance and availability of their systems. It provides valuable information about various aspects such as system health, latency, error rates, user behavior, and resource utilization. By leveraging telemetry, DevOps practitioners can proactively identify and address issues, make informed decisions, and continuously improve their systems and applications.

Tenable.Io

Tenable.io is a comprehensive vulnerability management platform designed to help organizations improve their security posture and reduce risk. It integrates seamlessly into the DevOps pipeline, providing continuous visibility into the vulnerabilities within an organization's infrastructure. With Tenable.io, organizations can easily identify and prioritize vulnerabilities, enabling them to take proactive measures to prevent potential cyber attacks. It offers a wide range of features and capabilities to support the DevOps workflow, including vulnerability assessment, asset management, and remediation planning.

Terraform Modules Usage

Terraform modules are reusable components that encapsulate a set of resources and configurations in order to achieve infrastructure as code (IaC) principles. They help automate the deployment and management of infrastructure resources in a consistent and efficient manner. Modules in Terraform serve as building blocks for creating and managing infrastructure. They allow DevOps teams to define and version infrastructure in a modular manner, breaking down complex systems into smaller, reusable components. These modules are reusable entities that can be instantiated multiple times with different input parameters to create multiple instances of the same infrastructure configuration, enabling teams to scale and manage their infrastructure more effectively.

Terraform Modules

Terraform Modules are reusable and self-contained pieces of code used in Infrastructure as Code (IaC) practices within the DevOps context. These modules encapsulate a set of resources and configurations to deploy and manage infrastructure components, such as virtual machines, networking resources, and storage resources. By using Terraform modules, DevOps teams can abstract and standardize the deployment process of infrastructure resources across different environments and projects. These modules provide a way to define and manage infrastructure components in a declarative manner, allowing teams to version, share, and reuse them efficiently.

Test-Driven Development (TDD)

Test-Driven Development (TDD), in the context of DevOps, is a software development technique that emphasizes writing automated tests before writing any production code. It follows a cycle of designing and executing tests, implementing the minimal amount of code required to pass those tests, and then refactoring the code to improve its design and maintainability. TDD enables teams to deliver high-quality software by ensuring that the code meets the specified requirements and remains stable throughout the development process. By writing tests before the implementation code, developers gain clarity on the desired functionality, ensuring that the code meets the business requirements and supports the desired use cases.

TestComplete

TestComplete is a software testing tool that helps in the execution of automated tests for various software applications, including web, mobile, and desktop applications. In the context of DevOps, TestComplete plays a crucial role in ensuring the quality and reliability of software throughout the development and deployment process. DevOps, which stands for Development and Operations, is a software development approach that emphasizes collaboration, communication, and integration between development teams and operations teams. It aims to streamline the software development lifecycle and accelerate the delivery of new features and updates. TestComplete aligns with the principles of DevOps by enabling continuous testing and integration within the development process. It allows developers and testers to automate the testing process and integrate it seamlessly with continuous integration and continuous deployment (CI/CD) pipelines. With TestComplete, developers can write automated test scripts that cover various test scenarios and execute them in a repeatable and consistent manner. These test scripts can be integrated into the CI/CD workflow, triggering automatic tests whenever there are code changes or new deployments. By incorporating TestComplete into the DevOps workflow, teams can ensure the early detection of bugs, improve overall software quality, and minimize the risk of introducing defects into production environments. It enables faster feedback cycles, as automated tests can be executed quickly and provide immediate results, allowing developers to identify and fix issues promptly. TestComplete also offers integrations with popular DevOps tools and frameworks, such as Jenkins and Docker, further enhancing its capabilities in a DevOps environment. These integrations allow for seamless integration of automated testing with other aspects of the development process, such as build and deployment automation. In summary, TestComplete is a software testing tool that aligns with the principles of DevOps by enabling continuous testing, integration, and automation. It facilitates the delivery of high-quality software by ensuring early bug detection, improving overall software reliability, and accelerating the software development lifecycle.

Threat Modeling

Threat modeling is a structured approach used in the field of DevOps to identify potential threats, vulnerabilities, and risks in software systems or applications. It is a proactive measure taken during the development and deployment stages to ensure that appropriate security controls are implemented to protect against potential attacks. Threat modeling involves the analysis of various components of a system, such as the technical infrastructure, data flow, user roles, and external dependencies, to identify potential threats and their associated attack vectors. It aims to systematically identify and prioritize potential threats based on their impact and likelihood, allowing organizations to allocate their resources more effectively towards mitigating the most critical risks.

Traefik

Traefik is a modern, open-source edge router and load balancer designed specifically for microservices and containerized environments. It is a popular choice among DevOps teams for managing and routing traffic, as well as providing essential functionalities such as SSL/TLS termination, circuit breakers, service discovery, and request tracing. With its container-native approach, Traefik integrates seamlessly with popular container orchestrators like Docker, Kubernetes, and Swarm. It dynamically listens to changes in the infrastructure and automatically adapts its routing configurations based on the available services and containers. This automatic discovery and configuration make Traefik highly scalable and flexible, allowing DevOps teams to easily add or remove services without manual intervention.

Travis CI

Travis CI is a cloud-based continuous integration and deployment platform that is widely used in the field of DevOps. It provides automated build, test, and deployment functionality, ensuring that software projects are built and deployed consistently and reliably. The main purpose of Travis CI is to integrate the process of continuously building, testing, and deploying software changes into a single, streamlined workflow. It allows developers to automate the repetitive tasks involved in software development, such as running tests and deploying code to various environments. By automating these tasks, Travis CI helps improve the efficiency, quality, and reliability of the development process. Travis CI integrates seamlessly with popular version control systems like Git and GitHub, making it easy to trigger builds and deployments whenever changes are pushed to the repository. It supports a wide range of programming languages and frameworks, providing developers with the flexibility to build and test their code in their preferred development environment. One of the key features of Travis CI is its ability to run tests in parallel, allowing developers to test their code quickly and efficiently. It provides a scalable infrastructure that can handle large-scale builds and tests, ensuring fast feedback and reducing the time it takes to detect and fix issues. Travis CI also provides extensive logging and reporting capabilities, allowing developers to easily track the progress and results of their builds and tests. It provides detailed information about build failures, including error messages and stack traces, making it easier to identify and fix issues. Overall, Travis CI plays a crucial role in the DevOps process by automating the build, test, and deployment stages of software development. It helps teams deliver high-quality software faster by reducing the manual effort required for these tasks and providing valuable insights into the health and stability of their codebase.

Trello

Trello is a web-based project management tool that allows teams to collaborate and organize their tasks and projects in a visually intuitive way. It is widely used in the context of DevOps to streamline and improve the efficiency of software development and deployment processes. With Trello, teams can create boards to represent projects or workflows, and within each board, they can create lists to represent different stages or phases of the project. Each list contains individual cards that represent specific tasks or user stories. These cards can be moved between lists as they progress through the project pipeline.

Trunk-Based Development

Trunk-Based Development is a software development approach that emphasizes continuous integration and rapid delivery in the context of DevOps. It involves the practice of maintaining a single, main branch, known as the trunk or master branch, as the central source of truth for the application codebase. In Trunk-Based Development, all developers work directly on the trunk branch, committing their changes frequently and integrating them with the existing codebase. This approach encourages a culture of collaboration and transparency, as any changes made by developers are immediately visible and accessible to the entire team. The key principle of Trunk-Based Development is continuous integration, where developers merge their changes into the main branch multiple times a day. By doing so, potential conflicts and integration issues are identified and resolved early, reducing the risk of merge conflicts and enabling faster delivery of features. Trunk-Based Development relies heavily on automated testing and validation processes to ensure the stability and quality of the codebase. Continuous integration pipelines are set up to perform a series of automated tests and checks whenever changes are pushed to the trunk branch. This allows developers to receive immediate feedback on the impact of their changes and catch any issues early in the development cycle. In addition to continuous integration, Trunk-Based Development also promotes continuous delivery and deployment. As changes are merged into the main branch, they undergo further automated validation and are ready to be deployed to production environments whenever required. This enables a fast and reliable release process, ensuring that new features and bug fixes can be delivered to end users quickly and safely. Overall, Trunk-Based Development aligns well with the DevOps philosophy by promoting collaboration, automation, and continuous feedback. It allows teams to develop and deliver software more efficiently, while maintaining a high level of code quality and stability.

Unleash

Unleash, in the context of DevOps, refers to the practice of deploying software or updates to production systems in a controlled and automated manner, ensuring continuous delivery and minimizing the risk of downtime or errors. It involves the process of releasing software changes into production environments, making them available to end-users. When implementing DevOps principles, organizations strive to automate and streamline the deployment process to eliminate manual errors and reduce the time between code commits and production deployments. Unleashing software allows for frequent releases, enabling developers to quickly respond to user feedback and market demands.

UrbanCode Deploy

UrbanCode Deploy is a software tool used in the context of DevOps to automate the deployment of applications and infrastructure changes across various environments. It provides a platform for continuous delivery, enabling organizations to deliver software updates more frequently and reliably. UrbanCode Deploy streamlines the deployment process by automating the manual steps involved in deploying applications, such as copying files, running scripts, and configuring servers. It allows developers and operators to define the entire deployment process as a series of logical steps or stages, which can be easily managed and tracked.

Value Stream Mapping

Value Stream Mapping is a visual representation and analysis technique used in the context of DevOps to identify, understand, and optimize the flow of value within a software development or IT operations process. It provides a detailed view of all the steps and activities involved in delivering a product or service, highlighting areas of waste, inefficiency, and bottlenecks. The goal of Value Stream Mapping in DevOps is to streamline and improve the end-to-end delivery process, ultimately increasing the value delivered to customers while reducing the time, effort, and resources required. It provides a holistic perspective on the entire value stream, helping teams and organizations to gain insights into both the technical and non-technical aspects of their processes.

Value Stream Optimization

A value stream is a series of steps or activities that deliver value to the customer. In the context of DevOps, value stream optimization refers to the continuous improvement of the process and flow of value delivery. It involves analyzing and eliminating wasteful activities, reducing handoffs and delays, and maximizing the flow of value through the entire software development and delivery lifecycle. Value stream optimization in DevOps focuses on streamlining and accelerating the end-to-end process of creating, testing, deploying, and delivering software. This optimization is achieved by adopting practices such as continuous integration, continuous delivery, and automation.

Vault

Vault is a secure software product used in the context of DevOps to manage secrets and protect sensitive information. It provides a centralized platform to securely store and access passwords, API keys, tokens, and other confidential data that is used across various applications and environments. With Vault, organizations can adopt a more secure approach to managing secrets by eliminating the need for hardcoding sensitive information into application code or configuration files. Instead, Vault offers a secure way to dynamically retrieve secrets at runtime, ensuring that only authorized entities can access the sensitive data.

Vendor Agnostic Tools Selection

Vendor Agnostic Tools Selection is a process in the context of DevOps that involves identifying and choosing software tools and technologies that are not tied to a specific vendor or provider. These tools are designed to work seamlessly with different platforms and environments without requiring any modifications or customizations. The primary objective of vendor agnostic tools selection in DevOps is to promote flexibility and interoperability within the software development and operations lifecycle. By using tools that are not vendor-specific, organizations can avoid vendor lock-in and reduce dependency on a single vendor, ensuring that they have the freedom to switch or integrate with different vendors in the future as per their requirements.

Vendor Agnostic Tools

A vendor agnostic tool refers to a software or system that is designed to work seamlessly with various vendors' technologies and platforms. In the context of DevOps, which emphasizes collaboration and integration across different stages of the software development and IT operations lifecycle, vendor agnostic tools play a crucial role in facilitating interoperability and flexibility. By being vendor agnostic, these tools are not tied to any specific vendor or technology stack, allowing teams to choose and integrate the best-in-class tools and technologies for their specific needs. This means that organizations can adopt a mix of tools from different vendors without facing compatibility issues or vendor lock-in. It also enables teams to evolve their toolchain as their requirements change or new technologies emerge.

Veracode

Veracode is a comprehensive application security platform that helps organizations integrate security testing into their DevOps processes. It provides a set of tools and services that enable developers to identify and remediate vulnerabilities in their code, as well as ensure compliance with industry standards. The Veracode platform offers a wide range of security testing capabilities, including static analysis, dynamic analysis, software composition analysis, and interactive application security testing. These different testing techniques help detect various types of security flaws, such as code vulnerabilities, configuration issues, and open source components with known vulnerabilities. By integrating Veracode into their DevOps workflows, organizations can effectively manage and mitigate security risks throughout the software development lifecycle. Developers can submit their code for analysis directly from their integrated development environments (IDEs), and receive clear and actionable results within minutes. These results include detailed information about the vulnerabilities found, such as their severity level and recommendations for remediation. Veracode also offers a policy-driven approach to security testing, allowing organizations to define their own security requirements and automatically enforce them throughout the development process. This helps ensure that applications meet the necessary security standards and regulations, such as the OWASP Top 10 or the Payment Card Industry Data Security Standard (PCI DSS). In addition to its testing capabilities, Veracode provides comprehensive reporting and analytics features that help organizations track and manage their application security posture. By gaining insight into their security risks and vulnerabilities, teams can prioritize their remediation efforts and make informed decisions to strengthen their overall security posture.

Version Control

Version control is a fundamental concept in DevOps, which refers to the management of changes made to software code, documents, or any other set of files in a collaborative development environment. It enables teams to track and control modifications, coordinate work between multiple contributors, and maintain a comprehensive history of every change made. In practice, version control systems (VCS) provide a mechanism to systematically record and manage different versions of a file or a set of files. The primary objective is to ensure that any modifications are traceable, reversible, and can be easily merged with other changes. VCSs allow developers to work concurrently on different branches or copies of code, preventing conflicts and facilitating collaboration.

Vulnerability Scanning

Vulnerability scanning in the context of DevOps refers to the process of identifying and assessing vulnerabilities or weaknesses in software applications and systems. It involves systematically scanning and analyzing these applications and systems to identify any security flaws or potential vulnerabilities that could be exploited by hackers or unauthorized personnel. The purpose of vulnerability scanning is to proactively identify and mitigate security risks in a DevOps environment. By conducting regular vulnerability scans, organizations can identify and address potential vulnerabilities before they are exploited, reducing the likelihood of security breaches and minimizing the impact of any potential attacks.

Water-Scrum-Fall

Water-Scrum-Fall is a software development model that combines elements of Waterfall, Scrum, and DevOps. It is an approach that is commonly used in large organizations where the traditional Waterfall model is entrenched, while also incorporating some Agile practices like Scrum and integrating DevOps principles. The Water-Scrum-Fall model is characterized by a sequential flow of activities where requirements are gathered upfront in a traditional waterfall manner. This means that the project starts with defining all the requirements, creating a detailed plan, and then proceeding with the development phase. The development phase follows a waterfall approach where each stage is completed before moving on to the next. This includes design, coding, testing, and deployment. This phase is typically longer and is focused on stability and predictability. The Scrum aspect of Water-Scrum-Fall comes into play during the development phase. While the overall project follows a traditional waterfall approach, development teams utilize Scrum practices such as time-boxed iterations, daily stand-up meetings, and backlog management. Scrum allows for increased flexibility and collaboration within the development team, providing a more iterative and incremental approach to development. This agile aspect helps address changing requirements, allows for feedback from stakeholders, and ensures continuous improvement throughout the development process. Finally, the DevOps principles are integrated during the deployment and operations phase of the Water-Scrum-Fall model. DevOps emphasizes collaboration and communication between development and operations teams to automate the deployment process, increase deployment frequency, and improve overall stability and efficiency. In the Water-Scrum-Fall model, DevOps practices are adopted to ensure a smooth transition from the development phase to operations, including continuous integration, continuous delivery, and continuous monitoring.

Wavefront

Wavefront is a cloud-native metrics monitoring and analytics platform that helps organizations in the field of DevOps successfully manage and optimize their applications and infrastructure. It collects, stores, and analyzes real-time data from various sources, enabling teams to gain valuable insights into the performance, availability, and reliability of their systems. With Wavefront, DevOps teams can easily track and monitor the health and performance metrics of their applications and infrastructure across different environments, such as on-premises data centers or cloud platforms. The platform offers a highly scalable and reliable architecture that can handle massive amounts of data, allowing teams to monitor their systems at any scale. Wavefront supports a wide range of data sources, including popular open-source metrics frameworks like Prometheus, as well as various agents and integrations for collecting data from different systems, services, and tools. This flexibility enables teams to easily integrate Wavefront into their existing monitoring and observability stack without disrupting their current workflows. One key feature of Wavefront is its real-time analytics capabilities. It provides powerful query language and visualization tools that allow teams to create custom dashboards and reports, as well as conduct advanced analysis on their metrics data. This empowers DevOps teams to detect anomalies, troubleshoot issues, and optimize performance quickly and efficiently. Another essential aspect of Wavefront is its alerting system. It supports flexible alerting policies that can be customized to meet specific needs, ensuring that teams are notified promptly when certain metrics or conditions reach predefined thresholds. This enables proactive monitoring and incident response, helping teams to minimize downtime and maintain high system availability. In summary, Wavefront is a cloud-native metrics monitoring and analytics platform specifically designed for DevOps teams. It provides a scalable and flexible solution for collecting, analyzing, and visualizing metrics data in real-time, facilitating effective monitoring, troubleshooting, and optimization of applications and infrastructure.

Wercker

Wercker is a DevOps platform that helps streamline the software development process by automating the workflow and providing continuous integration and delivery. It is designed to simplify the deployment of applications and services, allowing developers to focus on writing code and delivering new features quickly and efficiently. With Wercker, developers can automate the building, testing, and deployment of their applications, reducing the time and effort required for manual intervention.

WhiteHat Security

WhiteHat Security is a leading provider of application security solutions, offering services and technologies that help organizations protect their software throughout the entire development lifecycle. In the context of DevOps, WhiteHat Security plays a crucial role in ensuring the security of applications deployed in continuous integration/continuous deployment (CI/CD) pipelines. As organizations embrace DevOps practices, the traditional approach to application security must be adapted to fit within the fast-paced, automated CI/CD workflows. WhiteHat Security specializes in providing security testing and vulnerability management solutions that seamlessly integrate with the DevOps toolchain, enabling developers to rapidly identify and address security weaknesses in their code.

Wrike

Wrike, in the context of DevOps, is a collaborative work management platform that assists development and operations teams in efficiently executing their tasks throughout the software development lifecycle. The platform offers a comprehensive set of features and functionalities to foster seamless collaboration, automate repetitive tasks, and enhance overall productivity. Wrike's DevOps capabilities enable teams to streamline their workflows, align their objectives, and deliver high-quality software at a faster pace.

XebiaLabs

DevOps is a collaboration and communication practice that aims to bring together the development and operations teams within an organization to improve efficiency and deliver high-quality software products. XebiaLabs is a leading provider of DevOps software solutions that enable organizations to streamline their delivery processes and accelerate the time-to-market for software applications. With the increasing complexity of software development and the need for faster delivery, DevOps has emerged as a crucial approach to bridge the gap between development and operations. It emphasizes collaboration, automation, and continuous delivery to ensure that software is developed, tested, and deployed in a timely and efficient manner. XebiaLabs offers a range of software tools and solutions that help organizations implement DevOps practices effectively. These tools include release orchestration, deployment automation, and continuous delivery software that enable teams to automate their software release processes, reduce manual errors, and increase efficiency. One of the key features of XebiaLabs' DevOps solutions is release orchestration. This feature allows organizations to plan, coordinate, and manage the entire release process, from development to production. It provides a centralized platform where teams can define release plans, track progress, and ensure that all the necessary steps are executed in the right order. Another important aspect of XebiaLabs' DevOps solutions is deployment automation. This feature enables organizations to automate the deployment process, eliminating manual and error-prone tasks. It allows teams to define deployment workflows, manage configuration files, and ensure consistent deployments across different environments. In addition to release orchestration and deployment automation, XebiaLabs' DevOps solutions also include continuous delivery capabilities. This feature enables organizations to automate the software delivery process, allowing them to release new features and updates more frequently and reliably. Overall, XebiaLabs' DevOps solutions provide organizations with the necessary tools and capabilities to implement and scale DevOps practices effectively. By enabling collaboration, automation, and continuous delivery, XebiaLabs helps organizations achieve faster time-to-market, higher quality software, and improved customer satisfaction.

ZenHub

ZenHub is a DevOps tool that enhances project management and collaboration within software development teams. It is specifically designed to integrate with GitHub, providing a seamless workflow for developers. With ZenHub, teams can visualize and track their work directly within their GitHub repositories. It enables teams to plan, prioritize, and manage their projects using Kanban boards and issue tracking capabilities. This helps in streamlining the development process and ensuring that all team members are on the same page. One key feature of ZenHub is its ability to create and manage pipelines, allowing teams to set up different stages for their workflow. This helps in visualizing the progress of each task and identifying any bottlenecks in the development process. Another important aspect of ZenHub is its collaboration features. It enables teams to have discussions, provide feedback, and coordinate their work through its built-in commenting system. This promotes effective communication and enables teams to resolve any issues or concerns in a timely manner. ZenHub also provides various analytics and reporting tools to help teams measure their performance and identify areas for improvement. It offers metrics such as cycle time, lead time, and burnup charts, allowing teams to gain insights into their productivity and make data-driven decisions. In summary, ZenHub is a powerful tool that enhances project management and collaboration within software development teams. It integrates seamlessly with GitHub and offers features such as Kanban boards, issue tracking, pipeline management, collaboration tools, and analytics. By using ZenHub, teams can streamline their workflows, improve communication, and make informed decisions to deliver high-quality software efficiently.

Zero Downtime Deployment

Zero Downtime Deployment refers to a software release process in the field of DevOps that allows updates or changes to be implemented without causing any disruption to the availability or performance of the application or system. During the traditional software deployment process, there is typically a period of downtime, during which the application or system is unavailable or inaccessible to users. This downtime is necessary to perform various tasks such as stopping the application, deploying the updated code, and restarting the application. However, this approach can lead to negative consequences, such as loss of revenue, decreased user satisfaction, and even potential business reputation damage. Zero Downtime Deployment aims to mitigate these issues by implementing strategies and techniques that enable the smooth transition from the current version of the application to the updated version without any interruption in service. This can be achieved through various practices, including: 1. Load Balancers: Employing load balancers to distribute incoming requests to multiple instances of the application. This ensures that even if one instance is taken offline for the deployment process, others can handle the traffic and maintain availability. 2. Blue-Green Deployment: Utilizing a blue-green deployment strategy, where two identical environments (blue and green) are maintained. The blue environment represents the current version of the application, while the green environment represents the updated version. Traffic is initially directed to the blue environment, and once the green environment is successfully deployed and tested, traffic is switched to it. This ensures no downtime for end users. 3. Rolling Updates: Implementing rolling updates, where the deployment process takes place incrementally across different instances or components of the application. This allows for continuous availability as each component is updated one by one, without affecting the overall functioning of the system. By adopting these practices and other related techniques, Zero Downtime Deployment aims to ensure that software updates or changes can be seamlessly deployed without any negative impact on the availability or performance of the application. This not only enhances user experience but also reduces the associated risks and costs of downtime, making it a critical aspect of modern DevOps practices.

Zero Trust Architecture (ZTA)

A Zero Trust Architecture (ZTA) is a security framework that focuses on securing the access to resources and systems in a DevOps environment. It recognizes that traditional security measures, such as perimeter-based defense, are no longer sufficient in modern cloud-based and dynamic infrastructures. In a Zero Trust Architecture, every interaction and access request is treated as potentially malicious, regardless of whether it originates from within or outside the organization's network. The ZTA model assumes that no user or device can be trusted by default and requires verification for every access attempt. The key principles of a Zero Trust Architecture in the context of DevOps are: 1. Least Privilege: Users and systems are granted the minimum level of access necessary to perform their tasks. This reduces the potential attack surface and limits the impact of compromised accounts or systems. 2. Microsegmentation: The network is divided into individual segments, or microsegments, to prevent lateral movement within the infrastructure. This helps contain potential breaches and limits the spread of attacks. 3. Multi-Factor Authentication (MFA): Users are required to provide multiple forms of authentication, such as passwords, biometrics, or tokens, to verify their identities. This adds an extra layer of security and reduces the risk of unauthorized access. 4. Continuous Monitoring: Security controls, such as logging, auditing, and anomaly detection, are implemented to monitor and detect any suspicious activities or deviations from normal behavior. This allows for timely response and mitigation of potential threats. 5. Encryption: Data is encrypted both at rest and in transit to protect it from unauthorized access or interception. This ensures that sensitive information remains secure even if it falls into the wrong hands. By implementing a Zero Trust Architecture in a DevOps environment, organizations can enhance the security of their systems, data, and resources. It shifts the focus from relying solely on perimeter defenses to a more holistic approach that validates every access request and monitors for any signs of compromise or malicious activities. This helps mitigate the risks associated with modern cyber threats and provides a more robust security posture in the dynamic and distributed nature of DevOps.

Zero Trust Network Access (ZTNA)

Zero Trust Network Access (ZTNA) is a security model that provides a more secure approach to network access in the context of DevOps. It is designed to enhance security by assuming that both internal and external networks are untrusted, and therefore requires verification and authentication for every access attempt, regardless of user or device. In the traditional network access model, once a user or device is granted access to a network, they are typically given unrestricted access to all resources within that network. This approach poses security risks, as it assumes that all users and devices within the network are trustworthy. However, with the introduction of cloud services, remote work, and increasing cyber threats, this trust-based model is no longer sufficient. The Zero Trust Network Access model eliminates the concept of a trusted network. Instead, it focuses on verifying the identity and trustworthiness of each access request. Every access attempt, whether from an internal or external source, must go through a strict authentication and verification process before access is granted. ZTNA enforces the principle of least privilege, meaning that users and devices are only granted access to the resources they actually need to perform their tasks. It follows a user-centric approach, where access policies are based on the user's identity, device health, and other contextual factors. This ensures that only authorized users, using trusted devices, can access specific resources. By incorporating ZTNA into the DevOps process, organizations can enhance security and minimize the risk of unauthorized access or data breaches. ZTNA can be implemented through various technologies, such as virtual private networks (VPNs), software-defined perimeter (SDP), and zero trust architectures. In conclusion, Zero Trust Network Access provides a more secure approach to network access in the context of DevOps. It focuses on verifying the identity and trustworthiness of each access request, eliminates the concept of a trusted network, and enforces the principle of least privilege. By implementing ZTNA, organizations can enhance security, mitigate risks, and ensure only authorized users and devices can access specific resources.

Zero Trust Security Models Implementation

A Zero Trust security model, when implemented in the context of DevOps, is an approach to securing applications and systems that assumes no trust is granted to any entity, whether it be within or outside the organization's network perimeter. This model requires strict identity verification and authentication for all users and devices, regardless of their location or network access. In a traditional security model, once a user or device gains access to a network, they are often granted significant privileges and trusted to access various resources. However, in the Zero Trust model, trust is never assumed, even for entities that have already gained access to the network. This ensures that each user, device, or application is continuously authenticated and authorized based on granular policies and context-aware information. Implementing a Zero Trust security model in the DevOps environment involves several key elements: 1. Identity-centric approach: The model focuses on establishing and validating a user's or device's identity before granting any access. This includes multi-factor authentication, privileged access management, and continuous identity verification. 2. Micro-segmentation: The network is divided into smaller segments, and access between these segments is controlled based on policies and least privilege principles. This limits the lateral movement of threats and reduces the attack surface. 3. Device trust assessment: All devices, whether they are company-owned or personal, are assessed for security posture and compliance before being granted access. This ensures that only trusted devices can connect to the network or access sensitive resources. 4. Proactive monitoring: Continuous monitoring and analysis of network traffic, user behavior, and security events are essential for identifying and mitigating potential threats. Real-time analytics and anomaly detection help detect and respond to any suspicious activities quickly. By implementing a Zero Trust security model in the context of DevOps, organizations can strengthen their security posture, reduce the risk of data breaches, and protect critical assets. This approach aligns security with the principles of agility and automation in the DevOps environment, allowing organizations to secure their systems while maintaining a fast-paced development lifecycle.

Zero Trust Security Models

A Zero Trust security model, in the context of DevOps, is a holistic approach to securing software systems, data, and infrastructure that assumes no implicit trust between any entities, both internal and external. It shifts the traditional perimeter-based security approach to a more granular, identity-focused strategy. The fundamental principle of the Zero Trust model is to verify and authenticate every user, device, or application that tries to access resources or services within the system, regardless of their location. It eliminates the assumption that everything inside the network is inherently trustworthy. Instead, it treats each access request as potentially malicious and requires appropriate authentication and authorization measures at every interaction point.

Zero Trust Security

The concept of Zero Trust Security in the context of DevOps refers to an approach that assumes no trust towards any user, device, or system, regardless of whether they are inside or outside the organization's network perimeter. It recognizes that traditional perimeter-based security measures are no longer sufficient to protect modern IT environments that consist of multiple cloud platforms, on-premises systems, and remote devices. In a Zero Trust Security model, every user, device, and system must verify their identity and meet certain security requirements before gaining access to any resource or data. This is done through different layers of authentication and authorization, as well as continuous monitoring and assessment of their behavior and risk level. The goal is to minimize the potential attack surface and reduce the impact of any potential breach or unauthorized access. Zero Trust Security relies heavily on automation and integration within the DevOps practices. It requires implementing secure development practices, such as code reviews, vulnerability assessments, and security testing, throughout the software development lifecycle. It also requires the use of strong encryption and secure communication protocols to protect data both in transit and at rest. Furthermore, continuous monitoring and logging are crucial in a Zero Trust Security approach. It involves collecting and analyzing logs, events, and metrics from various sources to detect anomalies or malicious activities. This enables rapid response and remediation to mitigate potential threats and vulnerabilities. Implementing Zero Trust Security in a DevOps environment requires close collaboration between security teams and development teams. It involves integrating security controls, such as access controls, identity and access management, and privileged access management, into the DevOps workflow and automating security tasks wherever possible. Overall, Zero Trust Security in the context of DevOps provides a comprehensive and proactive approach to protect organizations' sensitive data and resources in an increasingly complex and distributed IT landscape.

Zuul

Zuul is an open-source gateway service in the context of DevOps. It operates as a reverse proxy and provides dynamic routing and load balancing capabilities for microservices-based architectures. With Zuul, organizations can implement a centralized entry point for all incoming requests to their microservices. It serves as a traffic cop, receiving API requests and directing them to the appropriate microservice based on predefined routes and rules. Zuul plays a crucial role in maintaining security and protecting the backend microservices from direct exposure to the internet. It acts as a shield, authenticating and authorizing requests, validating tokens, and applying access control policies. The dynamic routing capabilities of Zuul allow for flexible and efficient routing of requests. It can distribute traffic across multiple instances of a microservice to achieve load balancing and high availability. By utilizing intelligent routing algorithms, Zuul can adaptively route requests based on factors like service health, latency, and geographical proximity. Furthermore, Zuul provides customizable filters to intercept and modify requests and responses. These filters enable organizations to implement various cross-cutting concerns such as logging, request tracing, rate limiting, and response manipulation. By employing these filters, DevOps teams can ensure consistent and controlled behavior across their microservices. In addition to routing and filtering capabilities, Zuul integrates seamlessly with other DevOps tools and services. It can work in conjunction with service registries like Netflix Eureka for automatic service discovery and registration. Moreover, it supports metrics and monitoring systems, enabling organizations to gain insights into the performance and behavior of their microservices. Zuul is highly scalable and extensible, making it suitable for deployments in large-scale and complex microservices architectures. It can handle high volumes of traffic while maintaining low latency and providing resilience. In summary, Zuul is a powerful gateway service that offers dynamic routing, load balancing, security, and filtering capabilities for microservices-based architectures. It plays a fundamental role in ensuring efficient and controlled communication between clients and microservices, enhancing the overall resilience and scalability of DevOps systems.